TRACKING POP

SERIES EDITORS: JOCELYN NEAL, JOHN COVACH,
ROBERT FINK, AND LOREN KAJIKAWA

TITLES IN THE SERIES:

Soda Goes Pop: Pepsi-Cola Advertising and Popular Music
by Joanna K. Love

The Beatles through a Glass Onion: Reconsidering the White Album
edited by Mark Osteen

The Pop Palimpsest: Intertextuality in Recorded Popular Music
edited by Lori Burns and Serge Lacasse

Uncharted: Creativity and the Expert Drummer
by Bill Bruford

I Hear a Symphony: Motown and Crossover R&B
by Andrew Flory

Hearing Harmony: Toward a Tonal Theory for the Rock Era
by Christopher Doll

Good Vibrations: Brian Wilson and the Beach Boys in
Critical Perspective
edited by Philip Lambert

Krautrock: German Music in the Seventies
by Ulrich Adelt

Sounds of the Underground: A Cultural, Political and Aesthetic
Mapping of Underground and Fringe Music
by Stephen Graham

Rhymin' and Stealin': Musical Borrowing in Hip-Hop
by Justin A. Williams

Powerful Voices: The Musical and Social World of Collegiate A Cappella
by Joshua S. Duchan

Bytes and Backbeats: Repurposing Music in the Digital Age
by Steve Savage

Are We Not New Wave? Modern Pop at the Turn of the 1980s
by Theo Cateforis

Soul Music: Tracking the Spiritual Roots of Pop from Plato
to Motown
by Joel Rudinow

I Don't Sound Like Nobody: Remaking Music in 1950s America
by Albin J. Zak III

Sounding Out Pop: Analytical Essays in Popular Music
edited by Mark Spicer and John Covach

Listening to Popular Music: Or, How I Learned to Stop Worrying and
Love Led Zeppelin
by Theodore Gracyk

SODA GOES POP

PEPSI-COLA ADVERTISING AND POPULAR MUSIC

Joanna K. Love

UNIVERSITY OF MICHIGAN PRESS
Ann Arbor

Published in the United States of America by the
University of Michigan Press
Manufactured in the United States of America
Printed on acid-free paper
First published July 2019

A CIP catalog record for this book is available from the British Library.

Library of Congress Cataloging-in-Publication Data

Names: Love, Joanna K. author.
Title: Soda goes pop : Pepsi-Cola advertising and popular music / Joanna K. Love.
Description: Ann Arbor : University of Michigan Press, 2019. | Series: Tracking pop | Includes
    bibliographical references and index. |
Identifiers: LCCN 2019007780 (print) | LCCN 2019013242 (ebook) | ISBN 9780472124329
    (E-book) | ISBN 9780472074020 (hardcover : alk. paper) | ISBN 9780472054022 (pbk. : alk.
    paper)
Subjects: LCSH: Music in advertising—United States—History. | Advertising—Soft drinks—
    United States—History. | Popular music—United States—History and criticism. | PepsiCo,
    Inc.
Classification: LCC ML3917.U6 (ebook) | LCC ML3917.U6 L68 2019 (print) |
    DDC 781.5/9—dc23
LC record available at https://lccn.loc.gov/2019007780

The University of Michigan Press gratefully acknowledges the support of the AMS 75 PAYS
Endowment of the American Musicological Society, funded in part by the National Endowment
for the Humanities and the Andrew W. Mellon Foundation, for the publication of this volume.

Cover image: Cola bottle © iStock / Boarding1Now; Music notes © iStock / RKaulitzki.

To my parents: John and Kathleen Love

CONTENTS

Acknowledgments   ix

**PART I: EARLY POP JINGLES AND PEPSI'S SHIFT
TO YOUTH MARKETING**

Introduction: Hitting the Spot and Spotting the Hits   3

1. The Pepsi Generation "Now and Then": (Re)composing the Cola Wars   28

**PART II: POP SONGS, CELEBRITY SPECTACLE,
AND THE MTV GENERATION**

2. Big Soda and Celebrity Pop: Pepsi Meets Michael Jackson   59

3. The Choice of a Neoliberal Generation: Pepsi Models the Perfect Consumer   86

4. Chasing "Bad": Pop Fantasies and Teleological Fiction   121

5. A "Wish" and a "Prayer": Pepsi Faces the Limits of Redaction   149

**PART III: MILLENNIAL MUSIC MARKETING:
REDACT, REUSE, RECYCLE**

6. Humorous Hits, Nostalgic Notes, and Retro Refrains in the 1990s   179

Pepsi Coda. Twenty-First-Century "Pop" and the Branded Future   214

Notes   235

Bibliography   279

Index   303

Digital materials related to this title can be found on
the Fulcrum platform via the following citable URL:
https://doi.org/10.3998/mpub.9536286

ACKNOWLEDGMENTS

It takes a village to write a book, especially one that is almost a decade in the making. I would have to write another one as long as this to properly honor all of the wonderful mentors, colleagues, friends, and family members who have supported me along the way. Since the interest of space prevents such an endeavor, I name as many as possible here and hope that those, both named and unnamed, are aware of my deep and sincere appreciation.

I first thank my brilliant mentors at the University of California, Los Angeles, who helped me to cultivate many of the ideas present in this book. I am especially appreciative of Timothy D. Taylor, Mitchell Morris, and Douglas Kellner. I owe a very special note of thanks to Robert Fink, who guided me through each step of this process.

I express my sincere gratitude to my amazing colleagues who took the time to read and comment on individual chapters. I thank Marianna Ritchey, Alexandra Apolloni, Ross Fenimore, Jillian Rodgers, Samuel Baltimore, Lindsay Johnson, Sarah Gerk, and Danielle Sirek, as well as colleagues at the University of Richmond, including Rania Sweis, Mariela Méndez, Erika Damer, Julianne Guillard, and Eric Grollman. I extend my deepest gratitude to Danijela Kulezic-Wilson, who read the entire manuscript and offered insightful feedback to prepare it for review. I am also deeply appreciative of Karen Ahlquist and all those involved with the 2015 publication of the *Journal for the Society of American Music* article that would become portions of chapter 2.

I am further grateful for the opportunity to workshop various sections of this book at the first two Junior Faculty Symposiums sponsored by the

American Musicological Society's Popular Music Study Group. There were unfortunately too many attendees and mentors to name here, but I do want thank those who offered substantial feedback on early drafts, including Robynn Stilwell, Neil Lerner, Susan Fast, Brian Wright, Dan Blim, Kim Mack, and Katherine Reed. I especially thank the symposium coordinators, Eric Hung and Daniel Goldmark.

The University of Richmond has also provided me with invaluable resources for this project. I sincerely thank the Department of Music, and especially Jessie Fillerup, Andy McGraw, and Jeffrey Riehl for their support. I also acknowledge our wonderful music librarian and musicologist Linda Fairtile for helping to locate various materials. This project surely would not have been feasible without funding from the School of Arts & Sciences, Dean's Office under the direction of Kathleen Skerrett and Patrice Rankine. I am further grateful for summer support allocated by the Faculty Research Committee.

I express my sincerest gratitude to the American Association of University Women, which made the completion of this book possible with a 2016–17 American Post-Doctoral Fellowship. I also thank those who provided access to essential archival materials, including Kay Peterson at the Archives Center of the National Museum of American History, Smithsonian Institution, and Martin Gostanian, who not only guided me through the materials available at the Paley Center for Media in Los Angeles but recommended excellent sources outside of the collection.

As always, I thank my strong network of family and friends. There are too many to name here, but I am forever indebted to John and Kathleen Love; Bill, Judy, and Kellen Evans; Christin Schillinger; and of course my rock and beloved, Mark Sanborn. Not least, I thank the University of Michigan Press and its exceptional faculty, staff, and reviewers. I am especially appreciative of Mary Francis who skillfully shepherded this book across the finish line along with Sarah Dougherty, Susan Cronin, and Kevin Rennells.

PART I

Early Pop Jingles and Pepsi's Shift to Youth Marketing

Introduction

Hitting the Spot and Spotting the Hits

Forty-one years after a North Carolina pharmacist named Caleb D. Bradham compounded a fountain drink that would become known as Pepsi-Cola, Walter Mack was appointed the company's president and chief executive officer (CEO). The year was 1939, and the Phoenix Securities firm had been put in charge of mitigating the losses and lawsuits that plagued Pepsi and its parent company at the time, Loft Inc.[1] Mack was cofounder and vice president of the securities company, but he would soon resign to devote his full attention to running the nascent soda brand.

The once failing company had finally begun to see gains due to its promise of 12-ounce bottles for only a nickel—a bargain that doubled Pepsi's profits during the 1930s depression era. But even with its recent success Mack recognized that the brand needed a major image makeover to sustain its profitability. He knew the company's future rested on the ability of its consumers and franchised bottlers to invest in the company name, so he set out to streamline the look of its logo, as well as the product's packaging. He also hired the Newell-Emmet advertising agency to create a nationwide marketing campaign that would solidify Pepsi's value and win over potential consumers. The new campaign produced highly successful skywriting promotions, as well as a cartoon comic strip called *Pepsi and Pete*, which featured characters similar to the Keystone Kops created by Mack Sennett. The most enduring outcome of Walter Mack's efforts with the Newell-Emmet agency, however, was the creation of the first nationally broadcast jingle for a national product.[2] It was called "Nickel, Nickel" and composed by Alan B. Kent and Austin H. Croom-Johnson. Although it was common at the time for jingles promoting local products to air on regional stations, this tune would prove extraordinary in changing the future of the company, as well as the advertising industry.

As recounted by writers J. C. Louise and Harvey Yazijian, and more recently by ethnomusicologist Timothy Taylor, the success, importance, and longevity of Pepsi-Cola's 1939 "Nickel, Nickel" cannot be overstated. Indeed, it would set the standard for broadcast, stand-alone "singing jingles."[3] By 1941 it had aired an estimated 296,426 times on 469 radio stations and was rearranged in "all variations and tempos for all occasions from concerts and theater to the World Series."[4] A full version of the song, renamed "Pepsi-Cola Hits the Spot," was orchestrated, recorded, and requested for use in some 100,000 jukeboxes.[5] In 1942, the jingle was dubbed the "best-known tune in America."[6] Two years later it was translated into 55 languages, and its lyrics were updated numerous times so that its melody could run in various formats for an entire decade.[7] Most important for the growth of the company, the tune played a major role in boosting sales profits to $8.5 million in 1940 and even higher to $14.9 million the following year.[8] Pepsi's jingle thus truly "hit the spot," precipitating the boom of the post–World War II jingle business and laying the groundwork for the professional upsurge of jingle composers to come.[9]

By all accounts, the jingle's success hinged on Mack's insistence that the brand steer away from current advertising trends that relied on the insertion of a narrated product description into the musical pitch.[10] Mack only wanted 15 seconds of jingle music—a request that substantially shortened the typical run time for advertising spots and displeased the Newell-Emmet agency as well as some of the radio stations on which he sought airtime.[11] Eventually however, everyone caved to the CEO's requests. As it turned out, Mack's instincts were right: the jingle's lyrics proved sufficient to carry the brand's message, including the product's ability to satisfy one's thirst ("Pepsi-Cola hits the spot") and its bargain price ("Twice as much for a nickel, too . . .").[12]

But the length and lyrics alone were not enough to make "Nickel, Nickel" a juggernaut. The musical score itself grabbed listeners' attention and communicated Pepsi's sales pitch for an entire decade. The jingle's composers carefully selected and structured the tune's musical tropes to produce its pleasing affect. They first attached the brand's short and pithy slogan to a well-known melody borrowed from a nineteenth-century English hunting ballad called "John Peel."[13] This strategy of choosing songs in the public domain for advertising purposes was common at the time since there were no royalty fees for songs outside the constraints of copyright laws.[14] Kent and Croom-Johnson also claimed to have chosen the song because of its "light mood."[15] Beyond this, the composers and Pepsi's marketing creatives knew that attaching a product to a song already popular on its own would increase the likelihood that audiences would take to the jingle and remember the product.

Kent and Croom-Johnson were therefore careful to use the basic tenets of the borrowed English ballad, but they also updated it to fit modern popular culture. Most noticeably, they added energetic pep to the song by substantially increasing its tempo and bookending the familiar tune with syncopated rhythms and scatted lyrics (too-do-dee-da-da-da) that proved reminiscent of the big band and jazz favorites topping the charts at the time.[16] Meanwhile, the slogan-bearing section of the jingle preserved the simplicity of the "John Peel" melody. With an opening third interval common to children's songs and a diatonic motion, the tune was easy to sing and remember. The melody also remained mostly stepwise, like its prototype, but retained the single octave leap on which the composers cleverly placed the lyrics, "Twice as much," to aurally highlight the unique selling proposition (USP) (example intro. 1, measure 1).[17]

Example intro.1. An octave leap highlights the USP. ("Nickel, Nickel," PepsiCo. Inc., 1939. Transcription by the author.)

Twice   as   much   for   a   nick - el   too! _____

The melody's A-A-B-C form further followed the expected trajectory of well-known English ballads and American parlor songs, allowing for a quick statement and repetition of the first two phrases (A), a brief climax in the third (B, example intro. 1), and a satisfying tonic resolution at the end (C). For the extended version that circulated as sheet music and jukebox recordings, Kent and Croom-Johnson kept the original ballad's familiar verse refrain and strophic (repeated) form, allowing the C section—their reworked refrain turned tagline ("Pepsi-Cola is the drink for you!")—to carry over not only from verse to verse, but throughout future iterations of the song.[18] Finally, the composers removed the ballad's pick-up notes to shift the tune's metric accent from beat four to the first beat in each measure. This removed the lilting that produced the original song's folksy gait, thereby giving Pepsi's version a duple meter pulse that could take on a quicker tempo, a bouncier quality, and an overall more modern sound. The musical decisions made by the composers—their selection of a pre-existing and (once) popular song, addition of contemporary musical tropes, and preservation of certain aspects of the tune while reworking others—proved key to making the jingle catchy, familiar, singable, modern, and wholly effective, thereby revealing the potential for using popular music to communicate branding aims.

Pepsi's advertising, and especially its television commercials, would continue to push the limits of musical marketing and set new trends well into the twenty-first century. Indeed, by the end of the twentieth century, the brand's interests would converge with those of the American popular music industry. The degree to which this partnership flourished was confirmed in a television commercial that aired during the premiere of the *X Factor–U.S.* reality talent show on September 21, 2011. The spot promised the show's contestants an unusual prize: in addition to a five-million-dollar recording contract, the winner was slated for a starring role in a Pepsi-Cola commercial set to debut during that February's televised Super Bowl sporting event. The 45-second cross-promotional spot, titled "Music Icons," showcased the potential exposure afforded by this once-in-a-lifetime opportunity. A visual mash-up of the soda giant's commercials featuring past pop legends like Michael Jackson and Britney Spears was set to a "Pepsi Exclusive Remix" of the hook to "Tonight Is the Night"—a single by up-and-coming rapper Outasight (Richard Andrew).[19] The spot's music and images thus promised to induct the would-be *X Factor* winner into the musical legacy achieved by Pepsi's impressive roster of superstar endorsers. Despite the fact that Outasight did not appear onscreen, the presence of his music was meant to inaugurate him into the iconic lineup while simultaneously communicating Pepsi's self-proclaimed status as a purveyor of cutting-edge popular music trends.

The treatment of the commercial's pop signifiers demonstrated just how adept Pepsi's marketers had become at revising popular music's sounds and imagery to promote the brand's agendas in the decades since its illustrious "Nickel, Nickel" campaign. In its original context, Outasight's lyrical hook ("Tonight Is the Night") had nothing to do with the soda or singing competition, but it was recontextualized with the commercial's images to refer to that very evening when the *X Factor* program and its Pepsi sponsor would make someone a star. While Outasight's music intended to appeal to contemporary audiences, the artist's newly acquired fame could not rival the iconicity of stars like Michael Jackson or Britney Spears. Pepsi's mar-

Fig. intro.1. Pop aspirations. (Still from "Music Icons," PepsiCo. Inc., 2011; clip from "Now and Then," PepsiCo. Inc., 2002.)

keters therefore rearranged the song's simple hook and generic pentatonic melody to provide a bland backdrop for highlighting the more famous musical acts onscreen (see fig. intro.1). The silenced images of these larger than life "music icons" were synchronized with Outasight's stripped-down soundtrack to support the soda giant's claim that the next global superstar would emerge from the pool of *X Factor* contestants. The rewritten track therefore functioned like the traditional jingles on which Pepsi had once relied. It was catchy enough to remember but simple enough to serve the intended message of the *brand*. "Music Icons" thus stood as a testament to the soda giant's mastery of incorporating popular music's codes into its branding agenda; by doubly displacing these pop stars into a commercial about commercials past, Pepsi reimagined American popular music history as the history of (soda) branding.

Pepsi's marketers were skillful in revising 30 years of pop music history to fit into a 45-second valorization of the soda giant in their attempt to position the brand's commercials as a necessary rite of passage for successful pop singers. The underlying message encouraged audiences to consume the product (with the added *X Factor* plug), but the spot proved distinct in its additional call to viewers to help the brand anoint a future pop star. "Music Icons" therefore suggested that the soda giant had worked intimately from within the music industry to become a key player and authority figure in popular music. The commercial made it clear that the soda giant no longer merely borrowed popular tunes, nor did it simply sponsor America's pop megastars. Its use of new music and iconic images proclaimed that Pepsi had joined the *X Factor* franchise in becoming a new kind of tastemaker, producer, and innovator in twenty-first-century musical culture.

Pepsi's 2011 *X Factor* spot raises important questions about the evolution of relationships between popular music and corporate advertising; namely, was a soda brand indeed responsible for steering the careers of America's biggest musical stars? For what reasons did advertising get involved in the creation, production, and dissemination of popular music? When and how did commercials featuring popular songs and celebrities become the norm? How and why have commercials historically reduced popular music aesthetics to benefit branding aims? What effect has Pepsi's music marketing practices had on other corporate brands, the advertising industry, and popular music? And what implications might this have for the future?

Soda Goes Pop answers these questions by examining the mediating role that Pepsi's commercials have played in forging lasting relationships between the American music and advertising industries from its 1939 "Nickel, Nickel" jingle to its pair of 2011–12 *X Factor* commercials. It historicizes and analyzes widely disseminated Pepsi commercials for its signature and diet colas, focusing largely on well-known television spots and charting their evolution from stand-alone broadcast jingles to celebrities singing the latest pop songs and styles in its campaigns. In chronicling Pepsi's shift from mid-twentieth-century advertising practices to the experiential approaches common to early-twenty-first-century branding, this book integrates close musical analysis with interdisciplinary scholarship on advertising and American popular culture to examine the process of *redaction*—the practice marketers have used to select, censor, and restructure musical texts to fit commercial contexts in ways that revise their aesthetic meanings and serve corporate aims. This book thus argues that it was advertising's ability to get *inside* musical texts that eventually allowed corporate brands to play key roles in popular music's dissemination and production. The following chapters investigate *how* Pepsi-Cola marketing has historically appropriated meanings from hit songs and celebrity musical endorsers, *what* new meanings its well-known spots attempted to emit, and *why* these commercials shaped future relationships among the American music business, the advertising industry, and corporate brands.

Trade press journals, media outlets, and music critics have long argued about the origins of popular music's place in advertising. Some sources attribute its beginnings to Jovan perfume's underwriting of the Rolling Stones' 1981 tour.[20] Others gesture to the advent of MTV.[21] Some attribute it to the music industry's greed and resulting decline.[22] Still others argue that popular music has always been "commercial" and point to mixed media formats that have functioned as advertisements for records—television programs such as the *Ed Sullivan Show* and *American Bandstand* and films like Elvis Presley's *Viva Las Vegas* and the Beatles' *Hard Day's Night*—concluding that pop music's appearance in advertising was the next logical step.[23] This last argument has expanded further into discussions about popular music's implicit ties to advertising through its placement in media that have always been reliant on sponsorship and marketing dollars.[24]

More recently Timothy Taylor has demonstrated that popular music has had ties to advertising for more than a century, and he pinpoints Pepsi's shift to youth marketing in the early 1960s as the moment when Madison Avenue formed an insatiable appetite for the music industry's newest sounds.[25] He further attributes the brand's 1984 partnership with Michael Jackson as the deal that solidified the relationship between the two industries. Indeed, the unprecedented success, memorability, and lasting influence of Pepsi's relentless musical marketing endeavors testify to its impact. The focus on Pepsi-Cola throughout *Soda Goes Pop* therefore proves representative rather than limiting. As the pioneering leader in pop music marketing for more than seven decades, a close consideration of the brand's commercials provides important historical and aesthetic perspectives for understanding twentieth- and twenty-first-century partnerships among music, advertising, and corporate brands.[26]

Although many other consumer brands have used popular music in their spots, Pepsi-Cola was the first national brand to incorporate it into its coast-to-coast campaigns. In its fight to stay relevant as a parity product it was also the first soda brand to use television as an advertising medium in 1950.[27] Most significantly, Pepsi would find its edge in the early-1960s by turning its attention away from housewives and onto youth. As chapter 1 discusses, the creation of the "Pepsi Generation" slogan and interest in portraying what author Thomas Frank identifies as "hip" trends in its commercials instigated advertising's now commonplace alliances with top musical acts and hit songs.[28] This effort forever impacted the demographics and psychographics (lifestyles) the brand would pursue as it tailored its commercials to a new "generation" of "youthful thinking" consumers.[29] Instead of following the traditional approach—"Let us tell you why this drink is right for you"—Pepsi used music to communicate a soft-sell approach: "Let us show you why you are (or why you want to be) one of us." Phil Dusenberry, a creative director at the Batten, Barton, Durstine, & Osborn (BBD&O) agency responsible for the campaign, summed up the difference between Coke and Pepsi advertising, writing that Coke's campaigns focused on products while Pepsi focused on *people*.[30] Those people would be dubbed the Pepsi Generation, and the designation applied to "youthful types enjoying life to its fullest before the envying eyes of non-belongers."[31] The Pepsi Generation moniker became so popular that it entered the vernacular as a catchphrase describing the so-called baby boomers born after World War II, and it showed up in everything from studies on health and aging to criticism of the media, youth, and even the Vietnam War.[32] As described so elegantly by marketing historian Richard S. Tedlow, "By creating this identification of their product with this new generation, Pepsi's marketers took the world as it was and made it more so."[33]

Bethany Klein notes that Pepsi's relationship with popular music worked largely because the company was willing to take risks.[34] Indeed, the soda giant's commercials proved innovative due to the brand's willingness to experiment with various formats and media, including network television, radio, film, cable television, music videos, audio recordings, ringtones, and the internet. More significantly, the brand worked diligently to follow music industry trends and included the sounds of teen pop, girl groups, early soul, rock, adult pop, disco, and hip hop in its campaigns. Using these musics allowed its commercials to keep a pulse on the current ethos of the nation by supporting images of thrilling leisure activities, the counterculture, the sexual revolution, technological innovation, and even desegregation.[35]

It was therefore the brand's inclination to adopt musical tropes from groups not typically represented in commercials—those marginalized by age, gender, and race—that helped its campaigns to attract so much attention, both positive and negative. Moreover, as underdog brand Pepsi has always been obliged to appeal to diverse audiences, especially because many of its bottlers (who have controlled its advertising budgets) have relied on patronage from what the brand called "special markets," a term used to designate nonwhite consumers, especially African Americans and Latinos.[36] The brand's aim to attract the youth market from the 1960s onward also necessitated Pepsi's embrace of music made by and for Black communities because these songs would define the sounds of the twentieth century.

Appropriating this music was not easy, however, since ideological constructs of race and racial relationships in the United States remained in flux. As America grappled with the complex social and cultural ramifications of the post-civil-rights era, Pepsi's marketers, too, wavered over what, who, when, and how they would appropriate nonhegemonic (i.e., non-white, male, middle-class, and heteronormative) signifiers into its commercials. As chapter 1 illustrates, Pepsi (like other national brands) was initially hesitant to feature nonwhite musicians and musics in its coast-to-coast campaigns—especially those that alluded rock and roll, which was considered too controversial to attract mainstream consumers.[37] Pepsi's marketing decisions also hinged on its focused efforts to beat Coca-Cola—a feat that required shaking the reputation it had gained from its "Nickel, Nickel" days as the cheap and low-class "black Coke" to appeal to more white middle-class audiences.[38]

But once Pepsi hired Michael Jackson in the mid-1980s and realized the crossover impact that some African American artists—and even white musicians singing in black styles—could have on its national and later global campaigns, the brand (sometimes unwittingly) began taking even more risks with the musicians it hired and the demographic categories that its commercials would highlight (including class, sexuality, and even religion). At the insistence of these new stars, Pepsi and its marketing team were often forced to loosen their grip on the creative aspects and content of endorsed commercials, thereby permitting their celebrities' songs and images to become their guiding forces. So, in addition to becoming some of the most highly publicized, watched, and remembered commercials to date, the brand's pop music campaigns also represented the extreme ends of the spectrum for success. Whereas it received substantial acclaim for its early 1960s "Think Young" and "Come Alive" campaigns featuring Joanie Sommers's teen-pop vocals (chapter 1) and garnered numerous awards for its 1984 "The Choice of a New Generation" spots with Michael Jackson (chapter 2) and early 1990s Ray Charles commercials (chapter 6), its 1989 spot with Madonna (chapter 5) attracted substantial criticism and remained, until 2017, one of the most controversial commercials to date.[39] Consequently, by allowing the sometimes volatile and controversial musical tropes, personas, and agendas of their superstars to appear unfiltered in a historically conservative and fickle industry, the soda giant's commercials proved essential in establishing advertising's affiliation with the music industry. In sum, Pepsi's campaigns opened new paths for celebrity endorsements, turned the ad industry on to the use of new and emerging pop trends, and established the ground rules for future co-branding deals.

The attention Pepsi garnered for its campaigns not only forced its rivals, and especially the market leader Coca-Cola, to take notice but also inspired countless books, memoirs, and videos.[40] It even prompted the Smithsonian Institution to conduct an extensive "Pepsi Generation" oral history project in 1986 (cited throughout this book), which resulted in a museum exhibit and an archive focused on the brand's advertising efforts. Talk of the "cola wars"—the decades-long battle for market domination between Pepsi and Coke—has inundated the media, the advertising and television trade press, financial reports, literature, and cultural scholarship ever since Pepsi's "Nickel, Nickel" campaign. Even today the pervasiveness of the cola wars continues as the rivalry often extends beyond the typical television ad buy and into popular culture itself.

A fairly recent example of how ingrained these brands have become in popular culture occurred in 2015 during the second season of the Fox network's hip-hop-themed show *Empire* when it dedicated a story line to a composition contest in which one of the main characters won an appearance in a Pepsi commercial.[41] The scenes were strung out over three episodes and culminated in a filmed commercial that was integrated so seamlessly into the plot that it was difficult to separate the television show from the soda pitch. The enduring prevalence of the cola wars in American culture was also highlighted throughout the historically informed AMC drama *Mad Men*. The parity rivalry surfaced throughout its seven seasons, although the show's most striking homage occurred in the series finale when, during its final 60 seconds, Coke's famous 1971 "Hilltop" commercial was played in its entirety to suggest the bright future that lay ahead of the show's personally flawed yet professionally talented lead character.

For many who recount the story of the cola wars, it was in fact this legendary spot that established Coca-Cola's superiority over Pepsi due to the fact that its counterculturally themed jingle was turned into the successful chart-topping song, "I'd Like to Teach the World to Sing." However, as the first two chapters here elucidate, Coke may have won this particular battle but the war was far from over. Not only did Pepsi's relentless pursuit of the youth culture compel its rival to create this campaign, but a little over a decade later its soda sales would finally exceed Coke's, at least temporarily, as a result of its 1984 Michael Jackson spots. Jackson's campaign was remarkable in that it defeated the soda leader for the first time in history, solidified the permanence of popular music's place in advertising, and, as recently recounted in *The Atlantic*, effectively killed the prominence of specially composed jingles in American advertising.[42] Accordingly, this book's examination of Pepsi's marketing practices and its role in the cola wars does not merely retell the story of the battle between two American corporate giants but sheds new light on the *musical dimensions* of a commercially produced battle for cultural superiority.

AIMS

Conversations both within and outside of the advertising industry about the use of music in commercials largely revolve around the perceived "feelings" or "moods" that music is believed to promote within the context of a branded experience. It is therefore this book's task to investigate how and why campaign music creates, or is thought to create, these experiences. This study continues the momentum of previous scholarship on this topic, but differs in its scope and content. *Soda Goes Pop* integrates musical analysis with historical research and cultural theory to trace the evolution of well-known commercials for a single influential American corporate brand to demonstrate their reflection of larger changes in the music and advertising industries over a 73-year period. As explained earlier, the focus on Pepsi during this period is instructive due to its pioneering and relentless efforts to align itself with America's musical trends. The pages that follow are informed by research on the music and advertising industries, including autobiographies, firsthand accounts, pop culture magazines, and trade press journals. They also incorporate primary source multimedia, including archived tapes of newsreels, interviews, commercials, and award shows studied at the Smithsonian's National Museum of American History in Washington, DC; the University of California, Los Angeles (UCLA), Film and Television Archive; and the Paley Center for Media in Los Angeles.

Since the majority of the literature on music in advertising misses opportunities to analyze the sounds themselves, the approaches taken here are rooted in musical analysis and hermeneutic approaches common to musicology. It is important to clarify, however, that, although the analysis employed in this book often takes structural approaches similar to those employed by prominent music semioticians such as Phillip Tagg and even follows the basic tenets of semiotic theory as developed by Charles Sanders Peirce, Ferdinand de Saussure, Roland Barthes, and others, this is not intended to be a semiotic study.[43] In the effort to make this book accessible to a diverse readership, it instead aims to historicize and contextualize the range of meanings audiences have or may have gleaned from sights and sounds that the creators of advertising texts (intentionally or not) have used to construct them. The goal, then, is not to theorize or to create new analytic paradigms for parsing out musical meaning but to investigate the ways in which musical meaning informs and impresses on a historical narrative. *Soda Goes Pop* therefore occupies a middle ground between prominent culturally and economically focused inquiries about music's role in advertising and those containing terminology-laden musical analysis geared toward experts.

Because both American advertising texts and pop music are intended to circulate widely, this book recognizes that they generally operate within the presumed boundaries of their target audiences' experiences and decoding capabilities. This study therefore follows the notion accepted by cultural scholars that audience competencies—that is, the presumed decoding skills on which marketers rely—determine the outcomes of a text's meanings. All inquiries are therefore geared toward what musically "experienced" (mostly) US audiences have, might have, or were expected to have understood from these texts based not only on specific signifiers in the commercials, their history, and the accompanying evidence of their reception in media sources, but also on the premises of what their creators—corporate executives, marketers, directors, and musicians—claim to have intended to convey.

In the effort to untangle the complex interaction between media and cultural references in Pepsi's commercials, the musical analyses in this book are framed by interdisciplinary theories, methodologies, and texts familiar to scholars and students of American studies, popular culture, advertising, and broadcast media. All analysis is thus explained in a manner that nonspecialist audiences will understand and informs readers with varying degrees of musical knowledge how and why a close consideration of commercial sounds themselves are important for investigating larger questions about the advertising industry and popular culture.

This book also accounts for the subjective pitfalls of interpretive methodologies, which include the polysemic nature of music in particular and cultural texts in general, the fact that diverse cultural groups read and understand texts differently, and the fact that some approaches have viewed cultural artifacts as fixed rather than fluid and changing forms. It also acknowledges that some commercials have been intentionally left open ended in order to produce a variety of possibilities. The chosen case studies are thus framed within the bounds of the historical documents that inform them, as well as the particularities of each spot's cultural moment, context, creation, and reception. By recognizing that there are many ways to flesh out meaning, this book attends to the media, politics, technology, biographies, ideologies, and identities that have shaped the creation and reception of individual commercial texts.

Although *Soda Goes Pop* models some historical, theoretical, and hermeneutic modes for examining the aesthetic effects of a phenomenon that has become increasingly prevalent over the past 60 years, it does not attempt to offer a comprehensive study of popular music's inclusion in television commercials. The interdisciplinary nature of this subject, as well as the gamut of social, political, cultural, historical, and aesthetic factors, is far too expansive for any one project to untangle. Additionally, the possibilities for incorporating new music in commercials are endless, making no one analytical or theoretical model suitable for all cases. This is especially true when considering that each brand offers its own "unique" products and services, making the music its marketers choose work toward very specific meanings, feelings, and ideas.

Neither is this an all-inclusive study of popular music in Pepsi-Cola advertising. Examining all the radio, television, and internet commercials for the soda's "flanker" products, as well as the countless national and global brands PepsiCo has acquired since the days of "Nickel, Nickel"—beverages such as Mountain Dew and Gatorade and restaurant chains including Taco Bell and Pizza Hut—would surely require dozens of focused studies of their own.[44] Even within the bounds of Pepsi's own regular and diet soda commercials, these campaigns differ in their foci, messages, target audiences, regions, and approaches, making a comprehensive analysis beyond the scope of one book.

Instead, this study considers representative music-focused television commercials for Pepsi's regular cola and a few prominent spots for its name-bearing diet soda. It examines campaigns that were either made with US audiences in mind or used American music and celebrities to attract global consumers. As a qualitative study about the sounds of its advertising, it is this book's unique focus on the *music* in Pepsi's commercials that drives its narrative. This project thus chronicles the advertising practices of one brand and the commercials that have made it (in)famous.

SURVEYING THE FIELD

Soda Goes Pop expands most obviously on foundational scholarship about music's role in television commercials. It builds on work begun 20 years ago by music theorist Nicholas Cook, who was the first scholar to use formal analysis to consider how advertising uses pre-existing music.[45] Both Cook and (later) communications scholar Anna Lisa Tota demonstrated some of the ways in which classical music styles were applied to specific products and discussed how their sounds created new meanings in branded contexts.[46] In recent years, music scholars Ron Rodman and Nicolai Graakjær have developed systematic approaches for investigating this phenomenon as it applies to advertising soundtracks that feature a variety of musical styles. The pages that follow take into account Rodman's model for considering mediated elements that exist simultaneously within a commercial— music, images, narration, and so on—as well as Graakjær's call for a "cotextual" examination of their roles and meanings.[47] Ethnomusicologist Mark Laver's work on portrayals of jazz in advertising also provides a useful review of music's role in commodity culture. This book complements his chapter on a television commercial for a short-lived 2006 flavor called Pepsi Jazz by offering a larger historical overview of the brand's appropriation of well-known styles.[48]

As noted above, *Soda Goes Pop* builds on work by Bethany Klein and Timothy Taylor through a close investigation of Pepsi commercials that they have pinpointed as foundational to today's relationships between the advertising and music industries. Klein uses Pepsi as a case study in her 2009 book, which examines the prevalence and effects of popular music licensing. She documents that an ideological shift had taken place by the early twenty-first century as taboos over "selling out" had given way to the need for exposure. She also expresses concern for the future of popular music, warning that many listeners have simply surrendered to claims of necessity and failed to act as "wardens of culture" for advertisers who go too far in reinterpreting songs for branding purposes.[49] Taylor expresses similar sentiments, writing that American cultural forms have become inextricably linked to corporate interests to the point that he no longer hears a distinction between popular and advertising music.[50] He in fact provides the most thorough historical and ethnographic overview of music in advertising to date and illustrates how the balance of musical expertise and business once privileged by music industry executives has been gradually displaced by the strategic imperatives of marketing professionals.[51] Indeed, the prevalence of music sponsorship, licensing, and synchronization by industries and corporations that previously were outside the realm of music making and distribution has become today's status quo.[52] Taylor's and Klein's work therefore appears at various points throughout this study as it digs deeper into the aesthetic reasons for popular music's prominence in twenty-first-century commercial culture.

This project is further informed by interdisciplinary studies that have examined music's newest relationships with branding, technology, and late capitalism. This includes scholarship by Anahid Kassabian, who investigates the many ways in which pre-existing popular music has become a "ubiquitous" tool for creating branded atmospheres, as well as that of Leslie Meier, who discusses the "promotional" implications of popular music in current branding models.[53] As discussed in the latter chapters of this book, pop's newest roles in commercial culture can be attributed to a number of factors, many of which can be accredited to what David Harvey calls a "speed up" of the production and circulation of commodities at the end of the twentieth century—conditions felt by the postmodern consumer and made possible by neoliberal policies that have continued to encourage technology, globalization, and market "freedom" for four decades.[54] These factors have ultimately changed the concept of "brands" and "branding" itself in the early twenty-first century, extending beyond corporations and into practically every realm of American life, including people and places.

The chapters that follow implement ideas from Harvey and also from media scholar Douglas Kellner, who reads postmodern discourse into the images of musical stars, recognizing that since the 1980s "spectacle" has become essential to the branding of their celebrity personas.[55] More specifically, this book illustrates the numerous ways that Pepsi has embraced the spectacle of its stars and leveraged considerable publicity and media formats to make its spots into must-see primetime "events."

This book's "Coda" takes into account studies of music, ambience, and sound as key components in creating twenty-first-century concepts of "brand awareness." Where jingles and one-off licensing once reigned supreme as the sounds of corporate advertising, a more distinct and focused practice called "sonic branding" now encourages brands to invest substantial time and money in defining their sounds—sounds that can range from a few-note logo or ID to larger forms borrowed from licensed songs belonging to a specific artist or genre. As explained by branding expert Daniel M. Jackson, practitioners of sonic branding claim to promote the "emotive power" of a brand's "beliefs," "ideas," and "identities."[56] Media scholar Devon Powers has been quick to reveal the potential downside of sonic branding ideology, however, arguing that it is used as a way to penetrate the perceived vulnerabilities of aural perception.[57] She claims that sonic branding "mobilizes and actualizes a particular kind of expertise meant to understand, interpret, and control both music as sound and hearing as a sense, then buttresses those ways of understanding as a means of creating and *extracting value*."[58]

Powers's remarks resonate strongly with those made twenty-one years earlier by music cognition scholar David Huron. Although advertising looked and sounded different in 1989, Huron labeled advertising agencies as "research institutes for social meanings" due to the substantial amount of meaning-directed demographic research that marketers (continue to) undertake.[59] He concluded, "But it is the overt knowledge of objectives and the consequent desire to control and handle the tools of musical meaning which make advertising such a compelling object of musical study."[60] Taking Huron's and Powers's ideas together arrives at this book's explicit task: to investigate the various ways in which Pepsi's marketers have historically attempted to "control," "handle," and "extract value" from preexisting popular music. More specifically, *Soda Goes Pop* contributes to these and other critical conversations about intersections among American music, media, and popular culture by providing new ways to understand today's music licensing and sonic branding practices through the process of musical *redaction*.

REDACTION IN A BRANDED WORLD

Soda Goes Pop illustrates how corporate advertising's relationship with popular music has depended on piggybacking on the latter industry's aesthetics. As mentioned above and discussed in chapter 1, this practice gained prominence following the birth of rock and roll and the rise of the baby boomer generation—a time when popular music seemed to best capture the spirit of the 18- to 24-year-old demographic. Pepsi's mid-twentieth-century campaigns therefore featured soundtracks that combined older jingle practices and slogan material with fragments of best-selling pop songs and styles in an effort to attract youth. Unlike today's spots, the majority of Pepsi's early pop music commercials did not sample whole sections of pre-existing songs but borrowed, imitated, and rearranged signifying tropes, imagery, and stylistic features to align them with its branding messages. Consequently, the industry's now commonplace licensing of new pop songs resulted from a slow progression of co-optation that unfolded over time.

As illustrated by the examples at the beginning of this chapter, adapting pre-existing music requires considerable dexterity since marketers essentially de-compose songs created for other purposes and then re-compose them to fit within the time and contextual constraints of an advertisement. Accordingly, the music undergoes what is referred to throughout this book as the process of *redaction*. As a large-scale study of Pepsi's redactive practices, this book expands on the idea as defined by media scholar John Hartley, who was the first to apply the term to contemporary cultural media. Hartley initially used the concept to theorize the social function of journalism at the dawn of the twenty-first century, arguing that the journalist's role had become "redactional" to the point where he or she worked "not as an original writer but as a professional redactor" of already circulating information.[61] In the years since, Hartley has revisited the concept to describe various cultural phenomena, arriving at the conclusion that "redaction is the creative editorial process of bringing existing materials together to make new texts and meanings. Redaction has added value to the end of meaning's value chain."[62]

For the purposes of this book, it is the brand's marketers, executives, and occasionally the star musicians themselves who become the redactors. The following chapters thus extend Hartley's principles with musicological methods that closely examine the *aesthetic* implications of marketers' specific yet varied redactive practices on pre-existing popular music to explain their branded outcomes. In following Hartley's hypothesis that redaction allows a means for "gatekeeping," a study of Pepsi's redactive practices therefore sheds light on the soda giant's claim to musical authority in the new millennium as its marketers have cleverly applied a variety of strategies to co-opt the latest hits over a 73-year period.[63]

Much like Hartley, the following chapters extend the various definitions of the verb *redact* in the *Oxford English Dictionary* (OED) beyond "written texts" and into other cultural forms. These definitions include the following:

1. To bring together in a single entity; to combine, unite.
2. a.) To bring together or organize (ideas, writings, etc.) into a coherent form: To compile, arrange, or set down in a written document.
3. a.) To reduce to a certain state or condition, especially an undesirable one.
   b.) To reduce (a material thing) *to* a certain form, especially as an act of destruction.
4. a.) To put (writing, text, etc.) in an appropriate from for publication; to edit.[64]

The approaches taken here, however, differ in a significant way from Hartley's. Whereas he has argued that redaction operates as a form of production, *not* reduction, *Soda Goes Pop* explores redaction through the processes of both production *and* reduction. This book investigates how redaction *produces* newly commodified texts by "combining," "uniting," "organizing," and "compiling" musical signifiers together with (invented) product attributes (OED entries 1 and 2), *and* it examines how and why advertising "*reduces*" and "*edits*" pre-existing popular songs and styles in order to align them with branding aims (entries 3 and 4). In other words, although *redaction* is used to describe how marketers incorporate music to create new meanings for the product, the term is equally applied to study the process's effects on the musical texts themselves and is therefore used to illuminate the numerous ways that advertisers have learned to *select, censor,* and *restructure* pop sights and sounds in order to adopt their best-known features—an act that, as the OED definition suggests, is often "destructive" to the musical text and at times "undesirable" for audiences. This book thus studies the process of redaction at various points along a musical text's "meaning value chain," including its inception and original form(s) (as a single, music video, performance, etc.), its circulation and reception outside advertising contexts, its adaptation into commercials, and finally its newly acquired branded meanings.

The study of redaction here is further informed by Susan McClary's musicological work, which demonstrates how tonality, structure, and teleology effect the reception of popular songs.[65] It also engages with that of Robert Fink, who supports and extends McClary's discussions to show how specific musical genres intentionally subvert expected musical trajectories, generating what he calls "recombinant teleologies" that work to delay gratification.[66] Since commercial scores are structured to fit branding parameters, McClary's and Fink's concepts are extended here to demonstrate how popular songs and styles are redacted to rush toward, delay, or suspend musical resolution and increase the desire for Pepsi's product.

Soda Goes Pop also borrows concepts from Stuart Hall, who theorized that advertisements should be examined through three distinct but interrelated factors that produce various possible meanings: "encoding" (the decision making and production that go into creating an advertisement), "text" (the spot itself), and "decoding" (how the commercial is received).[67] The chapters that follow extend this framework to show how musical redaction occurs within the process of encoding. Just as a visual symbol or icon can be isolated and recontexualized among commodity signs to connote or denote something entirely new, so too can musical signifiers be treated this way. Redaction at the encoding stage thus affects the resulting text and decoding processes, creating the potential—for better or worse—for marketers to redirect and even omit the underlying social, cultural, and political implications of a track to fit advertising contexts. And because redactive processes effect how audiences perceive musical texts, the outcomes of the commercials investigated here (i.e., their decodings) are conceptualized as falling somewhere within what Hall defined as "preferred readings" (where meaning is received by audiences as intended by the brand), "negotiated readings" (where broad features of the message are accepted but the meaning is configured through personal experiences or knowledge), or "oppositional readings" (where advertising's ideologies run against the grain of its viewing audience).[68]

Influential conversations about the role that visual images have played in advertising ideology and meaning creation are also extended throughout this study to discussions about *music*. Scholars agree that, as potent cultural texts, advertising borrows, amplifies, and even shapes ideologies that pervade American society. Criticism of these practices can be traced back to the late 1950s when Vance Packard released his landmark book *The Hidden Persuaders*, which documented advertising's psychological effects on shoppers.[69] In the decades since, sociologists Judith Williamson and Sut Jhally, along with cultural studies scholar Raymond Williams, have likened advertising to a form of "magic" that animates inert commodities with personal and social meaning.[70] Jhally, in particular, postulates that the breakdown of the nuclear family and religious institutions has opened a space for advertising to step in and offer guidance to the general population. He claims that "advertising derives its power from providing meaning that is not available elsewhere."[71]

Jhally followed Williamson, who as early as 1978 used semiotic analysis to discuss the meanings conveyed by the imagery in print advertisements. She summarized viewers' relationships to advertising, writing, "Ads produce a universe of puzzles—one that we cannot move in without 'deciphering,' one that requires us to stop and work out a solution."[72] Grant McCracken's later work on meaning transfer shows evidence of her influence since Williamson had already argued that advertising works as a mediator for meaning that, as a result, produces a "'metastructure' where meaning is not just 'decoded' within one structure but transferred to create another."[73] Williamson even mentioned Pepsi advertising specifically in her pioneering study and pointed out the ways in which the brand created the myth of individuality only to reinscribe each "Pepsi Person" back into its fictional "clan."[74] These ideas are therefore prevalent throughout *Soda Goes Pop* as keys to examining the ways in which Pepsi's advertising has used musical meaning as a kind of cultural "currency" to attract audiences.[75]

Robert Goldman and Steven Papson's work also provides a foundation for considering redacted sounds. In particular they recoin terms first introduced by Williamson that describe how audiences relate to ads. These include the terms *appellate* (how ads invite audiences in), *alreadyness* (the ideological assumptions and experiences audiences bring to ads), and *equivalence* (the link made between the product and the promised result).[76]

Michael Schudson's notion of "capitalist realism" runs most obviously throughout this book. Like his predecessors, Schudson discusses the various ways in which advertising borrows cultural forms. More specifically, he focuses on the ways that art, specifically visual art, is made banal and posits that "abstraction is essential to the aesthetic and intention of contemporary national consumer-goods advertising."[77] He therefore likens the generic aesthetics of advertising to Soviet socialist realism, dubbing it "capitalist realism" since it "more often flattens than deepens experience." His insights are extended here to examine the various ways in which marketers have attempted—and sometimes failed—to redact complex musical structures by emptying out specific sonic signifiers to create banal and fantastic worlds of consumption.

ORGANIZATION

This book is organized in six chapters, which are framed by an introduction and coda and divided into three parts. Each chapter focuses on key Pepsi-Cola commercials that feature popular music and celebrity images, the majority of which were designed to cater to youth or at least "youthful-thinking" consumers. These commercials were chosen based on the prominence they gained from a combination of factors: their wide circulation, lofty budgets, high production values, extreme popularity, technological innovation, aesthetic novelty, financial success, and prominent mention in primary sources and media. While Pepsi remains at the center of these analyses, this study accounts for elements that influenced the historical moment of each spot, including the brand's relationships with key competitors (especially Coca-Cola), other influential national brand campaigns, technological advances, social and political factors, and transformations in the music and advertising industries.

"Part I: Early Pop Jingles and Pepsi's Shift to Youth Marketing" provides a broad historical overview of the popular marketing practices employed by Pepsi and its competitors in the mid-twentieth century. More specifically, it demonstrates how and why the brand changed its focus to target "those who think young," and it provides the early history of the use of pop music in commercials, laying the groundwork for the case studies to come. Chapter 1, "The Pepsi Generation 'Now and Then': (Re)composing the Cola Wars," continues the story detailed earlier with "Nickel, Nickel" by investigating Pepsi's early years of borrowing and emulating an array of popular styles in order to appeal to its newly sought-out demographic. It builds on influential work by J. C. Louise and Harvey Yazijian, Stanley Hollander and Richard Germain, Thomas Frank, and Timothy Taylor, that has considered the brand's appeal to youth culture.[78] More specifically, this chapter re-hears the brand's well-known 1960s–70s campaigns through the lens of its nostalgic 2002 commercial featuring pop princess Britney Spears. These analyses are supported by archival materials that illuminate marketers' aesthetic decisions, confirm sales outcomes, and highlight the brand's midcentury battles with Coca-Cola. A closer examination of the music and images in Pepsi's original commercials against their millennial remakes thus reveals the motivations behind the brand's redactive methods and creates a clearer picture of marketers' unrealized intentions for its landmark campaigns.

"Part II: Pop Songs, Celebrity Spectacle, and the MTV Generation" features case studies that closely analyze the various ways in which Pepsi borrowed, redacted, and redirected musical signifiers in its most popular campaigns of the 1980s. This section is the largest due to the fact that the 1980s represented a pivot point for pop music marketing as a result of the increased prominence of neoliberal economic policies (including globalization and rapid technological advances), as well as the advent of the cable network MTV (Music Television) as an innovative and highly profitable multimedia music distribution venue. Consequently, the commercials from this era are not only the best remembered, but they also set trends and defined the standards for using popular music and celebrities in corporate advertising.

Chapter 2, "Big Soda and Celebrity Pop: Pepsi Meets Michael Jackson," examines the pioneering 1984 "The Choice of a New Generation" campaign, which was intended to boost Jackson's visibility and lend cultural credibility to the brand. This chapter outlines how Jackson's commercials drastically changed the look and sound of celebrity endorsements by investigating the aesthetic reworking of both his image and hit pop song "Billie Jean." It further extends advertising theories by Judith Williamson and Michael Schudson and employs close musical analysis to deduce how Pepsi's marketers isolated memorable musical themes and reordered the harmonic structure in "Billie Jean" to create new meanings for the song in the campaign.[79] This case study reveals how Pepsi's successful appropriation of Jackson's iconic visual "symbols" and redaction of the musical structures in his original track changed it from a cautionary tale about paternity to a family-friendly soda slogan.

Riding the success of Jackson's campaigns, Pepsi created more of its "The Choice of a New Generation" commercials, this time with baby boomer artists Lionel Richie (1985), Tina Turner (1986–88), and David Bowie (1987). Chapter 3, "The Choice of a Neoliberal Generation: Pepsi Models the Perfect Consumer," chronicles how the brand gave way to the ideologies of neoliberalism and redacted the performances, videos, and songs of these veteran musicians to reimagine the ideal late capitalist soda customer. It contextualizes these commercials within the ideologies of technology, globalization, and upward social mobility promised by the new neoliberal marketplace as theorized by David Harvey and recently expanded upon by music scholars.[80] It further illustrates how the coupling of increased spectacle with these aging stars' middle-of-the-road styles actually complicated the image Pepsi had established with its Jackson campaigns. Primary sources and close analysis illuminate how the soda giant's attempt to lure consumers under the guise of the MTV spectacle sent inconsistent and confusing messages to viewers of all ages.

In 1987 Pepsi created a second campaign with Michael Jackson. Chapter 4, "Chasing 'Bad': Pop Fantasies and Teleological Fiction," highlights the historical precedents this campaign set as the first-ever episodic series of spots that told a long-form story. Its commercials also looked more like music videos than any others to date and proved enormously successful in publicizing Jackson's newest album, video, and tour. Most significantly, this campaign marked a pivotal moment in advertising's transition away from the jingle: its spots incorporated a unique hybrid of Jackson's original lyrics to "Bad" and soda slogan material. Formal analysis reveals how marketers reshuffled the song's teleological harmonic structures to bolster the incredulous action sequences onscreen and worked to literally harmonize Jackson's lyrical assertion of superiority—his badness—with Pepsi's product. By blending hermeneutic inquiry with foundational theories about simulation and recent scholarship on Michael Jackson by Joseph Vogel and Ruchi Mital, among others, this chapter chronicles how and why marketers attempted to redact Jackson's music and his controversial physical appearance to put a positive spin on his image for these spots.[81]

Chapter 5, "A 'Wish' and a 'Prayer': Pepsi Faces the Limits of Redaction," chronicles the global controversy that resulted from one of the most notorious campaigns in US advertising history—Madonna's "Make a Wish." By re-engaging with foundational interdisciplinary scholarship on the commercial, this chapter investigates the brand's missteps in its move away from the jingle and branded slogans and demonstrates that it was the soda giant's inability to fully redact the pop star's song that unintentionally positioned it at the center of Madonna's controversial agenda for her newest single.[82] Close analysis shows how the superstar's musical choices questioned dominant racial and religious ideologies and how the transfer of these sonic signifiers into the commercial caused Pepsi's images to grapple with the same politics. In revisiting Schudson's ideas about capitalist realism and considering the spot through a modernist Brechtian lens, this chapter further illuminates how and why Pepsi's naive approach to Madonna and her music—including an agreement not to change any of the song's lyrics or to omit the politically charged musical tropes—caused marketers to lose control of its densely coded sonic signifiers and open themselves to considerable backlash from religious groups worldwide.[83]

The book's final section, "Part III: Millennial Music Marketing: Redact, Reuse, Recycle," investigates the evolution of musical marketing at the turn of the new millennium. From the 1990s onward, the soda giant and its competitors embraced a diversity of musical genres, expanded the potential for co-branding opportunities, and experimented with various media and distribution venues. Chapter 6, "Humorous Hits, Nostalgic Notes, and Retro Refrains in the 1990s" demonstrates how Pepsi combined the lessons it learned from its earlier pop music endorsements and the traditional midcentury jingle practices on which it had once relied. In order to widen its demographic reach, the soda brand expanded its musical repertoire to include the hip hop flow of M. C. Hammer and the classic soul sounds of Ray Charles, as well as references to older rock, Motown, and disco hits. With the support of recent work on humor in advertising by Fred K. Beard, as well as Michael D. Dwyer's scholarship on nostalgia and Simon Reynolds's musings on the rise of retro in pop culture, this chapter demonstrates how the brand largely steered its marketing tactics away from focusing on newly released music.[84] Instead its commercials redacted pre-existing songs that were not humorous, nostalgic, or retro on their own into texts that roused these responses and catered to all of Pepsi's past and present "generations."

"Pepsi Coda: Twenty-First-Century 'Pop' and the Branded Future" brings this book full circle to investigate how its pair of 2011–12 *X Factor–*

U.S. spots exemplified the converged interests of the music and advertising industries in the twenty-first century. The first pages draw from the analytical methods employed in previous chapters to discuss how the soda giant's reinvoking of its most successful campaigns in "Music Icons" attempted to revise pop music history and promise new democratic possibilities for its sponsorship of hot musical talent. An examination of the follow-up commercial, "King's Court," investigates Pepsi's claim to create a new utopian musical culture through the reality talent show and its inaugural winner, Melanie Amaro. Kellner's theories about "technocapitalism" and the "infotainment society" help to untangle the complicated relationships that the soda giant formed with the various industries involved in the show's production.[85] Additionally, scholarship by Nicholas Carah, Henry Jenkins, Katherine L. Meizel, and others illuminates the reality of viewers' labor for the competition.[86] Media sources and public opinion further help to explain the reasons for Amaro's short-lived single and the X Factor show's fast descent into obscurity, thus clarifying why Pepsi's guarantee for creative innovation proved both unconvincing and unsuccessful. This chapter thus confirms that, despite the brand's long history of music marketing, Pepsi's stake in popular music continues to reside in its sponsorship and *redaction* of the latest sights and sounds—not in their creation. In completing a narrative that reveals as much about the long-term effects of popular music on corporate advertising as it does the other way around, the book's final pages take a step back to consider the brand's complicated history with the musical texts it sponsored and suggests further avenues for inquiry.

CHAPTER 1

The Pepsi Generation "Now and Then"

(Re)composing the Cola Wars

Pepsi-Cola would solidify its place as America's number-two soft drink in the 1960s with innovative marketing campaigns that would force its rival, Coca-Cola, and the advertising industry as a whole to restrategize their approaches. The fierce competition between the two soda brands, famously dubbed the "cola wars," gained momentum in the decade's first year when Pepsi's newly hired advertising firm, BBD&O, confirmed that product-focused marketing efforts had proven useless due to the soda's parity status. These findings explained the minimal successes the brand had gained with 1950s campaigns that stressed the product's qualities. Despite featuring endorsements by celebrities such as James Dean and Polly Bergen, audiences were only mildly persuaded with promises about the soda's energizing and dietary potential, namely "More Bounce to the Ounce" and "Have a Pepsi, the Light Refreshment."[1] Pepsi's 1958 efforts fared even worse when its new CEO, Alfred Steele, demanded that the brand take a more sophisticated approach.[2] The resulting "Be Sociable" campaign was a stark departure from the brand's affordable depression era image in its picturing of formally dressed, "debonair" couples dancing ballroom style to an acoustic jazz quartet onscreen. Although Pepsi's new jingle vaguely alluded to popular trends of the era, its composer, Hank Sylvern, used the sounds of what has been dubbed "George Shearing–style" jazz to suggest the aspirational mobility of the white middle class.[3] These lofty sights and sounds were intended to "kick Pepsi 'upstairs' into the prestige class, [and to] make it a family drink and have it poured in the living room not just the kitchen."[4] But, much to Steele's dismay, "Be Sociable" failed to convince audiences of Pepsi's elite cultural capital or to attract acclaim, thus demonstrating that it could not challenge Coca-Cola's reputation for quality nor compete with its image as a promoter of "traditional" American values.[5]

Pepsi thus willingly took the advice of its new marketing firm and refocused its advertising dollars to attract the ideal cola consumer—adolescent, post–World War II baby boomers. Philip Hinerfeld, the vice-president and director of Pepsi marketing at the time, outlined the strategies of the company's first youth-focused campaign in a 1961 article, noting its appeal "to young families and to those who 'think young.'"[6] He justified the brand's new direction, saying, "American society places a premium on youth, the maintaining of youth, the image of youth, young vigor, and the youthful approach." With the help of BBD&O, Pepsi would thus fashion itself as the soda for the young and the young-at-heart. As this chapter illustrates, this move prompted the brand to rely heavily on music—especially popular music—to communicate its new message.

Much has been written about Pepsi's efforts to dominate the youth market from the 1960s onwards, including a mid-1980s exhibit created by the Smithsonian National Museum of American History. In addition to plentiful trade press and media coverage, scholarship from a variety of fields has documented the economic and cultural implications of Pepsi's marketing practices, including that of J. C. Louise and Harvey Yazijian (1980), Stanley Hollander and Richard Germain (1993), Thomas Frank (1997), and Timothy Taylor (2012). This chapter builds on these historical documents and critiques to pinpoint the ways in which Pepsi and its marketing targeted this new demographic in its redaction of the concept of "youthfulness" into its commercial soundtracks. Rather than rehashing well-worn points, the analysis here takes a different approach by rehearing the brand's pioneering "Pepsi Generation" spots—especially those from the 1960s and early 1970s—through their re-creation 40 years later in a retrospective commercial that featured teen-pop idol Britney Spears. A closer examination of Pepsi's 2002 "Now and Then" commercial illuminates the company's keen awareness of its own history and its aim to venerate and even remake its past through a nostalgic lens that aimed to attract Spears's millennial fans while also reengaging aging boomers with its use of old jingles.

To unpack the brand's strategies, the following pages engage with recent literature by Michael D. Dwyer and Svetlana Boym, who argue that nostalgia is a longing not just for place, as in its early definition, but for a different *time*.[7] They also stress that nostalgia does not have to be historical or accurate but that it ultimately tries to cope with and perhaps repair a sense of loss felt in the present. In Dwyer's work on the fluidity of pop culture's relationship to its own past, he confirms, "Nostalgic longing . . . can be used in efforts to remake the present, or at least to imagine corrective alternatives to it."[8] He defines nostalgia as a "critical affective response" that "forces us to confront the contingencies that shape our ever-changing responses to texts: history, culture, politics, intertextual networks, even our subjectivity."[9]

As discussed further in chapter 6, nostalgic and retro signifiers of pop's past had become prevalent in advertising campaigns from the 1990s onward. It comes as no surprise, then, that Pepsi would mobilize nostalgia as a "critical affective response" to cope with the brand's 2002 anxieties about its steady decline in soda sales.[10] What is most revealing, therefore, about viewing Pepsi's iconic mid-twentieth-century spots through the lens of its 2002 re-creation is that the millennial commercial does not provide a simple re-presentation of past commercials: "Now and Then" remakes the campaigns, sometimes completely, to paint a more nuanced picture of the brand's targeting of youth—methods that were sometimes incorporated into its marketing and public outreach venues but did not always appear in its nationally televised commercials. Moreover, in viewing Pepsi's original campaigns in light of its newly redacted versions, the 2002 campaign highlights the soda brand's struggle from the 1960s onward to incorporate the signifiers that its marketers thought would appeal to youth while simultaneously avoiding sonic tropes deemed potentially volatile due to their association with what was broadly defined as "rock and roll." These "corrections" therefore offer insight into Pepsi's original intentions, aspirations, and views about the role its commercials played in the early years of the cola wars, and, most significantly, they provide further perspective into how the company, in hindsight, might have liked to define music's role in them.

BABY BOOMER AESTHETICS AND MADISON AVENUE

Pepsi shifted its advertising strategies at the precise moment when America's new generation of war babies would define the ethos of an entire decade. The influence of this generation was profound to say the least, in large part due to its size: by the mid-1960s, almost half of all Americans were under the age of 25.[11] Since the mid-1950s, music—and especially rock and roll—had proven central to the ideals and interests of this emergent youth culture, and many industries jumped at the chance to profit from its spending potential. Rooted in "race" and "hillbilly" musical styles, rock and roll had left an indelible mark on the United States in the 1950s, inspiring adolescent rebellion, alarming white middle- and upper-class adults, and turning the entertainment industry upside down. Consequently, when a series of scandals and unfortunate events slowed the genre's momentum in the decade's final years, rock and roll's initial upset of hegemonic norms and subsequent bust had already laid the groundwork for the simultaneous hopefulness and insecurity of the early 1960s.[12]

Indeed, the ideological precarity of the nation was confirmed in 1960 by the election of John F. Kennedy as the youngest-ever president of the United States. America's industries mirrored the growing rifts between up-and-coming boomers and older generations as some obviously clung to the social, economic, and religious decorum of the 1950s while others welcomed the change that rock and roll and President Kennedy had promised (but in the end did not fully deliver). These binary views manifested even further in conflicts about the Vietnam War and social movements advocating for civil rights and reproductive health (among others). As pointed out by the writer Thomas Frank, advertisements for Pepsi and Coke perfectly encapsulated the country's escalating tensions. Content with its position atop the cola market, Coke was slow to change its tactics, whereas Pepsi's conscientious shift to youth marketing in 1961 would leave an indelible mark on the soda and advertising industries, making waves in an industry that was always a few steps behind.[13]

It was not until the early years of the post-payola and pre-Beatles early 1960s that Madison Avenue would change its focus to the youth culture on which the entertainment industry had already capitalized (and some might say cannibalized) for more than half a decade.[14] According to Frank, a Creative Revolution took hold and marketers became obsessed with youth and the counterculture ideals that emerged from them.[15] These interests stemmed from a newer generation of copyists and art directors who yearned to upend the stodginess and lack of creativity they felt had befallen the industry in the 1950s. Advertisers therefore zeroed in on characteristics that Frank terms "hip" and "cool"—features that marketers believed defined countercultural young people. As a result, the advertising industry gradually turned to the soft sell and began to use consumer-centric lifestyle images and slogans.[16] By 1962 advertisements for beer, cigarettes, cosmetics, automobiles, and of course cola, were being fashioned specifically for youthful customers.[17]

Marketers were also well aware that music was at the heart of boomer culture and central to the "hip" and "cool" authenticity they were after— ideologies centered on individuality, creativity, and a deviation from the cookie-cutter conformity of the 1950s.[18] But, as Timothy Taylor has pointed out, executives struggled with how to incorporate new sounds without offending older audiences still wary of rock and roll and its associations with drugs and sex. Much of this anxiety stemmed from marketers' unfamiliarity with the language of popular music as a whole and their struggle to define it. As a result, there was a sizable disconnect between advertisers and youth because the term *rock and roll* meant different things to each group.

For advertisers *rock and roll*, later shortened to *rock*, was (and still is) a blanket term used to describe popular music intended for youth.[19] On the contrary, young people apprised of emergent 1960s trends knew that music had experienced a splintering of rock and roll's key idioms—its syncopation, amplification, controversial and anti-establishment lyrics, instrumentation, and, above all, its appeal to nonhegemonic ideologies and desires. New genres continually emerged to target even more specific segments of the youth population based on race, region, and gender. Recoiling from the backlash incurred by its rock and roll predecessors, music in the early 1960s—including girl group pop, surf and folk rock, rockabilly pop, and soul music—appeared, at least on the surface, to be more restrained and refined than the so-called abrasive and wild sounds that had dominated the charts in the previous decade. Later British invasion rock would unabashedly reclaim the original (furthering arguably white and masculine) ideologies of rock and roll, and their styles would extend to the psychedelic, punk, and funk genres that would fragment even further in the 1970s.

Marketers and brands that therefore attempted to stay on top of musical trends usually fell behind, partly due to the lag time common between the culture and advertising industries and partially due to the fear of scaring off consumers with music that the middle-aged executives who approved creative marketing decisions did not understand. And, while the advertising industry might have done more to keep up, new media technologies further accelerated the rise and fall of musical trends. Consequently, in an era of swift social, cultural, and political change, the accompanying evolution of musical styles proved difficult to capture while hot and even more impossible to predict, especially for outsiders who were neither young nor part of the counterculture.

According to Taylor, a few select brands did manage to capture the latest trends. The soft drink company 7 Up led the charge to attract youth as early as 1960 when it released a promotional recording and four commercials featuring the hit group the Kingston Trio.[20] The group's close vocal harmonies and country pop influences emanated from commercials that featured lengthy rationalizations of the group's endorsement as well as hokey scenarios that accompanied sung praises about the sponsor's ability to quench their seemingly insatiable thirst.

The following year Pepsi became the next and most memorable—and, as it would turn out, the most consistent—brand to latch onto youth.[21] Executives fearful of excluding loyal patrons, however, made it clear that the brand was targeting "attitude" not age—a philosophy that continues to be in flux even today.[22] Frank has detailed how Pepsi's early 1960s television commercials realized the brand's philosophy of "youthfulness" through its images, lyrics, and narration, explaining that the brand linked itself to the counterculture by the mid-1960s with a focus on "individuality" realized through anarchic and carnivalesque scenarios that conveyed to audiences that "Pepsi meant *vitality*, a colorful call to recreation, excitement, daring, and fun."[23] Indeed, its commercials featured quick visual cuts bolstered with narrated lines that highlighted the terms *active, lively*, and *energetic* to describe the soda and its ideal consumer. These tropes also assured viewers that the brand was up to date on what was "new" and "modern." And, as the following analysis demonstrates, Pepsi's winning formula paired these vivid images and selling points with carefully composed musical tracks that reflected a branded vision of what it was to be young in the 1960s.

HEARING PEPSI'S GENERATIONS, BOTH "NOW AND THEN"

Pepsi's nostalgic 2002 "Now and Then" retrospective commercial illuminates the many ways in which the brand attempted to place musical and visual signifiers of youthfulness at the forefront of its mid-twentieth-century campaigns. Table 1.1 outlines the form of the 90-second spot and shows how Pepsi's original commercials were reworked into vignettes of iconic campaigns that spanned 40 years.[24] The spot's narrative is notably dominated by four of the brand's most memorable campaigns from the

Table 1.1. "Now and Then" form

"Now and Then" Dates	Actual Campaign Years	Original Composition	Original Celebrity Performer	Commercial Inspiration
JINGLE: *"Now It's Pepsi, for Those Who Think Young"*				
1958	1961–63	Set to the 1928 tune "Makin' Whoopie" by Gus Kahn and Walter Donaldson	Joanie Sommers	"Soda Fountain" (1961)
JINGLE: *"Come Alive! You're in the Pepsi Generation."*				
1963	1963–67	Original jingle by Sid Ramin	Joanie Sommers *Later radio spots:* The Hondells, Martha and the Vandellas, and Del Shannon	None
JINGLE: *"The Taste That Beats the Others Cold, Pepsi Pours It On"*				
1966	1967–69	Original jingle by Anne Phillips	*Radio spots included:* The Turtles, The Four Tops, The Hondells, and the Trade Masters	"Surf Football" (1968)
JINGLE: *"You've Got a Lot to Live, and Pepsi's Got a Lot to Give"*				
1970	1969–73	Derived from a protest song by Joe Brooks	*Radio spots included:* Tina Turner, James Brown, and Lynn Anderson	"Young America" (1970)
JINGLE: *"The Choice of a New Generation"*				
1989	1984–1991	Redaction of Robert Palmer's 1988, "Simply Irresistible"	Robert Palmer	"Simply Irresistible" (1989)
JINGLE: *"Joy of Pepsi"* (*renamed from "Joy of Cola"*)				
2002	1999–2002	Original jingle by Mary Frisbie Wood and Clifford Lane	*Various artists, including:* Aretha Franklin, Issac Hayes, Faith Hill, and Britney Spears	N/A
JINGLE: *"Now It's Pepsi, for Those Who Think Young"*				
1958/2002	1961–63	"Makin' Whoopie" hook + added USP	Joanie Sommers	"Soda Fountain" (1961)

Source: Transcribed from PepsiCo. Inc., 2002.

1960s and 1970s: "Now It's Pepsi, for Those Who Think Young," "Come Alive! You're in the Pepsi Generation," "The Taste That Beats the Others Cold, Pepsi Pours It On," and "You've Got a Lot to Live, and Pepsi's Got a Lot to Give."[25] Rehearing the brand's original campaigns through its 2002 remake therefore illuminates Pepsi's triumphs and failures in redacting the pop signifiers it thought would best target its new demographic. By revisiting these campaigns at the turn of the millennium, the soda giant also reminds twenty-first-century audiences of the various cultural, political, and social forces that defined its earliest and most famous generations of consumers.

Thinking Young: A Classic Tune Meets an Ingénue

Pepsi's first youth-focused campaign, "Now It's Pepsi, for Those Who Think Young," made its radio premiere on February 20, 1961.[26] The television spots began airing on March 5 and continued for 11 weeks during prime-time breaks on all three major networks: ABC, NBC, and CBS. Marketers were careful to place Pepsi's first youth-oriented campaign during programs that would reach the right demographics (based on age) and psychographics (lifestyles) to enjoy the product. These included a musical variety special by actress Jane Powell, the Pepsi-sponsored *Miss America Pageant*, and fictional programs about deep-sea exploration and the Wild West.[27] By all accounts Pepsi poured considerable resources into this campaign, and its efforts paid off handsomely. *Sponsor* magazine reported that the brand's 29 percent increase in its advertising budget led to a net sales gain of $16 million in 1961.[28] By 1962 the success of the campaign's reach was confirmed by market research indicating that 81 percent of teenagers and 16 percent of young adults recognized the slogan.

The famous 1961 slogan set Pepsi-themed lyrics to the well-known melody of Gus Kahn and Walter Donaldson's 1928 musical number "Makin' Whoopee." Marketers made relatively simple lyrical, syntactic, and structural adjustments to redact the song into a jingle format suitable for the brand's new catchphrase.[29] The completed version printed in the March 1961 issue of *Pepsi-Cola World Magazine* (renamed there as the "The Pepsi Song") adheres to the original hit's A-A-B-A Tin Pan Alley song form (table 1.2, column 1).[30] Kahn's lyrics are completely rewritten for the spot. In lieu of the song's warning about the pitfalls of succumbing to bodily desires that necessitate marriage and result in unhappiness (i.e., "makin' whoopee"), the new Pepsi jingle declares that modernity and youthfulness now *happily* necessitate soda consumption. The redacted tune turned jingle thus calls attention to the brand's name by changing the "makin' whoopee" hook to the assertion "Now It's Pepsi." Marketers also inserted the USP tagline "For Those Who Think Young" after each of the A sections.

The 1961 jingle was recorded in various styles for radio commercials meant to attract audiences with diverse backgrounds.[31] For its run on television, it was cut down to fit the time constraints of the purchased segments. As column 2 of table 1.2 demonstrates, the original 1961 "Soda Fountain" commercial omitted the jingle's second A section to shorten the pitch to 60 seconds. For the 2002 remake, marketers redacted it even further to accommodate only the first verse (A) with a cut to a modified version of the final hook and tagline.

While the brand's 1961 marketing approach energized some of Pepsi's executives and marketing creatives, the bottlers who funded the company's advertising efforts expressed some reservations. Marketers were therefore tasked with explaining to the concerned parties that they had chosen a "universal tune" with "a proven record of popular appeal."[32] Ad executives cited recordings by Frank Sinatra, Rosemary Clooney, and Julie London to demonstrate the song's enduring popularity and verify that it had been brought "up to date."[33] Although these recordings supported the case for the song's popularity, it was likely the fact that the tune was not ultra

Table 1.2. "The Pepsi Song" form and its redactions

	"The Pepsi Song" (full jingle)	"Soda Fountain" (1961 TV spot)	"Now and Then" (2002 TV excerpt)
A	"The lively crowd . . ."	"The lively crowd . . ."	"The lively crowd . . ."
USP	"For those who think young."	"For those who think young."	Omitted
A	"The active set . . ."	Omitted	Omitted
USP	"For those who think young."		
B	"When you say 'Pepsi please' . . ."	"When you say 'Pepsi please' . . ."	Omitted
A	"So go ahead . . ."	"So go ahead . . ."	Cut to end of hook and USP:
USP	"For those who think young."	"For those who think young."	"Pepsi, for those who think young."

trendy that actually eased bottlers' fears about losing older customers. So, despite the fact that Pepsi's remake featured a slightly faster tempo and swapped the sappy strings heard in Eddie Cantor's famous rendition for a spritely woodwind and glockenspiel version played by the Mitchell Ayres band, the commercial arrangement itself was actually not all that more "modern" than the 1928 original.[34] Moreover, although recent recordings surely kept the tune alive, Sinatra, Clooney, and London were well out of the brand's targeted baby boomer age bracket, and so were their fans. Thus the jingle's message of youthfulness was not aurally conveyed in either the song selection or the treatment of the track, but instead in the brand's choice to feature 20-year-old Joanie Sommers singing the jingle's *vocals*.[35] Paired with onscreen images of smiling young people, it was Sommers's voice that helped Pepsi find its winning strategy.

Like Britney Spears, Joanie Sommers was a teen idol, and her impact on Pepsi's commercials was profound to say the least. Her vocals would not only define the sound of youthfulness in Pepsi's commercials, but when she was hired again to sing the brand's new "Come Alive!" jingle just two years later she became known as the "voice" of the "Pepsi Generation."

Unlike Pepsi's future stars, Sommers did not appear onscreen in its commercials. She in fact claimed that her participation was kept quiet due to concerns about the impact that associating herself with a brand would have on her rising career.[36] For young fans not exposed to the advertising trade publications that did happen to mention her name (something of which Sommers also must have been unaware), the artist believes that it was the unique quality of her voice that gave her away.[37] Indeed, her rich alto timbre, jazz-like syncopated delivery, and polite, clear articulation proved unmistakable.

For the "Think Young" television commercials, Sommers's "smoky" voice was dubbed over images of "youth in action."[38] Photographer Irving Penn approached the spots with innovative lighting, shadowing, angles, and close-up effects that were atypical for television commercials at the time. For the "Soda Fountain" commercial in particular, the camera focuses on a young blonde woman whose appearance and mannerisms suggest her embodiment of an innocent yet fun-loving girl next door. Sommers's recitation of the jingle narrates this young woman's actions as she quietly takes in the bustle of the soda fountain with a polite smile and distant gaze (fig. 1.1). By pairing these onscreen markers of white, virginal femininity with Sommers's smoky voice, the commercial upholds charac-

Fig. 1.1. The young ingénue enjoys her Pepsi. (Still from "Soda Fountain," PepsiCo. Inc., 1964.)

teristics of the modern ingénue: an adolescent female whose "in-between" image is simultaneously wholesome and flirtatious.[39] A typical media caricature of the time, Pepsi's commercial uses Sommers's voice to aurally suggest the fun consumers will have with the product while visually modeling the reserved decorum still expected of young women.

Forty years later Pepsi re-created the iconic signifiers of "Soda Fountain" with spokesperson Britney Spears (table 1.1). To heighten the commercial's nostalgia, the opening film appears in black and white while the sound of a film projector confirms its setting in the distant past. Middle-class, mostly white youngsters dressed like the cast of the film *Grease* mill about. Like the 1961 original, a male narrator introduces the scene, declaring that "People who think young say 'Pepsi, please.'" At that moment, Spears is handed a Pepsi cup and the camera focuses on her batting her eyelashes as she takes a polite sip. Inspired by the soda commodity, she then sings the first line of the "Think Young" jingle made famous by Sommers (table 1.2, column 3).

As the incorrect year (1958) superimposed at the bottom of the 2002 spot suggests, the scenarios depicted in 1961's "Soda Fountain" proved more fitting for the unnatural and staged celebrity cameos that upheld

Fig. 1.2. Spears gives viewers a knowing wink. (Still from "Now and Then," PepsiCo. Inc., 2002.)

the conservatism of the 1950s. The 2002 version reflects this by depicting the pop princess in a smart sweater set, capri pants, and pearls. Much like the onscreen actress in the original version, she projects an overtly mechanical demeanor. Spears's cropped and perfectly curled blonde wig (placed over her own long, bleached hair) further suggests the same sexual innocence and racial purity projected by her predecessor.[40] Spears's vocal performance deviates from the original, however, by mirroring her sweet onscreen actions. Despite her ability to sing with a range and timbral richness comparable to Sommers's, Spears instead employs an uncharacteristically quiet and whispy tone that proves more restrained and polite than that of her predecessor. Spears's innocent act does not last long, however, cracking just slightly toward the end of the segment. Following the crooning hook sung by a male trio in letterman sweaters, Spears switches to what has been dubbed her "fuller, more sensuous lower register" to sing the USP.[41] Her vocal gesture is followed by a gaping mouth and a knowing wink that is synchronized with an equally corny, crisp tonic cadence punctuated by high winds and a glockenspiel (fig. 1.2)

Decades after conversations about "selling out" had generally shifted in favor of musical celebrity endorsements, "Now and Then" features Spears onscreen in order to capitalize on the brand's missed opportunity to spotlight its first teen spokesperson, Joanie Sommers. Additionally, Spears's performance—her vocal delivery, choreography, clothing, and facial expressions—work to overly exaggerate and even parody the rigidity of early 1960s advertising practices, thereby highlighting their strangeness for millennial audiences. The "critically affective" nostalgic response created by the brand here thus results in a twenty-first-century pop-star spin on the image of the ingénue. Pepsi uses Spears's celebrity to update and unify the voice and image of the brand's vision for its (then) "modern" consumer.

The Cola Wars "Come Alive": Adventurous Sounds and the Battle for Top Pop Trends

At the completion of "Think Young," Spears's vignette fast-forwards to 1963 to feature her performance of another groundbreaking Joanie Sommers Pepsi campaign, "Come Alive! You're in the Pepsi Generation" (table 1.1). Following the early 1960s success of "Think Young," Pepsi and its bottlers committed well over $36 million to the 1963 "Come Alive!" campaign, 55 percent of which was earmarked for television advertising on 400 local and network stations.[42] The brand also changed its strategy so that it could market the regular and diet versions of its signature cola together. "Come Alive!" made its television debut on September 12, 1964, during the brand's cosponsored *Miss America Pageant* finals on CBS.[43]

The jingle, created by Sidney Ramin, was selected from a pool of submissions.[44] Ramin claims to have designed the tune with Joanie Sommers's "brassy" voice in mind.[45] His knowledge of the lyrics and the singer's vocal capabilities compelled him to write what he calls a "fanfaric" vocal melody where the first three notes signal the "heraldic" theme. Indeed, the major fourth interval between the first two notes (B♭ to E♭) has long been associated with forewarning horn calls in Western Art music traditions (example 1.1).[46] The opening three-note hook thus perfectly complements the slogan's call to action.

Example 1.1. "Come Alive!" jingle hook. ("Amusement Park," PepsiCo. Inc., 1965. Transcription by the author.)

The remainder of the musical score aurally signifies the brand's ideal consumers with a fast-paced, swinging big band sound that includes tight saxophone and woodwind runs, sharply articulated calls and responses, and dizzying flourishes. Ramin claimed that he composed the jingle to sound "bold, and big, and confident, and almost commanding."[47] His affinity for the energy of the big band sound is therefore evident throughout, as is his avoidance of references to the rock and roll style that he claimed to dislike.[48] Its exuberance thus obviously mirrors the optimistic ethos that pervaded the early 1960s prior to the assassination of John F. Kennedy or the escalation of the civil rights movement and Vietnam War protests.

Ramin's energetic score matches the images of the 1963–68 television spots that depicted young people's activities outdoors. "Amphibicar," for example, pictures a couple driving through various types of terrain in an automobile that converts into a boat. "Amusement Park" highlights the brand's (former) partnership with the then newly opened Disneyland theme park as the camera follows a young couple enjoying various rides.[49] Louise and Yazijian explain that these commercial images became metaphors for the brand:

> Modernity, leisure, sparkling technology, and newness were exalted over nature, which was pictured as dry, even barren, full of hardships and lacking in contemporary conveniences. Pepsi's central image—that of youth, with its sparkling cleanliness and lively activeness—was nothing more than an adjunct to the underlying symbolism of culture.[50]

Ramin's tight, quick, big band score thus complements these notions of "sparkling cleanliness" and "lively activeness," as does the dizzying camerawork and its accompanying voice-over, which explains that the product's "spark" and "swing" make it the drink of "today's generation." The startling and quick descent down a B♭-dominant-7th chord that opens many of the spots further helps to convey the "danger" of the onscreen antics by aurally mimicking the rush presumably felt by the commercial's actors as they plummeted down a roller coaster or winding road.[51]

Other than the preservation of Ramin's basic melody, the "Come Alive!" vignette performed by Spears possesses little resemblance to the original campaign. Instead of depicting high-energy outdoor recreation, the 2002 spot pictures a black-and-white indoor staging of a live television show.[52] The camera focuses on Spears performing in a doo-wop style while two women in matching lamé dresses and blond wigs follow each of her phrases with syncopated "shoos" and "bops." Spears and the youth who dance around her also perform iconic 1960s choreography that compliments the newly stylized musical score. Spears's routine here largely conforms to the character she plays in the scene, but we again get a glimpse of her twenty-first-century persona with a touch of vocal fry on the final statement of the USP ("You're in the Pepsi Generation").

As an obvious throwback to the iconic *American Bandstand* television show, Spears's trio stands in as a Caucasian version of the African American girl groups who dominated the charts in the early 1960s. Pepsi's remake thus better connects with the musical trends of the era, and the disparity it creates with the original campaign actually highlights the real-life aesthetic struggles that young marketers faced when trying to sell the newest sounds of the youth culture to their conservative superiors. Indeed, BBD&O adman Hilary Lipsitz admitted that he had pleaded with executives to hire Diana Ross and The Supremes (or any famous group, for that matter) before Coke did.[53] His request was met with resistance and the nearsighted comment that Motown's music (and likely girl groups in general) would never be successful.

Because the higher-ups dragged their feet, Pepsi's competitor snatched up The Supremes for its popular campaign "Things Go Better with Coca-Cola." Launched in response to Pepsi's "Think Young" and released the same year as "Come Alive!," Coke not only beat its rival to Motown's audience but also to the folk, rock, pop, and country fans to whom its various radio jingle styles were targeted.[54] Audiences quickly took to Coke's new jingle because it possessed all the qualities of a Top 40 hit, including its use of musical giants such as Ray Charles and Aretha Franklin.[55]

In explaining the aesthetic differences between the two soda giants' 1963 campaigns, Frank expands on Jackson Lears's hypothesis that twentieth-century American advertising oscillated between messages of "personal efficacy" and the "carnivalesque." Frank hypothesizes that Coke's pop-sponsored slogans touted the product's promotion of "workplace order," while Pepsi's "Come Alive!" imagery suggested the "leisure-time anarchy of pure consuming."[56] Louise and Yazijian note a similar change in Coke's ads mid-decade when the Vietnam War and social and economic uneasiness overtook the optimism of previous years.[57] Coke thus pushed its soda's ability to maintain "efficiency" and act as "an instrumental element of work"—key elements relayed in the lyrics sung by its celebrity endorsers.[58] At the opposite end of the spectrum, *Pepsi-Cola World* defined its brand against Coke by hyping "Come Alive!" as a "fresh approach" aligned with the "face of a changing, and more youthful America," noting further that it left "the competition" in "its staid, dull pleasures of yesterday."[59]

While Pepsi's visual images of consuming for consumption's sake certainly got it noticed, its use of musical trends in mainstream advertising campaigns trailed behind that of its rival. Despite their inclusion of Sommers's youthful timbre, the swinging television versions of "Come Alive!" did little to convey the idea that Pepsi was on the cutting edge of popular styles. However, in 1966 the brand retooled its approaches after market research revealed that its soda was not properly distributed at "Youth Market gathering places." Pepsi therefore commissioned disc jockeys (DJs) to push its product by playing reworked versions of Ramin's "Come Alive!" jingle with hit makers The Hondells, Martha and the Vandellas (also a Motown girl group), and Del Shannon.[60] Although Pepsi was proud to hire these artists, it continued to misunderstand the diversity of the youthful styles its endorsers performed—harmonized surf rock, girl group soul, and solo pop-rock—and its marketing materials simply lumped them together under the umbrella of "rock-n-roll."[61]

That same year, Pepsi pushed its product at a new "avante-garde," non-alcoholic dance club called Cheetahs in New York City.[62] In 1967 it would go further to reach young audiences by sponsoring a short-lived youth-themed variety television show called *Go!!!*[63] Most significant, it would again hire Sid Ramin—this time to create a new jingle for Diet Pepsi, one that would finally bring musical acclaim to the brand.[64]

In 1966 Ramin created "Music to Watch Girls By" for a new Diet Pepsi campaign titled "Girl Watchers." The spots placed young women in scenarios where their figures became the focus of the camera's (i.e., the male) gaze. Ramin conceived the new jingle with a complete song form and based its title on contemporary popular recordings that were intended to accompany everyday tasks (such as "Music to Study By" and "Music to Eat By"). He confessed that he was asked to compose the tune in the style of Herb Alpert and the Tijuana Brass and added that he simultaneously modeled it on the title theme he wrote for the television show *The Trials of O'Brien*.[65] As a result, "Music to Watch Girls By" perfectly complimented the sex appeal of the women onscreen with its sultry and laid-back qualities—namely, its swinging bossa-nova-style syncopation and shifting major and minor modes. The tune became an instant hit and was so popular that radio audiences called into local radio stations to request it. Ramin soon received requests from various musicians to re-record the tune, and the instrumental version released by Bob Crewe actually reached number 15 on the *Billboard* charts.[66] The success of Ramin's jingle turned chart topper eventually became free advertising for Pepsi since its association with the brand had been firmly established. Consequently, the campaign won the award for "Best Soft Drink Commercial" three years in a row, and its winning tune boosted Diet Pepsi sales to number one.[67]

Considering the gains Pepsi made in attracting youth in the years immediately following the release of its "Come Alive!" campaign, it makes sense that the 2002 version recomposes it to better reflect the brand's fluency in pop trends. Pepsi thus uses the lens of nostalgia to blur and remake this campaign's history with a potpourri of redacted 1960s signifiers. By reimagining Ramin's "Come Alive" as a doo-wop hit rather than a dated swing anthem, "Now and Then" amplifies the retrospective view that Pepsi was hip to youth trends and to its culture.[68] And despite the fact that it was not "Come Alive!" but Ramin's other jingle ("Music to Watch Girls By") that became a pop sensation, the 2002 version challenges the notion that Pepsi's understanding of the mid-1960s youth culture was based primarily on its deployment of *imagery* as Frank and others have suggested. Rather, the new commercial more accurately reflects the brand's affiliation with the entertainment crazes of the moment: its (retroactive) creation of pop celebrity radio commercials, its product placement at the Cheetahs dance club, and its sponsorship of the *Go!!!* television show. The updated version of "Come Alive!" further provides the soda giant with another opportunity to benefit from the iconicity provided by Spears as its hit artist, who again, unlike Sommers, is permitted to perform onscreen. Perhaps most ironically (and unintentionally), the vignette's portrayal of America's penchant for whitewashing and redacting African American musical trends also offers a compelling critique of both music and advertising industry practices during this era.

Pepsi Pours on the Hard Sell: Detours into the Madison Avenue Sound

A descending glissando segues Spears's spot from her performance in the black-and-white television dance show to the full color world of a 1966 surf contest (table 1.1). The new scene combines the soda giant's famous mid-1960s "Surf Football" commercial and a playful parody of the teen beach movies that dominated the era. Pepsi's use of beach romp imagery here proves reflexive of its own iconography, as its 1961 "For Those Who Think Young" slogan had become a colloquialism—so much so that United Artists adopted it for the title of a 1964 teen-themed film.[69]

Despite the momentum created by its two previous campaigns, Pepsi chose to redirect its 1967–69 slogan away from its successful customer-centric messages and back onto the product itself. The brand thus budgeted $30 million to herald the revamped USP: "The Taste That Beats the Others Cold, Pepsi Pours It On." The new slogan derived from market research showing that customers preferred Pepsi over other soda brands when properly chilled.[70] According to Pepsi advertising executive Alan Pottasch, the company switched strategies due to the belief that the "Come Alive!" campaign's focus proved too narrow in its efforts to attract young people.[71]

BBD&O executive John Bergin candidly aired his disappointment about Pepsi's insistence on reverting to the hard sell but noted that he and his team made a concerted effort to keep the cola's youthful message at the forefront by continuing to feature active lifestyle imagery.[72] Their efforts were best realized in the campaign's iconic "Surf Football" spot and its use of what marketers called a "stroboscopic effect"—the practice of slowing and blurring multiple frames together—to highlight the action of a young man throwing a football.[73] The BBD&O admen were further encouraged by the fact that the brand had finally recognized the potential of hiring popular musicians to sing in its radio spots.[74] Marketers were therefore permitted from the outset to record versions of the jingle that featured the close folk-rock harmonies of The Turtles and the polished soul sounds of The Four Tops.[75] Other radio spots starred The Hondells and The Trade Masters.

Despite its pop-focused efforts, Pepsi's use of musical stars had little effect on the campaign's reception. As its executives would later admit, the new slogan proved "bland, too cute, and too product oriented," and it destroyed the continuity and momentum of the "Pepsi Generation" theme.[76] Indeed, Frank confirmed that by 1967 American life had changed dramatically and those who identified with the counterculture had moved beyond the innocence and bubbliness depicted in the "Pepsi Pours It On" commercials, thus rendering Pepsi's happy-go-lucky beach scenes dated and out of touch.[77]

The musical score, too, betrayed the campaign's lack of hipness by featuring the clichéd "Madison Avenue choir" sound. This jingle style dominated advertising in the 1950s and 1960s and was easy to discern due to its sharp distinction from chart-topping music trends and other media programming at the time. Accordingly, "Pepsi Pours It On" featured all the characteristics quintessential to this well-worn sound: close vocal harmonies, clear diction, a fast tempo, a big band backing ensemble, and a direct and harmonized praise of the product and its features.[78] So, despite the use of chart-topping vocalists and the youthful characteristics Anne Phillips composed into the score—including a brief surf guitar riff and frequent excitement-inducing modulations—its hard-selling jingle sounds trumped any efforts to match the youthful ethos of the moment.

Marketing historian Richard S. Tedlow summarized the track's less than memorable quality, saying:

> Pepsi's advertising agency shipped a camera crew to California beaches and shot thousands of feet of tape of young, beautiful, alluring, healthy looking adolescent women and men playing a pick-up game of touch football (American football, that is) at the water's edge. *There was a jingle in the background and words being spoken, but the real message was in the picture of beautiful, insouciant youth . . .*
>
> A written description does not do justice to this advertisement nor to the series of those like it produced by Pepsi. The essence of the message was in the *image* presented to the public. The Pepsi Generation would have been impossible without television.[79]

Tedlow's observations thus recognize the effort Bergin and his team put into preserving the campaign's youthful images and confirm that these visuals bore responsibility for driving home Pepsi's message while the music and slogan proved largely forgettable.

In visiting the campaign 35 years later in the "Now and Then" remake, marketers seemed to acknowledge its pitfalls by parodying its failures. The 2002 version shows Spears alternating between a diegetic performance of the jingle and overacting the roles of participating, winning, and celebrating a surf contest victory (fig. 1.3). Low-quality computer graphics emphasize the B-rating attributes of the beach movies it mimics, while the images of youth enjoying the sand, sunshine, and water serve as a reminder of the overexuberance and fun that Pepsi had promised to boomers. The Madison Avenue choir sound of the original is also re-created here by mixing Spears into the soundtrack's chorus of peppy voices. Other than placing Spears and her endorsement at center of the

Fig. 1.3. Spears parodies the hard sell. (Still from "Now and Then," PepsiCo. Inc., 2002.)

storyline, the remake of "Pepsi Pours It On" largely remains faithful to the visuals of the original "Surf Football" spot.

Depoliticizing the Counterculture: Pepsi's "Live/Give" and Coke's "Hilltop"

"Now and Then" transitions seamlessly to the year 1970 by morphing Spears from a beach babe into a countercultural sweetheart. Just as her beach buddies hoist her into the air, the soundtrack abruptly shifts to the slow communal jingle chorus to Pepsi's 1969–73 campaign, "You've Got a Lot to Live, and Pepsi's Got a Lot to Give" (table 1.1). The 2002 version harks back to prominent signifiers from the late 1960s counterculture as the camera follows young people with long hair, headbands, and bright flowing clothing. Images of tents, Volkswagen buses, and white horses reinforce the idyllic view of those who followed Timothy Leary's call to "tune in, turn on, and drop out." Flowers are also prominently displayed throughout to suggest beat poet Alan Ginsberg's famous "flower power" proposition for passive resistance. The onscreen images further imply the ideals of communal living and "free love." Unlike the previous vignettes, Spears is not always the central figure here, and her voice is buried in the soundtrack to heighten the communal ethos.

"Now and Then" loosely resembles Pepsi's original campaign and more specifically to a spot called "Young America." The 1970 *Pepsi-Cola Media Ordering Catalog* describes the commercial as depicting "the exuberance and love and joy of growing up in America . . . the beauty and strength of our land in the faces of our youth."[80] As evident in this description and that of the scenes discussed above, the images in "Young America" and the "Live/Give" campaign as a whole attempted to brush the surface of countercultural ideology without getting overly political. Frank confirms that the commercial's images inferred the counterculture's "live and let live" ethos with scenes that captured a variety of racial, age, and lifestyle designations in nonsensical scenes that made subtle references to flowers and long hair.[81] For Frank, the real message of the "Live/Give" campaign lay in the "plentitude" of things to do and consume (hence its USP).[82] He concludes that these commercials supplied a "sanitized" and "depoliticized" version of the countercultural myth accessible to everyone. A closer listen to the commercial's television score supports these claims.

Pepsi's "Live/Give" jingle is based on a protest song written by Joe Brooks.[83] Marketers shied away from the music's potential for controversy by reworking the song and its accompanying images to make it "politically ambiguous," but they preserved enough of it to "tug on the heartstrings" and offer healing and optimism to a country hurting from war and social turmoil.[84] The 1969 *Pepsi-Cola Media Ordering Catalog* best summarized this intent: "Here's a great new theme for Pepsi-Cola. And for the whole country. It reminds Americans that life has never been so full. There's never been so much living to do or so much to live for. And Pepsi belongs in a life like this."[85]

Marketers were conscientious about pairing Pepsi's hopeful message with musical tropes that aligned with the youth generation's musical affinities. BBD&O chairman Allen Rosenshine believed that the score was Pepsi's "first expression of spirit through song" and described it as "truly soaring" and "uplifting."[86] Marketers suggested that the jingle's musical inspiration came from the Beatles, and, as Taylor documents, executives classified "Live/Give" as "jubilation rock" or "gospel rock."[87] Indeed, the jingle's chorus delivers the message of hope and faith through close vocal harmonies, a slow tempo, a prominent bass line, a recognizable backbeat, and fanfaric-sounding brass that all prove reminiscent of the Beatles's saccharine 1967 "All You Need Is Love." The thinly textured, mid-tempo verses, however, more closely resemble the country- or folk-inspired singer-songwriters of the era. Taylor, in fact, writes that he hears the jingle as more pop than rock oriented. This is likely due to the avoidance of rock's affinity for aggressive and political elements, including the guitar, volatile lyrics, and often unrefined vocal delivery. Pepsi instead chose professionally trained singers to deliver a clearly articulated message over a subtle folk- and gospel-inspired track. The redaction of Brooks's charged lyrics and employment of carefully selected, non-offensive (i.e., rock-adjacent) signifiers therefore allowed the "Live/Give" television commercial soundtrack to perfectly support the "sanitized" and "depoliticized" version of the counterculture Frank reads from the images. Accordingly, the benignly optimistic jingle paired with the onscreen scenarios to declare that Pepsi played a vital role in this "new generation's" (branded) experience of the world.[88]

Three years into the "Live/Give" campaign, Pepsi's rival would surpass its efforts to co-opt the musical signifiers of the counterculture. Indeed, Coca-Cola's 1971 "Hilltop" commercial featured a folk-like jingle that became an instant success. For many it was the musical and visual suggestion of not just American unity but a global community that created its powerful affect. In a story recounted dozens of times, "Hilltop" included hundreds of extras lip-syncing "I'd Like to Buy the World a Coke" on an Italian hillside. The commercial re-created the multicultural bonding its makers claimed to have experienced when stranded in an Irish airport.[89] The commercial's musical track became an instant hit, and, according to a retrospective in the *Washington Post*, Coke's bottlers received more than 100,000 letters while radio DJs reported that people requested it as if it were a pop hit.[90]

An appropriately named group, the Hillside Singers, recorded the commercial version of Coca-Cola's hit jingle. When the track reached number 13 on the *Billboard* charts, creative director Bill Backer removed explicit references to the brand, renamed the tune after its second verse ("I'd Like to Teach the World to Sing"), and re-recorded it with the New Seekers.[91] The new version reached number seven on the charts and boosted soda sales, confirming that Coke's marketing for its regular soda had managed to accomplish what Pepsi's efforts had not: the "Hilltop" campaign established Coca-Cola as a popular music icon while confirming its status as the number-one regular soda on the market. "Hilltop" demonstrated that Coke was indeed "the Real Thing."

In his discussion of the musical score, Ron Rodman asserts that the jingle's length and production made it convincing for audiences.[92] The tune possessed other significant qualities, too, that made it approachable as a song rather than a jingle. It differed, for example, from Pepsi's recent campaigns in that an offscreen narrator did not interrupt the song with a hard-sell explanation. Even with the jingle's blatant mention of the product name, its repeated refrain ("I'd like to") and its contrapuntal ending (bolstered by overlapping suspended chords—"It's the Real Thing" harmonized underneath "I'd Like to Buy the World a Coke") created an inclusive, campground sing-along sound that was punctuated by an uplifting fade-out on the USP. Additionally, the lyrics upheld important ideologies of the counterculture with their suggestion of the power of music ("I'd like to teach the world to sing"), connection to nature ("trees," "bees," and "turtledoves"), and ties to a global community (by encouraging "harmony" and "love").

Although Coke's 1971 spot would ultimately win the battle to emulate the contemporary sound of the counterculture, Pepsi's "Live/Give" was not without success. Just prior to the release of "Hilltop," *Pepsi-Cola World* reported that audiences of all ages and various walks of life had sent more than 10,000 letters of praise about the campaign to the brand's headquarters and another couple of thousand to bottlers.[93] The BBD&O agency also received thousands of congratulatory phone calls. After the release of Coke's "Hilltop," Pepsi hired more stars to sing the "Live/Give" radio jingle—including Tina Turner, James Brown, and Lynn Anderson. These stars considerably raised the brand's Neilsen ratings and propelled its sales to come within "an eyelash" of those of its rival.[94] Pepsi's "Live/Give" thus laid the groundwork for Coke's "Hilltop" achievements, and in the end the campaigns proved mutually beneficial as they challenged one another to delve deeper into music-focused marketing. Moreover, the positive reception of "Live/Give" and subsequent acclaim for "Hilltop" marked the moment when countercultural practices had become mainstream. Indeed, Frank credits this moment as the point where these ideals truly became "all American."[95]

Pepsi's original "Live/Give" campaign obviously aimed to redact and mobilize the least volatile signifiers of countercultural music and imagery in order to provide mainstream audiences with an optimistic outlook in a post-Altamont era of stagnant civil rights progress and continued war abroad. But thirty years later the brand no longer feared offending audiences with straightforward images of hippies and their notions of "peace, love, and harmony." With its loose suggestion of communal living, drug-induced euphoria, and free love, Pepsi's 2002 remake strove to recapture the height of the countercultural ethos while simultaneously employing what its original commercials lacked—namely, the political ideals that Coke's jingle had more effectively conveyed. And while the music was almost identical to that of the original spots, the images in the 2002 version more accurately upheld the intentions Brooks had for his song, as well as the amiable picture of the youth culture that Pepsi had so desperately wanted to capture. Much like the other vignettes in "Now and Then," this remake offered yet another "critical affective response" that reached longingly into the (branded) past while simultaneously correcting the shortcomings in the soda giant's original deployment of youthful signifiers.

"Irresistible" and "New Millennium": A Quick Nod to Pepsi's Newer Generations

"Now and Then" takes a humorous turn when a man's voice is dubbed over the mouth of the white horse used for the countercultural scene. The commercial then skips over 19 years of the brand's advertising to segue into a version of Pepsi's 1989 co-optation of Robert Palmer's "Simply Irresistible" (table 1.1). As discussed further in part II of this book, Pepsi had finally established solid relationships with top musical celebrities by the late-1980s and had become adept at borrowing the music industry's latest hits for its commercials. Spears's version of Palmer's "The Choice of a New Generation" endorsement is therefore visually faithful to the original commercial, which in turn was nearly identical to Palmer's MTV video for his hit song. The 1989 spot appropriated images of him nestled between dozens of identically dressed, stone-faced models and redacted them into an homage for the soda by inserting the brand's colors, product, and logo. The spot's musical score was similarly identical and changed very few words from Palmer's first verse, bridge, and refrain, merely exchanging the object of his affection, "she," for "it" (the soda) and replacing the word "course" with the slogan's key word, "choice." The 2002 remake redacts Palmer's song even further as an androgynously dressed Spears is also surrounded by stoic models as she belts out the famous hook that bookends the original song's riff.[96] The soft-sell slogan and focus on visual spectacle here make it a perfect representation of the brand's MTV era commercials.

The "Now and Then" soundtrack cuts quickly to Spears's request to "turn [her] up" while its visuals flip through each of the historical vignettes shown thus far and lands on a climactic rendition of the brand's newest "Joy of Pepsi" jingle.[97] As an homage to the opening 1958 "Soda Fountain" vignette, Spears and her entourage perform in front of a 1950s-style drive-in. The pop star sports her on-trend long and straight bleached hair and midriff-revealing shirt as she sings to an upbeat track that touts "the joy all around" and hails "each generation's" sense of "style." Her call to "shout it out" transitions to the current campaign's hook—a string of scatted, non-sense "Ba-ba-ba-ba-ba" syllables that culminate with the "Joy of

Pepsi" USP. Spears's recitation of the brand's newest hook takes viewers one last time through the Pepsi's 1960s–70s campaigns just visited by picturing her and the other dancers performing identical choreography on each of the sets. A climactic, arpeggiated A minor, sharp-seventh chord leads to one last a cappella recitation of the "Think Young" hook as the scene flashes back to the trio of 1950s college men pictured early in the spot. Their recitation of the brand name is followed by a cut to Spears in her 2002 streetwear holding a Pepsi can at arm's length and reciting the "For Those Who Think Young" USP (table 1.1 and fig. intro.1). Reminiscent of the opening vignette, her wink is punctuated by one last cadential glockenspiel chime to confirm the spot's completion. The screen then goes black and the brand's logo and USP fill the frame.

SELLING SPEARS

In 1964 Pepsi executive Alan Pottasch told bottlers, "When you stop to think of it, we are doing something in advertising bigger and broader in meaning than anything we've ever done: *we're naming a whole era and its people after our product.*"[98] As demonstrated above, this was a lengthy and complicated process that required Pepsi to redact and appropriate a myriad of signifiers that it thought might best convey concepts of youthfulness in its campaigns. Marketers thus featured images of young, active, fashionable people and included musical scores that included celebrity vocals ("Think Young," "Come Alive!," and the late 1960s–'70s radio spots), featured energetic tempos and lively scores (Ramin's "Come Alive!" and Phillips's "Pepsi Pours It On"), and alluded (vaguely) to contemporary styles ("Live/Give" and "The Choice of a New Generation"). So, although its musical scores were not always cutting edge, Pepsi's consistent efforts to attract youth proved impactful to its sales and the aesthetics of the advertising industry as a whole.

It is doubtful that the brand had any idea just how much impact its "Pepsi Generation" concept would have on its future image, but four decades later "Now and Then" demonstrated the extent to which the slogan remained central to the brand's philosophy. The 2002 spot thus strove to recapture the optimism and innovation of its most memorable campaigns, especially those familiar to its first adopted "generation." Significantly, marketers did not simply replicate this history: they *re-composed* it by focusing on specific campaigns while discarding others, repositioning their spokesperson as a diegetic performer, re-dating some spots, and altogether remaking some of their musical scores and storylines to better reflect the brand's support of youth culture activities in other marketing arenas. "Now and Then" therefore used a nostalgic lens to repair the sense of loss the brand had for its glory days.

To accomplish these ends, the soda giant placed Britney Spears at the center of its revisionist history and relied on signifiers from her celebrity image and musical career to provide continuity for the spot.[99] Notably, Pepsi selected the pop princess to extend its "Joy of Cola" campaign at the same time that she was looking to transition her image from teen wonder to young adult.[100] At 19 years of age, her 2001 self-titled album communicated the difficulties of this reinvention with songs like "I'm Not a Girl, Not Yet a Woman." Pepsi signed on to help Spears redirect her image in the hopes of using her iconicity to attract more consumers. Dawn Hudson, a senior vice-president for strategy and marketing, confirmed the brand's belief in her star power, saying, "Britney Spears is in transition from kid star to broad-based pop star. . . . She's going to surprise a lot of people."[101]

Accordingly, the commercial's countercultural, coming-of-age tale hinges on audience familiarity with Spears's controversial image and real-life transition into adulthood. Although Spears's reputation for straddling line between "immaturity and eroticism" had the potential to tarnish the brand, it was precisely her liminality—what scholars call her "mixed signals"—on which Pepsi's storyline drew.[102] Spears's twenty-first-century struggles to define her subjectivity as a young woman thus perfectly embodied the changing roles of women from the early 1960s onward that she played onscreen. While exaggerated in "Now and Then," the pop star exemplified the new forms of liminality that some women navigated when the previously accepted transition from child to wife and mother was complicated by the birth control pill, women's liberation, and a breakdown of the nuclear family.

Spears thus became Pepsi's mouthpiece in its attempt to revisit twentieth-century culture, especially the 1960s and early 1970s spots that dominate "Now and Then." Just as these decades oscillated between optimism and insecurity, and liberal and conservative values, the pop star's reputation confounded the binary values Frank located in cola wars commercials. This is demonstrated in the commercial's very first scene, where Spears captures and even parodies the trappings of middle-class, blonde innocence in the early 1960s by playing the ingénue intended for teen admiration and male adoration—one who was virginal yet playful—and then thwarting it with her low-register vocals and wink at the end. By performing the "mixed signals" she had skillfully cultivated, the pop star expertly embodied various roles in the campaign: from the innocent yet cheeky girl next door ("Think Young") to television pop star ("Come Alive!); from the all-American beach bum ("Pepsi Pours it On") to liberated, countercultural woman ("Live/Give"); and finally from the androgynous rock star ("The Choice of a New Generation") to millennial sensation ("Joy of Cola"). Musically, her vocal timbre supported these developments, moving from restrained and sweet in "Think Young" to folksy and communal by "Live/Give" and assertive and dominant by the "The Choice of a New Generation." Consequently, the spot used Spears's vocal performance as much as her image to suggest an idealized and commodified version of what it was like for both boomers and Spears to "grow up" in a "pop" world.

Most obviously, Spears's onscreen performances supplied "Now and Then" with the musical cultural capital necessary to align Pepsi's refashioning of its early slogans with the reputation the spot intended to honor. While the brand's promotional support of television shows and dance clubs, as well its employment of celebrity voices, had demonstrated its affinity for youth culture in the past, these subtle cues were not enough to convince twenty-first-century audiences accustomed to hearing the latest pop hits in commercials. Spears thus proved essential to (re)establishing the brand's credibility. Her iconicity was funneled simultaneously into the concept of the "Pepsi Generation" and the soda commodity to drive home the claim that the brand had been a reliable supplier of "pop"—soda as well as cultural trends, especially music—to youth for more than 40 years.

REDACTION AND RECEPTION

Examining the process of redaction reveals a lot about music's roles in marketing, not only by studying what is included but also by considering what is left out. Notably, "Now and Then" skipped over most of Pepsi's campaigns from the 1970s ("Join the Pepsi People: Feeling Free" and "Have a Pepsi Day"), early 1980s ("Catch that Pepsi Spirit," "Pepsi's Got Your Taste for Life," "Pepsi Now," and "The Pepsi Challenge") and every 1990s slogan that predated 1999's "Joy of Cola." Additionally, by keeping the blonde-haired, fair-skinned Spears and her poppy sound at the center of the commercial, it also left out references to key campaigns and marketing efforts that the brand made for African American and Latino consumers—those who belonged to what Pepsi called "special markets."

Indeed, Pepsi's nationally broadcast campaigns from the 1940s onward had tried to distance its mainstream image from the "negro Coke" moniker it had gained from its midcentury focus on its bargain price. Bottlers in regional markets, however, knew that African American and Latino consumers constituted sizable sales. Many therefore sponsored promotions and materials that benefited these communities. In 1965, for example, the brand created an educational long-playing record (LP) titled *Adventures in Negro History* that featured 300 years of "historic contributions" by African Americans.[103] In 1967 marketers targeted Texas consumers by featuring special full-color commercials with accompanying mariachi soundtracks.[104] In 1968 Pepsi sponsored jazz festivals and recordings in the American South that included participants from historically black colleges.[105] The brand also supported black radio programming in the 1970s (defining then as "soul" and "heavy rock"), as well as a television show, *Black Journal*, on PBS.[106] Pepsi also continued to hire black artists such as Roberta Flack for its radio campaigns in the 1970s, and late in the decade its national television commercials even featured all black casts in "Have a Pepsi Day."[107]

Given the brand's historical focus on special markets and its long list of prominent African American celebrity endorsers (detailed throughout this book), it might seem curious that "Now and Then" preserves the whitewashed images of Americana prevalent in the brand's 1960s and early 1970s national television campaigns. This makes sense, however, when considering that Spears's role as provocateur yet all American (white) girl best upheld the long-held vision of the "Pepsi Generation" that Frank notes was essential to the brand's 1960s campaigns: "Whether playing wildly at the beach, speeding on motorcycles, or dancing to rock music, the Pepsi Generation was acting out 1960 notions of rebellion and corporate America's vision of the *model consumer*."[108]

Moreover, Pepsi's maintenance of a familiar Americana image was pertinent to the cultural moment and likely deemed safest at a time when the United States was reeling from the recent September 11, 2001 attacks on the World Trade Center in New York City. "Now and Then" ran less than five months later, on February 2, 2002, during the first quarter of Super Bowl XXXVI.[109] The event itself was overtly nationalistic: it was self-conscious in foregrounding patriotic musical acts to bolster confidence and even ran antidrug campaigns to offer hope.[110] The US had not faced such uncertain times since the mid-1960s, and the revisiting of this decade in "Now and Then" fit well within post-9/11 idealistic propaganda. The spot's picturing of Pepsi's carefree commercials mixed with a peaceful countercultural ethos could be read as patriotic, and in this way it offered a critically affective, nostalgic lens through which it could remind audiences of the nation's resilience.

Viewers, however, did not respond to the spot as expected. *USA Today* reported, "The 90-second ad, which cost Pepsi about $5.8 million to air— was the third-lowest-rated Pepsi spot ever among the 52 rated by Ad Meter."[111] Panelists notably seemed to appreciate mainly humorous commercials that year, and one viewer in particular openly criticized Pepsi for selling Spears instead of soda, thereby suggesting that Spears's presence failed to convey the message that marketers had hoped. The soda giant's re-envisioning of its most famous campaigns was thus apparently lost on (or at least unimpressive to) contemporary audiences in need of a post-9/11 comedic distraction. By the end of the year, Pepsi would drop Spears as its spokesperson, replacing her with up-and-coming R&B powerhouse Beyoncé Knowles.[112]

Pepsi's "Now and Then" suggested that it had kept a pulse on popular music since the late 1950s when in reality the cola maker actually spent decades struggling to find its perfect "pop" sound. This book's coda revisits Pepsi's affinity for redacting its own advertising history, but first part II delves deeper into its quest to attract a "new generation" in the 1980s. The next few chapters examine the many forms of redaction that the brand applied to the texts and celebrities it appropriated, thereby creating some of the most famous (and *in*famous) campaigns of the twentieth century.

PART II

Pop Songs, Celebrity Spectacle, and the MTV Generation

Big Soda and Celebrity Pop

Pepsi Meets Michael Jackson

On February 28, 1984, Michael Jackson stood at the pinnacle of his success.[1] That night he won a record eight Grammy awards, including Album of the Year for *Thriller* and Record of the Year for "Beat It."[2] Jackson was also recognized for his mastery in a variety of musical styles, taking home awards for Best Male R&B Vocal Performance ("Billie Jean"), Best Male Rock Vocal Performance ("Beat It"), and Best Pop Vocal Performance ("Thriller"). But arguably the most groundbreaking event of the evening happened between Jackson's repeated trips to the stage. During the commercial breaks, Pepsi-Cola unveiled its latest attempt to win its decades-long battle to beat Coca-Cola with a pair of television commercials titled "The Concert" and "Street." The commercials featured Jackson and his brothers singing the praises of Pepsi over an edited version of the instrumental backing track to "Billie Jean." Months of media hype turned the unveiling of the commercials into an "event" not to be missed by Grammy viewers and fans—all 83 million of them.[3] Earlier that week MTV had contributed to the excitement by devoting a half-hour special to the premiere of the now infamous "Concert" commercial.[4] The craze for all things Michael Jackson had also been fueled by heavy rotation of his music videos on MTV and his riveting performance of "Billie Jean" less than a year earlier during the *Motown 25: Yesterday, Today, and Forever* television special.[5]

Pepsi unveiled its new campaign at the precise moment when fans could not get enough of their favorite pop star. Jackson's "Choice of a New Generation" commercials became so popular that according to Roger Enrico, Pepsi's CEO at the time, a year after their premiere 97 percent of the American population had seen the commercials more than a dozen times.[6] In less than a month, Pepsi's sales had climbed high enough to make its product the fastest-growing regular cola on the market and the most purchased soft drink from grocery retailers.[7] The campaigns were also notable accomplishments in the advertising world, and BBD&O garnered 74 creative awards for the spots.[8] The venture paid off handsomely for Michael Jackson, too, as *Thriller* stayed on the charts for more than two years, spent 37 weeks in the number-one spot, and became (what remains) the best-selling album of all time.[9] The buzz generated by the campaign was unmatched as networks begged for small clips of the commercials to air before their premieres at the Grammys and on MTV. Phil Dusenberry, the campaign's creative and musical director, believed it was "perhaps the first time in history when a commercial was more anticipated than the television show surrounding it."[10] In Jackson's own words, the deal was "magic."[11]

Jackson's 1984 "The Choice of a New Generation" campaign proved remarkable not only for the reasons listed above but also because this was the first set of American television commercials to successfully co-brand a hit musician's *current* album and upcoming tour with a household product. Prior to this campaign, jingles and "classic rock" songs dominated advertising soundtracks.[12] Bethany Klein and Timothy Taylor have each highlighted the importance of Pepsi's move to new music marketing with "The Choice of a New Generation" campaign, noting that its innovative appeal to youth through the employment of MTV sounds and images was a turning point in relationships between the music and advertising industries.[13] Echoing these statements, most other sources on the topic have attributed Pepsi's convincing appropriation of Jackson's performances of his then biggest hit as the key to forever changing the way musical endorsements look and sound.

What has remained unexamined is *why* and *how* a family-friendly brand was able to spin Jackson's taboo tale of promiscuity, paternity, and betrayal into an acclaimed soda-sipping message. This chapter investigates these questions by incorporating cultural and media theories with musical analysis to reveal the processes undertaken by marketers to carefully encode Pepsi's commodity into the pop star's iconic pre-existing texts and symbols. The analysis here is therefore informed by scholarship on meaning making in multimedia formats that asserts that the transfer of meanings between music and images is a two-way street whereby the music brings outside associations to the images and the images have the potential to give new meanings to the music.[14] In particular, Lawrence Kramer argues that how much and what meaning the music contributes to the reception of an "imagetext" depends on both how much prior experience the listener has with the music and how subordinate the soundtrack is to the visual elements.[15] He adds that music and images have the potential to bring various signifiers together and that these signifiers affect how each might be perceived.[16] Anders Bonde has more recently asserted that audience interpretations of pre-existing music in television commercials are made through "multimodal interactions" among the various audiovisual texts in which the music has been contextualized (music video, film, commercials, etc.).[17] He further coined the phrase "meaning potentials" to explore the modification and negotiation of pre-existing music in these contexts.[18] Ron Rodman has also demonstrated the various ways that music mediates a commercial's various sonic and visual elements— what Nicolai Graakjær calls "cotextual" elements—to create branded narratives.[19] Taking these ideas together, the following pages perform a "multimodal" analysis of the "meaning potentials" for audiences who may have encountered "Billie Jean" both outside and inside Pepsi's campaign. What follows thus serves to illustrate how the redaction of Jackson's signifiers created specific "cotextual" elements that conveyed new narratives on the terms of the commodity.

This chapter also extends well-established theories about the function that visual imagery plays in advertising texts to the roles performed by a commercial's music track. The very year in which Jackson's Pepsi commercials aired, Michael Schudson published a book that showed how American advertising borrowed visual art and other cultural forms to abstract and redirect previously formed aesthetic meanings to fit branded contexts. In it, he analyzed how marketers reworked iconic images, including those of celebrities, to "simplify" and "typify" (break down and typecast) their signifiers in order to appeal to the widest possible audience.[20] In the preceding decade, Judith Williamson demonstrated just how skillful marketers had become at spinning culturally constructed signs and signifiers to fit branding agendas. She argued that "advertisements use 'meanings' as a currency and signification as market. . . . [T]hey can always exchange them, take anything out of its context and replace it: *re*-presentation."[21] By extending these ideas to Jackson's commercial performances, the following sections unpack how Pepsi's marketers "re-presented" his well-known track and star image through a skillful process of "simplifying" and "typifying" his most familiar signifiers.

MICHAEL JACKSON'S "BILLIE JEAN"

Jackson's "Billie Jean" track circulated as a single more than a year prior to its inclusion in Pepsi's campaign. In his late 1980s memoir, *Moonwalk*, Jackson claims that he wrote "Billie Jean" to reflect the awkward situations faced by his brothers during their time in the Jackson 5.[22] The lyrics lay out the scenario of a lover causing a "scene" (actually a court battle) after tracking down a former flame to tell him he is the father of her child. The song outlines the clichéd tale of a celebrity who falls prey to a dissatisfied ex- or wannabe lover, and it evokes betrayal and lies through a skillful pairing of poetic lyrics with harmonic, melodic, and rhythmic instabilities. As the story unfolds, Jackson shifts the narrative among his past experiences, flashbacks to his encounters with Billie Jean, and the story's moral lesson. The music emphasizes the seriousness of the story line as the backing track continually gravitates toward the ♭VI to subvert desired or expected cadential closure.[23] Accordingly, the ♭VI (represented by D♮) frequently disrupts sections in the F♯ Dorian mode, causing a strong pull toward F♯ natural minor, and the precariousness of the half-step oscillation of the sixth degree (D♯ and D♮) renders both modes unstable (table 2.1). Frequent moves to the ♭VI thus seem to metaphorically cast doubt on Jackson's claims of innocence by appearing at critical points in the story and subverting resolutions. In fact, resolution is something that the song never attains; the storyline is left open-ended and the harmonies never reach a satisfying tonic cadence.[24]

The "Billie Jean" track opens slowly with a synthetic-sounding rock groove followed by a bass line that winds around what at first sounds like the tonic and fifth degrees of F♯ minor (table 2.1).[25] When inverted F♯ minor and G♯ minor chords enter eight bars later, the introduction of the D♯ indicates that the bass line's hint at F♯ minor was misleading and that F♯ Dorian is actually the correct mode for this section (example 2.1).[26] These chords build nervous energy as the top voices move up and down on a major second and land precariously off the second beat of each measure. The careful addition of new timbral, melodic, and rhythmic layers over the course of the extended opening groove indicates the structural importance of these individual textural elements as they set up and support the song's tenuous story line.

Example 2.1. Opening bass and synthesizer groove. (Michael Jackson, Thriller, 1982. Transcription by the author.)

Table 2.1. "Billie Jean" form and its harmonic diagram

Form	Mode
Opening drum kit and bass groove	Sounds like F♯ minor
Intro synthesizer chords	Confirms F♯ Dorian with D♯
Verses 1 and 2	F♯ Dorian with 3 x 2 mm iterations of F♯ minor (D♮ as ♭VI)
Bridge	F♯ minor (D♮) and momentary cadence on V
Chorus	F♯ Dorian with multiple iterations of F♯ minor (D♮ as ♭VI)
Verses 4 and 5	F♯ Dorian with 3 x 2 mm iterations of F♯ minor (D♮ as ♭VI)
Bridge	F♯ minor (D♮) and momentary cadence on V
Chorus (2x)	F♯ Dorian with many iterations of F♯ minor (D♮ as ♭VI)
Guitar riff	Oscillation between I and ♭VI scale degrees
Chorus (excerpt repetition)	Features F♯ Dorian to F♯ minor (D♮ as ♭VI) slippage
Chorus (fragments and fade-out)	F♯ Dorian supported by guitar riff on I and ♭VI

Note: "Billie Jean" transcription from Michael Jackson, *Thriller*, Epic, EK 38112, 1982, LP.

As the verses unfold, Jackson interrupts testimony about his relationship with Billie Jean with brief metaphorical visions of "dancing" around her desires and accusations. These memories mysteriously float among the couple's past, present, and future encounters. The song's tension comes to the fore during these refrain-like interruptions by halting the tonal progression in favor of dark B minor-seventh chords that introduce the flat-sixth scale degree (D♮) and momentarily subvert the Dorian mode (example 2.2, measures 2–3). During these harmonic shifts, the bass line abandons its smooth eighth-note pattern by jumping over beat three to land safely on the familiar F♯—a move that seems rhetorically to "dance around" the B minor-seventh intrusion. These interruptions happen reg-

Example 2.2. Dancing around the ♭VI and the bridge shift to F♯ minor. (Michael Jackson, Thriller, 1982. Transcription by the author.)

ularly in each verse (six in total; table 2.1). The ♭VI works in conjunction with Jackson's narrative asides to cast doubt on and displace the Dorian mode, and, further, these visions of dancing around the antagonist might be interpreted as either a euphemism for their past sexual encounters or simply as contradicting testimonies between Jackson and his accuser. The harmonic deviations here also foreshadow the upcoming move to F♯ minor in the bridge.

The D♮ makes its most intrusive appearance on the bridge's downbeat, where Jackson tells the moral of his story (example 2.2, mm. 6). Here the groove drops out and the ♭VI becomes the root of D Major chords that trick listeners into hearing it as a temporary tonic. However, the motion here actually changes the mode from Dorian to F♯ minor. Up to this point Jackson's voice has remained in a comfortable middle range, but here he highlights the anxiety expressed in the lyrics by driving his voice into the upper octave and changing the metric accent from off-beats to the down-beats where sustained block chords support his warning against playing lovers' games. Jackson's vocal line creates even more tension by singing the word *careful* on the intrusive sixth degree (example 2.3). The D♮ acts decep-tively throughout the bridge as the VI chords resist cadencing through the dominant until the last possible moment. Once the C♯ Major chord finally appears in the last measure of the bridge, it heightens the dramatic action by illuminating cautionary words about the nature of lies and sexual advances. These two assertions of the dominant provide the only "true" cadential points in the song. The resistance to authentic harmonic reso-lution here thus aurally supports the deception described in the storyline.

At the arrival of the chorus, the opening groove is reinstated to push the song back into F♯ Dorian, making the bridge sound like a temporary detour (table 2.1). The decision not to stay in F♯ minor renders the song's

Example 2.3. ♭VI warning and half cadence on C♯. (Michael Jackson, Thriller, 1982. Transcription by author.)

turmoil irresolvable because the ♭VI continues to reappear and be suppressed. In fact, the unstable harmonic motion from the verses returns to alternate between the F♯ Dorian and F♯ minor modes with synthesized intrusions of the D♮ (similar to example 2.2). During these minor-mode passages, Jackson repeatedly denies paternity despite the lack of an alibi. The vocal's melodic line complicates the lyrics as his syncopated phrase lands squarely on D♮ to highlight the possessive pronoun "*my*" (example 2.4). Jackson thus takes brief ownership of the ♭VI, alluding either to the extent of Billie Jean's betrayal or to his own guilt.

Example 2.4. Jackson sings the ♭VI (D♮) to assert his position as the "accused." (Michael Jackson, Thriller, 1982. Transcription by the author.)

Adding further precariousness to the story line, dreamy-sounding synthesizer flourishes interject to dance once more around D♮ (example 2.5). The falling F♯ minor arpeggio (which never stops to rest on the C♯) repeats several times, seeming to question Jackson's declaration of innocence. These little melodic frills act as musical echoes of the protagonist's struggle to deny the opening Dorian mode. They therefore help to preserve the ambiguity of the song's modal center and thus its overall "truths" or "meanings."

Example 2.5. Synthesizer flourish. (Michael Jackson, Thriller, 1982. Transcription by the author.)

Listeners are ultimately left guessing as to how the story ends as the song fades out on Jackson's famous denial: "Billie Jean is not my lover." A guitar riff accompanies this phrase by moving between the tonic and ♭6 scale degrees. The ability of "Billie Jean" to maintain harmonic tension throughout thus effectively supports the anxiety and uncertainty fundamental to its storyline.

Jackson's music video for "Billie Jean" notably does little to resolve the questions raised by the song. If anything, the video heightens its uncertainty by depicting the pop star as a mysterious yet magical man who is impossible to pin down. The final scenes of the video even seem to call Jackson's proclaimed innocence into question by showing him getting into bed with an unknown person and disappearing. He eventually emerges as a tiger—enacting the metaphor of a man's sexual appetite being like that of a wild beast—and then vanishes into the night.[27]

When considering the implications of the song's messages and video imagery, it is highly unlikely that Pepsi would be willing to associate its brand with these sordid situations. It is not surprising, then, that the brand would decide to go in a dramatically different direction with its own version.

PEPSI'S NEW CHALLENGE

By all accounts, it was the unusual and often difficult terms set by Jackson that dictated the aesthetic direction of Pepsi's commercials.[28] In *The Other Guy Blinked: How Pepsi Won the Cola Wars*, Roger Enrico gives an entertaining account of how, under his leadership, the second-largest soda manufacturer in America collaborated with the biggest musical superstar of the 1980s to create the most popular and expensive campaign to date. According to Enrico, an entrepreneur named Jay Coleman called him one day to talk about the possibility of sponsoring Michael Jackson.[29] Coleman had just started publishing a magazine called *RockBill*, that featured pictures and articles about the latest musical acts and the advertisements they made with corporate sponsors. Enrico claims he took the meeting because he had heard of Michael Jackson but was completely unaware of the pop star's success with his new album, *Thriller*. Two hours into their first meeting, Enrico decided that the five-million-dollar figure requested by Coleman for the endorsement was ridiculous and nonnegotiable. But, after a follow-up (and rather farcical) meeting with Jackson's manager, Don King, as well as dozens of conversations with various men along Pepsi's chain of command, Enrico finally agreed to the unprecedented price tag.[30] In return Pepsi was promised two commercials starring Michael Jackson and his brothers, sole sponsorship of their upcoming tour, and personal appearances at press conferences.[31]

Soon after the contracts were signed major glitches began to plague the deal, including offers from other sponsors to hire Jackson for more money, the pop star's notorious insecurity about his appearance, and dire warnings from fellow celebrities that doing the commercials would be career suicide.[32] After some coercion by his lawyers and family (mainly his father), Michael Jackson finally sat down with Pepsi to renegotiate a deal that worked for both parties. During the meeting, Jackson claimed that he was worried about overexposure. He also did not like the jingle Pepsi had written for him and was concerned with the excessive amount of time he would be onscreen. In a simultaneous attempt to encourage Pepsi's marketers to be more creative and meet them halfway, Jackson did something that would forever change the way commercials would look and sound: he offered them the use of "Billie Jean" and his "symbols"—the iconic glove, red jacket, spats, and shoes made famous in his performances and MTV videos—in exchange for four total seconds of face time, one close-up, and only one of his iconic dance spins.[33] Elated that Jackson would offer the company his current and most popular song, Pepsi gladly took the deal along with the many months of headaches that followed (including the negative publicity that followed the singer's on-set injury and trip to the hospital).

Jackson's desire for creative perfection became the campaign's ruling force.[34] Everyone involved admitted that Jackson's input was essential to the project's positive reception and acknowledged that his willingness to lend the soda giant the full force of his image and music made these spots appealing to its targeted youth demographic. This could be attributed to the fact that the pop star challenged Pepsi to represent him as a performer and icon rather than showing clichéd close-ups of him drinking the product. In the end, a careful wedding of Jackson's "symbols" and Pepsi's slogan proved flattering to both parties. Dusenberry noted, "Michael's instincts were right. The more you hold back the more people will clamour. The brief, lightning-quick flashes of Michael's face actually made viewers eager for more of the sudden glimpses that had been so carefully portioned out."[35] Pepsi's marketers thus worked meticulously to interweave visual and musical tropes that showed the superstar doing what he did best: entertaining audiences.

Dusenberry later confirmed that entertainment was a central idea for the campaign.

> Pepsi's advertising would exalt the user rather than sanctify the product. . . .
> Pepsi was the first to use celebrities in a way that went beyond their celebrity . . .

the first to use entertainment as the primary appeal of a commercial, more primary than the selling proposition.[36]

Although Pepsi's focus on musical entertainment was a new concept for the company at the time, it actually fit well within with the company's long history of depicting "vitality," "liveliness," and "leisure" in visually and sonically edgy commercials—a strategy that aligned with its concept of lifestyle advertising.[37] Thus, as detailed in chapter 1, the soda giant was after what Thomas Frank called "hip consumerism" to entice youth to purchase its product.[38] "Billie Jean" was certainly "hip" at the time due to its massive success and the input it received from Jackson's entourage of old-school talents, including its producer Quincy Jones. Its success was further propelled by the pop star's own achievements as a young Motown artist, his recent performance of the song on the *Motown 25* special, and his riveting music videos.[39] What better way, then, to represent Pepsi's "New Generation" than to use the very music its target audience already loved— music whose energy could encourage them to buy a soda?

Jackson's fan base, in fact, turned out to be a perfect match for Pepsi as it permitted the brand to continue its focus on targeting "youth" while also focusing on older Motown fans who wanted to *feel* young.[40] Rather than an age designation, "youthfulness" in these commercials therefore applied to anyone who enjoyed the pop star's performance. The venture thus had a greater potential to pay off, largely because both the sponsor and the endorser's products were carefully aimed at consumers who had a greater potential to buy both. The soda giant's optimistic sales projections also proved realistic considering that audiences could consume Pepsi just as often as they consumed the pop star's music and videos.

JACKSON'S ICONICITY AND MTV AESTHETICS

The soda giant made two commercials that captured only the positive aspects of Jackson's celebrity image and the catchiest sections of the backing track to "Billie Jean." Enrico and Dusenberry confirmed that Pepsi banked on the fact that much of its national audience would recognize the song. Marketers therefore attempted to encapsulate the "essence" of Jackson's superstar persona by co-opting and controlling as many of his musical and visual signifiers as they could.[41] These sources also indicate that the soda giant was clever to pick up on the trend, later noted by musicologist Andrew Goodwin and sociologist Jaap Kooijman, that mid-1980s audiences favored performances and texts that re-created music video imagery.[42] In fact, Pepsi's marketing team strategically hired Bob Giraldi, then a top music video director, to film the campaign in a way that embraced the facets of performance spectacle most important to the emerging aesthetic of MTV.[43]

Goodwin argues that musical aesthetics in the 1980s became increasingly dependent on images after MTV and other video formats had redefined the matrix of meaning in popular music from the sounds alone to include the visual aspects of an artist's performance.[44] As a defining characteristic of MTV programming, this change was fostered by an increasing reliance on the pairing of visual iconography and recorded sound.[45] Kooijman echoes Goodwin in his analysis of Jackson's *Motown 25* performance and subsequent reenactments of that night. He notes that Jackson's performance marked a turning point in popular music aesthetics in which the audience was fascinated not by the entertainer's musical skills (considering that he lip-synced his hit song), but by the way he looked and moved onstage.[46] Eighties pop was then realized and experienced more than ever before through the onstage spectacle of costuming, elaborate sets, and dancing.[47]

Jackson's appearance as the performer therefore added an important level of signification to his music. Pepsi, however, faced a considerable challenge when Jackson instructed it to use as few camera shots of his face as possible. Luckily for the soda giant, the superstar's music had become an aural representation of the spectacle of his performances to many fans, which allowed his images and sounds to mutually refer to one another. Similar to the way scholars have discussed Hollywood icon Fred Astaire (to whom Jackson has often been compared), both Kooijman and Mercer note that isolated aspects of Jackson's appearance (his costuming in particular) and bodily movements and gestures (especially the moonwalk) work, even today, to signify him.[48] Kooijman further argues that in the years following *Thriller*'s release, the star himself became a "postmodernist sign, a visual representation."[49] He concludes by observing that the pop star's visual signifiers had the ability to work separately from his voice and music to act as representations of his performances and/or performing self.

Due to the fluidity of his signifiers, it makes sense, then, that any of Jackson's three primary areas of signification—his physical appearance, dancing, and music—could effectively stand in for and represent the other aspects of his performing persona.[50] This point is supported by the fact that he openly acknowledged to Pepsi that he had carefully crafted his "symbols"—his costuming and signature moves—to become representational parts of his image.[51] These signifiers would effectively place Jackson throughout Pepsi's commercials despite the fact that his onscreen face time was severely limited.

"The Concert"

In his autobiography, Enrico described how the first spot, "The Concert," was designed to look.

> The commercial starts with the Jacksons—but not Michael—drinking Pepsi and relaxing in their dressing room before a concert. There's a flash of Michael in front of the makeup mirror, and then we move behind the stage, where Michael's about to make his entrance, and we are tantalized anew with glimpses of Michael's look—his symbols. Then the set opens, and with a flash of fireworks, Michael dances and spins into a full-fledged concert, singing the reworded "Billie Jean" to a mob of screaming kids in the audience.[52]

Enrico's account captures the commercial's attention to spectacle and movement. As a whole, the spot cultivates excitement by rapidly progressing through a montage of frames that depict a youthful audience gearing up for a concert, the Jacksons getting ready to perform, and Michael Jackson's "symbols" interspersed with Pepsi's. The camera works to keep the images moving at a pace equal to that of the music's soundtrack by cutting sporadically between the bustle backstage, screaming fans, and the staged excitement of the concert. The piecemeal style of editing used here is similar to that of music videos; the cinematography never focuses on any one scene for more than a few seconds as it works to manipulate the viewer's sense of moving through time.

The commercial opens with a panning shot over a sea of spectators. A pared-down version of the opening groove to "Billie Jean" begins the soundtrack.[53] Here the aggressive synthesized backbeats heard the original are replaced with a much lighter snare figure that gently accents beats one and three (table 2.2).[54] The song's distinctive bass riff, which is noticeably more prominent in this arrangement, enters next to accompany the bustle backstage and glimpses of Michael Jackson's white glove and sparkly

Table 2.2. "Billie Jean" form comparison

Jackson's "Billie Jean"	Pepsi's "Billie Jean"
Opening drum kit and bass groove	*Opening drum kit and bass groove*
Backbeat accents	Groove accents shifted to beats one and three
Sounds like F♯ minor	Prominent bass line and adjusted timbres
	Sounds like F♯ minor
Intro synthesizer chords	*Intro synthesizer chords*
Confirms F♯ Dorian with D♯	Hints at F♯ Dorian with D♯ and paired with Jackson's iconic symbols
Verses 1 and 2	*Verses 1 and 2*
F♯ Dorian with 3 x 2 mm iterations of F♯ minor (D♮ as ♭VI)	Omitted
Bridge	*Bridge*
F♯ minor (D♮) and momentary cadence on V	Splice to F♯ minor sounds exciting with a D major chord at the entrance of Pepsi's lyrics
Opening D major chord sounds striking against previous Dorian mode	Half cadence on C♯ accentuates the spot's visual and lyrical climax
Chorus	*Chorus*
F♯ Dorian with iterations of F♯ minor (D♮ as ♭VI)	Conflicts between D♯ and D♮ downplayed while D♮s slide by as passing tones
Verses 4 and 5	*Verses 4 and 5*
F♯ Dorian with 3 x 2 mm iterations of F♯ minor (D♮ as ♭VI)	Omitted
Bridge	*Bridge*
F♯ minor (D♮) and momentary cadence on V	Omitted
Chorus (2x)	*Chorus (2x)*
F♯ Dorian with many iterations of F♯ minor (D♮ as ♭VI)	Omitted
Guitar riff	*Guitar riff*
Oscillation between I and ♭VI scale degrees	Quick fade-out foregrounds Pepsi's slogan
Chorus (excerpt repeated)	*Chorus (excerpt repeated)*
Features F♯ Dorian to F♯ minor (D♮ as ♭VI) section	Omitted
Chorus fragments and fade-out	*Chorus fragments and fade-out*
F♯ Dorian supported by guitar riff on I and ♭VI	Omitted

Note: "Billie Jean" transcription from Michael Jackson, *Thriller*, Epic, EK 38112, 1982, LP; "The Concert," PepsiCo. Inc., 1984.

jacket, which are reminiscent of his famous *Motown 25* costume. At the entrance of the Dorian-inflected synthesizer chords (example 2.1) marketers weave quick cuts to Jackson's other iconic symbols between clips of his brothers sipping from Pepsi bottles and cups. In the original track, these synthesizer chords set up the song's tonal tension, but here the imagetext clearly gives them a *positive* connotation, complementing the anticipation and energy displayed by the performers and the crowd.

The first two stanzas of Pepsi's slogan enter a few measures later and are mapped onto the bridge of "Billie Jean" (table 2.2). Departing from traditional marketing practices, in which the slogan material is intended to be remembered, the instrumental track is mixed at a higher volume than its new lyrics to increase the likelihood that audiences familiar with Jackson's music would easily recognize the tune and make the association with the hit single. Although the slogan played a lesser role in hooking viewers than did Jackson's remixed track, marketing executives worked diligently with the superstar to ensure that the commercial's new words complemented the company's long-standing history of lifestyle advertising.[55] The verbs used—*dancing, grabbing, lovin'*, and so on—evoke the vitality that Pepsi ascribed to its "New Generation" of consumers. When substituted over the backing track of "Billie Jean," their poetic meter lines up perfectly with the harmonic changes on the downbeats to highlight key action words and the product name. In the original version, Jackson shifted the metric accents in this bridge section to give weight to the story's stern moral warning against "messing with young girl's hearts." But in the Pepsi spot, these accents emphasize the carefree, positive message of the brand.

To make "Billie Jean" fit within the confines of a 60-second ad, marketers simply cut out the song's verses. This move is not only practical and efficient (the song's most identifying features are in fact the riff and the chorus hook), but it is also aesthetically pleasing because it effectively eliminates the tension created in Jackson's verses by removing the struggle between the D♯ and D♮ (the Dorian mode and an intrusive ♭VI). The resulting splice from the opening groove to the bridge causes the prominent D Major chord (♭VI in the original song) to sound unambiguously "major" and exciting, especially in the context of the images and the commercial's reworked lyrics (table 2.2). It is here where Schudson's, Williamson's, and Bonde's theories can work together to illuminate how the "simplified" and rearranged musical fragments "re-present" the song's signifiers in a way that creates new "meaning potentials" for the commercial version of the

Fig. 2.1. Jackson's iconic socks and loafers. (Still from "The Concert," PepsiCo. Inc., 1984.)

track. This moment thus reveals the extent to which Pepsi's marketers had gained facility in redacting and redirecting musical signifiers to complement branding needs.

A tracking shot then follows Jackson's sparkly white socks and black loafers as they dance through a tunnel of backstage fans to the words "Put a Pepsi in the motion" (fig. 2.1).[56] The camera follows with cuts to images of his brothers running onstage. Just before the stars come into view, an announcer's voice cuts through the music to introduce them, causing the crowd to go wild.

Jackson's recognizable sequined jacket finally comes into focus on the key phrase of Pepsi's lyrics where the brand encourages viewers to choose its product (example 2.6, second line). This phrase is harmonically highlighted by the first and only time that the aurally and structurally satisfying C♯ dominant chord is heard in the commercial. By minimizing the Dorian versus minor harmonic uncertainty and putting musical and visual emphasis on a strong structural dominant, Pepsi and Jackson musically encourage their target demographic, represented in the diverse faces of the onscreen audience, to take action. At this point Pepsi's slogan conspicuously replaces Jackson's lines about deceit and sexual advances with an encouraging slogan about drinking its soda. It is at this moment that the extent of advertising's prowess in forging new contexts for familiar musical signifiers becomes strikingly evident and emblematic.

Example 2.6. Jackson's ♭VI warning (top) is replaced with an innocuous soda slogan (bottom). (Michael Jackson, Thriller, 1982; "The Concert," PepsiCo. Inc., 1984. Transcriptions by the author.)

As if these structural changes are not enough to signify the positive qualities of Pepsi's product, the omission of the original song's verses further allows the postponed dominant heard in the bridge to simply sound like an exciting climax at the downbeat of the commercial's chorus (Example 2.7, mm. 1–2). Indeed, without setting up the anxious stew-

Example 2.7. Dominant C♯ sets up the aurally satisfying chorus slogan. ("The Concert," PepsiCo. Inc., 1984. Transcription by the author.)

ing of the ♭VI, the otherwise precarious alteration between the minor and Dorian modes at this moment is downplayed by Pepsi's rousing images and welcoming slogan (table 2.2; see the first chorus). As a result, this move to the chorus drives the onscreen audience members to their feet as they finally get a clear view of Michael Jackson, who hails them as the "Pepsi Generation."

Amid the pandemonium and pyrotechnics, the music becomes fully diegetic as the Jackson brothers entice fans to drink Pepsi. The word *thrill* is syncopated and sung on the highest note heard thus far, aurally elevating the excitement for the product and subtly reminding viewers of Jackson's hit album *Thriller* (example 2.8). In the original song, this passage falls on the accusation: "She says that *I* am the one." The commercial version changes the meaning potential of the original song by diffusing the ♭VI on the second syllable of the product name, and allowing the precarious note to highlight the brand instead of bearing the weight of Jackson's denial of paternity (compare example 2.8, mm. 2–3, and example 2.4). Further, the synthesizer motives that "danced around" the deceptive ♭VI lose the rhetorical function they had in the original track. Here they merely act as recognizable, glittery ornaments, much like the sequins on Jackson's costume.

Example 2.8. Jackson's hook reworked into Pepsi's slogan. ("The Concert," PepsiCo. Inc., 1984. Transcription by the author.)

Following a close-up of each performer, the vocal line loops back to the opening measures of the chorus to reiterate that Pepsi's viewers are "a whole new generation" of consumers. The music decrescendos while the commercial's slogan, "Pepsi. The Choice of a New Generation," slides to the center of the screen over a sea of screaming fans. The commercial's soundtrack ends the same way as the album version of "Billie Jean" does, fading out on the repetition of the hook, underpinned by the rhythmic guitar vamp that oscillates between the F♯ tonic and ♭VI.

"The Concert" operates like MTV fictionalized performance videos that use close-ups and tracking shots of backstage footage to put the viewer on a more personal level with the musicians. Pepsi's concept of youthfulness is also displayed onscreen in the faces of the concertgoers and performers and is perpetuated by the energy expressed in the lyrics and musical track. By ending on a shot of a pumped-up crowd, the images leave viewers hanging in suspense, unable to experience the entirety of the performance, which is presumed to continue after the camera stops rolling.

"Street"

The second commercial, "Street," offers yet another interpretation of "Billie Jean" and Michael Jackson's iconicity by placing him and his brothers in an urban neighborhood. This spot mimics music videos that depict audience members embodying the personas of their favorite performers. Musically, much of the track is the same as "The Concert," although it works to bolster a different plot line.

The spot opens with extramusical sounds such as car horns and video arcade noises that sonically place the action on a busy city street. Once Pepsi's version of the "Billie Jean" opening groove enters (table 2.2), it is extended to give the camera more time to set the scene. The groove gives way to a glimpse of Michael Jackson wearing his well-known symbols as he strategically walks past Pepsi's logo posted in the window of a pizza parlor. A quick cut to his sparkling white socks and black loafers sets off the reworked groove to promote an energetic pace for the ensuing bass riff (example 2.1). At the entrance of the bass line, a dozen children happily bounce into the street wearing outfits resembling those worn by the rival gangs in Jackson's "Beat It" video. One of them carries a boom box, suggesting that the music in the scene is diegetic and that the children are dancing to the original version of "Billie Jean." Multiple shot-reverse-shots create an eyeline connection between images of the Jackson brothers hanging out and images of the kids drinking soda while they dance. Jackson's glove comes into focus the moment the groove's synthesizer chords enter the soundtrack (example 2.1). The linkage of his most famous symbol with the opening Dorian riff perfectly pairs Jackson's redacted musical and visual signi-

Fig. 2.2. Jackson's child impersonator emerges. (Still from "Street," PepsiCo. Inc., 1984.)

fiers. This moment solidifies his iconicity and confirms for the viewer that the song is indeed "Billie Jean."

A boy then slides out of a doorway dressed identically to Jackson's character in the video for "Beat It" (fig. 2.2).[57] As the child makes his way into the street, he performs all the pop star's signature moves. Michael Jackson's voice enters at this point with the first phrase of Pepsi's slogan placed over the bridge to "Billie Jean" (table 2.2). Direct word painting occurs when the children's dancing onscreen syncs with the reworked bridge.[58] After one of the Jackson brothers spots them, the group walks out join the fun. Just before the two groups collide, Michael Jackson sings, "Put a Pepsi in the motion." At that same moment, the boy begins to moonwalk as he dramatically gulps from a Pepsi can. The impersonator's reward for literally putting his Pepsi into "motion" is that he unknowingly slides into his idol. The boy turns around on the dominant C♯ to see Michael Jackson (example 2.7, mm. 2–3). The "King of Pop" then sings the chorus directly to his astonished young fans, identifying them as Pepsi's new generation.

For the remainder of the chorus, the boy and his friends eagerly perform side by side with the famous brothers (fig. 2.3). It is no coincidence that the performance here resembles the final dance number in "Beat It" because the commercial's director (Bob Giraldi) and choreographer

Fig. 2.3. The Jacksons dance with their admirers. (Still from "Street," PepsiCo. Inc., 1984.)

(Michael Peters) had also worked with Jackson on the music video. What is obviously different is Pepsi's replacement of violent street gangs with children dancing alongside the Jacksons—one of America's most friendly family acts. So, much like the conclusion of "The Concert" spot, the concluding guitar riff and final images suggest that the Jacksons serve as models for consumption for all of Pepsi's current and future generations.

Taking the two commercials together, it is clear that Pepsi distanced itself from the implications of adultery, deceit, and legal obligations laid out in Jackson's version of "Billie Jean" by showing only positive images, rewriting the lyrics, and wholly redacting the musical track. Visually, Jackson's Pepsi performances perfectly exemplify the concept of youthfulness that continued to prove central to the soda giant's branding aims. In "The Concert," marketers pair "Billie Jean's" energetic track with Jackson's costuming, dancing, and extravagant pyrotechnic entrance to enhance his perceived "hipness" and "coolness." The pop star's "wide appeal" is evident onscreen in the eager expressions of the staged audience members, who represent all ages, genders, and various racial groups. "Street" reinforces Pepsi's re-presentation of Jackson's mass popularity by showing young kids from various racial backgrounds dancing together to his music. The campaign thus follows historical trends established in past Pepsi spots by showing spirited consumers enjoying leisure time while they take pleasure in Jackson's performance and Pepsi's product.

Most important for the commercial's positive reception, marketers redacted the track by isolating the musical features that fans had the most potential to recognize. Marketers thus disassembled "Billie Jean" and rearranged it to create an innocuous version that avoided the anxious connotations created by the harmonic and melodic subversions so carefully set up in the original. This transformation was achieved first by reworking the opening groove, a feat that included shifting its metric accent to make the drums sound less aggressive (and more friendly) and increasing the prominence of the well-known bass line (table 2.2). Second, the tension set up in the original by the slow unfolding of the opening groove and the chorus's intrusive synthesizer flourishes was avoided by re-presenting them as short, isolated sound bytes (examples 2.1, 2.5). Most prominently, the commercials simply omitted Jackson's verses, eliminating the immanent conflict created by the opposition between the natural minor and Dorian modes (table 2.2). The tension in Pepsi's new track was therefore understated from the very beginning: the introduction of the major ♭VI chord on the downbeat of the bridge was no longer striking or volatile but instead exciting and positive when paired with the onscreen images (table 2.2). So even though some harmonic ambiguity was preserved in the sections left intact, in its new context the pivotal ♭VI actually worked to delay gratification for Pepsi's product instead of manifesting unresolved anxiety. Accordingly, the arrival of the bridge's dominant chord worked to achieve at least a partial resolution when viewers finally got a good glimpse of Michael Jackson and learned the "moral" of both commercials: drink Pepsi (not Coke). Pepsi marketers were therefore clever to combine various redacted "cotextual" elements within the commercial—the song's most memorable sound bites, friendly slogan, and exciting onscreen images—in a manner that promoted excitement for the product and performers and replaced the apprehensive stewing and themes of deception and illegitimacy that were prevalent in the original track. Marketers' ability to pick "Billie Jean" apart, redact its themes, stitch them back together, and present a new version to audiences thus successfully altered the song's original meaning potentials and proved to viewers that Pepsi was as hip to MTV and the latest trends as it was to its superstar endorser and his fans.

Advertising scholars agree that viewers of television commercials decipher meanings based on their "alreadyness": the previous knowledge they bring to a commercial's sounds and images.[59] Based on the discussion above, the soda giant obviously assumed that viewers' alreadyness with Jackson's hit song would make the campaign's soundtrack readily identifiable and therefore relatable. More specifically, its marketers hoped that hearing snippets of "Billie Jean's" catchiest tropes would allow audiences to bring their prior knowledge of his iconicity into the context of the campaign, giving them the potential to simultaneously recognize portions of the original song and make new connections with his music in Pepsi's branded context. And, as detailed at the beginning of this chapter, this tactic paid off handsomely as the overwhelming popularity of the campaign and the dramatic increase in soda sales indicated that the presence of the visual and musical elements of Jackson's persona offered a convincing and entertaining depiction of the star.

What remains puzzling, however, is that well-informed audiences—fans familiar with the original storyline of "Billie Jean" and its mysterious video—did not ridicule the song's placement in the spot, but instead willingly reconciled the contradictory meanings created by Pepsi's representation of Jackson and his music with their knowledge of the song in other contexts.[60] This begs the question: even if the campaign was received purely as entertainment, how was it that the appearance of Jackson and portions of his backing track fostered an acceptance of Pepsi's reconstruction of the pop star with its product? More specifically, why did audiences accept that the soda giant had twisted Jackson's celebrity by showing him as an endorser of a product he refused to drink, and why did they respond positively to the fact that it had changed his cautionary lyrics about the risks of fame to a more blandly inclusive message about an ideologically constructed "generation" of consumers? How were viewers persuaded to literally buy into Pepsi's claims with such a substantially redacted version of the original "Billie Jean"?

The answer is that these discrepancies were reconciled through the fabricated worlds of advertising under what Schudson calls "capitalist realism." For Schudson, late-twentieth-century American advertising resembled Soviet socialist realism in that it stripped down the complexities of visual art forms to propagate streamlined messages about corporate products to consumers.[61] Extending Schudson's argument to pre-existing popular music's role in advertising reveals how Pepsi's marketers accomplished similar ends by stripping a complex, modern song down to its most recognizable generic bits and rearranging them to fit 60- to 90-second spots. The success of these commercials suggests, then, that viewers accepted what was presented to them on the terms of capitalist realism, knowing on some level that the scenes of Jackson performing were not real, that his life as an entertainer was fabricated, and that the song in the commercial was not in fact "Billie Jean." Pairing these ideas with Judith Williamson's aforementioned theories on advertising's use of "meanings as currency" reveals how the most recognizable sonic signifiers of "Billie Jean" were successfully "re-presented" as a celebration of passive consumerism. Pepsi and Jackson thus created a new and striking example of capitalist realism that fit well within the constructed fantasy world of youthfulness, soda, and pop music. In this way, the song's tale of betrayal was made suitable and appealing to cater to both Jackson's and Pepsi's core audiences through a careful redaction of the original musical score—a practice that allowed it to become *the* model capitalist realist text that would solidify advertising's relationship with hit songs.

THE PEPSI-JACKSON LEGACY

Pepsi's "The Choice of a New Generation" campaign with Michael Jackson created a template for a new kind of celebrity endorsement—one that featured top performers singing new and current hit songs to endorse their recordings alongside corporate products. Sources report that Pepsi gained a volume share of 8 percent despite the fact that the rest of the soft drink industry had stagnated.[62] These co-branding efforts proved for the first time that musical celebrity endorsements could produce lucrative sales in both industries while their overwhelming success indicated that consumer sentiment about famous musicians appearing in commercial contexts had begun to shift. Pepsi's success made it evident that MTV viewers were not only eager to consume music and material goods together but also that they (at least temporarily) offered notably fewer criticisms of these endorsements than previous generations had showered on past artists who had similarly "sold out" their iconic images and music to promote goods.

Pepsi's decision to hire the star for such an extraordinary fee was also significant in increasing the amount of publicity, money, and potential record sales for musical endorsements. In the desire to match the quality of advertising Pepsi had financed, other companies rushed to pour more money into their own advertising budgets.[63] Many corporations (including Pepsi's rival, Coca-Cola) scrambled to hire well-known musicians for their campaigns, and some offered two to three times what Pepsi had paid Jackson in an attempt to gain the same level of notoriety.[64] The increase in cash flow resulted in good press for highly paid musicians and corporations that could shell out millions to hire them and allowed brands that offered the right deal at the right price to attract top artists.

Perhaps most important, Pepsi changed the way the advertising industry did business by working as diligently to (re-)present Michael Jackson and his music as it did to promote its own product. The level of control Jackson maintained during production allowed future stars to have more input in the creative aspects of the spots in which they appeared. By forcing Pepsi to work harder than ever to please its star, Jackson persuaded marketers to be more imaginative and suggested that celebrities did not even have to touch a product to represent it well. This new marketing style encouraged other brands to replace older, unnatural, and staged endorsement techniques.

The attention Jackson's sponsorship attracted also indicates that his commercials were not viewed simply as product endorsements but as highly efficient mini–music videos. The creative director at BBD&O reflects:

> Critics say that when an ad agency resorts to celebrity advertising, it's a sign that the agency is out of ideas. That's true if you're still locked into the 1950s, plunking a familiar face . . . in front of the camera to read provocative lines. . . . But we . . . [used] the biggest one we could find and put him . . . in a carefully scripted scenario that functions like a mini-movie, with a beginning, middle, and end.[65]

Indeed, the costuming, sets, dancing, and performance of a hit song by a young star all helped these commercials to look like music videos. Furthermore, the energy evoked by the melodies, harmonies, rhythms, and new lyrics coupled with the fast-paced editing, enthusiasm of the performers, and excitement of the onscreen audiences and actors emulated the very essence of MTV programming.

This last point is particularly important since the advertising industry was working diligently at that time to defeat a new set of adversaries that proved equally if not more challenging than parity marketplace rivalries; 1984 had become known as the "year of the zapper" due to the rapidly growing cable industry, which had prompted the wide distribution of the videocassette recorder (VCR) and remote control device (RCD), and these new technologies allowed consumers to take unprecedented control over their programming choices.[66] The RCD "zapper" and VCR "zipper" not only offered viewers ease in changing channels and fast-forwarding through shows from the comfort of their couches, but they also sparked major concerns for marketers who realized that these habits were directed primarily at commercial breaks.[67] Anxieties over these devices were so significant that talk of them dominated the 1984 *Advertising Age* awards show. The show's host, Fred Danzig, opened his monologue with the statement that the zapper had led to "ad agencies working late into the night. More than ever before, the creative challenge in 1984 was to find the production elements that would make viewers forget about the buttons when the commercial came on."[68] As the show cycled through the year's big winners, Danzig explained that agencies were attempting to "cure zapper fever" with high-tech effects, computer graphics, sound effects, and, of course, popular music. Just before screening Michael Jackson's "Street" Pepsi commercial, Danzig noted:

> Pepsi-Cola also managed to confound the zappers of '84 with a big event commercial. . . . It's a commercial aimed at building a leadership image among today's youngsters for Pepsi-Cola. It linked the "Pepsi Generation" with the leading edge of rock music.[69]

That "leading edge" of course referred to the music video format on MTV and its parent, cable television—ironically the very technologies that necessitated the RCD and VCR. The year 1984 therefore marks a historical moment when the rapid convergence of media technologies—computers, music videos, cable television, recordings, and playback devices (VCR, cassette tapes, etc.)—had an unprecedented impact on the advertising industry. Ultimately this technology even had the potential to force commercials to the brink of extinction. Marketers therefore were scrambling to integrate computer graphics and music video formats into commercials to prevent their jobs from becoming obsolete. As Danzig points out, Michael

Jackson's Pepsi commercials perhaps best encapsulated this new vision and made pop music marketing a hot topic.

Pepsi's 1984 campaign thus opened new possibilities for experimenting with musical co-branding. But, as the next few chapters demonstrate, the soda giant's transition away from the jingle and toward the incorporation of pre-existing songs proved challenging. Admen sometimes learned the hard way that a pop star's larger than life personality was not the only factor that had the potential to redirect marketing aims. Audiences were also growing increasingly savvy, and not every artist would have Jackson's charisma or his power to attract broad-based consumer interest. Most important, marketers found that the loaded signifiers composed into contemporary hit tracks sometimes proved difficult to control and could yield unintentional and unwanted outcomes. Pepsi's marketers would therefore use the better part of the decade to test multiple possibilities for redacting new pop songs, leading to variable outcomes along the way.

CHAPTER 3

The Choice of a Neoliberal Generation

Pepsi Models the Perfect Consumer

Pepsi's 1984 "The Choice of a New Generation" campaign with Michael Jackson prompted an explosion of musical celebrity endorsements. Following the directives of the brand's CEO, Roger Enrico, its advertising continued to use hit songs and MTV aesthetics to combat Coca-Cola, as well as the new possibilities for zipping (VCR fast-forwarding) and zapping (remotely changing channels) that had the potential to stifle sales.[1] Even prior to the completion of Jackson's commercials, Pepsi was aggressively pursuing what Enrico termed the next "big idea."[2] Pepsi executives had yet to witness the magnitude of their success with the megastar, but they knew that securing an edge in the soft drink market meant maintaining sponsorship deals with top musicians and continuing to wield pop music's sounds and imagery to define their "new generation." The brand therefore hired MTV veteran and ex-Commodore Lionel Richie for its 1985 campaign. In addition to sponsoring the Live Aid charity concert in the summer of 1985, Pepsi would also cut a deal in 1986 with rock star Tina Turner, who was gaining publicity for her starring role in the film *Mad Max: Beyond Thunderdome*; her newest album, *Private Dancer*; and her public revelations about surviving domestic abuse.[3] In 1987, Pepsi hired Turner for a second campaign—this time for a short-lived commercial duet with glam rocker David Bowie that depicted the new possibilities for dating in the age of personal computers.[4]

Pepsi's mid-1980s commercials proved noteworthy not just for their lineup of big names but also because their content underscored developing US neoliberal policies. These spots chronicle the soda giant's struggle to define its new generation alongside the larger reinvention of America's citizenry under President Ronald Reagan's support of market-driven logic as it applied to the autonomy of individuals and pushed for technological innovation, "free" global trade, and of course consumerism.[5] According to David Harvey and Wendy Brown, the ideology of "freedom" defined the core tenets of neoliberalism.[6] Pepsi's "The Choice of a New Generation" slogan thus perfectly encapsulated the language of neoliberal ideology by suggesting a semantic correlation between the concepts of "freedom" and "choice," specifically consumer choice. The words *free* and *choice* had actually appeared in Pepsi commercials since 1974.[7] Fittingly—as explained by Phil Dusenberry, the BBD&O creative director responsible for "The Choice of a New Generation" campaigns—the brand's historical focus on youthful "generations" was selected to "conjure appealing visions of American values such as *freedom*."[8] Dusenberry's marketing team and Pepsi executives therefore agreed that combining these two long-held concepts into the "The Choice of a New Generation" slogan worked well to maintain the brand's consistency, as well as the youthful image it had curated for two and a half decades. It was also (perhaps unwittingly) aligned with the neoliberal agenda that characterized American economic policy in the 1980s. The slogan's success therefore prompted the brand to continue its run well into the following decade.

Following Michel Foucault and others, music scholars Timothy Taylor, Andrea Moore, and Marianna Ritchey have demonstrated how 1980s neoliberalism has shaped today's musical culture and production.[9] More specifically, they illustrate how these policies led to an age of increased technological possibilities for musical creation and dissemination yet narrowed the chances of success within a declining (and arguably dismantled) twenty-first-century music industry. Their work has investigated the ways in which musicians from all genres increasingly turned to corporate brands in the last decades of the twentieth century due to their ability to offer crucial alternatives.[10] Indeed, even before the late 1980s, when the industry began to lose its grip because of new technologies that allowed for easy at-home replication (cassette tapes, compact discs, and later MP3s), high-stature artists had already started to use commercials to supplement the promotional power offered by music labels without involving the labels themselves.[11] From the 1980s onward, corporate sponsorship therefore allowed artists to achieve the heightened levels of exposure necessary for boosting album and tour sales in an increasingly saturated and fast-paced neoliberal economy that demanded constant innovation. In exchange, a growing number of musical stars were willing to lend not just their images but also their new or fairly recent hit songs to peddle consumer goods. Not only did these musicians serve corporate interests, but their music did too.

Pepsi's music-centered advertising agenda should have aligned seamlessly with the neoliberal values promoted by the Reagan administration—especially since its commercials had encouraged consumerism through fabricated and managed promises of youthful "freedom" for the better part of the twentieth century. But, as this chapter demonstrates, the brand's mid-1980s commercials exhibit the complexities of the cultural work necessary to effectively persuade audiences at a time when the advertising industry itself was also struggling to navigate new technologies and evolving aesthetic tastes in an increasingly competitive global marketplace. This chapter thus foregrounds Pepsi advertising's role in the developing years of neoliberalism in the United States, not only through an exploration of the ways in which it borrowed pre-existing melodies and harmonies, but also by revealing its transformation and redaction of musical and visual tropes in order to impose developing political agendas, which in this case aimed to exemplify Pepsi's (and America's) perfect consumer. Hence, the soda giant's deployment of successful pop stars in its mid-1980s campaigns modeled the *potential* of the new neoliberal individual. Marketers' manipulation of specific pop tropes communicated the qualities that would best exemplify this "new generation" of consumer citizenry as autonomous, upwardly mobile, family oriented, dazzled by spectacle, globally minded, and technologically savvy. The brand's Lionel Richie, Tina Turner, and David Bowie commercials, each in its own way, provide an early sonic blueprint for advertising's negotiation and integration of neoliberal values. They also illuminate the role that advertising played in promoting new neoliberal agendas—though not always to great acclaim.

LIONEL RICHIE MODELS A NEW GENERATION OF STYLE, SENTIMENTALITY, AND DEVOTION

Pepsi's commercials with Michael Jackson attained unprecedented success, but the company's sponsorship of his Victory Tour revealed the true costs of pop musical endorsements. The brand lost money on concert ticket sales and found distribution and scheduling incredibly difficult. Furthermore, when fans later realized that Jackson did not drink caffeinated products, Pepsi's credibility was questioned.[12] Some soft drink brands therefore remained cautious and refused to support music tours or sign deals with big names. Others were undeterred, including the Canada Dry beverage company, that hired singer and supermodel Grace Jones as its spokesperson.[13] Of course Coca-Cola also remained focused on winning the cola wars and regaining its status as the soft drink leader. In addition to hiring stars such as Julio Iglesias, Coke marketers used the likeness of Max Headroom—a fictional Artificial Intelligence figure—to appear as the brand's sassy and "hip" endorser.[14] By 1986 Headroom had appeared in a series of commercials that took direct aim at Pepsi and encouraged kids to give New Coke another chance. For its low-calorie soft drink, the brand hired pop sensation Whitney Houston to sing its Diet Coke jingle that same year. Vocal veterans the Pointer Sisters and Manhattan Transfer took up the charge in 1987.[15]

Once it seemed certain that Coca-Cola had secured Iglesias, Pepsi wasted no time in aggressively pursuing Lionel Richie. The former lead singer of the Motown group, the Commodores, had recently launched a solo career and was riding the success of his second solo album, *Can't Slow Down*.[16] The album produced five hit singles, including "Running with the Night," which Pepsi would co-opt for its campaign.[17] Richie's Pepsi deal included a multi-million-dollar payout that was reported to be competitive with Jackson's, sponsorship of two upcoming tours, several promotional funding opportunities, and matching contributions to the star's favorite charities.[18] In return the singer would appear in Pepsi's 1985 campaign and write a new jingle.[19]

In the year following Richie's Pepsi agreement, his fame would sky-rocket with a successful international tour and a performance at the closing ceremony of the 1984 Olympics in Los Angeles.[20] Pepsi executives thus elected to follow the formula they had created with Jackson and once again released their big campaign at the height of their new endorser's fame. Richie's commercials premiered on February 26, 1985, during the 27th annual Grammy Awards broadcast.[21] Richie was nominated for four awards during the Grammy event, and he won Album of the Year for *Can't Slow Down*, as well as Producer of the Year (nonclassical).[22]

The Grammys were the perfect venue to host the campaign's debut since the content of the spot blended almost seamlessly into the celebrity appearances and performances on the program. Indeed, Richie's acceptance of his awards was as much a promo for his album as for the soda campaign itself. This blurring of programming and commercial content was precisely what the advertising industry sought in its attempt to discourage channel changing and fast-forwarding during commercial breaks.[23]

Prior to the awards show, Richie's Pepsi campaign was hyped for its two-million-dollar production price tag and its uniqueness in being three minutes long—the lengthiest spot to air up to that point in prime time history.[24] The broadcast was also noteworthy because Pepsi reportedly paid the CBS television network an unprecedented one million dollars for the six consecutive 30-second slots needed to air the entire campaign.[25] The content that ran that night consisted of three separate, smaller spots titled "New Styles," "Homecoming," and "Block Party."[26] Pepsi marketers planned to air the three-minute compilation for its Grammy telecast premiere and then break the episodes into three individual 60-second segments. Eventually they would reduce each to 30 seconds.[27]

Each of the three spots features a unique story line and a distinct soundtrack that defines specific qualities that the soda giant and its marketers believed the new generation to possess. As explained in the *Los Angeles Times*, Pepsi's "mini-rock video[s]" show Richie talking and singing about the "style, heart, and beat" of the "new generation."[28] By extension, these traits were intended to glorify the brand and its product.

Although the campaign's high-quality cinematic and music video production values work to enhance the spectacle, it is the musical track that carries the weight of the campaign's message. Richie's compositional style sonically unifies each of the tunes used in the three segments. These include a new Pepsi jingle, "You're Looking Pepsi Style"; an arrangement of his 1983 single "You Mean More to Me"; and "Pepsi Feels So Right," which features the backing track to his more recent hit, "Running with the Night."[29] The three tracks (when played consecutively on the Grammy Awards show) follow a large-scale, ABA harmonic form that provides a guiding aural trajectory and ushers viewers through moments of climax, suspense, and resolution (table 3.1). In addition to beginning and ending in C Major, the melody also begins and ends on the same note (E), allowing the commercial's track to end in the familiar key where it began. The ABA form is reinforced with two danceable midtempo, synthesizer-saturated tracks ("New Styles" and "Block Party") that act as bookends for the slow, classically orchestrated middle segment ("Homecoming").[30] This form aligns closely with the images onscreen to guide viewers through Pepsi's identification of and communication with its new generation.

"New Styles"

The first commercial focuses on the look and lifestyle "choices" of Pepsi's ideal consumers. The campaign begins with a close-up of Lionel Richie, who is sharply dressed in a gray suit. He strolls casually down an empty city street, and as he walks toward the camera he recites a brief introduction that highlights the campaign's main points. The "new generation," he says, distinguishes itself with "new rhythms, new feelings, [and] new styles." As outlined in table 3.1, these traits correspond directly to the message in each of the following commercial segments.

An abrupt transition then takes viewers to the first spot, where Richie sings his newly composed pop jingle, "You're Looking Pepsi Style."[31] The tune bears his trademark solo sound, with layered synthesizer grooves, a prominent bass line, and smooth lyrical clarity. A pulsing drum groove propels its energy. Other than the avoidance of tonic or dominant resolution, the jingle works like a mini–pop song with an instrumental introduction, two verses, and a repeated chorus. In fact, the tune sounds so much like one of Richie's Top 40 hits that multiple sources referred to it not as a jingle but as a Pepsi "theme song."[32] This is perhaps due to the fact that the jingle's opening phrases closely mirror the chorus of Richie's 1982 hit "You Are."[33]

Visually, "New Styles" bears the aesthetics of an MTV video. Specifically, the dark setting in a city street, trendy consuming, and quick editing closely resemble the scenes that the commercial's director, Bob Giraldi, had also filmed when making the video for Richie's "Running with the Night" (a track reworked and featured later in the spot). The choreography is also similar, as is the staged scenario of young attractive singles—twenty- and thirty-something professionals—getting ready for a night on the town (fig. 3.1). Richie's lyrics accompany Giraldi's commercial footage by hailing the "new generation" as "free," "fine," and "right," and he emphasizes its desire to live in "Pepsi Style." The outro hook proclaims, "We made our choice, makin' it Pepsi. Looking Pepsi Style." As shown in table 3.1, the excitement of the images and lyrics is reinforced by a climactic key change up a step to D Major, followed by the repetition of the chorus's hook and a fade-out on F♯. When paired with Richie's jingle, the images make it clear that those who "choose" to be part of Pepsi's new generation are single, urban, young professionals who are concerned with their appearance and desire a nightlife fueled by Pepsi-Cola. Hence, as upwardly mobile consumers they represent the brand's target audience: youthful neoliberals.

"Homecoming"

The second commercial in the campaign, "Homecoming," provides a sharp contrast to the first. As the track enters the "B" section of the campaign's form, Richie's upbeat, poppy, and youth-themed opening jingle

Table 3.1. Lionel Richie's three-minute Pepsi commercial

Form	Commercial Title	New Generation Qualities	Song Title	Song Form	Key
Speaking intro					
A	"New Styles"	"Style"/ "Look"	"You're Looking Pepsi Style"	Verse 1	C Major
				Verse 2	C Major
				Chorus (2x)	D Major
B	"Home- coming"	"Heart"/ "Feelings"	"You Mean More to Me"	Piano and spoken intro	D Major
				Chorus/ refrain	D Major
				Verse	D Major
				Chorus/ refrain	E♭ Major
				Fermata/ dialogue	E♭ Major
Transition/ crowd cheers					
A	"Block Party"	"Beat"/ "Rhythms"	"Pepsi Feels So Right" (lyrics set to "Running with the Night")	Instrumental intro	C Major
				Verse 1	C Major
				Chorus	C Major
				Coda/chorus variation to fade	C Major

Note: Transcribed from "New Styles," "Homecoming," and "Block Party," PepsiCo. Inc., 1985.

Fig. 3.1. A stylish single enjoys his soda. (Still from "New Styles," PepsiCo. Inc., 1985.)

gives way to a slow and sentimental tune more suitable for adult contemporary radio.[34] As a result, the track aligns well with the balladeer reputation Richie had built to attract older audiences.[35]

"Homecoming" begins with a smooth elision of the F$\sharp$ from the previous commercial that supports a visual transition to Richie sitting alone at the piano in Los Angeles' historic Embassy Auditorium.[36] Languishing block chords outline a D Major triad to confirm the commercial's new key area and its sentimental affect (table 3.1). Richie looks directly into the lens and explains, "[This is] the heart of a new generation. The way we feel about each other." He then croons the first phrase of "You Mean More to Me," from his first solo album. During his performance the camera offers a (fictional) flashback to a little girl who once pleaded for his autograph as he rushed through a sea of fans. Despite his hurry, Richie decided to take a moment to talk with the child, sign her Pepsi cup, and share a hug (fig. 3.2). The scene is reminiscent of Richie's performance of the same song during the historic *Motown 25* special a few years earlier when he sang to a similar-looking girl named Lynette Butler, known as one of the "Sickle Cell Poster Children."[37] This visual cue adds yet another layer of familiarity, media

Fig. 3.2. Pepsi takes Richie on a sentimental journey. (Still from "Homecoming," PepsiCo. Inc., 1985.)

convergence, and sentimentality to the already syrupy music and visuals. More specifically, by alluding to Motown—a well-known black owned and operated label—as well as the sickle cell epidemic, the campaign attempts to make a direct connection with African American audiences who continued to be an essential demographic for the brand.

The sentimentality of this moment is heighted by Richie's musical score, which works cinematically to comment on the heartfelt scene. Most notably, the newly redacted lyrics steer clear of the romantic affection communicated on the album. The track's redirected meanings are highlighted when direct word painting illuminates the inserted phrase "Just to see you smile" as the little girl looks at Richie with delight. Soaring strings punctuate the kindness of his gesture. The swelling musical score thus connotes the significance of this moment to the commercial's overall message: as the spokesperson for Pepsi's new generation, not only does Richie's pause to fulfill the child's wish demonstrate his likability and sincerity but his signature on Pepsi's cup validates its symbolic value. Richie therefore literally inscribes the commodity with his own cultural capital (his autograph) and transfers his best traits—his popularity, earnestness, and kindness—to the brand. Put another way, Richie "fills Pepsi's cup" with the very traits that the commercial's sights and sounds exaggerate.

A series of quick visual cuts then continues to alternate between this scene and his solo diegetic performance in Embassy Auditorium. Eventually Richie's flashback moves to another series of crosscuts between various stages of airplane and taxi travel—the very trip he risked missing when he stopped to interact with his young fan. The star finally arrives at an undisclosed location—one in which viewers have been misled to believe is his home. An unexpected half-step key change up to E♭ heightens the onscreen anticipation and works to foreshadow the upcoming plot twist (table 3.1). Richie's acousmatic voice repeats the song's refrain one last time while the camera follows him into a private garden. Once inside he does not greet his wife or child but unexpectedly surprises his 91-year-old grandmother.[38] Soaring high strings once again underscore the scene's sentimentality, and the commercial ends with a pause on their embrace.

Pepsi's product is notably absent in the final moments of "Homecoming," making it easy to forget that this is indeed a commercial. The wholesome images and cinematic score distance it from "New Styles," as well as Pepsi's previous new music marketing commercials with Michael Jackson. In lieu of a high-energy pop tune, the track tugs at viewers' heartstrings by combining tropes from a slightly dated adult contemporary song with Hollywood-esque film scoring.[39] The reworked lyrics to "You Mean More to Me" and thick orchestral underscoring in "Homecoming" thus support its distinct message: Pepsi's new generation is as generous and loyal to its family and community as it is to the brand. In this way, the spot strongly alludes to other well-known 1970s and early 1980s campaigns made for Kodak, Polaroid, and President Ronald Reagan's 1984 reelection campaign, which similarly attempted to reinforce constructions of "American values"—namely, those of the nuclear family and patriotism.

As a result, the commercial's suggestion of a nostalgic "return" to an idyllic home and "traditional" family aligned perfectly with President Reagan's 1980s political rhetoric and the rise of the "New Right." As noted by Michael D. Dwyer and David Harvey, these tropes emerged in 1980s popular culture, movies, videos, and music that strove to promote the decade's emerging neoconservative values: cultural nationalism, moral righteousness, family values, and (a revisionist) history.[40] And, although they contradicted many aspects of the neoliberal agenda (such as opposing the "moral permissiveness" that usually accompanied individualism and the restoration of class power), neoconservative ideologies successfully appealed to the working class and helped to keep Reagan era policies—those that fostered a relentless focus on maintaining individuality, the free market, and class hierarchies—from breaking the country apart.[41]

Pepsi's "Homecoming" commercial thus perfectly captures the powerful ideological veil that neoconservative values provided while simultaneously supporting neoliberal consumerist agendas. It gives the consumer a break from the hard sell and instead offers the potential for a nostalgic and sentimental connection to Richie's personal life through the brand. More specifically, the commercial's extensive redaction of Richie's original track—including its redirection of the lyrical content and focus on only the most climactic moments of a largely restrained yet sensual adult contemporary ballad—repurposes it from an overtly romantic gesture to a platonic neoconservative anthem. In tandem with the images, the music not only helps to paint Richie as the perfect example of an upwardly mobile, entrepreneurial, and consumerist neoliberal citizen, but he is also presented as a model of morality and tradition.

"Block Party"

The final spot in Richie's three-minute campaign reignites the energetic pace established in the opening "New Styles" commercial and aligns most closely with Pepsi's new music marketing strategy. "Block Party" begins with the commotion of a cheering crowd, which mediates the musical track's unexpected leap up a seventh (B♭ to A). When paired with the visible excitement of the onscreen crowd, the upbeat tempo of the ostinato from Richie's "Running with the Night" establishes a playful mise-en-scène. Pepsi is again careful to redirect its star's adult-themed lyrics into something more appropriate for national television audiences: it redirects a story about going out on the town, drinking, and making love into a branded anthem. "Running with the Night" is therefore treated much like Jackson's "Billie Jean," and the album's lyrics are completely replaced with a new Pepsi slogan. The harmonic trajectory of the backing track is also reworked, but this time the melody is subtly altered to heighten anticipation for Richie's performance and also to support the onscreen devotion to Pepsi's product.

The commercial's opening frames introduce a large crowd waiting for an outdoor evening concert to begin.[42] To increase suspense, the spot swaps the original track's opening VI-IV-V syncopated chord progression with the A ostinato that follows it (example 3.1). Visually, the film is edited so that all cuts and onscreen movements are perfectly synchronized with each pulsating beat (mm. 1–5). As Carol Vernallis points out in her examination of music videos, when images are edited to correspond to the music's rhythmic pulse, the forward motion, or "flow," is heightened by what appears to be a reciprocal reinforcement of forward motion between the track and the visuals.[43] Consequently, the pairing of the pulsing A with the motion onscreen effectively builds excitement for Richie's entrance.

Example 3.1. Opening synthesized ostinato and guitar (score reduction). ("Block Party," PepsiCo. Inc., 1985. Transcription by the author.)

Once the Richie runs onstage, the syncopated VI-IV-V progression heard at the beginning of the original track is spliced in to sonically reinforce his image with the familiar chords (mm. 6–9, example 3.1). At this moment the music does most of the work to appellate viewers since, unlike Michael Jackson, Richie had no flashy or iconic "symbols" to incorporate into the spot. Instead, the singer's costuming blends in with the crowd, and his rigid, bouncy singing posture noticeably lacks the pizzazz of Jackson's slick choreography. Marketers therefore had to trust that audiences would find familiarity in hearing the song's introduction and would simply recognize Richie's face from his MTV videos.[44]

Richie's onstage vocal performance opens with two re-lyricized phrases set to the first verse of the backing track to "Running with the Night." In lieu of singing about the thrills of experiencing the bustling city with his lover, Richie waxes poetic about the "beat" of Pepsi's new generation and its desire to have fun with the aid of the soda brand. Close-ups of the star are interspersed with an occasional wide pan of the stage and the generically "diverse" all-ages crowd that surrounds it. The track then forgoes a smooth transition to the neighboring notes of Richie's first chorus and instead cuts to a reworked version heard much later in the original song. The jarring leap up a fifth (to G), thus aurally emphasizes the product name (example 3.2). This new chorus replaces Richie's allusions to urban escapades and sexual encounters veiled by the cover of nightfall with a slightly more wholesome suggestion of "dancing 'til the sun shines."

Direct word painting then illuminates Richie's lyrical command. As his vocal line moves upward on the directive to lift their Pepsis "high," the crowd obeys by raising their soft drinks in solidarity and acting out key action words. At one point the lens even makes an eyeline connection between Richie and an eager young listener who takes the pop star's advice to "get down before [Pepsi's] magic gets away."[45] It is in these scenes that viewers witness the extent of advertising's ideological power as the commercial literally names the "magic" that Pepsi creates for its consumers. This magic, as advertising scholars have long argued, ultimately works to replace religious devotion with loyalty to the commodity.[46] In this way, the spot depicts an all-ages crowd of ideal consumers coming together to celebrate the "Church" of Pepsi as led by "Reverend" Richie. The pop star leads his congregation with constant praises offered to the corporate power, and his followers show their devotion by following his commands and moving ecstatically to the redacted score. Advertising's magic thus animates the Pepsi commodity with personal and social meanings for the onscreen crowd—ideas that the brand hopes will translate easily to viewers at home.[47]

Example 3.2. A melodic splice highlights the product name. ("Block Party," PepsiCo. Inc., 1985. Transcription by the author.)

As this third commercial comes to a close, new lyrics cleverly substitute Richie's affection for the brand—"Pepsi Feels So Right"—for the romantic lust communicated in his original ("Girl, it was so right"). This repeated final phrase becomes the commercial's hook, switching Richie's role from an adventurous lover to a corporate mouthpiece.

After three minutes of spectacle, sentimentality, and Pepsi pop slogans, it is obvious that the brand offers its drink as the *only* "choice" for those who wish to be included in the new generation. The first number, "You're Looking Pepsi Style" foregrounds the product by featuring Richie's specially composed jingle set in a generic adult contemporary musical style. Images of young professionals demonstrate how the ideal neoliberal consumer should look and act. The second scene transitions to one of Richie's recognizable older hits, "You Mean More to Me." Not only are its lyrics modified to fit the commercial's family-friendly, sentimental story line, but Pepsi gives viewers a momentary break from the hard sell. This allows Richie to embody the ideal citizen and demonstrate that despite his success he maintains the moral values important to neoconservative audiences. The campaign's final vignette, "Pepsi Feels So Right" is set to the tune of Richie's recent hit "Running with the Night." This commercial brings viewers into advertising's (and more specifically into Pepsi's) most recent trend: the performance of new(er) hit songs injected with lyrics that showcase the brand and offer guidance to those who seek fulfillment in the commodity.

WHOSE GENERATION? RICHIE'S MIXED RECEPTION

Richie's campaign was in many ways a mirror image of Jackson's. Not only was it released at the same event just one year later, but the same filmmaker, Bob Giraldi, directed it. Accordingly, the street and concert scenarios in "New Styles" and "Block Party" look largely identical to those in Jackson's commercials. What made Richie's different was that they featured people and scenarios appealing to consumers both within and well beyond the MTV demographic. Whereas the first scene showed Richie instigating the nightlife of young urban professionals, the middle and final spots aimed for audiences of all ages and various racial groups by highlighting the star's sentimental feelings for children and the elderly and his ability to bring everyone together to celebrate his music alongside the endorsed product. Pepsi's 1985 campaign thus attempted to cover the gambit of ideal neoliberal consumers. Not only were they single, hip, and young, but they could also be racially diverse and in any age bracket. Moreover, members of Pepsi's "new generation" might have the ambition and cash to experience city life, dress fashionably, and go out in the evening or they might be family oriented and enjoy traveling and attending concerts. Regardless, these consumers exemplified the types of aspirational middle-class lifestyles that would presumably allow them to consume Pepsi during leisure time spent with their friends, family, and community.

Pepsi soon learned, however, that casting such a wide demographic net clouded its message. Sources contemporary with the commercial indicate that its reception was lukewarm at best. One positive yet brief mention was published in the *New York Times* recap of the awards show, where it was noted that "one of the night's highlights starred Lionel Richie, winner of the Best Album award, in a three-minute commercial for Pepsi-Cola. He sang the praises of 'a whole new generation of feelings, rhythms and styles.'"[48] But not everyone was as comfortable with seeing pop stars performing in commercials as the soda giant expected. One reporter was clearly unimpressed, writing:

Lionel Richie's music-video-ad for Pepsi—a sepia-toned slice of sentiment, featuring Richie's personal 91-year-old Grammy—did not bode well for the future marriages of rock videos, advertising and soft drinks. That Richie also won best album of the year will only encourage the continuing unhappy confusion between pushing product and spreading music.[49]

A writer for the *Washington Post* was downright hostile in his review, admonishing Richie for what he saw as an egregious case of self-promotion.

One of the big winners on this year's Grammy show, Lionel Richie . . . also appeared on the program in an outlandishly overproduced, new Pepsi-Cola commercial. . . . It was a three-minute mega-production that video ace Bob Giraldi was called in to direct. . . . And it had a cast as big as an old MGM musical. Maybe as big as "Ben-Hur." There were concert segments, with Richie leading huge mobs through the streets, and dramatic segments, with Richie hugging a fervently adoring little girl and traveling hundreds of miles to visit his grandmother.

This was selling out on an epic scale, boy. Lionel Richie wasn't just selling Pepsi; he was also selling Lionel Richie. And for all that money and all of

Richie's sickening saccharine posturing, it was still a lousy commercial. It was like the Duran Duran "Wild Boys" video: mawkishly humorless excess. Richie has replaced Barry Manilow as America's chief source of cloyingly syrupy quasi-musical pap, an ever-dependable reference point for presumptuous bad taste.[50]

A Canadian journalist shared similar sentiments in his reflections on the spot more than year later, labeling Richie's reworked rendition of "Running with the Night" as "bucklust blasphemy."[51]

Alternatively, those within the advertising industry expressed enthusiasm for the spots and recognized the market potential of Richie's commercial. A special report on the latest difficulties facing marketers praised its epic length and content, saying that it would surely distract viewers from acting on their new ability to zip or zap during commercial breaks.[52] Months later, when PepsiCo. declared a victory over its rival following Coca-Cola's announcement of its New Coke formula, the *New York Times* put a positive spin on the spot.

> Nowadays, Pepsi's jingles are more like No. 1 hits on the pop music charts. With Michael Jackson and Lionel Richie touting the drink as that of a "new generation." "Pepsi feels sooo right, sooo right," Mr. Richie croons as scores of young people dance in the street decorated with the red, white and blue colors of Pepsi.[53]

Additionally, Video Storyboard Tests, Inc., a company that analyzed recent trends in television advertising, ranked the campaign's final commercial, "Block Party," as the best ad of 1985.[54]

The discrepancies that arose between viewer reactions and those from inside the ad industry point to ideological disagreements about what constituted "selling out" at the time and further highlight the confusion about who exactly Pepsi intended to target with these spots. Some, like *Ebony* magazine, thought that the brand was aimed at black audiences. Its 1984 issue thus confirmed that hiring black celebrities like Michael Jackson and Lionel Richie not only bolstered the chances of the cola brand appealing to the $160 to $200 billion African American consumer market but had proven effective in selling products to white consumers as well.[55] Pepsi's CEO, however, stated that hiring these stars was *not* intended to increase the brand's black market share but instead to create media buzz and capture "youthful ideas and attitudes."[56] So, while the upward mobility of African Americans is highlighted throughout (as exemplified by Richie, his onscreen fans, and references to Motown), Pepsi claimed to have intended its star's image to appeal across age groups.[57] What marketers did not realize was that Richie's musical style would complicate his reception with both black and youthful audiences.

Indeed, by 1985 Richie had garnered a reputation as a 1970s soul and funk singer turned love song balladeer. His material was therefore hardly as cutting-edge or popular as Michael Jackson's. As perhaps best summarized by a *Washington Post* critic, Richie's appeal was complex.

> In this age of boogie-downs and permafunk, Richie's mainstream pop instinct reflects an old-fashioned romantic optimism and supple melodicism that owe much to Sammy Cahn and Burt Bacharach and the Tin Pan Alley tradition in general. Some gag at Richie's sometimes saccharine tendencies, but his blend of popcraft and sentimentality has obviously struck a responsive chord.[58]

As this and other contemporary sources allude, Richie's affinity for old (and arguably white) standards caused him to struggle to maintain the interest of African American fans who were once faithful to his Commodores catalog.[59] But in addition to his music's potential to alienate black audiences, which represented a sizable portion of Pepsi's consumer base, it was even more problematic that marketers missed the fact that Richie's style would prove ineffective in reaching the *youth* demographic the brand intended to retain.

As detailed in chapter 1, Pepsi had originally marketed itself as the soft drink for "those who *think* young." By making the concept of youthfulness a tool for lifestyle marketing, the adage was not initially intended to be an age designation but was meant to appeal to anyone who exemplified the "vitality" the soda giant ascribed to its consumers.[60] Pepsi's campaigns thus had wavered in their focus since the 1961 "Think Young" campaign as they strove to attract a broader consumer base without being overly exclusive. However, the brand's move to new music marketing and use of music video imagery in 1984 suggested a redefining of its audience: the new catchphrase implied that it catered specifically to the savvy MTV demographic (18- to 34-year-olds). Indeed, Philip Hughs, president and CEO of the Beverage Products Corporation franchise at the time, said that he believed the new campaign returned the brand to youth-targeted advertising after years of attempting to reach too broadly.[61] Alan Pottasch, director of creative services for Pepsi, also confirmed that the strong appeal of both Jackson and Richie across the country was intended to help the company target slightly younger audiences: 12- to 24-year-olds.[62] Executives knew that Michael Jackson had worked well as the initial "The Choice of a New Generation" spokesperson because his long career bridged the gap between mature audiences familiar with Pepsi's (and Jackson's) previous image and the teens and young adults attracted by the flashiness of the superstar's music, dancing, and MTV culture—that is, those in the presumed *new* generation. But by hiring thirty-four-year-old Lionel Richie to sing what many regarded as overtly sentimental, adult contemporary tunes, Pepsi actually clouded this new message.[63]

Indeed, professionals within the advertising industry itself openly disagreed on the purpose of hiring Richie. An interview with a beverage analyst in the *New York Times* noted, "When Pepsi began using rock stars like Michael Jackson and Lionel Richie, it identified 'the Pepsi generation' as teenagers."[64] From the opposite vantage point, the *Washington Post* claimed that Richie's spots transcended age categories.[65] Jay Coleman, president and founder of *RockBill* magazine (and the man responsible for pairing Jackson with Pepsi), offered a third perspective. He saw Jackson and Richie as appealing to two different audiences.

> To reach the nation's 22.8 million teenagers, for example, PepsiCo, the soft-drink company, signed on Michael Jackson and his brothers. To reach a somewhat older audience, Pepsi announced a deal with the singer Lionel Richie.[66]

Accordingly, Coleman and others recognized that Richie was aging out of the MTV demographic. And, although his videos did appear regularly on the network, they were certainly not as popular as Jackson's and were not always well received.[67] Pepsi's marketers thus obviously intended to ride out what they saw as a winning approach to new music marketing: hiring a black male MTV artist to sing hit songs to adoring fans. So, while they were correct in recognizing Richie's popularity, BBD&O marketers and Pepsi executives were perhaps not as careful in assessing *who* his fans were or, more accurately, to whom his musical style would most effectively communicate.[68]

Just as Richie was looking to reinvent his career as a soloist, baby boomer rock star Tina Turner was doing the same. Around the time Richie had signed his deal with Pepsi, the star had asked Turner to perform the opening act for his 1984 tour.[69] That year her new solo album would climb the charts, and the following year it received acclaim during the 1985 Grammy Awards show on which Richie's Pepsi commercial premiered.[70] Pepsi recognized Turner's success and was quick to seize the media frenzy around her hit album, the public disclosure of her personal struggles, and her new film role. Its executives thus offered to sponsor her upcoming tours along with a multiyear endorsement deal reported to be worth around $4.5 million.[71]

Turner's 1986 campaign was marketed worldwide, thus demonstrating the potential of the international marketplace. For this campaign, Pepsi-Cola International hired a marketing team at the Ogilvy and Mather agency to devise a plan that could appeal to fans both in the United States and overseas.[72] The team conceptualized a series of commercials that it could build from core footage filmed in 1986 in Honolulu and Los Angeles. The initial take featured Turner singing a new Pepsi jingle called "We've Got the Taste" to a staged audience. For each country where the spot was aired, marketers added clips of local rock stars singing in their native languages alongside the American icon. According to the press release, only about six rockers actually had the opportunity to sing live with Turner, while others were simply added using computer graphics technology. On March 17 the first commercials aired in Puerto Rico, Mexico, Brazil, and Thailand.[73]

In many ways, Tina Turner was a more convincing spokesperson than Lionel Richie. First of all, Turner claimed to be an avid Pepsi drinker.[74] Marketers could therefore film her not only touching the product but actually drinking it. Following the buzz that surrounded the revelation that Michael Jackson did not drink caffeine, it was important for the brand to find an endorser who could be a credible advocate.

Second, Turner had developed iconic symbols that Pepsi could place throughout the campaign. Her new "natural" hairstyle, toned legs, and high heels had become her trademark look.[75] And when mixed with her distinctive gravelly voice, these signifiers would prove unmistakable to her fans. Turner's recognizable iconography thus likely inspired Pepsi's marketers to make its commercials resemble key scenes from her music video for "Show Some Respect."[76] As a bonus, the video's scenario worked well within Pepsi's newly cultivated oeuvre of musical celebrity commercials by continuing the thread of live concert themes realized in both Jackson's and Richie's spots. More specifically, its mix of private backstage footage with performance shots closely mimicked Jackson's 1984 "Concert" commercial.

"We've Got the Taste" proved further significant in its emblematic portrayal of the universalizing vision of neoliberalism by skillfully tapping into the potential profits from foreign markets with its integration of American rock culture and local talent. The campaign also followed rapid advances in technology that had already facilitated an increased exportation of American products. Not only did satellite technology spread the MTV phenomenon to global youth, but with the aid of computer graphics this same technology could also hype local musicians alongside big name international stars—all while pushing American goods (in this case, soda). As a hallmark of the kind of free marketplace interactions that pushed Ronald Reagan's economic and political agendas, Turner's campaign was a potential win-win for everyone involved: local, lesser-known musicians received unprecedented press and cultural capital from their association with Turner and Pepsi-Cola, while Turner and Pepsi benefited financially from the economies of the host countries.

The following sections examine two versions of "We've Got the Taste" that reveal the essential role that the musical track played in facilitating Pepsi's multicultural, neoliberal agenda. The first analyzes Turner's solo spot, which was created for US audiences and acted as the baseline footage for her later duets with foreign musicians (some real and others dubbed in with computer graphics). The second examines the commercial made for audiences in Thailand, which features Turner singing live with local rocker Pu Anchalee Jongkadeekij.[77] Comparing the commercials side by side reveals that the presence of Jongkadeekij and her Thai fans adds little to the original US spot, thereby confirming the campaign's focus on cultural assimilation rather than exchange.

"We've Got the Taste" (Solo Version)

Turner's solo version of "We've Got the Taste" begins the same way as her music video for "Show Some Respect" as viewers are offered a private glimpse of her getting ready for a show backstage. The commotion made by eager fans fills the dressing room where she rats her hair, applies eyeliner, and takes a dramatic gulp of Pepsi. Turner puts on her signature sexy high heels and walks onto the stage, giving the camera a coy look before she exits the dressing room. Onstage Turner's rich vocal timbre cuts through the crowd as she soulfully belts out the first phrase of Pepsi's jingle. The jingle's form follows a truncated version of a standard verse-chorus pop song with a brief solo instrumental bridge (table 3.2). Turner's lyrics attempt to establish a personal connection with her fans by repeatedly using the first-person plural "we" throughout the performance. This departs significantly from Pepsi's previous "The Choice of a New Generation" slogans where Jackson and Richie address fans as "you" and do not explicitly include themselves as part of Pepsi's target audience (although their endorsement certainly implies it).

A slow unfolding of the verse here gives way to a drum fill and shift to a quicker tempo that builds an energetic pace for the jingle's hook and USP. Turner's band responds emphatically to each sung phrase in the chorus with accented B♭ tonic chords on beats four and one of every other measure (example 3.3). The call-and-response figures that occur between

Table 3.2. Jingle analysis of Tina Turner's solo spot

Form	Performing Forces	Harmonic and Melodic Area
Intro	• Keyboards • Suspended cymbal • Slide guitar	A♭ Major
Verse 1	• Turner (a cappella) • Keyboards (second phrase) • Drum fill	A♭ Major pentatonic
Chorus	• Turner and band (call-and-response)	B♭ Major pentatonic
Bridge	• Saxophone solo • Band accompaniment	Begins in F (V of B♭), ends on C (V/V)
Verse 1 (repeated)	• Turner and full band • Crescendo	A♭ Major pentatonic
Chorus	• Turner and band (call-and-response) • Fans sing along • Everyone punches the air on tonic accents	B♭ Major pentatonic

Note: Transcribed from "We've Got the Taste," PepsiCo. Inc., 1986.

Turner and her band, as well as the repeated "We've got," loosely resemble "Show Some Respect," especially the obvious syncopation and punctuation of the final words in each phrase (mm. 2 and 4). The commercial differs in its tempo and lyrical content as Turner confesses her insatiable thirst for Pepsi-Cola.

Example 3.3. Chorus call-and-response between vocals (top) and band (bottom, score reduction). ("We've Got the Taste," PepsiCo. Inc., 1986. Transcription by the author.)

A massive neon Pepsi sign illuminates the stage, and the camera jumps among images of the cheering crowd, members of the band, and Turner's performance. Pepsi merchandise is prominent throughout the set, and the piano itself becomes a prop for soda bottles and cups. During the bridge, an extended shot of Tim Cappello (a musician also featured in "Show Some Respect") showcases a quintessential 1980s saxophone solo. Cappello's provocative gestures and muscle-revealing shirt add another element of sex appeal to the commercial.

A return to the short verse and repeat of the chorus accompany Turner as she leaves the stage and walks into the crowd (table 3.2). Her fans joyfully gather around her and sing along. They help to punctuate the end of the jingle by pumping their fists in unison on the final two accentuated B♭ chords. The action onscreen and B♭ tonic resolution closes the commercial with a gratifying sense of finality. To round out the spot, cheers and a freeze-frame of Turner's smiling face fade to a black screen.

The visual signifiers here construct a generic scenario of the spectacle of a 1980s American rock concert, while the musical structure of the "We've Got the Taste" jingle makes it aurally accessible to audiences. The jingle's

Fig. 3.3. Fan swap, US version. (Still from "We've Got the Taste," PepsiCo. Inc., 1986.)

simple harmonic progression and tonic resolution offer the spot satisfying closure. Moreover, the deployment of simple, pentatonic three-note melodies makes it easy for audiences to sing along, as modeled by the onscreen fans. The jingle's singability thus makes it the perfect earworm for at-home viewers to remember, and it also makes the tune easily adaptable and "exportable" to the commercials filmed later that would feature international stars.

"We've Got the Taste" (Turner and Jongkadeekij Duet)

Turner's spot with Pu Anchalee Jongkadeekij epitomizes the neoliberal push for globalization and, more specifically, Pepsi's desire to dominate international soda markets.[78] Marketers were shrewd in modifying Turner's solo commercial to appeal to worldwide audiences and made very slight adjustments to the original footage.[79] Visually, Turner wears the same costume and the concert's setting is unchanged. The frame-by-frame editing is also largely similar with pans to the crowd interspersed with close-ups of the performers. The most notable changes occur with the omission of the two bookending scenes—Turner's opening dressing room shots and her journey into the crowd for a sing-along—which are replaced with sequences of her duet with Jongkadeekij.

Fig. 3.4. Fan swap, Thailand version. (Still from "We've Got the Taste," PepsiCo. Inc., 1986.)

Fan close-ups are also swapped out to reinforce the new setting. In both commercials, the crowd is largely a blur with the exception of one close-up of a fan who hands Turner a Pepsi bottle. For the Thai commercial, the blonde woman shown in the US spot is simply replaced with another fan to give the appearance of relocating the commercial in the host country (figs. 3.3 and 3.4).[80] This obvious moment of tokenism proves common in advertising contexts as it reduces "cultural difference" to mere appearances. This gesture thus suggests that no matter the location Pepsi drinkers are identical in their devotion to American music and its commodities.

Although both commercials have the same run time (60 seconds), the music for the Thai commercial is expanded and rearranged to allow for adequate participation by Jongkadeekij. Along with the omission of the introductory dressing room scene, the track that accompanies it is also removed and replaced with an additional verse—this time in a key even farther from the tonic (E♭ Major pentatonic; compare tables 3.2 and 3.3). As Turner sings about "breaking rules," Jongkadeekij joins her onstage playing a guitar (table 3.3). The lyrical metaphor is paired with a roaring crowd that welcomes Jongkadeekij into the spectacle while hailing Pepsi's ingenuity in engineering such an elaborate cultural export of American music and products. An abrupt shift up a fourth draws further attention to

Jongkadeekij as she belts out the second verse in Thai, which is actually the opening verse in Turner's solo spot (table 3.2). By giving Turner a new verse to sing prior to Jongkadeekij's entrance, the revised harmonic progression builds anticipation for the Thai star's vocal entrance. Perhaps more important, it also establishes Turner as the spot's central figure (table 3.2).

After the second verse the track moves up another full step to heighten the climactic energy of the jingle's chorus. The commercial's hook is established clearly in both languages as the stars trade lines. Pepsi's aim for its product to be integrated into the global economy is thus metaphorically

Table 3.3. Jingle analysis of the Turner and Jongkadeekij duet

Form	Central Performing Forces	Key Area
Short Intro	• Turner runs onstage	E♭ Major
New Verse 1	• Turner sings (English) • Jongkadeekij appears playing guitar	E♭ Major pentatonic
Verse 2 (1st in Turner's solo spot)	• Jongkadeekij sings (Thai)	A♭ Major pentatonic
Chorus	• Turner sings two phrases (English) • Jongkadeekij sings three phrases (Thai)	B♭ Major pentatonic
Bridge	• Tim Cappello on saxophone	Begins on F (V of B♭); ends on C (V/V)
Verse 2	• Turner reiterates in English	A♭ Major pentatonic
Chorus	• Jongkadeekij sings (Thai) • Turner responds (English) • Jongkadeekij repeats (Thai) • Turner finishes her phrase (English) • Jongkadeekij hails the product (Thai) • Turner confirms her insatiability (English) • Turner and Jongkadeekij sing the "We've Got the Taste" refrain together (English)	B♭ Major pentatonic

Note: Transcribed from "We've Got the Taste," PepsiCo. Inc., 1986.

Fig. 3.5. Turner and Jongkadeekij sing together. (Still from "We've Got the Taste," Thailand version, PepsiCo. Inc., 1986.)

showcased during this second chorus, which demonstrates the collaboration between the two stars, and by extension signifies the exportability of the new convergences among American pop culture, its media, and commodities (i.e., music, advertising, and soda products). A close multicultural dialogue between Turner and Jongkadeekij thus unfolds to replace the call-and-response exchanged between Turner and her band in the solo commercial (example 3.3). For the second chorus, the two stars trade every other phrase as the Thai singer takes the lead and Turner echoes the hook in English (table 3.3). Turner then completes the lyrics, and in a metaphorical moment of cultural solidarity the two belt out the final iteration of "We've Got the Taste" in unison in *English*. Two tonic cadential B♭ chords harmonically close the commercial and, by extension, confirm the success of the branded partnership (fig. 3.5).

Taylor reminds us that "one of the effects of globalization under neoliberal capitalism has been the increased desire of Western Musicians to work with non-Western ones under the ideologies of 'collaboration.'"[81] Taylor and Louise Meintjes have criticized this approach—specifically Paul Simon's *Graceland* album and the surrounding practices that fueled the late-twentieth-century "world music" craze—for glorifying the Western appropriation of subaltern musics and using Western stars to act as "brokers" for non-Western musicians. Released in the same year as Simon's *Graceland,* Pepsi's international "We've Got the Taste" commercials were similar in their expression of the one-sided relationships these scholars describe. Although the campaign sought the reverse of the world music phenomenon that sold non-Western music to American audiences, Pepsi used the same Western-centric tactics to sell American music and soda to non-American audiences in an effort to invite them (and their capital) into its new generation. These aims therefore fit well within the parameters of neoliberalism that Marianna Ritchey identifies as operating under a universalizing strategy—one in which promises for freedom (in this case, the "choice" of soft drinks) infiltrate global life and transcend cultural and national boundaries.[82]

Pepsi's Thai version of "We've Got the Taste" thus encapsulates the media spectacle and technological advances that had permeated the music and advertising industries in the mid-1980s, as well as the neoliberal practices that sought to expand the influence of American products abroad. As a redaction of the American rock concert experience and its customs, the music and images work together to paint a perfect one-directional picture of the possibilities for cultural partnerships. The commercial's favoring of a recognizable American musical style and household product confirms that this is not a true exchange but an *exportation* to, and perhaps even a colonization of, Thai culture. While the spot gestures toward a cultural partnership by translating the jingle into Thailand's native language, the rock concert as a whole aligns with Western musical tropes in terms of its instrumentation, staging, harmonic language, performance practice, vocal gestures, and showcasing of Turner as the headlining star. These characteristics are thus meant to lend further credibility to Jongkadeekij, whose music had already embraced Western idioms. The choice to feature Jongkadeekij in the spot was therefore logical due to the possibility that she could appeal to local fans already familiar with these sounds, even if they were not necessarily fans of Turner.

THE CHOICE OF A TECHY GENERATION: BOWIE MEETS TURNER

In 1987 Tina Turner made another Pepsi commercial, this time with David Bowie, who was working on his own musical comeback.[83] The commercial was released in the United States during the last week of July to kick off both Bowie's and Turner's Pepsi-sponsored world tours.[84] Bowie is reported to have collected $2 million, while Turner earned another $6 million, and the spot is rumored to have been filmed in Europe.[85] Pepsi timed the spot to replace Michael Jackson's latest round of soft drink commercials which had been postponed several times to accommodate the delayed release of his *Thriller* follow-up album, *Bad*.[86] Instead of turning to the new music marketing strategy used with Jackson and Richie, Pepsi's marketers borrowed the hook and backing track to one of Bowie's older tracks, "Modern Love," a moderately successful single from his 1983 album *Let's Dance*.[87] Although the original song might be understood as a struggle to define a romantic or spiritual relationship within contemporary society and negotiate that love with a religious ceremony (marriage), Pepsi uses here it to narrate a scenario similar to that of the 1985 film *Weird Science*, wherein a scientist creates the perfect woman with the help of his computer and the soda product. "Creation" therefore translates the lyrics expressed in Bowie's tale of anxiety over spiritual righteousness to more literally address new potentials for finding "modern love" with the aid of computer technology—a prospect still considered science fiction at the time.[88]

"Creation" was unique in its omission of the diegetic performance sequences that had become clichéd in earlier "The Choice of a New Generation" spots. Instead, it depicts pure fantasy, with Pepsi's musical endorsers performing not as themselves but as sci-fi actors. This concept likely stemmed from Bowie's long history of theatrics and Turner's film and television roles.[89] Falling somewhere in the fantastical gap, the musical track does not support simulated concert outtakes like the brand's former campaigns but instead is laid over the scene to lyrically, stylistically, and timbrally signify the identities and actions of the silent onscreen protagonists. Viewers are therefore expected to connect Bowie's and Turner's images with their singing voices and to reconcile their real-life status as rock stars with their roles as actors in the spot.

The commercial kicks off with a rock drum backbeat and a syncopated synthesizer groove. The camera tracks through a window into a neon-lit office with wall-to-wall electronics. The original track's introductory G Major chords are piped over the scene, but Bowie's spoken introduction is left out to highlight his movement around the room as he pushes buttons, turns wheels, and examines printouts. The star's large framed glasses and white coat are paired with digital computer sounds to confirm his occu-

Fig. 3.6. Ingredients for the perfect woman. (Still from "Creation," PepsiCo. Inc., 1987.)

pation as a "pop" scientist. A printout of an attractive woman prompts Bowie to feed paper images of body parts—legs, eyes, and lips, as well as a crayon drawing of a heart and a leather stiletto boot—into the computer (fig. 3.6).[90]

Following the song's introduction, the commercial's track jumps to the second verse of "Modern Love," and for the first time in any "The Choice of a New Generation" commercials, this spot preserves a considerable portion of the original lyrics from an endorser's pre-existing song. Equally as unique, there is no mention of the product's name. Marketers are sly, however, to restructure and replace specific lyrics to complement the action in each scene and to subtly allude to the brand's slogan. For instance, the lyrics, "there's no sign of life," are borrowed directly from Bowie's second verse and placed over the opening Frankenstein-esque scenario in which the "mad" scientist attempts to create a "superwoman."[91] This verse continues to unfold like the album until the final line, where Bowie's lyrics "I never say bye-bye," are swapped for the line "they always wave goodbye" to communicate the onscreen protagonist's failure to find love.

The pop scientist soon takes a break and accidentally spills his Pepsi into the computer. An acousmatic, high-pitched "whoo" is followed by the first lines of the chorus to synchronize with a series of explosions that blow off Bowie's lab coat and glasses and free his ponytail. Looking much more stylish, the pop scientist is greeted by his accidental, Pepsi-influenced creation. A close-up reveals that the black leather stiletto boot fed into the computer is now worn by a (yet) unknown woman. The entrance of Turner's distinctive vocal timbre reveals her identity and complements the subsequent eyeline connection between her and Bowie. Turner completes Bowie's phrase with a voice-over of the hook, confirming that she embodies the possibility of "Modern Love" in the computer age.

Bowie and Turner exchange longing glances and come together to run onto a street illuminated by neon signs and Pepsi machines. A quick game of cat and mouse brings the scientist and his creation together to dance to the reworked chorus (table 3.4). Any mention of anxiety about love or religion expressed in Bowie's original track is removed here to create a positive connotation. In Pepsi's version, "modern love" does not "walk on by" but stays "at my side." Perhaps the most brilliant moment of redaction happens when marketers redirect the song's message by borrowing Bowie's technique of slowly replacing the refrain's lyrics by simply changing the words to fit the slogan. No longer "terrified" about getting to the "church on time," Bowie and Turner sing "the choice is mine" USP. This phrase

Table 3.4. "Modern Love" lyric comparison with harmonic motion

"Modern Love" Original Chorus	"Modern Love" Pepsi Redaction	Harmonic Motion
Never gonna fall for, modern love.	Never gonna fall for, modern love.	C Major
Walks beside me, modern love.	Walks beside me, modern love.	D minor
Walks on by, modern love.	At my side, modern love.	E minor
Gets me to the church on time.	Now I know the choice is mine.	F Major C Major
Church on time.	The choice is mine.	
Terrifies me.	Satisfies me.	D Minor
Church on time.	Choice is mine.	
Makes me party.	Makes me party.	E Minor
Church on time.	Choice is mine.	
Puts my trust in God and Man.	Puts my choice in my hand.	F Major C Major
God and Man.	Modern love . . . (Repeat and fade)	

Note: Transcribed from David Bowie, "Modern Love," 1983; "Creation," PepsiCo. Inc., 1987.

is not only consistent with the campaign's message, but it rhymes so well with the original lyrics that the replacement is seamless (table 3.4).

As further demonstrated in table 3.4, marketers were also careful to maintain the cyclic harmonic progression heard in the original (C through D and E to F), which allows the track to aurally climax multiple times, first, on the USP and then on lyrics that highlight Pepsi's convenience as the "choice" (i.e., soda) placed "in my hand." The lyrical revisions of the second climax thus cleverly swap Bowie's wavering trust in "God and Man" with the assurance of the Pepsi commodity—a promise that offers viewers comfort in the permanence of the brand. A repetition and fade-out of the hook concludes with a fairy tale ending that pictures the new couple spinning before a wall of showering sparks.

"Creation" demonstrates just how astute Pepsi's marketing creatives had become in redacting pre-existing music into brand-worthy messages only three years after its first campaign with Michael Jackson. Marketers used a substantial portion of Bowie's track to draw in experienced audiences and were careful to change the lyrics only at the most climactic musical moments. Equally as important, the spot preserved the anxiety composed into the original track—its pacing introductory chords, the verse's restless E Minor melody, and the chorus's ascending four-chord cycle—to add gravity to Pepsi's final hook, which provided reassurance in the availability of the commodity. Consequently, it is in the final seconds—where Bowie's anxious ruminations about faith in romance and religion are traded for faith in the soda brand—that marketers literally realize advertising's unique ability to offer guidance in the modern world. In other words, politically complicated concerns about marriage and spirituality are replaced here with commodity-laden images and lyrics that address more contemporary anxieties over the possibilities of computer innovation.

In its focus on technological advances, "Creation" pictured tropes that fit neatly into neoliberalism's push for innovation. The commercial is curious, however, in its blatant fetishizing of Turner's body, which causes her to become what one critic called, Bowie's "Private Dancer."[92] Where a preferred reading might suggest that computer innovation has the potential to offer even the oddest men true love (a prevalent theme in *Weird Science*), a negotiated reading reveals that a woman is made up of her parts, as suggested by the legs, pretty face, sparkling eyes, heart, and stilettos that Bowie feeds into his computer. An oppositional reading further acknowledges that Turner is also racially fetishized in the spot: while it is no secret that her legs and hair had become her trademark symbols (largely due to the sexualized image her ex-husband insisted she curate), nothing suggested that a black entertainer would be produced from the Caucasian and crayoned body parts fed into Bowie's computer.[93] The commercial's visuals are thus extraordinary in their suggestion that Bowie's spilled Pepsi is the key ingredient in creating an African American woman. While this may have been an effort to appellate the marginalized demographics to which the brand historically catered, and also perhaps to welcome new audiences into its generation, the commercial is perplexing in its less than empowering representation of a veteran spokesperson who had fought so hard in real life to regain her agency.[94] In its portrayals of the possibilities offered by new technologies, the commercial thus expertly supports a neoliberal agenda while continuing to perpetuate timeworn (and troublesome) marketing stereotypes.[95]

GLOBAL GAINS AND AESTHETIC LOSSES

Pepsi's campaigns with Jackson, Richie, Turner, and Bowie made use of the global marketplace to increase the corporation's visibility and intensify its pressure on Coca-Cola. Indeed, by 1987 Pepsi's Canadian market share had nearly doubled. Analysts credited these gains to music celebrity commercials, especially those featuring Jackson and Richie.[96] Across the globe, in what was dubbed the "Australian Cola Wars," it was Turner who joined Jackson on the front lines. Jackson's 1986 Victory Tour had bumped up Pepsi's share of the Australian cola market by 60 percent in October and 85 percent in November, resulting in a 40 percent increase in sales across the continent and making Pepsi the first music marketer in Australia to make such substantial gains.[97] In an effort to duplicate this, the soda giant pulled out all the stops to endorse Turner's 1988 tour. The brand spent more than $5 million on promotions, which included radio and television spots featuring "We've Got the Taste" and contests promising winners a chance to see Turner live in Japan. Her Australian success even prompted Pepsi to sponsor the country's local rock musicians in the coming years.[98]

By contrast, Turner and Bowie's duet commercial received little more than a passing nod in US and London markets. Just four months after "Creation" aired, it was pulled following allegations of sexual assault made against Bowie by his makeup artist. Pepsi executives denied that the incident was linked to their decision to stop showing the spot and claimed it was simply time for Michael Jackson's next set of commercials to take center stage.[99] As demonstrated above, "Creation" should have proven useful as a placeholder since it aligned neatly with the neoliberal focus on technological innovation and further extended the star power of the brand's pop music endorsements. Viewers, however, admitted that they had grown weary of Pepsi's concert outtakes and nightlife imagery. By this point Pepsi was competing with an array of musical endorsements (including Run-D.M.C.'s famous track and video, "My Adidas," which praised their favorite sneaker brand). Consequently, many dismissed Turner's and Bowie's campaigns as mere gimmicks intended to reboot their careers. For this reason, Turner's age became a hot topic of discussion among news outlets.[100] Now in her mid-forties, she was well outside MTV's target audience. In London, the press called her a once "fading rhythm-and-blues star" and an "old star . . . reborn."[101] Bowie, too, appeared out of date, even to longtime fans. The elaborate staging of his Pepsi-sponsored Glass Spider Tour seemed passé, as noted by biographer Paul Trynka, who reported that Bowie looked "tired" compared to younger stars like Michael Jackson, Prince, and Madonna.[102] So, while the tour was a financial success, many deemed it a creative failure and capitalist ploy. Trynka summarized fans' disappointment with Bowie's on- and offstage marketing, writing,

> The impression that this was an emotionally empty exercise in generating cash deepened with the announcement that Bowie's huge earnings were being further bloated by a predictably clichéd commercial in which David and Tina Turner camp around a vending machine yelping, "[It] puts my choice in my hand," to the tune of "Modern Love."[103]

Bowie's and Turner's spots were not the only pop-themed commercials Pepsi banked on at the time. In an attempt to appeal to baby boomers and fans of the *Miami Vice* television show, Pepsi featured a diegetic snippet of its theme song, "You Belong to the City," and starred the song's composer, former Eagles lead singer Glenn Frey, alongside the show's lead actor Don Johnson. Pepsi also appealed to the growing Latin American population by releasing commercials in both English and Spanish that featured Miami Sound Machine.[104] The redaction of Frey's and Miami Sound Machine's music was similar to that of the spots discussed above, where themes of youth, individuality, upward mobility, and globalization were infused into each narrative. Additionally, Pepsi packed notable sports, television, and film celebrities into other spots, including Joe Montana, Dan Marino, Teri Farr, and Billy Crystal. Film and television star Michael J. Fox and vice-presidential candidate Geraldine Ferraro also made memorable commercials for Pepsi's low-calorie Diet Pepsi.

The spots discussed in this chapter prove exemplary of the way that mid-1980s commercial texts integrated pop music into neoliberal discourses. Pepsi's commericals communicated these ideals by fetishizing the concept of "freedom" promoted through the "choice" it offered audiences in selecting its product over its competitors'.[105] As demonstrated in the spots featuring Lionel Richie, Tina Turner, and David Bowie, choosing the Pepsi commodity equated with being the ideal consumer (and citizen), one that was stylish, sentimental, family focused, globally minded, and technologically savvy. The ability for marketers to get into the musical texts themselves and to redact their content to uphold these values demonstrates how these commercials do considerable cultural work by skillfully undoing and remaking the cultural objects from which they borrow.

But, as noted above, mid-1980s audiences were not completely comfortable with music marketing practices. The same year in which "Creation" aired, the Nike athletic clothing brand received significant backlash and even incited a legal battle when it used a beloved version of the Beatles' 1968 song "Revolution" in a campaign for similar ends. Because the living Beatles members did not own the rights to the song and did not approve its use in Nike's "Revolution in Motion" campaign (Michael Jackson had licensed it without their permission), the spot reignited debates over copyright laws and the presence of pre-existing music in advertising.[106] Fans who believed that the Beatles' track upheld countercultural ideals that specifically included anti-consumerism were furious that it was stripped of its original meanings to peddle athletic gear. The onslaught of negative responses to "Revolution in Motion" indicated that, despite the successes achieved by Pepsi and other brands that followed its new music marketing model, some audiences continued to hold an unwavering stance against musicians who "sold out" to corporate interests. The negative response to this commercial, as well as the less than enthusiastic responses to Pepsi's post-1984 Jackson spots, demonstrated the limits of neoliberal influence at the time. Some cultural icons and texts, especially those from 1960s baby boomer culture, were simply not (yet) for sale.

As the following chapter demonstrates, Pepsi did not give up on exploring the possibilities for new music marketing. In 1987 the brand made another set of commercials with Michael Jackson, who had pushed its sales to the top of the soft drink market just a few years earlier. This time however, the stakes were considerably higher for both parties as Jackson's favor with fans and the media was strained by his intentional hiatus from the spotlight. In order to stifle mounting criticism, Pepsi's marketers used every possible resource to convince audiences that they and Jackson were still the obvious choices for the new generation.

CHAPTER 4

Chasing "Bad"

Pop Fantasies and Teleological Fiction

By the spring of 1986, Pepsi was riding a colossal wave of celebrity endorsements. Since its successful partnership with Michael Jackson two years earlier, the soda giant had scored commercial deals with music industry icons Lionel Richie, Tina Turner, and David Bowie as well as stars of television and the silver screen that included Michael J. Fox, Don Johnson, and Billy Crystal. Pepsi's CEO, Roger Enrico, was satisfied with the company's marketing and sales achievements to date and confident that the corporation had reached its pinnacle—that is, until he received another phone call from Jay Coleman, the publisher of *RockBill* magazine and the man responsible for the company's first deal with the King of Pop. Enrico was surprised to learn that Michael Jackson wanted to make more Pepsi commercials and jumped on a plane to Los Angeles to discuss the possibilities of a second arrangement.[1] After Jackson was promised a more extensive partnership that included more money, safeguards against overexposure, and the option of co-directing or directing a future commercial, the megastar agreed to another landmark deal to create a new set of "The Choice of a New Generation" spots under the direction of the legendary commercial director and filmmaker Joe Pytka.[2] This time Jackson appeared without his brothers and the campaign was scheduled to coincide with the unveiling of his much-anticipated third solo album, *Bad*.[3] Pepsi poured more than $50 million in the project.[4] Described as a "multiyear creative partnership," the pop star received yet another incredible sum from Pepsi for the use of the title track—estimated to be somewhere around $10 million—and a sponsorship of his first solo tour.[5] The conditions of the new agreement allowed the commercials, as well as Jackson's concert tours, to expand to an international market. The spots were eventually released in the United

Kingdom, Canada, Japan, and Russia and the tour covered much of the United States, Europe, Japan, and Australia.[6]

As they did with previous campaigns, Pepsi's marketers expertly crafted a publicity storm around the new commercials. They ran into difficulties along the way, however, when Jackson delayed the release of his album numerous times, forcing the brand to postpone the air dates of the commercials until almost a year and half after announcing the deal (see table 4.1).[7] Pepsi had become an expert at weathering the pop star's ever-changing demands, and its executives took the setbacks in stride, saying, "One of the things we've learned in association with music marketing is that music is an art, and art shouldn't be rushed."[8] Instead of bemoaning the fact that its blockbuster campaign would not air as originally planned during the summer of 1987, the company took the opportunity to showcase its Tina Turner and David Bowie "Creation" spot.[9]

Table 4.1. Timeline for the release of Pepsi's 1987–88 Jackson spots

May 6, 1986	Pepsi announces a second deal with Jackson
Winter 1987	Joe Pytka films staged concert footage
February 24, 1987	Teasers of the concert footage debut during the Grammy awards on CBS
August 31, 1987	The *Bad* album is finally released
August 31, 1987	More concert footage teasers debut during the commercial breaks of *Michael Jackson: The Magic Returns*, a CBS special designed around the premiere of Jackson's music video for "Bad"
Week of September 3, 1987	Another teaser with concert footage runs during prime time to advertise forthcoming premieres of the completed commercials
October 30 and 31, 1987	Two full-length commercials featuring the same concert footage ("Concert" and "Backstage") premiere on an MTV special, *Rockin' the Pepsi Generations*
November 1, 1987	The "Backstage" and "Concert" commercials run during network and local broadcasts of *Family Ties*, a sitcom starring another Pepsi spokesperson, Michael J. Fox
January 1988	Pepsi bottlers view "The Chase," a four-and-a-half-minute episodic spot that incorporates Pytka's concert footage into a fantasy story line
March 2, 1988	"The Chase" premieres during the Grammy awards on CBS

The media and Jackson's fans were, unfortunately, less forgiving. Trade press publications reported that the public was complaining just as loudly about waiting for the spots as for the music itself.

> For endless months, newspapers, magazines and broadcast outlets have been reporting on the progress of the Michael Jackson album, 'Bad,' the Michael Jackson tour and the Michael Jackson Pepsi commercials. It was a publicity bonanza that played right into Jackson's hands—the multiple delays, of course, having been calculated to create pent-up demand.[10]

Jackson's new album finally hit shelves on August 31, 1987, more than six months later than promised. That same day Pepsi aired teasers about the new campaign during *Michael Jackson: The Magic Returns*, a CBS television special designed to unveil the music video for the title track.[11] The *Bad* video (or short film, as Jackson called it) was hyped for its super-star roster, which included its director, Martin Scorsese, and cameos by Jackson's longtime producer, Quincy Jones, and up-and-coming actor Wesley Snipes.

The simultaneity of these events marked a pop culture milestone: for the first time in advertising history, commercials for a household corporate product became a key promotional tool for a top artist's newest album, solo tour, documentary special, and music video. Jackson's 1987–88 commercials were therefore groundbreaking in their convergence of so many traditionally disparate media and technologies.[12] While Pepsi's previous pop star commercials adhered to more conventional marketing practices that mainly served the needs of the brand, its 1987–88 commercials were conceptualized *alongside* Jackson's album and video, becoming an important tool in the promotion of the music and its accompanying media spectacle. During the time it took Jackson to finish the *Bad* album and create the short film for its title track, marketers worked closely beside him to carefully incorporate his most prominent musical and visual signifiers into the soda spots. The album, video, and commercials thus collapsed into one another, further eroding the aesthetic and corporate boundaries between the three mediums.

Enhancing its prestige, this deal marked the first time a popular song had ever been licensed for a commercial *before* it aired on the radio or proved itself on the charts—a practice that would become mainstream a little more than a decade later. So, in addition to significantly raising the bar for creative and economic investment in future co-branding arrangements with a production budget that far surpassed any other, Michael Jackson's 1987–88 Pepsi campaign became a turning point for the jingle, signaling how American popular music would soon displace it by creating a template for a new kind of celebrity endorsement—one that featured top performers singing *new* songs to endorse their latest recordings, tours, and videos alongside corporate products. This deal thus sounded different than Pepsi's previous commercials. As detailed in chapter 2, the 1984 spots featured the most prominent elements of the backing track to "Billie Jean" (which had already been in circulation for months), but the words were completely reworked into a jingle re-recorded by Jackson and his brothers.[13] For Jackson's newest campaign the commercials worked to hype *Bad during* its release, which required marketers to use much more of the song's original track and lyrics in order to to familiarize audiences with the single. In sum, by incorporating more *new* pop music and lyrics than ever before, Jackson's second Pepsi campaign moved the American advertising industry to the brink of its transition away from jingles and toward today's commonplace practice of incorporating whole sections of the latest tracks in commercials.

Pepsi and Jackson would soon realize, however, that achieving mainstream success would prove more complicated than either had initially realized. As explained in the pages that follow, Jackson's complicated public image would intimately affect the way the campaign's texts were both created and received. This prompted both the superstar and Pepsi to work harder than ever to convince audiences that neither party had lost its edge. This campaign therefore marks a precarious moment in the brand's history of musical marketing when its endorser's image and aesthetics not only proved challenging to redact, but their incorporation also risked ruining the selling proposition.

ESCAPING THRILLER

Now 29 years old, the superstar attempted to create a more mature look and sound to showcase his newest album. Pepsi appreciated this as it also was intentionally extending its marketing to reach slightly older audiences.[14] In the years following *Thriller*, the album's achievements, as well as the issues that plagued Jackson's Victory Tour, loomed large over the pop star and his image.[15] The relentlessness of the media and his fans prompted him to seclude himself from the public gaze, which in turn made the paparazzi even more ravenous. As he began work on his new album, Jackson was determined to quiet ongoing criticism and speculation by (once again) superseding his previous achievements.[16]

In his absence from the limelight, Jackson noticed that record sales for his pop rivals, Madonna and Prince, were flourishing and that they had gained considerable media attention for the controversial sexual imagery and political statements they deployed in their videos. Jackson followed their lead and worked carefully to "re-brand" his persona from the shy, ubiquitous, former child star into an edgier artist.[17] Consequently, *Bad* was more direct in addressing social issues and adult themes. These included poverty and homelessness ("Man in the Mirror"), standing up for personal honor ("Bad"), and seduction ("Dirty Diana"). Musically, the album was eclectic: from the sensual love ballad "I Just Can't Stop Loving You" to the funk grooves in "Bad," the heavy backbeat and metal guitar in "Dirty Diana," to the gospel-tinged "Man in the Mirror," this album confirmed the diversity of Jackson's musical range. He also wrote many of the songs himself and relentlessly experimented with different sounds, using the latest synthesizer technology to create new timbres and employ extramusical samples throughout.[18]

Jackson's *Bad* image also proved to be edgier than *Thriller*'s. His crossover look incorporated androgynous signifiers from glam, punk, and heavy metal. His locks were long and curly, and he wore makeup, large boots, and ostentatious buckles and chains.[19] Notably, this feminized look was bolstered by rhythmic falsetto exclamations made throughout his songs. His performance of the title track, however, was simultaneously hypermasculinized and hyperracialized as he wore a leather-looking motorcycle gang outfit, grunted incessantly like his idol James Brown, and made forceful gestures toward his crotch.[20] As a result, Jackson's new "bad boy" image seemed to complicate well-worn Stagger Lee stereotypes that assumed African American men to be overly sexual and aggressive. His new iconography was therefore difficult to reconcile as masculine or feminine, black or white, heterosexual or queer. In anticipation of the album, the *Washington Post* published an article that summarized the problems Jackson would face.

Questions about his masculinity, rumors of homosexuality (he's not gay) haunted him during the 1984 Victory Tour, but would that Jackson's problems had ended there. As he begins his new quest for greater heights, he faces an enormous image problem, helped in part by media overkill, his shyness and refusal to talk to the press (save *Ebony* magazine, which published an interview with him in December 1984) and his sometimes eccentric behavior.[21]

Jackson thus embodied what scholar Joseph Vogel identifies as the opposite of President Ronald Reagan's "dualistic worldview" and instead "represented all the complexities and ambiguities of the new America (and world)."[22] These "complexities" and "ambiguities" opened the pop star up to even more public criticism once *Bad* was released. An article in *Adweek* confirmed this, saying,

> We're fascinated by his talent but we're also taken with his persona because it expresses much of the ambiguity of America in the '80s: the sexual confusion, the pursuit of fulfillment at any cost (remaking his face), the obsession with making money, including the marketing of himself to a giant, conservative corporation whose product he doesn't use, all while maintaining the image of innocence.[23]

Media outlets therefore directed much of their attention to Jackson's new look, which he had hidden and revealed all at once for the album's premiere. In a *New York Times* review, Jon Pareles wrote, that Jackson "portrays himself in conventional pop terms, as a lover and as a rather tame outlaw; when he insists he's 'really, really bad' in 'Bad,' he's not too believable."[24] The pop star's chiseled face, lighter skin color, and long hair had made him look more ambiguous than ever, and, as discussed below, these factors made audiences uncomfortable. Jackson's once-glistening image would therefore wane considerably under the pressure and scrutiny. As a performer, he was still admired by the 4.4 million fans worldwide who flocked to see his concerts and buy his album.[25] But as an African American man he was criticized for blurring the boundaries between his personal life and the spectacle of the performance space he embodied in his music videos and concerts. Most notably, his private amusement park (the Neverland Ranch) and adoption of a pet chimpanzee fueled rumors—some spread as hoaxes by Jackson himself—that he slept in a hyperbaric chamber, was best friends with zoo animals, and had purchased the Elephant Man's bones.[26]

In the decades since, cultural scholarship by Kobena Mercer, Tavia Nyong'o, and Harriet J. Manning, among others, has confirmed that Jackson's life became media fodder due to his confrontation and negotiation of long-held American ideological boundaries between markers of race, sexuality, and gender, as well as values about musical authenticity, notions of childhood, and definitions of personal identity.[27] Writer James Baldwin concluded that the media preyed on Jackson because he did not live up to social expectations of how an African American heterosexual man should look and act—especially one who was so threatening with his prolific artistry and financial success.[28] Baldwin noted that Jackson had reached the level of "freak" due the fact that he "helped people to realize their most profound desires and fears."[29] *Thriller* thus became the albatross that would follow Jackson for the remainder of his career: it was the pinnacle that late-twentieth-century American social norms permitted him to reach, and any accomplishment beyond that proved difficult (if not impossible) for the mainstream media to accept.

So, while Pepsi executives were aware that the star's reputation was under attack when they agreed to his endorsement, they would not witness the extent of media's wrath until after the album and commercials were released.[30] Indeed, Jackson's previous success with promoting the brand and his greater willingness to cooperate quelled any doubts that Pepsi had about the outcome. The brand thus hoped that by once again borrowing the icon's most prominent signifiers it could help propel *Bad* past the accolades both parties had reaped from *Thriller*.

Pepsi's new campaign playfully confronted the realities of Jackson's fame and wholly incorporated his "Bad" signifiers into its three commercials. Figure 4.1 demonstrates that the superstar's appearance in Pepsi's spots was largely identical to the images he donned on his album cover and in the *Bad* music video. Akin to Jackson's 1984 campaign, the first commercial released was titled "Concert" and it closely tracked the pop star's movements around the stage as he entertained a stadium packed with fans. The second spot, "Backstage," closely resembles "Street" (another 1984 commercial) and highlights the antics of a young fan who sneaks into the pop star's dressing room, tries on his icon's costume, and envisions himself onstage until an amused Jackson discovers him.

Fig. 4.1. Jackson's "Bad" image. (Still from "Concert," PepsiCo. Inc., 1987.)

The following pages focus on "The Chase," the third and final commercial made for the campaign. This final spot reportedly cost almost $2 million to produce and was hyped as the industry's first set of episodic commercials.[31] "The Chase" is far removed from run-of-the-mill celebrity endorsements. It ran four and a half minutes long, was composed of four parts—"The Chase," "The Chopper," "The Museum," and "The Finale"—, and was spread over multiple commercial breaks as a mini-drama that premiered during the 1988 Grammy Awards on CBS. Each episode ended with a teaser that encouraged viewers to stay tuned, thereby enticing fans to keep watching both the awards show and the remainder of the commercial's storyline.[32] By making "The Chase" an integral part of the program, CBS once again benefited from the publicity along with Pepsi and Jackson, adding yet another layer of convergence and profitability to the already media-saturated campaign.

"The Chase" complemented and closely mirrored themes that pervaded the *Bad* album and its accompanying promotional videos and films. Vogel refers to *Bad* as a set of cinematic "dream capsules" that create "fantastical scenarios."[33] Pepsi emulates one such scenario as depicted in the song "Speed Demon," where the theme of escape from a variety of oppressive forces emerges.[34] Throughout the song's video—which was featured as part of Jackson's promotional film *Moonwalker*—the star uses every means possible to elude the frenzy of fans and media, including morphing into a cartoon rabbit that becomes his alter ego.

For Pepsi's "The Chase" the King of Pop also adopts an alter ego to avoid his admirers—this time as a stuntman. Functioning more like small-scale mini-dramas than ads, the spots depict a fantastic and metaphorical narrative of Jackson's life as an entertainer. They interweave Jackson's concert performance with a trance-like dream in which he runs offstage and (much like in "Speed Demon") carries out dangerous and extraordinary feats to escape the clutches of the media and overzealous fans. Pepsi's CEO acknowledged the fictional nature of the spots, saying that were intended to add "the sense of fun and the fantasy that are so much part of Michael Jackson's persona."[35] In his discussion of the similarly fictional vignettes present in the *Moonwalker* film, scholar Ruchi Mital notes that they work to conflate various historical symbols with tropes from science fiction to establish the King of Pop as a historical and messianic presence. Mital argues, "Jackson's presence, however, is always part of performance, revealing the performative nature of history. It is a history of clips, an edited history with a soundtrack, made more real on film than the real."[36] So, too, does "The Chase" focus on the "performative nature" of Jackson as a historical figure, similarly providing an "edited history with a soundtrack." In Pepsi's version, its commodity—and thus late (neoliberal) capitalism—becomes essential to the tale.

As a capitalist realist text, "The Chase" constructs a "surreal" world around Jackson's iconicity, and the superstar himself becomes the dreamer.[37] Viewers thus follow him as he slips between fantasy and reality. Notably, Jackson's "reality" is loosely defined in the moments during and just after his concert performance; that is, the spectacle he puts on *is* his reality. Jackson's staged Pepsi performances might therefore be understood through a Baudrillardian lens as "neither real nor unreal" but *hyper*real, as defined by the "universe of simulation" the commercial creates around it.[38] Indeed, by 1988 simulation had become a well-worn advertising trope for celebrity brand endorsements. Robert Goldman and Stephen Papson build on Baudrillard's definitions of *simulacra* and *simulation* to argue that celebrity commercials appropriate "not the biography of the man himself, but rather the media representations of him."[39] Michael Schudson further notes that in commercials "the person played is not the actor or athlete as a human being but the actor or athlete flattened into a celebrity persona."[40] "The Chase" therefore presents audiences with a compelling simulation of Jackson's *Bad* celebrity persona. It blurs the hyperreality of him as a hardworking entertainer with the fantasy of his escape from the spotlight. By placing the viewer inside a simulation of the pop star's imagination, it reinforces the notion that his day-to-day life is literally unbelievable and only Pepsi-Cola can help him navigate the chaos of his stardom. It is thus through hyperreality—what Umberto Eco defines as the process of "fabricating the absolute fake" and blurring boundaries between "game and illusion" to confirm "the real thing" (ironically the slogan of archrival Coca-Cola)—that the soda giant allowed audiences to gain entry into Jackson's world.[41]

Much like the process marketers undertook with "Billie Jean," they impose the soda giant's commodity into *Bad* by redacting Jackson's image and music. "The Chase," however, visually departs from Jackson's previous Pepsi commercials in that close-ups of his face are equally, if not more, prominent than his onstage symbols—which (as noted above) had evolved past his *Thriller* era white glove and sparkly socks. Accounts of this second deal report that Jackson was much more obliging in lending his image to the spots.[42] This newfound willingness to become the focus of the camera's gaze permitted Joe Pytka to film extended tracking shots that made "The Chase" look more like the performance footage and action sequences common to music video formats and cinema than traditional brand advertising.

The most prominent way in which Pepsi inserted itself into Jackson's iconicity occurred through the reworking of his pre-existing musical track. This was accomplished in part by creating hybrid lyrics that combined original "Bad" material with the soft drink slogan. Even more significant, "The Chase" offered an important lesson in *crafting musical teleology to suit consumer patterns of desire*: sections taken from "Bad" were treated as modular themes and recombined in each episode to build to (sometimes multiple) premature aural climaxes that inhibited the song's resolution until the final scene in episode 4 (see table 4.2). When paired with the onscreen images, marketers created what Robert Fink calls "recombinant teleologies": by leaving audiences in suspense, marketers generated desire for subsequent episodes and, by extension, for the soft drink as well.[43]

Episode 1: "The Chase"

Episode 1 is the longest in the series and focuses both visually and aurally on Jackson's role as an entertainer. This clip features an extended close-up of him doing his signature hip thrusting, spinning, and James Brown–inspired, fancy footwork moves, thereby creating a believable simulation of his celebrity persona. His musical performance adheres closely to the structural and harmonic integrity of the "Bad" single, retaining the musical styles and devices used in the track, including dissonant jazz harmonies, Motown horn lines, grunts, and the latest synthesizers and drum machines.[44] The tropes employed—many of which signify and pay homage to his African American musical predecessors—prove key to promoting his message of "badness."[45]

The commercial's soundtrack begins with cheers from an adoring audience followed by a synthesized riff played on the first five notes of a blues scale on A (example 4.1). Its syncopated entrance on the upbeat of every other measure perpetuates a two-bar cycle. The drum machine adds aggression to the riff by accentuating the rhythmic motion with a forceful bass drum and a steady subdivision on the tom-tom. Much like the riff in "Billie Jean," this one remains virtually unchanged throughout most of the original track, making it contagious and identifiable. When transferred to Pepsi's commercials, the riff's cyclic structure—its completion on an upbeat and the dominant (instead of the tonic)—makes it perfectly suited for use as a modular section to facilitate the transition between each episode in Pepsi's series (last column in table 4.2).[46]

Example 4.1. Borrowed synthesizer riff. ("The Chase," PepsiCo. Inc., 1988. Transcription by the author.)

Following two cycles of the riff, Jackson sings hybridized lyrics that incorporate Pepsi's product into fragments taken from the track's verses (example 4.2). The pop star's vocal skills are showcased here with phrase elisions, syncopation, and guttural vocalizations. Moreover, Jackson's diegetic solo line noticeably clashes with the harmonic structure under-

Table 4.2. The rearrangement of the teleological form for "Bad" in each episode

EPISODE 1: **"THE CHASE"**

Crowd noise	*Opening riff*	**Verse**	<u>*Pre-chorus*</u>	<u>**Chorus**</u> with stop-time tagline + USP ("It's Cool")	Crowd noise	*Opening riff*
	(4 mm)	(8 mm)	(4mm)	(8 mm)		(2 mm)

EPISODE 2: **"THE CHOPPER"**

Opening riff	<u>*Pre-chorus*</u> without vocals	<u>**Chorus**</u> variation with transitional tagline	**Verse** without vocals	<u>*Pre-chorus*</u>	<u>**Chorus**</u> with stop-time tagline	*Opening riff*
(2 mm)	(2 mm)	(8 mm)	(6mm)	(4 mm)	(4.5 mm)	(2 mm)

EPISODE 3: **"THE MUSEUM"**

Opening riff	**Verse** without vocals	<u>**Chorus**</u> variation with transitional tagline	**Verse** without vocals	<u>*Pre-chorus*</u>	<u>**Chorus**</u> with stop-time tagline	*Opening riff*
(2 mm)	(4 mm)	(8 mm)	(4mm)	(4 mm)	(8 mm)	(2 mm)

EPISODE 4: **"THE FINALE"**

Opening riff	<u>*Pre-chorus*</u>	<u>**Chorus**</u> variation with transitional tagline	**Verse** without vocals	<u>**Chorus**</u> with stop-time tagline + USP ("It's Cool")	Crowd noise
(2 mm)	(4 mm)	(8 mm)	(8mm)	(4.5 mm)	

Note: Transcribed from "The Chase," PepsiCo. Inc., 1988.

neath it to create grating dissonances that underpin the song's message of "badness." In particular, Jackson sings a C♮ against the descending synthesizer line to create a tritone. The C♮ also conflicts with the D♮ in the riff, producing a major 2nd. The pulsating sound of the synthesizer combined with the clashing dissonance produced by the tritone and major 2nd establish a noticeably rough and edgy "bad" sound. Jackson leans on these dissonances in the commercials as much as in the original track to effectively highlight key words in Pepsi's slogan—"right" and "good" and "up"—and to reinforce the soda giant's message about the positive qualities of its product. Much like its other recent campaigns, the action words

Example 4.2. Tritone + M2. ("The Chase," PepsiCo. Inc., 1988. Transcription by the author.)

inserted here ("show," "feelin'," "reachin'," and "choice") also encapsulate the energy and agency of Pepsi's new generation. As documented in table 4.2, variations of Jackson's verse can be heard throughout the other episodes in the campaign, but his voice is only present in the first. The omission of the verse's lyrics in episodes 2 through 4 relegates the musical track to transitional and subordinate material, thereby reinforcing the strangeness of the pop star's dream world.

The pre-chorus enters next as the song's harmonies tease listeners and stir the desire for resolution by pacing back and forth between the minor ii and iii (table 4.2). At the end of this section, the harmonic motion finally moves to a half cadence on E. The commercial intentionally holds off on naming its soda product until this moment—the one and only time the track reaches an aurally satisfying harmonic cadential point (example 4.3,

Example 4.3. Product placement on the dominant and the "Bad" chord entrance. ("The Chase," PepsiCo. Inc., 1988. Transcription by the author.)

mm. 1). Jackson thus sings "Pepsi's comin' through" on the downbeat of the dominant's entrance, which is supported by a trumpet and saxophone horn line that blares E7♯9 chords on each word.[47] Like the musical material in the verses, the pre-chorus is treated as a modular unit inserted at convenient times throughout other episodes in the series (table 4.2). During these moments, this section is often stripped of its vocal track and shortened to fit the onscreen action. Marketers surely recognized that, even without the vocal track, the cadential horn line would effectively build excitement for Jackson's stunts and, by extension, for the product.

Up to this point, the camera has focused on Jackson's onstage performance. Once the chorus begins, viewers finally get a good glimpse of his ethnically diverse and youthful fans in between carefully edited shots of the superstar's movements. It is obvious from the attention that the camera pays to them that a preferred reading would permit viewers to identify with these onscreen simulations of the "new generation" who enjoy drinking Pepsi and listening to Jackson's music.

A tonic Am7 chord finally arrives once the hybrid "Bad"/Pepsi chorus-slogan enters the track (table 4.2 and example 4.3). While the constant reiteration of the tonic chord should aurally ground the track in a stable harmonic pocket, striking dissonances (also heard in the original) occur on every other iteration of the lyrics "bad" and "cool" (beat three of measures 2 and 4). This dissonance further perpetuates the harmonic motion and makes the hook's melody catchy and easily identifiable. Jackson's vocal line adds even more tension by pushing forcefully against these underlying harmonies to sing a G over a D9 chord. In the absence of an E dominant chord, the vocalized G grates against the A sung in the backup vocals, as well as the F# played below it, creating what hereafter is referred to as "the bad chord" (example 4.3).[48]

The "badness" of Jackson's solo line is further intensified here by the concluding rhythmic tagline (table 4.2 and example 4.4). Underneath Jackson's sung tonic note (on A), the harmonies continue to pace between IV and I and end on the subdominant instead of the tonic. The song's resolution then comes not from a harmonic cadence but from the vocal reiteration of the tonic and Jackson's stop-time, scatted whisper "It's Cool." Other than the extra note added to accommodate his recitation of the brand's name (the second sixteenth-note of beat one in measure 2), the most noticeable change from the original is marketers' alteration of the lyrical cadence from "Who's bad?" to "It's cool."

It is this moment that becomes one of the most startling examples of the brand's efforts to appropriate Jackson's badness. On the album, the superstar uses the tagline to rhetorically assert that *he* is the one who is "bad"—so much so that he creates musical resolution using only his voice. In the commercial, marketers reassign his agency to the product, insinuating instead that it is the "coolness" of the soda that is "bad," effectively redacting it to fit the brand's USP. As would be expected, marketers pair these crudely modified sections from the chorus—which stands as the soundtrack's most quintessentially "bad" section—with images of his daring stunts in episodes 2 through 4. And when Jackson's voice is stripped from the verses in the remaining episodes, the presence of the lyrics in the reworked chorus-turned-slogan (USP) carries more weight.

Example 4.4. Stop-time chorus and altered tagline turned USP. ("The Chase," PepsiCo. Inc., 1988. Transcription by the author.)

At the conclusion of Jackson's staged performance, multiple shot-reverse-shots cut to and from the screaming audience and footage of the star racing outside to escape an approaching mob (table 4.2). Shrieks from his fans take up the soundtrack as he runs onto a rooftop to catch a waiting helicopter. At the last minute, Jackson realizes that he must run the other way to escape the hoard, but he reaches a dead end. A title card reminis-

Fig. 4.2. Jackson reaches a dead end. (Still from "The Chase," PepsiCo. Inc., 1988.)

cent of Hollywood silent films appears under his distraught face to signal that the story will continue (fig. 4.2). Two measures of the opening riff once again enter the soundtrack to aurally reinforce the fact that there is more to come (table 4.2 and example 4.1). This positioning of Pepsi's logo over Jackson (who has noticeably changed out of his onstage costume) further hints that Pepsi's product will become his saving grace.

Episode 2: "The Chopper"

Much like Jackson's video for "Speed Demon," episodes 2 through 4 of the commercial follow Jackson as he performs a variety of impossible feats to escape his fanatical pursuers. As always, the brand's logo is prominently distributed on cups, cans, bottles, vending machines, neon signs, and so on. The spot's later episodes rely even less on the pop star's "Bad" signifiers (the black leather costume, spinning, and falsetto grunts), and the camera's view of Jackson remains fragmented, often focusing on isolated parts of his body—most prominently his face, hands, and feet. These shots make it clear that he has been freed from the costuming he had meticulously developed, thus shedding his musical persona to fully represent a Pepsi-fueled, action hero fantasy.

Throughout the remaining episodes, the superstar has flashbacks to his performance in episode 1.[49] When remembering his time onstage, Jackson's voice is diegetic. It quickly becomes non-diegetic during the action sequences. This movement between diegesis and the fantastical gap indicates that his onstage performance narrates his daydream. The music therefore plays a central role in the later episodes since its movement does not follow the original song's trajectory. Instead it is truncated and rearranged to emphasize the implausibility of his stunts (table 4.2).

Episode 2 begins like the first with a quick statement of the opening riff (example 4.1). The track then deviates abruptly to the last two measures of the pre-chorus (table. 4.2). The now familiar cadential E7#9 chords blare from the soundtrack and lead to a premature musical climax (example 4.3, mm. 1). These chords mimic the energy Jackson exhibits onscreen in his jump from the rooftop to grab the runner of a hovering helicopter. The sound of the chopper's blades mix with the track's move to an abbreviated version of the reworded chorus, complete with its new hook and the dissonant "bad chords." The music here narrates the incredulousness of Jackson's ability to dangle from the helicopter. As a few more measures of the chorus play out, the camera tracks the chopper's move upward into the sky. In the next scene, the pop star-turned-action hero plunges onto a zip line that carries him safely to the street below. Marketers once again manipulate the chorus' final tagline, this time changing the nature of the stop-time whisper by *extending* the IV chord to play through the chant to "It's Cool." The continuation of the harmonic motion here noticeably deviates from Jackson's original track and pushes the soundtrack seamlessly into a wordless variation of the song's verse (table 4.2). From this point forward, the tagline is used repeatedly as modular, transitional material.

Once on his feet the pop star frantically surveys his surroundings to locate his next mode of transportation. The verse's funky guitar and synthesizer groove parallel the visual editing between flashbacks to the concert footage (recycled from episode 1) and Jackson racing through city streets in a Ferrari Tessarosa convertible.[50] As the fugitive pop star approaches a construction zone, the pre-chorus once again sneaks into the track. Here the E7#9 cadential horn chords build to a *second* aural climax, which accompanies the sound of screeching tires and images of Jackson's high-speed donut and subsequent escape from the car. At the repetition of chorus's final bars and the stop-time tagline, the approaching mob catches up to the pop icon and chases him onto the roof of a Pepsi delivery truck. Marketers reorder the soundtrack again and abruptly loop it back to the

Fig. 4.3. Jackson's leap leaves fans hanging. (Still from "The Chase," PepsiCo. Inc., 1988.)

opening riff. A still frame that signals the next episode suspends Jackson in the air as he jumps from the vehicle (fig. 4.3). By ending on the dominant and an upbeat, the track acts as an aural cliffhanger to compliment the final frame (example 4.1).

Episode 2 demonstrates that the structures in Jackson's original track are as breakable as the laws of physics in the Pepsi fantasy. Not only are the musical phrases cut short, but the harmonic movements through natural cadence points are also repeated multiple times and eventually suspended to compliment the action onscreen. By modifying and shuffling the musical fragments to "Bad," marketing creatives once again redact Jackson's music into "themes," which take on new functions that lead to alternative meaning potentials when aligned with commercial images. In this and subsequent episodes, each of the modular fragments borrowed from "Bad" takes on a specific role: the opening riff works to introduce the song and suspend the final action of each episode; the stripped-down verse serves as transitional material; the pre-chorus signals impending danger; and the chorus-turned-Pepsi slogan indicates that Jackson is in the midst of completing another "bad" stunt (table 4.2). The music thus supports the preferred reading of this and subsequent episodes, namely, that drinking Pepsi will allow viewers, too, to accomplish extraordinary feats.

Episode 3: "The Museum"

In episodes 3 and 4, Jackson's actions and the accompanying soundtrack take him even farther from his performance and into his stuntman fantasy. Following the now standard two-measure lead-in with the riff, the mob chases the star into a museum accompanied by the sounds of a short, four-measure snippet taken from the verse's instrumental track (table 4.2). The camera switches between shots of the mob and back to a dead-end where the pop star disappears and leaves his pursuers confused. The track then skips over the pre-chorus and moves straight into the chorus's hook and a transitional version of the tagline. The accompanying shot reveals the star's hiding place inside a painting of a 1950s soda fountain. During another jarring return to the verse and a quick edit to the final bars of the pre-chorus, Jackson realizes his hideout has been discovered. In the next shot he becomes a "simulation of his simulation" and materializes in a black-and-white television set positioned above the diner's countertop. The screen changes abruptly from black and white to color when the camera follows him into the television set, removing one of the many layers of distance he has been built between himself and the fans from whom he runs. The shot then pans out to show the pop star on a mountain, positioned precariously atop an Olympic-sized ski ramp. As he makes his way down, the chorus and Pepsi's modified stop-time tag are again cued up. The spot again literally leaves Jackson and viewers hanging with a still frame that suspends his jump, accompanied by another return to the opening riff.

A preferred reading of this episode magnifies Jackson's ability to wow audiences and defy expectations—a claim Pepsi hopes to associate, by proximity, with its product. The pop star's actions here not only offer an entertaining storyline, but they also make explicit references to his place in popular culture. His ability to jump into the painting reinforces his immortality as a cultural figure (a trope also prevalent in his *Moonwalker* film) while his appearance in the television set suggests the voyeuristic manner in which the media and audiences have tracked his every move. Most ironically, the television in this commercial becomes a place of *refuge* instead of scrutiny for the star. Instead of gazing at Jackson as a passive viewer, the camera unexpectedly follows him into the set, adding insight into the pop star's situation. The shot outside the TV shows only Jackson's face, but from within the viewer takes on his perspective from the dangerous perch to the ramp below. The episodic series can be viewed as liberating for the star since it appears that the Pepsi commodity gives him the (fantasy of) "freedom" to escape the pressures of his fame. This scene in particular sends viewers a strong message about the problems inherent in the media's narrow perspective of Jackson's life—a reading that perhaps also makes it safer for Pepsi to associate itself with such a controversial figure. The moral of episode 3 might be understood, therefore, as a cautionary tale about judging the superstar without having a grasp on the perils he actually faces. And, as confirmed by the chorus entrances at the height of each action sequence, the superstar's "badness" comes from his ability to handle media pressure and adapt to any situation—that is (of course), with the support of the cola brand.

Episode 4: "The Finale"

Pepsi's episodic sequence concludes with Jackson soaring through the clouds, parachuting from the sky, and unexpectedly landing right back onstage. Direct word painting reinforces these images as Jackson sings the first lines of the pre-chorus, "Well they say the sky's the limit . . . ," during his launch into the stratosphere. The chorus accompanies his journey into the sky and final flashbacks to his concert performance (table 4.2). Portions of the verse's backing track accompany his parachute landing, and once he is on the ground he is illuminated with spotlights to signal his onstage re-arrival. The final bars of the chorus enter the soundtrack one last time to round out the spot. Realizing that he cannot escape his fame, the King of Pop poses for the camera, re-embodies his carefully curated performing persona, and finishes his song for the adoring onscreen crowd.

Curiously, Jackson still wears the outfit that defined his daredevil Pepsi persona rather than his "Bad" costuming in this final scene. It is therefore unclear at this point whether his re-emergence onto the stage is part of his Pepsi-induced fantasy or if he never left. The open-ended nature of this scene is similar to the final minutes in *Moonwalker*, where Jackson returns to his role as a superstar after taking on various cyborg metamorphoses throughout the film. Mital reminds us that audiences are forced to accept his transformation back to the stage and come to terms with the fact that "the imaginary Jackson is completely imploded with the real: This real is still and always an *image*."[51] Thus, even Jackson's restored image as a performer in *Moonwalker*, and by extension in "The Chase," is simulacra; it is *hyper*real.

A negotiated reading might further attribute the incongruity of the commercial's final scenes to the capitalist realist outcomes that Schudson deems typical of advertising. Viewers had become skilled at reconciling these types of disparities as they appeared throughout Jackson's music video oeuvre. Moreover, as Mercer points out, Jackson's groundbreaking short film for "Thriller" proved captivating precisely because it "incorporates the pop video convention of switching from 'realist' to 'fantastic' modes of representation, but binds this into continuity and closure through its narrative."[52] "The Chase" works in a similar way, but, as the pages above illustrate, it is the *music* that leads the viewer toward or frequently away from a perceived "narrative continuity." Thus, "closure" in the final episode of "The Chase" comes from finally hearing the musical track come to an end after the proper placement of the re-lyricized stop-time tagline ("It's Cool"). The cheers that follow the soundtrack's resolution force viewers to accept the capitalist realist fantasy offered to them. They must acknowledge that Jackson's trance-like sequence is over and that at least some part of his physical or mental being has returned to the stage.

This final episode of "The Chase" obviously plays with public views of the superstar by depicting the stage as his perceived "home." Jackson's onscreen simulation exemplifies this by accepting and embracing his inability to escape his fame. Indeed, without hesitation the star looks directly into the camera and returns to what he is best at—performing. Episode 4 therefore serves as a reminder that it is Michael Jackson's ability to *entertain* that ultimately makes him "bad." Pepsi therefore encourages its viewers to realize their own potential—their "badness"—with the help of its soft drink. At this point, the brand has realized the full potential of its redactive practices as it has fully co-opted Jackson's demonstration of musical prowess, as well as his message of personal affirmation, for its own gain.

"The Chase" offers a compelling snapshot of the aesthetic evolution of new music marketing in the years since Pepsi's first campaign with Michael Jackson. Due to the star's intention for the commercials to work alongside the various promotional texts he created for the album (its videos, *Moonwalker* film, CBS documentary special, Grammy appearance, etc.), the brand was granted unprecedented access to his image and music.[53] Marketers could therefore fully integrate Pepsi into Jackson's legacy and even used the opportunity to add their own twist to his iconography. A review of "The Chase" reported that Pepsi had promised a "new look . . .

more sophisticated than *Bad* but rougher than *Thriller*."[54] This is accomplished once Jackson runs offstage in the first episode. Here the commodity literally transforms him as he dons a less opulent wardrobe and his "performances" are confined to the stunts required to escape his pursuers (fig. 4.2). Pepsi's reimagined version of Jackson thus obviously mimics the action hero characters featured in popular movies throughout the decade (*Die Hard*, *Lethal Weapon*, *Raiders of the Lost Ark*, etc.) and fits well within the ideologies and economies of Reagan era "hard-bodied" masculinity that Susan Jeffords defines as "indefatigable, muscular, and invincible."[55] By employing these tropes, marketers may have guessed this version of masculinity would be familiar to contemporary audiences. These images also aligned well with the "soul man machismo" persona Jackson had curated in his video for "Smooth Criminal"—another popular text in his *Bad* oeuvre that is featured in *Moonwalker*.[56] As musicologist Susan Fast notes, Jackson's "Smooth Criminal" character demonstrated "that a black man could inhabit that kind of powerful character as convincingly as white men had."[57] Jackson's character in "The Chase" similarly attempts to promote this agenda as he embodies the over-the-top, "hard-bodied" characters made famous by well-known white actors in leading roles, including those played by Bruce Willis, Mel Gibson, and Harrison Ford.

In some respects, decentering Jackson's performing persona fostered a safer, more family-friendly version of the star. But it also encouraged the possibility of circulating an alternative view of him that could be read as humorous, sympathetic, or both. Consequently, the commercial's fantastic narrative allows Jackson to escape from tabloid rumors in multiple ways: it pokes fun at the pandemonium caused by fans and paparazzi pursuers and offers a glimpse at what Jackson's embrace of "hard-bodied," heterosexual masculinity might look like—something the media demanded but that his "Bad" persona so obviously challenged. In doing this, the commercials (perhaps unintentionally) highlight the ridiculousness of both scenarios, coming across as camp or even drag. Pepsi's alternative image of the pop star therefore works to *legitimize* the importance of his celebrity. To borrow from Joseba Gabilonda, the fantastic serves to strengthen the reality of Jackson's androgynous and racially and sexually ambiguous hyperreal "Bad" image.[58] The act of returning the pop sensation to the stage affirms and supports his rightful place there, thereby allowing Pepsi's final scene to have an impactful message: while Jackson may have tried to escape the success and shadow of his former album along with the resulting oppressiveness of his fame, Pepsi helps to confirm what he already knows—that he cannot escape his destiny to be himself and neither should those who identify as part of the "new generation."

Marketers make this selling point clear through the redaction of the musical track. By making a hybrid of the jingle slogan with Jackson's pre-existing lyrics, they re-map the star's message of "badness" onto the brand. While the lyrics on the album challenge bullies to live up to honorable notions of manhood, the commercial supports a more generic notion of what being "bad" means: it equates "badness" with Jackson's celebrity and the literal and figurative "coolness" of the Pepsi commodity.[59] The pop star exhibits "badness" in "The Chase" not by standing up for truth or honor, as in the Scorsese-directed video, but more generically through his concert performance and the improbable and life-threatening stunts he performs to escape an ensuing mob. The spots venerate his ability to be daring, insinuating his "coolness" in the "hip" sense of the word.[60] By extension, then, marketers associate Pepsi's product with Jackson by inserting the brand name into the second line of the hook: "You know I'm bad, I'm bad. And Pepsi's cool, it's cool." Jackson's personal accolades are therefore followed with praises to his sponsor, directly correlating Pepsi with positive aspects of the pop star's image. The word *cool*, then, becomes the ideal pun with which to describe a product aimed at a young (or at least youthful thinking) "hip" generation of consumers. Viewers can easily deduce that a chilled Pepsi is "refreshing" and the "in" thing to drink. The commercial's images reinforce this concept by showing attractive, hip music lovers enjoying their cola as much as Jackson's concert. By rewriting the lyrics and blurring Pepsi's "coolness" with Jackson's "badness," the musical track is able to take on meanings connected to the product in each of commercial's episodes. As advertising critic Barbara Lippert writes, the reworked hook becomes "a perfect '80s-style blend of innocence and cynicism."[61]

These messages are further conveyed through the reordering of the song's teleological structure. Each episode of "The Chase" incorporates selected material from the opening riff, verses, pre-chorus, and chorus in distinct ways (table 4.2). Marketers isolated major sections of the musical form into modular chunks and then rearranged, shortened, or repeated them as necessary to fit the duration of each scene. Each version of the reworked track therefore supports the action onscreen by aurally reinforcing key moments of tension and resolution, as well as the transitions between Jackson's performance and stuntman fantasy. The musical fragments borrowed from "Bad" occur only in the correct order (except for some repetition) and as completed phrases in episode 1, which is a simulation of Jackson's concert performances. In the second episode, "The Chopper," Jackson's daydream takes shape and the music follows suit by moving sporadically between varied fragments of "Bad." Episodes 3 and 4 take viewers even deeper into his fantasy as the track's teleology becomes increasingly misdirected and unpredictable to mirror the incredulity of his stunts. Consequently, each episode's distinct arrangement of Pepsi's chosen musical fragments follows the various scenarios Jackson works through, creating unique narrative continuities for every segment. The redacted musical score thus plays a key role in shaping audience expectations throughout the storyline: by reworking the song's goal-directed teleology, marketers string audiences along and simultaneously fuel their desire not only for narrative closure but also for the promised products produced by both Pepsi and Jackson.

Put simply, "The Chase" depicts Jackson in a fantasy induced and perpetuated by the Pepsi commodity itself. Ultimately, this set of "The Choice of a New Generation" commercials redacts the messages in "Bad" and uses the King of Pop to invite consumers into a *capitalist's* version of "badness," the kind that comes from consuming soda and buying music. The commercials demonstrate how advertising, like Michael Jackson's image, works to collapse hyperreality with fantasy: simulacrum thus allowed both global icons—Pepsi and Jackson—to adapt, create, and evolve in ways that best suited their own "pop" agendas.[62]

"BAD" RECEPTION

The reworking of Jackson's image and music in "The Chase" was representative of the star's larger desire to adapt to new ideas, genres, and technologies throughout his career. Fast summarizes his aesthetics best.

> Jackson moved so fluidly among performance traditions and subjectivities that he might productively be (re)thought through the lens of posthumanism in the sense that it calls into question liberal humanist ideas about the individual, unified, unchanging self, with the clear demarcation of boundaries between the human and non-human, between species and technologies.[63]

Indeed, by his third solo album Jackson's persona was anything but "unified." He was constantly changing aspects of his physique, which drew intense ridicule and speculation. His look not only blurred the lines between "human and non-human" and "species and technology," but so did his dancing, according to Judith Hamera. She observes, "In his precise attack, preternatural cleanness and speed, explicitly mechanistic movement vocabulary, and recurring invocations of repetitive work, Jackson both incarnates and transcends the trope of the human motor, combining the virtuoso's seemingly mechanical exactitude with suprahuman charisma."[64] With the release of *Bad* it became evident that his music also blurred these boundaries. Davit Sigerson of *Rolling Stone* confirms that "Jackson's free-form language keeps us aware that we are on the edge of several realities: the film, the dream it inspires, the waking world it illuminates."[65]

Once *Bad* hit the airwaves, some critics, like Sigerson, recognized the hard work that went into the album's creation and considered it a success. His cautiously worded praise proclaims, "*Bad* is the work of a gifted singer-songwriter with his own skewed aesthetic agenda and the technical prowess to pursue it."[66] Many other contemporary reviewers, however, did not receive the album with the same enthusiasm. Even prior to its unveiling, some were openly skeptical that it could reach the musical "perfection" and popularity that Jackson's previous record had achieved.[67] These critics thought his seclusion from public view and rumored eccentricities indicated that his star had fallen. Others were influenced by tabloid headlines and dismissed the album altogether. A writer for *Time* magazine simply shrugged off the title track, calling it a "'Beat It' redux, a spectacularly snazzy hang-tough tune that warns against macho excess."[68]

Pepsi's incorporation of Jackson's image and music also attracted its fair share of criticism.[69] Trade press coverage of the campaign was cynical about the soda giant's ability to rescue Jackson from the ongoing media circus and skillfully picked each commercial apart. Bob Garfield, a writer for *Advertising Age*, expressed his disappointment with the two commercials released prior to "The Chase."

> The first spot, called "Concert," is a 90-second on-stage spectacular that isn't all that spectacular. We have a glittery, black-clad Jackson, bathed in the smoky pastels of stage lighting, singing and dancing in his spasmodic signature style— what has now become your basic, Michael Jackson simulated-concert outtake

spot. "You're a bad new generation, and Pepsi's comin' through," he sings (I think, because the sound track has a strangely distant quality). "I'm bad, I'm bad . . ."[70]

Garfield then singled out the potential humor in the second spot, "Backstage," (mentioned above), unleashing a sarcastic jab that resonated strongly with the tabloids at the time: "Now, never mind that in real life [the boy would] be instantly apprehended and maybe hermetically sealed in a giant, nitrogen-filled thermos bottle for display in Jackson's game room. This is fantasy, you know."[71] The cynicism that drips from Garfield's comments reveals that even the advertising industry had difficulty accepting Pepsi's lighthearted redaction of Jackson's controversial image.

Four months later "The Chase" received only a brief mention in reviews of the 1988 Grammy Awards show on which it premiered. Critics seemed to revel in the disappointment of the superstar's evening as *Bad* lost in all but one category and Jackson's live performances of "The Way You Make Me Feel" and "Man in the Mirror" were met with little acclaim. The *Washington Post* and *Toronto Star* used the opportunity to call the Pepsi spots "awful" and "execrable."[72] That April rocker Neil Young took direct aim at the commercials and wrote a song and video that poked fun at Jackson and his fellow music icon, Whitney Houston, who had become the spokesperson for Diet Coke.[73] The commercials attracted more negative attention months later when Pepsi released Jackson from his contract following revelations that he was addicted to pain medications.

Aside from the inferences that Jackson's fame had reached a saturation point and Neil Young's articulation of lingering baby boomer anxieties about "selling out," no source pinpointed exactly why the commercials themselves received so little positive attention. It can be easily inferred, however, from the language in the reviews that the commercial's faults lay in its approaches. Indeed, Jackson's previous campaign was venerated because its selling point was well disguised by its innovative and entertaining qualities. But Pepsi's tactics—especially those featuring staged concert footage—had become well worn and even clichéd by 1988, as noted by Bob Garfield and Neil Young and evidenced in previous chapters. More obviously, Pepsi's clumsy hybrid of slogan material and Jackson's lyrics drew attention to its co-branding intent. An obvious example occurs when the song's opening lyrics, "Your butt is mine, gonna tell you right," are rearranged with fragments that occur later in the original song: "Gonna tell you right, just show your stuff" (example 4.2). Here marketers substitute the strong nature of the opening phrase (slang for "I'm gonna kick your butt") with something more friendly and innocuous (show me your potential). These substituted phrases sound awkward when placed over the wrong rhythmic and melodic lines, especially at the end of the first phrase when the single-syllabic word *stuff* is stretched over two syllables. Viewers' expectations were thus thwarted when they were offered neither the original track nor a seamless substitute. Instead, Pepsi's less than subtle redactions highlighted the inelegance of the selling proposition, making it less of a soft sell than the 1984 campaign and therefore less appealing to audiences who were now fluent in the brand's music marketing language.

BAD LEGACY

Despite its negative reception, the 1987–88 commercials marked an important moment in the history of advertising. The fact that they received so much attention was a testament to the future potential that co-branding cutting-edge songs with corporate brands could offer. After all, the publicity generated by Pepsi's sponsorship helped the pop star's tour become the highest grossing of all time and aided in making *Bad* the first album ever to produce five number-one hits.[74] The partnership also helped Pepsi to (once again) expand its market shares in Australia and Japan.[75] Consequently, the campaign proved that even if consumers did not fawn over the commercials, their constant exposure to them kept Jackson's music and Pepsi's products fresh in their minds. Equally as important, Pepsi took a major gamble in incorporating such a large amount of the new music in its spots. The extensive reworking of Jackson's track revealed the degree to which pre-existing music could be applied to branding environments.

This campaign also taught the soda giant and its rivals that it was still tricky to negotiate the threshold for what audiences would allow their favorite musicians to do in commercial contexts. As detailed in chapter 5, audience approval at the end of the 1980s had much more to do with particularities of the musical *content* and the *context* in which it was placed than with how much pre-existing musical material was transferred to the commercials. The soda giant would therefore learn its hardest lesson yet: some pop stars create music that resists the kind of redaction required to make it appropriate for general consumption.

CHAPTER 5

A "Wish" and a "Prayer"

Pepsi Faces the Limits of Redaction

By 1989, commercials that used popular music inundated the airwaves. Many brands continued to use older hits to market products like alcohol and cars to appeal to adult consumers while some still hesitated to show the artists themselves. Even when commercials did feature performer cameos—such as Michelob's spot with Phil Collins or Diet Coke's George Michael and Whitney Houston endorsements—the brand's slogan and product placement usually overran the artist's pre-existing musical track. Pepsi-Cola therefore continued to lead the way in terms of placing new artists and their hit soundtracks at the forefront of its marketing endeavors.

The soda giant's continued desire to partner with young contemporary talent was evident in its ongoing sponsorship of the annually televised Grammy Awards show. In 1989, its commercials dominated the program's breaks with three separate music-focused co-branding deals. One of the most memorable spots mimicked Robert Palmer's steamy music video for "Simply Irresistible." As described in chapter 1, this commercial redirected his accolades for the uniformed and mute models onscreen to his love for the soft drink. Another landmark spot famously featured Spanish singing sensation, Chayanne and became the first Spanish-language Pepsi commercial to air on a mainstream US network.[1] The third spot was intended to garner the most hype as a promo for the brand's forthcoming commercial featuring Madonna—the number-one female pop artist at the time. The 25-second teaser told audiences to drop everything to hear Madonna singing her "latest release, 'Like a Prayer,' for the first time."[2] Curiously, this promo for Pepsi's future commercial featured images of an Australian aborigine roaming to find a television in the desolate outback. Marketers spliced his journey between glimpses of Madonna getting ready for the commercial's shoot, Pepsi paraphernalia, and images of her upcoming television appearance. Racial politics seeped through the visual montage and into the selling message as the commercial interspersed the dark-skinned tribal figure with glimpses of Madonna's pale face and seductive red lips. These provocative images were heightened by audio cuts that included a didgeridoo and snippets of the "Like a Prayer" chorus sung by an African American gospel choir.[3] Appropriately enough for a teaser, Madonna's voice never actually enters the track. As one reviewer put it, the promo was meant to invite "the global village into [Madonna's] living room"—a setting that, not coincidently, would also become the backdrop for her upcoming full-length Pepsi commercial.[4] With its exoticist yet neo-liberal universalizing message—that Pepsi and American musical culture had become ubiquitous and globally unifying commodities—these "cold clues" did little to prepare audiences for the even more perplexing and pro-voking signifiers to come.[5]

SEARCHING FOR A MIRACLE

Despite the notable sales increases Pepsi had achieved with endorsements from pop artists like Lionel Richie and Tina Turner, none matched the acclaim garnered by the soda giant's first commercials with the King of Pop. As a result, Pepsi challenged BBD&O to brainstorm new ways to regain its status at the top of the celebrity endorsement market.[6] The creative team eventually came up with the solution to make a global campaign featur-ing the second-biggest solo pop star to date—Madonna. During a meeting at her California home in October 1988, the would-be Queen of Pop not only agreed to begin negotiations but also offered the brand the title track from the new album she had in production. Three months later the soda corporation officially hired her to sing her yet to be released single "Like a Prayer" for its "A Generation Ahead" campaign. In return for the same five-million-dollar fee paid to Michael Jackson and the sponsorship of her upcoming tour, Madonna was persuaded to lend her dance moves and image to the spot.[7] Most notably, she agreed to market the song through the commercial on network and cable television *before* the album was released. This reversed the traditional order for a record promotion—album, video, and then commercial—indicating the central role that visual promotions played in record sales by the late 1980s. Hence, for the first time in history global audiences were exposed to new American pop music through a *television commercial* for a *consumer product* before they could buy the album in stores (table 5.1).

As they had done for Michael Jackson's second campaign (discussed in chapter 4), Pepsi and BBD&O sought out Joe Pytka to direct Madonna's first—and, as it happened, only—commercial. The spot, titled "Make a Wish," tells the story of a young girl (Madonna as a child) who gets a rare glimpse into her future with help of her 1980s superstar self. The commercial abides by MTV aesthetics, interweaving performance footage, colorful point-of-view shots, and nostalgic black-and-white dream sequences. A full two minutes long—twice as long as the standard 60-second spot—Pepsi's

Table 5.1. Timeline of "Like a Prayer" promotions, controversy, and release

May 5, 1988	Pepsi asks BBD&O's creative team to create an international commercial. Madonna's name comes up during the deliberations.
October 12, 1988	Madonna plays a "rough mix" of "Like a Prayer" for BBD&O creatives and offers it for the commercial
January 25, 1989	Madonna signs the contract with Pepsi. It is reported that she will make three global commercials.
January 26, 1989	*USA Today* publishes the deal on the front page
February 22, 1989	The promo for "Make a Wish" airs during the Grammy awards show
March 2, 1989	"Make a Wish" premieres globally
March 3, 1989	Madonna's "Like a Prayer" video premieres on MTV
March 4, 1989	Pepsi pulls "Make a Wish" from the US market
March 10, 1989	The American Family Association, led by Rev. Donald Wildmon, calls for a one-year boycott of Pepsi soft drinks. Two weeks later the bishop of Corpus Christi, Texas, calls for a boycott of all Pepsi products (including the Taco Bell and Pizza Hut chains).
March 21, 1989	The *Like a Prayer* album hits stores
April 4, 1989	Boycotts end after Pepsi officials announce that Madonna will no longer be featured in the brand's commercials
April 22, 1989	*Like a Prayer* hits number one on *Billboard*'s Top 200 chart and remains there for 77 weeks
September 6, 1989	Madonna's *Like a Prayer* music video receives the Viewer's Choice award during MTV's Video Music Awards show

mini-video for "Like a Prayer" premiered worldwide to create anticipation for the unveiling of the album and Madonna's video for the title track. The hype paid off, as media reports estimated that 250 million viewers in 40 countries watched the spot on the date of its premiere.[8]

"Make a Wish" set important precedents for the eventual and total convergence of corporate brands and pop music in the twenty-first century. As mentioned above, it was groundbreaking as the first globally advertised commercial to premiere a popular song in order to hype the *upcoming* release of an album and video.[9] Madonna's Pepsi commercial was also the first to use only the *original* lyrics and backing track from a new song. Consequently, the commercial contains *zero* slogan material and the brand name is never spoken, only integrated into the onscreen action. This deal thus marked the definitive end to Pepsi's (and by extension the advertising industry's) sole dependence on adapted or custom-composed jingles and ushered in the now commonplace practice of co-opting the newest musical hits to complement increasingly sophisticated branding imperatives.[10]

But, despite the commercial's innovative promotional model and its inclusion of MTV aesthetics, its content ignited a controversy that forced Pepsi to pull it off the air shortly after its premiere. As perhaps the most infamous co-branding blunder of the twentieth century, Pepsi executives failed to view Madonna's music video for "Like a Prayer" before airing "Make a Wish" and were caught off guard by backlash from conservative groups outraged by the video's sexually provocative, racially charged, and borderline blasphemous religious imagery. Outraged viewers demanded that both texts be pulled from rotation.[11] Following an onslaught of negative media attention, the soda giant released Madonna from her contract and pulled the commercial from most US stations after only a few days, leaving "Make a Wish" best remembered for the controversy that surrounded it (table 5.1).[12]

In the years since the commercial's fallout, scholars from multiple disciplines have weighed in on its meaning. Most have read the commercial, song, and MTV video primarily through the song's lyrical text, Madonna's appearance, and the onscreen imagery. Literary and cultural theorist Nancy A. Vickers and Renaissance scholar Carla Freccero have both produced compelling examples of this approach by using aspects of the pop star's biography to unpack the personal and religious themes within the spot.[13] Cultural critics Robert Goldman and Stephen Papson have also discussed the commercial's imagery, claiming that viewers were able to interpret neoliberal "concepts [of] (pseudo)individuality and upward mobility."[14] Media scholar Douglas Kellner reads the images as operating outside traditional commercial formats, noting that they instead work like an artistically driven and politically charged, modernist mini–music video.[15] More recent texts by Bethany Klein, Timothy Taylor, and Leslie Meier have framed the commercial within the trajectory of the advertising industry's history of licensing hit songs.[16] Only musicologist Susan McClary has provided insight into the musical track itself by briefly analyzing its role in setting up the imagery deployed in its video and commercial.[17]

This chapter takes advantage of 30 years of historical distance and builds most obviously on McClary's work to bring a closer consideration of the music's role—and, specifically, marketers' attempts to redact its politically charged signifiers—into these conversations. By integrating primary source trade press and media with advertising theory and close musical analysis, the pages below provide a clearer picture of why the commercial caused so much controversy. As we will see, Madonna's densely coded song ultimately proved too challenging to control, and her refusal to allow Pepsi to rework the politically charged musical signifiers encoded in "Like a Prayer" made the traditional capitalist realist imperatives of simplifying and typifying its musical structures impossible for marketers to achieve.[18] Moreover, with the premiere of the music video the following day, it became glaringly apparent that the commercial merely amplified the pop star's agenda and confirmed the degree to which Pepsi was unable to contain it. "Make a Wish" thus stands as a unique case study of *failed redaction* as its content usurped the traditional aims of corporate advertising.

MADONNA'S "PRAYER"

In an effort to remain faithful to the order in which 1989 audiences experienced each of Madonna's "Like a Prayer" texts, this chapter begins with an analysis of the single, which aired on the radio just before the release of Pepsi's campaign. Prior to the *Like a Prayer* album, Madonna was known largely for her "carefree" upbeat dance music.[19] But, as many critics and scholars saw it, her 1989 album and title song demonstrated a new musical and ideological maturity that stemmed from her personal reflections as a now 30-year-old woman. No longer viewed as tongue-in-cheek dance pop, *Like a Prayer* was blatant in addressing more "serious" issues as Madonna employed less of her breathy, high-pitched, girlish vocal delivery in favor of a smooth chest voice that gave many of the tracks a more soulful sound. Scholars, fans, biographers, and even mainstream media outlets weighed in on the meanings of the album's songs. An article in the *New York Times* reported, "The songs, which deal directly and very emotionally with her failed marriage to the actor Sean Penn, her family, and her Catholic girlhood, transcend the brassy dance-pop of her three previous records to reveal Madonna as a vulnerable human being."[20]

In their reading of the title track, some scholars zeroed in on Madonna's struggle with her Italian American Catholic upbringing during the turmoil of Vatican II. Carla Freccero explains that the confused relationship Madonna claims to have had with the proper aspects of her faith also stems from the fact that Italian American Catholics often mix the iconography of popular mysticism—which includes ecstatic interactions between the carnal and divine—with the austere patriarchal practices of American churches.[21] Additionally, her past struggles to "behave" as a headstrong and sexually aware adolescent have been attributed to her strict upbringing, the death of her mother, and the limitations she felt were imposed on her while attending Catholic schools.[22]

Adding to the speculation, discussions concerning Madonna's alleged confusion about her racial identity were rolled into media accounts reporting that she admitted her childhood friends had all been black and that she had, at one time, identified with them.[23] Critics, like scholar bell hooks, were thus quick to point out Madonna's privileged position and admonished her appropriation of black culture.[24] hooks and others documented their concern about the racialized visual tropes Madonna employed in her video—including the appearance of an African American choir and a romantic interaction with a black saint. But, as the analysis below indicates, it was also the pop star's deployment of the most prevalent *musical* tropes from African American culture—including the blues and gospel idioms—that proved equally (if not more) provocative in "Like a Prayer."

The song's ambiguity is set up in its lyrics, as "Like a Prayer" features long strings of similes that make it impossible to pinpoint from the text alone the object of its descriptive language. In some respects, it reads as a love song with its use of "like" before the words "prayer," "child," "angel," "dream." The title itself might then be understood as a simile for a romantic relationship that has the potential to rescue the pop star from being "lost" to life's "mysteries." However, the various coded religious expressions used in the text, including the "midnight hour"—a biblical reference to choosing faith at the last possible moment in life—and her multiple calls out to "God," all strongly suggest that the song is indeed representative of a spiritual struggle. This reading is confirmed by a 1989 interview in which Madonna admitted that the whole of her album dealt with inner conflicts with her Catholic faith, including her "guilt and shame" as a "sinner."[25]

The allusive nature of the lyrics are further compounded by spiritual metaphors that hint at double entendre as Madonna exclaims, "I'm down on my knees, / I wanna take you there. / In the midnight hour, / I can feel your power." It is not entirely clear whether the underlying sexual tension is meant to be physically or spiritually connotative, but it is likely that Madonna intended to describe an experience evocative of both religious mysticism and sexual pleasure. One of her biographers agrees, writing, "Indeed, double entendres and ironies abound in 'Like a Prayer.' ... While the song feels distinctively religious, the underlying sexual tension is undeniable."[26] Kellner, too, reads double entendre into these lines, writing that they "could either refer to religious or sexual ecstasy."[27]

Using sexual terminology to describe ecstatic Christian religious experiences is a well-worn practice, and accounts of mystical unions with the divine are documented as far back as the tenth century to Hildegard von Bingen's works. McClary notes:

> In Saint Teresa's writings, religious ecstasy is described through images of sexual ecstasy, for the intensity of her relationship with the deity could only be expressed verbally to other human beings through the metaphors of submission, penetration, even orgasm.[28]

Freccero adds that being raised as a child of Italian immigrants would have exposed Madonna to a form of Catholic mysticism that would have embraced experiences of corporeal unions with the divine. At the time of the album's release, the superstar offered an interpretation of the title song that aligns with this reading: "'Like a Prayer' is the song of a passionate young girl so in love with God that it is almost as though He were the male figure in her life. From around 8 to 12 years old, I had the same feelings. I really wanted to be a nun."[29] Madonna's confession here confirms that the lyrics simultaneously reference religious and secular idioms, making them provocative as a vehicle for questioning God's presence in her life. Moreover, growing up in 1960s Detroit, Madonna would not have had to go farther than her own living room radio to be exposed to African American soul traditions derived from gospel and blues that also used coded language to mask carnal desires and secularize religious texts and tunes.[30] Twenty-six years later Madonna references "Like a Prayer" during a 2015 *Rolling Stone* interview, saying, "There's no law that says that you cannot be a spiritual person and a sexual person. In fact, if you have the right consciousness, *sex is like a prayer.*"[31]

A secular (and sexual) interpretation of these lyrics therefore opens their interpretation to numerous dialectical possibilities. As demonstrated in tables 5.2 and 5.3, the song's backing track supports and magnifies the tensions laid out in the lyrics. The lyrical evocation of religious imagery is

Table 5.2. Dialectical tensions in "Like a Prayer"

Lyrical tensions	
• Literal interpretation	• Metaphorical interpretation
• Spiritual devotion/love	• Human devotion/love
• Religious metaphors (Catholic/Pentecostal)	• Sexual metaphors (double entendre from religious expressions)
• Hope for salvation	• Despair over being "lost"

Structural tensions (religious pentatonic)	
F Major	*D minor*
• F Major pentatonic choruses: Catholic and Pentecostal	• D minor pentatonic bridges and verses: Catholic and Pentecostal
• Divinity, heaven, spiritual, transcendent (hope for salvation)	• Humanity, earthly, corporeal, desire (despair over being "lost")

Textural tensions	
Choir (Pentecostal)	*Solo voice (Catholic)*
• Community and salvation	• Isolated and lost
• African American	• Italian American

Performing force tensions	
Contemporary pop music	*Traditional church music*
• Synthesizer	• Organ
• Drum kit	

Tempo/rhythmic tensions	
• Cut time (eighth notes)	• Slow (quarter notes)
• Rejoicing	• Somber and reflective

Note: Transcribed from Madonna, *Like a Prayer*, 1989.

Table 5.3. "Like a Prayer" song structure

FORM:	Instrumental intro	Intro/bridge	Chorus	Verses 1–2
KEY AREA:	D minor	D minor	F Major	Bb Major (IV/F)
PENTATONIC MELODY:	D minor: octaves and block chords	D-F-G-A-C-D	F-G-A-C-D-F	D-F-G-A-C-D
PERFORMING FORCES:	• Solo vocal pick-up • Solo electric guitar • "Slam" silences guitar • Choir "ooh" replaces organ pedal	• Prominent solo voice • Background choir • Background organ	• Prominent solo voice • Keyboard synthesizer • Drum kit	• Prominent solo voice • Background choir • Background organ • Triangle

FORM:	Chorus	Verses 3–4	(3x) Chorus variation 1:	Bridge variation
KEY AREA:	F Major	Bb Major (IV/F)	F Major	D minor
PENTATONIC MELODY:	F-G-A-C-D-F	D-F-G-A-C-D	F-G-A-C-D-F	D-F-G-A-C-D
PERFORMING FORCES:	• Prominent solo voice • Midlevel choir • Background organ • Keyboard synthesizer • Drum kit	• Prominent solo • Background choir • Background organ • Triangle	• Prominent solo • Prominent choir • Keyboard synthesizer • Drum kit	• Prominent solo • Contrapuntal choir • Electric guitar • Drum kit

FORM:	(3x) Chorus variation 2:	(2x) Bridge variation:	Outro
KEY AREA:	F Major	D minor/V of F	D minor/V of F
PENTATONIC MELODY:	F-G-A-C-D-F	D-F-G-A-C-D / F-G-A-C-D-F	D-F-G-A-C-D /F-G-A-C-D-F
PERFORMING FORCES:	• Choir only • Choir respondent • Keyboard synthesizer • Drum kit	• Prominent solo • Contrapuntal choir • Keyboard synthesizer • Electric guitar • Drum kit	• Prominent solo • Contrapuntal choir • Keyboard synthesizer • Electric guitar • Drum kit

Note: Transcribed from Madonna, *Like a Prayer*, 1989.

bolstered with pentatonic vocal melodies that foster a powerful dialectical tension that allows easy slippages between the two primary modes—the solemn D minor heard in the bridges and the celebratory choruses that operate in the relative major of F.[32] This opposition between major and minor pentatonic melodies and harmonies further reflects Madonna's musical upbringing in the Catholic Church, as these sounds can be traced to nineteenth-century compositional practices known as the "religious pentatonic." According to musicologist Jeremy Day-O'Connell, the opposition of major and minor pentatonic melodies aurally alludes to divisions between humanity and divinity, earthly and heavenly, corporeal and spiritual, and desire and transcendence (table 5.2).[33] In the same way, the single's pairing of traditional dialectical pentatonic tropes and the heavy use of the organ act as strong musical gestures toward Western European forms of Catholicism.[34]

The musical contributions of an African American gospel choir, led by the legendary Pentecostal singer Andraé Crouch, not only enhance the track's religious signifiers, but also work to complicate the song's racial signifiers (see the "Textural tensions" noted in table 5.2).[35] Not coincidentally, the way in which the pentatonic melodies of "Like a Prayer" oppose moments of solemn reflection and celebratory salvation align as much with African American gospel music traditions as they do with Catholic traditions.[36] As a prevalent sonic force, the choir further represents guidance from a saved (and arguably Protestant) collective against the isolation of the protagonist's (Catholic) struggle with "sin" and spiritual uncertainty (tables 5.2 and 5.3). We can hear this through Madonna's soft opening monologue, the lyrics "Everyone must stand alone," and in her repeated descents into D minor. As the images in the video and commercial highlight, the choir plays an important role in the latter half of the song as a guide for Madonna's languishing solo vocal line by attempting to redirect her melody (and presumably her faith) to the celebratory key area of F Major (table 5.3).[37]

McClary ascribes the lack of public approval for Pepsi's commercial to the tensions set up by the song's musical tropes and to general oppositions between Catholicism and Protestantism—ideas expanded on in tables 5.2, and 5.3. Moreover, she and Freccero both read the song and video as a confrontation between conflicting ideological perspectives about "appropriate" religious expression.[38] McClary concludes, "This song is about the possibility of creating musical and visual narratives that celebrate multiple rather than unitary identities, that are concerned with ecstatic continuation rather than with purging and containment."[39]

The following section expands on this reading to illustrate the ways in which the song confronts *racial* tensions as much as religious ones. More specifically, the analysis below aligns with work by bell hooks and Ronald B. Scott to reveal that the song's complicated and tense dialectical oppositions work to juxtapose musical, physical, and spiritual ideological divisions between *black and white communities*.[40] Accordingly, it is the track's multiple, overlapping confrontations with culturally policed boundaries—European Catholic mystical idioms versus African American Pentecostal devotion, divine versus carnal love, and dance-pop versus reserved religious devotion—that made Pepsi's project of *redacting* "Like a Prayer" challenging from the very beginning.

PEPSI'S "PRAYER"

"Make a Wish" opens with the diegetic sound of film moving through a projector (table 5.4). The camera moves from the back of a living room to focus on a black-and-white home movie of Madonna's eighth birthday. The image of the child unwrapping a doll unleashes the sounds of the song's opening D minor bridge. Madonna's minor pentatonic vocal melody fills the scene (tables 5.3 and 5.4). In the movie within the spot, the pop star is not yet visible, making the identity of the acousmatic voice unclear until she sings the word "mystery." In the context of the commercial the lyrics do not question religious propriety (as suggested in the album), but are literally reinterpreted to comment on the identity of the spectator, who has not been revealed until now: the reinvented, svelte, and brown-haired Madonna of 1989.[41] On the phrase "everyone must stand alone," Madonna appears to exchange glances with the onscreen version of herself. The isolation expressed by the lyrics and soulful delivery of her minor pentatonic solo line is mirrored in Pepsi's images to suggest a biographical insight into the pop star's climb to success. The opening bars thus work here with the images to convey a longing for her past innocence.

The underlying organ and wordless choir lend a mystical timbre to the track and provide the sonic envelope for the fantastical situation about to unfold. On the phrase, "I hear you call my name / and it feels like home," the two Madonnas switch places (fig. 5.1). The mysteriousness

Table 5.4. "Like a Prayer" form comparison

Original "Like a Prayer"	Pepsi's "Like a Prayer"
Instrumental intro: D minor	*Short intro: extra musical sounds*
• Solo electric guitar	• Film projector sounds
• Slamming sound silences the guitar	• Slamming sound silences the projector
• Wordless choir "ooh"	• Four *beat* choir and organ pedal cut to
• Four *measure* choir and organ pedal lead-in to bridge	bridge
	• Screening of Madonna's eighth birthday
Intro/bridge: D minor	*Intro/bridge: D minor*
• Prominent solo voice in D minor pentatonic	• Prominent solo voice in D minor pentatonic
• Background choir and organ	• Background choir and organ
• Vocal slide on "home"	• Vocal slide on "home"
• Sustained D minor chord for *four measures*; preps miracle cadence to chorus	• D minor chord sustained *for a few beats*; preps miracle cadence to chorus
	• Madonnas switch places onscreen
Chorus: F Major	*Chorus: F Major*
• Drum kit fill and keyboard synthesizer	• Drum kit fill and keyboard synthesizer
• Prominent solo voice in F major pentatonic	• Prominent solo voice in F major pentatonic
	• Keyboard synthesizer
	• *Splice to verse 3*
	• Black and white youth dance onscreen
Verses 1 and 2: B♭ Major (IV/F)	*Verses 1 and 2: B♭ Major (IV/F)*
• Prominent solo voice in D minor pentatonic	• Omission of verse 1 and most of verse 2
• Background choir and organ	• Last measure of *verse 2 later spliced onto the end of verse 3* when Madonna entices
• Triangle	schoolgirls to dance ("Heaven help me!")
Chorus: F Major	*Chorus: F Major*
• Prominent solo voice in F Major pentatonic	Omitted
• Mid-level choir and background organ	
• Keyboard synthesizer and drum kit	
Verses 3 and 4: B♭ Major (IV/F)	*Verses 3 and 4: B♭ Major (IV/F)*
• Prominent solo voice in D minor pentatonic	• Prominent solo voice in D minor pentatonic
• Background choir, organ, and triangle	• Background choir, organ, and triangle
	• *Includes only 7mm.* ("Like a child . . .")
	• End of verse 2 tacked onto the end ("Heaven help me!")
	• Young Madonna explores her future house; grown Madonna remembers her parochial school

Chorus variation 1: F Major	Chorus variation 1: F Major
• 3x with melodic shift down a third on repeat	• *Includes only first 8 mm.*
• Prominent solo voice and choir in F major pentatonic	• Splice to chorus variation 2
• Keyboard synthesizer and drum kit	• Melodic shift downward replaced with elision to an authentic V-I cadence on F tonic from chorus variation 2
• Slides back into D minor to repeat the bridge	• Prominent solo voice and choir in F major pentatonic
	• Keyboard synthesizer and drum kit
	• Grown Madonna dances again with multiracial youth onscreen

Bridge variation: D minor	Bridge variation: D minor
• Prominent solo and contrapuntal choir in D minor pentatonic	Omitted
• Electric guitar and drum kit	

Chorus variation 2: F Major	Chorus variation 2: F Major
• Choir only in F Major pentatonic (3x)	• Choir only in F Major pentatonic (3x)
• Three half cadences on C (V)	• Three half cadences on C (V)
• Choir respondent	• Choir respondent
• Keyboard synthesizer and drum kit	• Keyboard synthesizer and drum kit
	• Madonna dances ecstatically in front of African American Pentecostal congregation
	• Cuts off three beats early when young Madonna finds her doll and the fantasy is broken

Bridge variation: D minor/V of F	Bridge variation: D minor/V of F
• Soloist returns and changes to D minor pentatonic to cast doubt on promise of salvation (2x)	Omitted
• Contrapuntal choir, keyboard synthesizer, guitar, and drum kit	

Outro D minor/V of F	Outro D minor/V of F
• Prominent solo in D minor pentatonic	• Slamming sound taken from original track introduction prevents return to D minor
• Contrapuntal choir	• Madonnas return to their proper eras
• Keyboard synthesizer, electric guitar, and drum kit	• Film projector sounds
	• Madonna instructs her childhood self to "Make a Wish."

Note: Transcribed from Madonna, *Like a Prayer*, 1989; "Make a Wish," PepsiCo. Inc., 1989.

Fig. 5.1. The commodity allows the Madonnas to switch places. (Still from "Make a Wish," PepsiCo. Inc., 1989.)

of the onscreen action is complimented by the harmonic strangeness of Madonna's offbeat slide away from the implied F tonic of the following section to the lower third (d) on the word "home" (example 5.1). This musical slide and exchange of the two Madonnas indicate that they both are searching for a place to belong. The switch from color (i.e., the wisdom and "freedom" Madonna knows in the 1980s) to the constricting world of her 1950s–60s "black-and-white" childhood, acts as an overarching metaphor for the spot.

Example 5.1. Musical catalyst on "home" followed by the "miracle" cadence. ("Make a Wish," PepsiCo. Inc., 1989. Transcription by the author.)

The organ and choir sustain their D minor chord to lend rhetorical weight to the vocal line's lingering in the solemn opening key area. However, unlike the original track, it cuts off after only a few beats (table

5.4). Nevertheless, the momentary pause on this minor chord adds gravity to the subsequent move to F Major. This motion creates what Day-O'Connell calls the "miracle" cadence, a technique that aurally evokes the sound of heaven opening up by moving directly from vi to I (example 5.1, mm. 2–3).[42] In the context of the commercial, the cadence and ensuing F Major chorus work to establish Madonna's agency while subtly creating excitement for the Pepsi product. Remaining true to the fictionalized practices of advertising, this uplifting musical moment is commodified as the religious imagery suggested in the lyrics (and later depicted in the sacred iconography of Madonna's video) is replaced with a neon Pepsi sign that stands out in full color against the black-and-white scene in the commercial. The soda giant momentarily replaces religious guidance and supplies Madonna—and by extension everyone watching—with the fulfillment she seeks.[43] The Pepsi commodity thus delivers the opportunity for a "miracle" in the spot.

A splice to a transitional drum fill and a flurry of edits gives way to the grown-up Madonna as she diegetically sings the chorus on a street outside a fictional 1950s dime-store soda fountain. The placement of Madonna in the past during the upbeat F Major chorus reinforces the nostalgic tone of the commercial's opening shots and offers audiences a familiar taste of her pop dance style. The star's attire in this scene is noticeably out of place as she dons a black bustier, high-waisted pants, high heels, and a rosary necklace that falls along her cleavage. Her body, and presumably her sexuality, is prominently on display despite the inappropriateness of her dress in this conservative 1950s setting.

Back in the 1980s living room, eight-year-old Madonna watches her future self dance onscreen against a backdrop of African American and Caucasian youth in poodle skirts and letterman sweaters.[44] The multiracial youth shown dancing together here force the notion of "black and white" to occupy multiple levels of signification: black and white versus color functions not only as a visual representation of the past and present, but also as a literal reference to racial relationships—tolerance versus intolerance in this and future desegregated scenes—as well as right versus wrong forms of physical and religious expression. In this way, the images echo the musical track to bring the politics of racial, religious, and even gendered conduct into circulation. Although the commercial's message is intended to be one of conventionally upbeat capitalist realism—that is, everyone likes the same music and soda—visual icons familiar on their own are juxtaposed and redacted in ways that make them unfamiliar, or at least unrealistic, in these early moments of the spot. The commercial therefore unwittingly enacts the modernist Brechtian gesture of turning familiar "objects" (visual and musical signifiers) into something "peculiar, striking, and unexpected."[45] This moment thus requires engaged audiences to stop, question, and decode the onscreen action. As the commercial continues, these perplexing moments grow increasingly obvious, allowing Madonna's self-conscious, modernist agenda to seep into the spot.

In the next scene, the commercial's ensuing splice to the D minor pentatonic vocal line ("like a child . . .") is interpreted literally by showing images of young Madonna spinning in color in front of her future grand piano (verses 3 and 4 in table 5.4). On the repeated phrase, young Madonna is caught peering at a sexy poster of her future self.[46] Despite an abrupt return to the minor pentatonic, the child appears to find gratification in the realization of her potential as she explores her future living room.[47]

This living room scene is juxtaposed with film-noir-like images of grown Madonna visiting a parochial classroom. The images here closely mirror the song's minor pentatonic melody as the pop star sits silently, looking troubled and alone. The non-diegetic track then takes a clichéd poke at the concept of authority, as the words "You're in control" support images of uniformed girls walking in perfect rows.[48] In the next second, Pepsi's commercial cuts abruptly to an earlier moment from verse 2 of the original to highlight the exclamation "Heaven help me!" (table 5.4). This scene reinforces the song and the commercial's religious undertones while the camera focuses on grown Madonna dancing between the girls (fig. 5.2). Thus, in an ironic and winking gesture, the pop star does what she was taught by the very forces that displease her—what any "good" Catholic girl would do in troubled times—she (metaphorically) "prays" by calling to God for help. In the next moment, the girls throw up their hands and break their lines to demonstrate their potential to break free from conformity.[49]

Madonna's call to heaven aurally summons a full gospel choir to join her as she invites everyone to dance.[50] Pepsi's images cut to another fictionalized "unification" of black and white youth during the climactic repeat of the song's upbeat chorus (fig. 5.3 and table 5.4, chorus variation 1). This soda hop differs considerably from the image of whitewashed, female innocence depicted in Pepsi's own "Soda Fountain" spot from 1961—notably, its first-ever youth-oriented spot (see chapter 1). Accordingly, the scenarios portrayed in "Make a Wish" would have been

Fig. 5.2. Grown Madonna liberates her childhood memories. (Still from "Make a Wish," PepsiCo. Inc., 1989.)

unconceivable in Catholic girls' schools and the segregated public spaces common in the 1950s and '60s. These fictional scenes are thus extraordinary in their depiction of Madonna's ability to be in both eras simultaneously and in her ability to transcend the realities of their oppressiveness. As a child she has the potential to be something great once she realizes that life is more than the cookie-cutter world of her surroundings. As an adult she participates in all scenes as a confident 1980s woman, becoming the symbol of change and unity.

Pepsi aurally reinforces this climactic moment by splicing together an authentic harmonic and melodic V-I cadence on the key gospel phrase "I'll take you there" (example 5.2). Noticeably, this definitive musical resolution *never* happens in the single because the track slides quickly back into D minor (table 5.4, chorus variation 1).[51] The commercial therefore deviates structurally from the Madonna's record at its most critical moment by cutting directly to the gospel choir's variation of the F Major chorus. As a result, Pepsi's splice effectively "fixes" Madonna's fleeting vocal cadence by eliding the unsatisfactory resolution and replacing it with a different, later tonic chord. This splice both shortens the track to make it fit into the two-minute spot and produces a definitive harmonic resolution at the crucial moment of Pepsi's imaginary social and religious fusion. With this celebratory authentic cadence, it seems that both Madonnas have "resolved" their struggles in the realization of themselves as empowered pop queens.

Fig. 5.3. Grown Madonna enjoys an integrated 1950s soda hop. (Still from "Make a Wish," PepsiCo. Inc., 1989.)

Example 5.2. Pepsi's tonic cadence. ("Make a Wish," PepsiCo. Inc., 1989. Transcription by the author.)

you know I'll take you there. Just like a prayer, I'll take you there.

It would have made sense for Pepsi to end the commercial here since the images and musical track have resolved, but in a curious move the spot keeps going. The sights and sounds are then sutured together to move to a new scene picturing an African American Pentecostal choir joyously singing and dancing along with its congregation (fig. 5.4). In a striking and odd moment, Madonna confidently dances in front of this church while its members support her with three half-cadences on C (Table 5.4, chorus variation 2).[52] These images confirm that Pepsi's marketers could not help but literally depict the gospel-inflected finish of "Like a Prayer."

As viewers likely noticed, this scene does not reconcile easily with the rest of the commercial. The members of this Protestant congregation seem out of place (especially when shown opposite the Catholic girls' school),

Fig. 5.4. Grown Madonna dances before a 1950s Pentecostal congregation. (Still from "Make a Wish," PepsiCo. Inc., 1989.)

while Madonna's scant clothing, Catholic rosary, and provocative dancing conflict with the reserved images of black Protestant families in their Sunday best.[53] Equally peculiar is the fact that Pepsi's star endorser is no longer the musical focus and that this scenario reads (the most) unrealistically as an autobiographical vignette.

A negotiated reading, then, might view these final moments as a representation of Madonna's childhood as she might have preferred it: The music and images suggest that she rejects the restrictions imposed by her Catholic upbringing and embraces the emotional and spiritual "freedoms" offered by Pentecostal traditions. Hence, as an Italian American raised under the conservative ideologies of a mystic Catholic faith who grew up to create, sing, and dance to black music, Madonna is musically, spiritually, and physically taken in by the African American Pentecostal community with which she most closely identifies. In her public demonstration of love for her new community, she encourages viewers to find their own happiness with the help of the Pepsi commodity. The spot's final scene therefore not only proves strikingly similar to the setting of the same musical section in the MTV video that would air the next day, but it also reveals itself as another modernist, Brechtian moment within the commercial. Its peculiarities amplify the social and political commentaries on race and religious propriety that ran through the spot's previous settings, thereby offering viewers a proverbial peek behind advertising's curtain.

Pepsi's uplifting gospel scene ends with grown Madonna spinning in slow motion in front of the congregation while her younger version stumbles upon her birthday doll. The girl's encounter with the doll breaks the fantasy's spell. Pepsi's marketers give the spot a banal musical ending by inserting the slamming-door sound taken from the beginning of the original track (and also heard at the beginning of the spot) to prohibit a final return to D minor uncertainty (table 5.4).[54] With the major-key harmonic resolution and the return of each Madonna to her proper era, Pepsi assures viewers that anyone—even a rebellious Catholic girl who appropriates black culture—can achieve the "American Dream." In the final seconds, the pop star thus encourages her former self (and by extension the viewing audience) to "Make a wish." The eight-year-old then blows out her birthday candles, and the screen reveals Pepsi's logo and slogan.

THE NEXT 48 HOURS . . .

The following day, Madonna's *Like a Prayer* video premiered to a global audience on MTV. Directed by Mary Lambert, the video is a high-modernist, surreal text that aims for shock and awe. Less than 24 hours after the video's premiere, Pepsi was flooded with calls from people who thought the commercial was taken from actual scenes in the video. Nationally syndicated shows such as *Entertainment Tonight* found the controversy newsworthy and showed some of the most contentious clips from the music video, saying that religious groups had found it "blasphemous."[55] A Canadian news source pinpointed the problem: "Some religious leaders were incensed with scenes of Madonna singing in a field of burning crosses and caressing a priest."[56] Action against the spot was formally taken in the United States when Rev. Donald Wildmon pushed the American Family Association to threaten a boycott of Pepsi products if the brand did not stop running it (table 5.1). Across the globe, an Italian Catholic group warned that it would sue the soda giant if commercials continued to be broadcast as planned.[57] The confusion between the commercial and video even extended to the ad industry itself, as *Advertising Age* incorrectly conflated them in two separate reports, stating, "The company broadcast a new commercial for regular Pepsi featuring rock singer Madonna and *using clips from her new music video* 'Like a Prayer.'"[58]

On the other end of the spectrum, Pepsi and its sympathizers saw the commercial and Madonna's video as two separate and incommensurate texts. In a public statement, Pepsi executive Tod MacKenzie questioned Reverend Wildmon's actions, asking, "Why isn't he going after the video? . . . Why has he targeted really an innocent, wholesome commercial people have responded favorably to?"[59] Notably, those "favorable" to the spot to were largely those in the advertising world who recognized the work and ingenuity that went into the production. The same article added, "Madonna's 'Like A Prayer' video—*not the ad*—shows her kissing a saint, writhing on an altar and receiving the wounds of Christ."[60] An advertising trade press source concurred, "While 'Make a Wish' traveled back in time to the party on Madonna's eighth birthday and was light and joyful, 'Like a Prayer' deals with a young woman struggling with sexual and religious guilt, and contains inflammatory images like burning crosses and a romantic alliance with a saint."[61] *Adweek's* Richard Morgan liked the spot so much that he praised its soft-sell approach and called it a "media 'must-see' for impossible-to-reach teens."[62] He further criticized the fact that Pepsi had caved to the pressure put on it by religious groups, writing, "The video ain't the commercial, however, and never will be."[63]

Never one to shy away from controversy, Madonna was unapologetic and told one reporter, "Art should be controversial, and that's all there is to it."[64] MTV also held its ground. Now eight years old, the network had established a reputation for cutting-edge programming and refused to pull the video. It released the statement, "MTV has found the video, 'Like A Prayer,' to be acceptable for air. . . . Ultimately MTV supports an artist's right to interpret his or her music."[65] Pepsi executives, on the other hand, did not feel the same way and pulled the spot after realizing that the commercial's message was not being read or received as intended by large numbers of its consumers.[66]

FAILED REDACTION

Pepsi's "Make a Wish" attempted to paint the perfect picture of upward mobility by demonstrating that success, happiness, and the soda commodity go hand-in-hand. The commercial and the promo that preceded it fit perfectly under the umbrella of Reagan era neoliberalism: together they demonstrated that the soda brand embraced technological innovation (satellites that broadcast MTV), encouraged the economic gains of individuals

(Madonna as star), and catered to global audiences (little girls, Madonna's fans, and even aboriginals halfway around the world).[67] Audiences, however, were unable to arrive at this preferred reading due to the fact that Madonna's musical track and the subsequent release of her video clearly overran the brand's intentions. The politics of the shared track created an uncanny resemblance between the imagery in the MTV video and the soda commercial.

For the video, director Mary Lambert remained faithful to "Like a Prayer" by including the song in its entirety and adhering to the star's intentionally modernist and controversial agenda. The video therefore supports an often graphic scenario of a young woman who witnesses another woman's assault and struggles with freeing a wrongly accused black man for fear that she too will become a victim of the white perpetrators.[68] The character's moral struggle is intensified when she runs into a church to find guidance among mixed religious iconography (statues, a crucifix, a rosary, and later burning crosses) and has mystical encounters with African American spiritual leaders (a sexual union with a saint, heavenly guidance by a female soloist, and a provocative profession of faith in front of a black Pentecostal choir).[69] In this way, the video strings together a politically amplified barrage of religious and racial images that support Madonna's expressed aim to "provoke" audiences.[70] Moreover, the MTV video—like Pepsi's commercial—deliberately evokes a Brechtian anti-realist aesthetic as the final framing shots picture a stage, closing curtain, and final bows from the cast to reveal its status as a morality play within a play. As a late-twentieth-century modernist and multimedia attempt at epic theater, the video foregrounds inflammatory images alongside the track's dialectical musical shifts to intentionally confuse and alienate audiences.[71]

As demonstrated above, Pepsi's "Make a Wish" can be read in much the same way: its double-coded and politically charged signifiers create a similar type of alienation effect that prevents the typical cycle of passive viewing and mindless consumption encouraged by most advertisements.[72] Advertising, in fact, depends on what Schudson calls "low involvement learning," which allows most people to decipher ads quickly and read them as "trivial or transparent or both."[73] But as the fierce debate over the commercial indicates, the confusing array of sights and sounds in "Make a Wish" proved anything but "trivial" or "transparent." Fatally for the selling proposition, it made viewers think about controversial topics and resulted in oppositional readings that made the political content glaringly obvious. Consequently, while it can be argued that Pepsi's images are not as blatant or inflammatory as Lambert's portrayal of sexual assault and racism in the video, one only needs to replace its religious iconography with soda paraphernalia, and to reflect on the commercial's aspirational portrayal of desegregation, religious freedom, and personal expression, to find similarities in their agendas. Moreover, it is striking that both texts end in precisely the same way: with a robed African American gospel choir singing the final F Major chorus while a sparsely dressed Madonna gyrates ecstatically in front of them. Hence, neither director could deny the evocative potential of portraying the Pentecostal choir as a powerful diegetic force, allowing Madonna's proclamation of faith to act as a catalyst for resolution in both visual realizations of "Like a Prayer."

Where these texts deviate are thus in the moments when Pepsi's marketers attempted to take control of the musical track through the process of redaction. Indeed, the forced F major cadential resolution at the end of the commercial imposes a celebratory spin on Madonna's song. Conversely, the video's fidelity to the record enhances its volatility. By preserving the precarity between the F Major and D minor modal areas, the video confirms that a resolution of the signified racial and religious tensions are not, in fact, easy to attain (see table 5.4).

Unfortunately for the brand, its imposed cadential revision was not convincing. This was largely due to the fact that Madonna refused to allow Pepsi's marketers to change her lyrics, which prevented them from cutting up the track, neutralizing her message with a slogan, or placing important cadential moments on the name of the brand—the very tactics that they had employed so many times before. So, despite their attempts to splice and redirect the harmonic motion of the song, the fact that marketers were not allowed to make a jingle out of a song whose tropes could never be redacted enough to achieve the banality typical of corporate advertising, marketers were set up from the outset to fail in reworking the star's richly polysemic text into something suitable for global consumers.

Consequently, more than in any other campaign examined in this book, the *music itself* became the ruling force for this commercial: "Like a Prayer" was full of sonic tropes that confronted hot-button issues and resisted the type of abstraction Schudson postulated to be central to the contemporary "aesthetic and intention of . . . national consumer-goods advertising."[74] Hard-edged and polysemic, Pepsi's marketers simply could not be effective in redacting the music. "Make a Wish" thus transgressed the rules of capitalist realism because the images highlighted the tensions already laid out on the record. The commercial boldly pictured Madonna dancing not only with multiracial youth in 1950s desegregated public spaces, but even more provocatively with a black Protestant congregation and white-washed Catholic youth. The song's structures and tropes—its religious and sexually suggestive lyrical narrative, dialectical oppositions between major and minor key areas, and textural expansions from Madonna's singular Catholic experience to group participation by a black Pentecostal choir—therefore controlled the commercial's imagery and transferred the politically volatile signifiers of people and places into the brand. Not only did this usurp advertising's traditional reliance on generalizing (and reproducing) oppressive social conditions, but the song's lyrics and compositional structure also prevented marketers from breaking it into discrete and abstract musical moments. Madonna's questioning of ideologies that promoted racial divisions and inequality alongside religious conservatism (concepts amplified with the release of the music video) thus bled through the generalities of the commercial's mediated visuals. Accordingly, Pepsi's attempt to fix the song so that it ended with a reassuring major cadence was not enough to make audiences believe that they could simply drink a Pepsi and "make a wish" to rewrite the religious intolerance and racism of a "black-and-white" past.

Put simply, the political agenda encoded in the music became the ruling force in the commercial just as it had in Madonna's MTV video. Their largely untouched musical tracks and similar imagery caused viewers to conflate the two. Literary and cultural theorist Nancy Vickers summarized the ensuing scandal as "a fascinating case of guilt by association: it demonstrates the operative power (be it consciously planned or unconsciously enacted) of one Madonna production to silence another."[75] Indeed, the video amplified the modernist alienation effect that was set up by the commercial that preceded it, and in doing so it revealed the fundamental falseness at the heart of Pepsi's fantasy of hip consumerism.

INDUSTRY FALLOUT

Debates about the "appropriate" relationships between new popular music and corporate brands intensified in the wake of the campaign's fallout. Media chatter indicated that corporate executives and their advertising firms were thinking seriously about how far they should go in fusing the practices and aesthetics of the music industry with their own. Douglas McGill's 1989 *New York Times* article illustrated just how drastically the look, sound, and even the goals of late 1980s advertising had changed due to the recent flurry of soda commercials featuring pop stars.

> In their relentless focus on celebrities even more than on the product being advertised, the commercials exemplify a shift in modern advertising—from sales pitch to pure entertainment. And they have generated a debate among marketing professionals, not only about the effectiveness of the ads but also about the very purpose of modern advertising.
>
> Many of the current cola spots present themselves as one-minute movies, rock concerts or music videos. In some, the soft drink is scarcely mentioned or even seen. . . .
>
> Some say the ads stray from tested advertising principles, betray a lack of creativity, and ignore the essential task of any commercial: to make a sale.[76]

A few important points stand out in McGill's reflection on the state of the late 1980s advertising industry. The first is his claim that entertainment had usurped the primacy of the sales pitch. As discussed in chapter 2, the stated purpose of Pepsi's first campaign with Michael Jackson was to entertain viewers. McGill confirms that this strategy continued to prevail in subsequent years as co-branding deals with famous musicians proliferated. Second, he observes that the newest spots did not look anything like commercials but instead resembled "movies," "rock concerts," or "music videos." This confirms the degree to which the sights and sounds of late 1980s advertising were similar to those of other forms of media.[77] Third, the degree to which glitzy soda spots had infiltrated television sets all over the world reveals the extent to which the imperatives of globalization had enabled the music and advertising industries to push their goods into international marketplaces. Finally, McGill reveals that the industry had begun to realize that incorporating pre-existing popular music in commercials challenged the fundamental way that advertising had worked for decades—namely, the use of generic people, places, and scenarios to sell commodities to the largest possible audience. Marketers were thus clearly nervous about the fact that using superstar musicians and their pre-existing music brought an array of complex signifiers into commercials, and they worried that these aesthetics had the potential to shift the sales focus away from the conventionally narrow scope of the household brand.

The implosion of Madonna's Pepsi campaign had therefore made the risks of corporate advertising's new strategies painfully clear. Those interested in continuing their musical co-branding efforts had to evaluate whether or not their commercials could continue to harness pop music texts without compromising the selling proposition. Brands and their marketing agencies had to ask: At what point does a commercial become too "artistic," and too bound up in the aesthetics, ideologies, and agendas of an individual artist or band, and lose its status as a piece of mass marketing? While the advertising industry continues (even today) to grapple with this question, the ensuing media frenzy around "Make a Wish," along with the timing of McGill's article, and the decades of academic discourse that followed it indicate this commercial had become the limit case for this concern.

Madonna's Pepsi commercial thus demonstrated the worst-case scenario for what might happen when redaction fails. The spot confirmed just how unwieldy musical signifiers could be when not adequately manipulated to fit branding aims—especially signifiers that were so closely related to other circulating texts. It also reignited fears that had played out in celebrity lawsuits during the 1970s about the consequences of merging art and commerce.[78] The key difference this time was that the party at risk was not the artist but the sponsoring corporation: Madonna was not embarrassed, Pepsi was. The concern so dominant among fans and academics— that putting music in advertising contexts necessarily ruins it—actually proved irrelevant when applied to "Make a Wish" since Madonna's song actually ruined Pepsi's commercial and subsequent plans for its first-ever global new music campaign. Indeed, other than the usual grumbling and derogatory remarks Madonna had become accustomed to weathering, her losses were minimal. Pepsi still had to pay her $5 million, the album generated five hit singles, her tour was immensely successful, and the *Like a Prayer* video even won the Viewer's Choice award at the MTV Video Music Awards (table 5.1).[79]

As McGill observes, "Make a Wish" further revealed marketers' inexperience with the inner workings of the music industry and the practices of globalization. Pepsi executives and BBD&O obviously had no idea what they were getting into by hiring Madonna, attempting to control her image, and allowing her to have the final say on all aspects of the deal. In a remark that reveals the brand's obliviousness about the consequences of signing an edgy young artist, Alan Pottasch, Pepsi's senior vice president for advertising, stated:

> Music marketing is especially crucial to increase international sales. . . . Internationalism is a major part of the soft-drink business and music is one of the three things that transcend cultural barriers—music, sports and sex. We're not about to use sex, and we think sports has been somewhat overdone. Music is 100 percent universal.[80]

The belief that the corporation could hire Madonna and somehow avoid selling "sex" (or anything controversial) was naive at best. Furthermore, Pottasch's grasp at the "music is universal" bromide betrayed the assumption that musical meanings could easily be controlled not only to appeal to widely diverse US audiences but also to other cultures around the world. It was clear that Pepsi fundamentally misunderstood Madonna and her reputation. Executives not only missed the fact that her image and music were politically motivated but also the fact that her constant attempts to reinvent her image and sound also made the signifiers available and desirable for use in a family-friendly spot virtually nonexistent.[81] Marketers should have realized that the pop queen's visual iconography, musical oeuvre, and reputation were considerably less ubiquitous than Jackson's and far more controversial than Richie's, Turner's, and even Bowie's. And, although the soda giant was wise to avoid the image she was best known for—a retro Marilyn Monroe–like "bimbo"—the brand unintentionally made what should have been a clichéd neoliberal tale of "status transformation" and upward mobility volatile and incendiary.[82] Madonna's antagonism toward social norms was instead made explicit by the forces she opposed (Catholic institutions and segregation legislation) and the marginalized groups with which she interacted (girls, teens, and African Americans). Accordingly, Pepsi's attempt to project her as a sentimental, vulnerable, and "wholesome" person went not only against what experienced viewers knew about her, but (as the international outcry attests) religious groups figured out that their ideals were the ones targeted most directly as Madonna once again aimed to challenge hegemonic (and white) patriarchal doctrines of mainstream Christianity.[83] Pepsi was therefore ineffective in its attempt to stay on the cutting edge of musical marketing and to create a secular interpretation of a fundamentally religious construct (i.e., prayer). Thus, as McGill's article attests, the entire advertising industry took note when

"Make a Wish" failed to sustain the comforting illusions of capitalist realism and operated outside the realm of what advertising could safely reconcile.

McGill's article does well to illuminate the quick-moving and vast effects of America's neoliberal, capitalist agenda. Innovation and globalization were rapidly pushing the music industry toward a technologically saturated new millennium. Part III therefore focuses on the new relationships Pepsi fostered as it prepared to move into the next century. As the following chapter illustrates, the brand continued to incorporate popular music trends into its promotions, but it carefully reworked its strategies following the headaches incurred by "Make a Wish." Consequently, Pepsi's marketers would focus more on *emulating* particular styles in the 1990s rather than on incorporating the newest hit songs as they aimed to reach wider audiences.

PART III

Millennial Music Marketing: Redact, Reuse, Recycle

Humorous Hits, Nostalgic Notes, and Retro Refrains in the 1990s

The 1990s ushered in drastic changes that would define the American way of life in the new millennium. Rapid advances in technology allowed unprecedented access to personal computers and public internet services, while the economy saw massive gains and losses stemming from recession and an upsurge and later bust of dot-com industries. Social, cultural, and political shifts were characterized by extreme fluctuations between liberal and conservative values (hallmarked by the election and subsequent impeachment of President Bill Clinton); a war in the Middle East (begun by President George W. Bush Sr.); heightened national attention to racism and police brutality (due in large part to the Rodney King videotape); and increased concerns about media violence and its effect on adolescents (evidenced by high teen suicide rates and the Columbine High School shootings).

Pepsi-Cola, like most corporations, was forced to adapt quickly to these changing norms while also working to overcome new challenges arising in the beverage industry. In an attempt to confirm its iconicity in American culture, the brand followed Coca-Cola's World War II strategy and distributed 10,000 cases of soda to US troops deployed to Operation Desert Storm.[1] At home Pepsi's sales had reached $6.5 billion by 1990, but the brand and its competitors soon realized that the soda market was approaching a saturation point.[2] The cola giant therefore continued to expand beyond its legacy products and purchase more diverse beverage franchises.[3] Additionally, in the effort to improve its global gains, Pepsi tried to distinguish itself from Coke by redesigning its well-known red, white, and blue can to feature a new, more prominent shade of electric blue.[4]

Pepsi also continued to pour considerable resources into producing television commercials for its regular and diet colas. Its 1990s commercials still placed popular music at the forefront of the brand's selling messages, but it was clear that the damage done by its 1989 fiasco with Madonna had caused executives to abandon previous visions of merging with the evolving aesthetics of the music industry.[5] Consequently, marketers backed off from using anything overtly risky or risqué for the better part of the decade.[6] The soda giant also largely reframed its soft-sell approach, choosing instead to promote its products in ways that reminded audiences that selling *soda* was its primary agenda. Additionally, the company would phase out its "The Choice of a New Generation" slogan because, according to Phil Dusenberry—the BBD&O executive who had spearheaded the celebrity music campaigns that inundated the 1980s—marketers believed that the campaign's youthful target audience was proving too narrow.[7] Consequently, the eight-year campaign was succeeded by *product*-centered phrases, including "Gotta Have It," "Nothing Else Is Pepsi," and "Be Young, Have Fun, Drink Pepsi." Pepsi would not focus specifically on youth markets again until releasing its global "Generation Next" campaign toward the end of the decade, but this, too, would be quickly replaced with another product-focused slogan, "Joy of Cola," which extended into the new millennium.

As the soda giant moved toward the twenty-first century, its commercials revealed its processes for reconsidering who belonged in its current "generation" and what music would best attract them. Was it 1990s teenagers interested in rap? Those who grew up listening to Michael Jackson and watching MTV? Or the classic-rock- and soul-loving baby boomers who had initially brought so much success to the brand? More important, how could Pepsi attract new audiences while retaining three decades of aging consumers?

Marketers sought answers by adjusting the brand's aesthetic strategies. Visually, most of Pepsi's 1990s commercials reverted to older advertising styles that replaced previous attempts to disguise the selling proposition within the spectacle of an artist's performance and iconography. Other than its third and final campaign with Michael Jackson, Pepsi's 1990s celebrity spots focused explicitly on the star's endorsement of the product. Marketers also generally avoided the complicated story lines pitched in the previous "The Choice of a New Generation" and "A Generation Ahead" commercials. Instead they favored fictional spectacles that were exaggerated to the point that their positioning as Hollywood aggrandizements of soda commercials proved unmistakable. Simply put, the majority of Pepsi's 1990s pop music commercials looked like *commercials*.

The soda giant's spots also sounded different in this era as marketers combined the lessons they learned from the brand's 1980s pop music endorsements with strategies more closely aligned with traditional jingle practices. Pepsi therefore seemed less interested in breaking new singles than in expanding its tactics to harness the spending potential of *all* its generations, including (and perhaps especially) aging boomers whose increased affluence was highly sought after by many industries. As a result, some of the brand's music-centered spots did not include musical celebrities at all but instead used pre-existing clips or pastiches of older, well-known songs or genres. For the spots that did include celebrities, the brand's musical repertoire expanded to include past and present industry icons who could attract an array of possible consumers: MC Hammer, Ray Charles, and, for the last time, Michael Jackson.[8]

To appeal across age groups, Pepsi's marketing creatives foregrounded three affective strategies in particular: humor, nostalgia, and retro. Fred K. Beard confirms that in the 1990s most advertising executives believed that humor increased product awareness and brand recognition and fostered effective communication.[9] Advertisers also counted on humor's ability to encourage brand switching and hold viewers' attention.[10] According to Michael D. Dwyer, nostalgia, too, had become a dominant trope at the time, especially within the entertainment industry, where it permeated various media formats.[11] Music writer Simon Reynolds notes that the 1990s were similarly ripe for the emergence of retro tropes in music and fashion. He noted that increased cultural retrospection was influenced not just by postmodern aesthetics and technological innovation but also by the fact that there was simply a lot of pop history with which to work.[12] Pepsi thus garnered considerable acclaim in the 1990s by employing these industrywide trends and combining them with hit styles and big musical acts.

This chapter investigates the many ways in which Pepsi's marketers redacted portions of well-known pop songs and styles and paired them with onscreen scenarios to create sentiments of humor, nostalgia, and retro that could best serve branding aims. Part 1 unpacks the processes marketers undertook in combining pre-existing musics that were not humorous on their own with specific types of onscreen humor in order to redirect and reassign musical signifiers to take on new meanings. Part 2 outlines the way nostalgic and retro redaction proved equally effective as familiar songs and styles were pulled apart and remade into kaleidoscopic lenses that created new ways of experiencing the past through the branded present. Ultimately, marketers would combine these elements to produce a campaign with Ray Charles that became the brand's most successful of the decade and one of the most memorable of the twentieth century.

PART 1: HUMOR AND THE HARD(ER) SELL

Debates about the effectiveness of the hard versus soft sell continued among industry experts throughout the 1990s. Marketers questioned whether consumers should be presented with just "the facts" or if they should be encouraged to form an "emotional bond" with the product or brand.[13] Proponents on both sides believed that humor could effectively push either type of selling proposition as long as marketers adapted it to the social, cultural, and economic moment.[14]

Beard notes that there were three prevalent mechanisms for communicating humor in this era: "disparagement," "incongruity resolution," and "arousal safety."[15] "Disparagement" often used satire or put-downs to claim superiority and ridicule other people, things, or ideas. "Incongruity resolution" involved the juxtaposition of unexpected or normally incompatible elements; it often suggested two different interpretations, thus causing momentary confusion. "Arousal safety" was the most aggressive form and often dealt with physical harm, something shocking, and sexual innuendo. This last type might also cause tension or anxiety or encourage sentiment or empathy. While most instances of humor in advertising fit into one of these three categories, Beard acknowledges that some spots fell within several.

Pepsi's marketers used each of these approaches in the brand's humorous 1990s spots, sometimes in combination, and they often relied on preexisting popular music to deliver the punch line. More specifically, marketers redacted popular songs and styles that lacked humor on their own to produce musical comedy. To accomplish this, they frequently employed humorous techniques common to Western Art music compositions: musical parody, comic text, unexpected juxtapositions of syntax, comic references to particular styles, incongruence, references to past styles, and car-icaturing well-known pieces.[16]

Pepsi and BBD&O were frequently praised for their use of musi-cal comedy, especially for comparison ads that poked fun at Coca-Cola. One early 1990s example occurred in a commercial called "Shady Acres," which caught the attention of the *New York Times*. A feature story detailed how a top BBD&O executive, Lee Garfinkel, had used his experience as a stand-up comedian to add humor to the brand's pitch.[17] The commercial itself follows the results of Coke and Pepsi deliveries that are mistakenly switched between a fraternity house and a retirement community.[18] At the retirement village, elderly citizens drink Pepsi and party to a pastiche of Young MC's 1989 "Bust a Move" while discussing their affinities for rap and Jimmy Hendrix.[19] Meanwhile the frat house is shrouded in a unison string score that parodies Giacomo Puccini's "O mio bambino caro" and pictures students playing bingo, dozing off, and studying quietly while they sip Coke. The musical track drives home the message of Pepsi's superior coolness—a claim confirmed by the rhetorical play cue of a deliveryman who shrugs off the swap, saying, "Coke. Pepsi. What's the difference?"[20] Garfinkel confirmed that it was the "twist" offered by the dull music and images at the fraternity house that made the commercial funny.[21]

This spot is exemplary of the ways that musical humor has histor-ically relied on tactics similar to those of modern advertising—namely, caricatures and stereotypes—to effectively communicate ideological con-structs. Without the musical caricaturing of each genre in "Shady Acres," the humor would not work. Indeed, the signifiers have to align with commonly held ideas that tie each song's respective creators, performers, and audiences to specific demographic indicators. In this case, the spot's humor hinges largely on assumptions about age. For this reason, commu-nications scholar Bonnie Drewnainy critiques the stereotyping at play in "Shady Acres," concluding, "Pepsi uses out-of-touch imagery as a shortcut to depict rival Coca-Cola as old and boring. Pepsi is young and fun."[22] Moreover, as she later observes, it is not just the imagery at work but also the music. The conflicting musical styles thus most clearly articulate the commercial's message and confirm commonly held ideas that it would be unthinkable for senior citizens to appreciate (fun) rap and for college stu-dents to favor (boring) classical music. By correctly balancing the redacted musical styles—not using too much classical music nor employing overly loud or politically charged rap lyrics—the soundtrack carries the punch line. Drewnainy confirms that the message here only works by confirming stereotypes about lifestyle and musical tastes—a message that she warns is potentially damaging to all of Pepsi's generations.[23]

Beard's theories further illuminate the ways in which the spot's musical punch line relies specifically on "incongruity resolution" humor. In its underlying put-down of Coke and the elderly, it also reads as an example of "disparaging" humor—the kind that should come with moral reservations but does not. Beard defines this conundrum as "misattribution" and references Pepsi's commonplace use of disparaging humor, explaining that misattribution frees viewers from the ethical and social consequences of enjoying the spot. Put aptly, he notes that "none of us really feels personally responsible if Coca-Cola's feelings are hurt because Pepsi says only losers drink Coke" and "no one will probably think less of us if we laugh at an ad that says this."[24] In fact, market research has shown favor toward brands that are "feisty" in their competition with rivals.[25] Accordingly, Pepsi continued to use disparaging humor to establish its superiority throughout the decade, often earning considerable accolades from audiences and the ad industry.

Hip Hop Humor and MC Hammer

"The Switch," featuring MC Hammer (Stanley Kirk Burrell), was one of the final installments of the brand's long-running "The Choice of a New Generation" campaign. It packed both humor and contemporary popular music into a spot that featured a much harder sell than its predecessors. The commercial was reportedly filmed at the University of Tennessee and was scheduled to premiere around Thanksgiving of 1990.[26] "The Switch" was timed to follow the release of the rapper's *Please Hammer Don't Hurt 'Em*, an album that topped the charts worldwide.

"The Switch" works to capture the "eyeball-popping" energy for which the artist and his entourage were famous for putting into live shows.[27] In the 60-second version, the opening frames look more like a rap video than a commercial in their featuring of rough, and often blurry, disjunctive editing that immerses viewers into the liveliness of an exhilarated crowd watching a staged rap concert. The images alternate between black-and-white footage and full-color close-ups of the rap star wearing his signature baggy shirwal pants and gold chain necklace, while displaying his bare chest underneath a gold lamé jacket.[28] The camera also captures young fans mesmerized by the spectacle of lights, music, fashion, and dancing.

Although the commercial's images are metaphorically "loud," the music is not. The commercial features selected fragments of the title track to Hammer's 1988 album *Let's Get It Started*, and his rapped lines are mixed at a mid-level volume, likely to decrease the possibility of alienating viewers who might find hip hop unfamiliar or unappealing (table 6.1).[29] Hammer's polished sound, clean lyrics, and easy to follow flow—exemplified by his clear diction and structurally even phrases—make his Pepsi performance accessible to a wide range of audiences.

The spot's first scenes thus focus on Hammer and his posse as they execute athletic choreography over the song's rapped flow, forceful percussive backbeats, and accented horn lines. The track also reproduces one of the song's many samples—the syncopated bass groove from Rick James's once scandalous "Give It to Me Baby" (1981)—and it highlights the rhythmic scratching that had become an iconic signifier of the genre. In these first few seconds, marketers were therefore careful to present a family-friendly snapshot of hip hop culture while also featuring the ruptures, layering, and flow that African studies scholar Tricia Rose cites as essential to all facets of the genre, including the music, B Boy and B Girl dancing, and fashion pictured in the spot.[30] Fifteen seconds into the spectacle, a male narrator's voice enters the track to confirm its status as a commercial rather than a music video (table 6.1). The spokesman's precise pronunciation and bland yet commanding mid-range timbre sharply contrasts with Hammer's low tessitura and the melodic rhyming. Marketers must not have expected viewers to be as familiar with MC Hammer as with the cola's previous endorsers and therefore use this opportunity to formally introduce him as a "rap star" and "Pepsi drinker." Reminiscent of the brand's early 1980s "Pepsi Challenge" taste-test campaign, the narrator explains that Hammer's Pepsi has been switched for a Coke. He instructs viewers to follow along to "see what happens."

On cue, the rap star runs offstage for a quick soda break. After sipping the imposter's elixir he makes a strange facial expression and the camera captures an abrupt change in his demeanor. Confused and bewitched, Hammer emerges slowly onto the stage, visibly ignoring the bustle of high-energy dancers and music. Instead, he hesitantly lifts his microphone and begins to croon fragments of the first verse to Albert Morris's 1974 easy

Table 6.1. "The Switch" commercial form

Commercial Form	Song Redaction	Style	Performing Forces	Soda Brand / Feeling
Intro	"Let's Get It Started" Percussion only	Contemporary rap	*Crowd:* "Ham-mer" chant. *Percussion:* Rock beat. *Horns:* Pickup into verse.	Pepsi / excitement
Verse fragment and refrain	"Let's Get It Started" End of verse 2 and refrain	Contemporary rap	*Crowd:* Cheers. *Band:* Horns and percussion. *DJ:* "Give It to Me Baby" bass sample. *Hammer:* Rapping.	Pepsi / excitement
Chorus and narration	"Let's Get It Started" Chorus	Contemporary rap over narration	*Narrator:* Sets up the soda switch. *Crowd:* Cheers. *Band:* Horns and percussion. *DJ:* "Give It to Me Baby" sample and scratching. *Hammer:* Rapping. *Chorus response:* "You Know."	Pepsi / excitement
Bridge	"Feelings" Spliced fragments from verse 1	1970s easy listening ballad	*Hammer:* A cappella crooning. *Fan:* "Yo! Hammer." *Hammer:* "Proper."	Coke / shock and boredom
Chorus and outro	"Let's Get It Started" Chorus	Contemporary rap	*Crowd:* Cheers. *Band:* Horns and percussion. *DJ:* Scratching. *Hammer:* Rapping. *Chorus response:* "You Know."	Pepsi / excitement

Source: Transcribed from PepsiCo. Inc., 1990.

Fig. 6.1. A young fan offers MC Hammer a Pepsi. (Still from "The Switch," PepsiCo. Inc., 1990.)

listening hit "Feelings." His actions create a striking moment of musical incongruity, and the abrupt shift in style silences the crowd and causes the hip hop backing track to drop out (table 6.1). Everyone pictured onscreen stops cold, and the camera pans to various members of his band, dance troupe, and audience as they watch in disbelief. The star remains motionless, and he anxiously surveys their stunned faces while belting out an a cappella version of the mawkish tune. An exasperated gasp from the crowd prompts a young African American man to interrupt the offbeat performance and offer his idol the remedy: an ice cold Pepsi (fig. 6.1). One sip breaks the spell and allows the rapper to regain his hip hop swagger. Confirming that Pepsi has indeed helped him to regain his "cool," Hammer glances at the cup's logo and follows his sip with his signature catchphrase, "Proper." The musical track begins again with the hook to "Let's Get It Started" and the star resumes his rapping and aerobic dancing (table 6.1). The film's fast-paced editing is also reinstated, and the commercial closes to the sounds of a roaring crowd and rhythmic record scratching.

Hammer's spot takes direct aim at Pepsi's biggest competitor by using pre-existing tracks to communicate Pepsi's superiority and coolness. By juxtaposing the youthful and contemporary "Let's Get It Started" rap with the outdated middle-of-the-road tune "Feelings," the brand once again deploys disparaging humor to paint Coca-Cola as dull and square and Pepsi as lively and fun (table 6.1, see the final column). The redacted styles of each track are thereby mapped onto the corresponding brand: Pepsi is young, interesting, and active while Coke is old, boring, and slow. Sonically, these stereotypes are communicated through the contrasting lyrics and tempos and also by the opposing textures, performing forces, and vocal styles employed in each song.

As documented by Mickey Hess, Loren Kajikawa, and Charles Hiroshi Garrett, humor and parody have always been essential to hip hop performances and, as Garrett further notes, these tropes bled easily into advertising.[31] Pepsi's MC Hammer commercial thus logically followed its hip hop-themed "Shady Acres" spot (detailed above) to continue this trend. Accordingly, Hammer's "Let's Get It Started" works well to simultaneously support the commercial's narrative and its aim to project hipness and humor. More specifically, the refrain ("just put on the Hammer, and you will be rewarded. / My beat is ever boomin,' and you know I get it started") brags about the superiority of the rapper's music and the lasting influence of hip hop—qualities that marketers hoped would map easily onto the brand. Additionally, Hammer's encounter with Coke and momentary loss of coolness is cleverly interjected just after the first rapped statement of the hook ("Let's Get It Started"). The strategic placement of Hammer's sip of Coke with his performance of "Feelings" thus provides the humorous twist that works to heighten the strangeness of the sudden suspension of onscreen excitement; that is, it is the track's comic reference to a non-youth-oriented and dated musical style, as well as its positioning against contemporary rap, that makes it funny (table 6.1). The commercial delivers its final blow when Hammer's young fan intervenes with the Pepsi product. The literal insertion of the soda remedies the star and saves the performance by (re)starting the rap music.

A preferred reading might conclude that it is merely the historical distance between the two songs and their stylistic differences make them incompatible. An oppositional reading, however, reveals that there is more going on here; it is the depiction of racial and gendered codes embedded in the track—and more specifically the role of black masculinity, as it applies to the performance of hip hop—that drives home the spot's humor. As articulated by music philosopher Robin James, ideologies about race are intimately linked to other markers of identity, including gender.[32] In writing about how female rappers have operated within a male-dominated hip hop discourse, Tricia Rose argues that (like their male counterparts) women rappers "seize the public stage, demanding the audience's attention and winning their admiration. Their rhymes are embedded in an aggressive self-possessed identity that exudes confidence and power. Given this, rhymes that boast, signify, and toast are an important part of women rappers' repertoire."[33] Indeed, the foundation of Pepsi's commercial relies on establishing, momentarily thwarting, and then re-establishing the masculine-defined tenets of rap Rose describes: its demands, confidence, aggression, and power. At the commercial's outset, Hammer exemplifies these traits. He boasts about his ability to entertain ("get it started"), and his track employs obvious tropes from previous African American performers to signify his lineage (with record scratching, prominent horn lines, and sampling). Consequently, it is the loss of these markers of "confidence" and "identity"—the switch to Morris's sappy ballad—that temporarily forfeits his audience's "attention" and "admiration" and drives Pepsi's message home. The humor then comes only partially from the fact that he's singing an out-of-date song but is ultimately confirmed with the implication that switching Hammer's Pepsi for a Coke makes the singer sentimental—and therefore more feminine—as he drops the rapper's bravado, as well as the "athleticism, sexuality, and physical aggression" that musicologist Loren Kajikawa notes are central to the stereotypes of black masculinity often reflected in rap.[34] Drinking a Coke thus causes Hammer to sing a mournful, minor-key ballad about "feelings" that makes him appear vulnerable and confused. Hammer's black male fan comes to the rescue when he recognizes this loss of composure and swagger. The Pepsi soda therefore literally reinvigorates the black masculinity of the superstar, and it allows him to recapture the crowd's admiration by resuming his physically demanding, sexual choreography and confirming his ability not only to get it (re)started but to finish the show with the same commanding bravado with which he began it.

Hammer's Mixed Reception

According to a 2016 online retrospective, "The Switch" represented a landmark moment for the national recognition of hip hop music.[35] It was also, however, severely criticized by respected hip hop artists who questioned MC Hammer's authenticity in both the commercial and in real life. Indeed, as the star's new album was taking its place as one of the best-selling hip hop records of all time, it was clear that, much like the crossover Run-D.M.C. had achieved with white rock fans in the mid-1980s, Hammer, too, was bringing rap to mainstream audiences. Furthermore, Hammer had established a reputation as a healthy and disciplined entertainer and was even rumored to ban alcohol on his tours (save for designated parties) and to fine his entourage for onstage mistakes.[36] While Pepsi likely found that these qualities made him a positive role model, his pop sound, elaborate stage shows, and clean image attracted criticism from his contemporaries. Moreover, despite hip hop's long history of corporate endorsements—including Kurtis Blow's early 1980s deal with Sprite and Run D.M.C.'s 1986 single "My Adidas"—Hammer's deals with Pepsi and its KFC and Taco Bell franchises, as well as his production of a children's doll and his Saturday morning cartoon show, were viewed as overkill and as consumerist ploys.[37]

Notably, contemporary criticism of Hammer did not center on ideologies about "selling out" as it had been defined by white, counterculture rock enthusiasts. As author and music critic Dan Charnas explains, "making it" in hip hop actually included securing lucrative corporate endorsement deals. The problem was that Hammer's music did not seem "authentic" or "credible" enough to truly be considered hip hop, and his endorsements for Pepsi furthered this perception.[38] According to Charnas, many East Coast rappers and fans admonished Hammer for his extensive use of sampling, repetitive family-friendly lyrics, lack of flow, and showmanship. His background as an athlete and Navy soldier also contradicted the experiences of oppression, poverty, and street life that were central to the message of many hip hop songs. More generally, his catchy tracks seemed to lack creativity. Hammer was therefore critiqued for being too commercial in the sense that his message was intended to reach the widest possible audience with the broadest message, and insiders knew that this included reaching the white middle-class audiences that the pop industry had catered to by exploiting black musicians for over a century. So, despite Hammer's use of the most basic elements of hip hop—rapping, DJing, B boying/breaking, signifying, scratching, and sampling—his polished, non-edgy, and nonpolitical style came across to many as not "black" enough. Charnas quotes one of the most influential hip hop magazines of the era, The Source, as bemoaning Hammer's success, perceiving him not as a hip hop idol but a "singing and dancing minstrel."[39] Charnas summarizes these sentiments and links Hammer's reception to that of Vanilla Ice, his fellow chart topper of the moment, writing, "It was hard to imagine a worse fate for the culture. Except, of course, if that minstrel were White."[40] Hammer's perceived "blackness" was thus under debate in real life despite Pepsi's attempt to confirm it in the commercial.

Moreover, as disgruntled hip hop fans had pointed out, Pepsi did not help Hammer's image as the brand appeared overly conservative in its approach to the genre. The degree to which hip hop could be faithfully and effectively represented in commercials was not demonstrated until four years later when Sprite (a Coke subsidiary) found a way to avoid media criticism while maintaining the genre's core audiences. Spearheaded by junior brand manager and hip hop aficionado Darryl Corbin, Sprite's 1994 "Obey Your Thirst" campaign featured some of the most prolific but least mainstream DJs and Emcees—artists like Pete Rock, CL Smooth, Grand Puba, and Large Professor.[41] Sprite's initial hip hop campaign criticized the "hype" of endorsements by celebrities like MC Hammer and assured audiences that "Image is Nothing."[42] Corbin's vision for maintaining the credibility of the artists he hired was realized because he allowed their music and imagery to operate outside the traditional expectations of brands, marketing agencies, and the media. Sprite's commercials therefore often had the gritty look of the harrowing inner city streets and studios where hip hop thrived. Moreover, unlike MC Hammer's measured and polished Pepsi performance, Sprite's artists were allowed to freestyle, use slang, and make insider references in their flow. The spontaneous look and sound of Sprite's "Obey Your Thirst" commercials confirmed the talent and authenticity of the artists featured. They also highlighted Sprite's support of the genre on a national stage (and ultimately that of its Coca-Cola parent company), proving that hip hop was worthy of respect and attention.

Sprite's sales skyrocketed not just when "urban" consumers—African Americans and Latinos—favored the lemon-lime drink but, as confirmed by both Charnas and Taylor, when white youth also literally bought into its campaigns, propelling its sales beyond both Pepsi's and Coke's signature sodas.[43] Sprite's commercials thus seemed to uphold hip hop's authenticity by focusing on the virtuosity of its DJs and MCs and relocating it back to the streets where it started. This contrasted significantly with Pepsi's glitzy and staged MC Hammer commercial—a text that did not differentiate the genre from the brand's other pop music spots. Furthermore, Sprite did not use hip hop to execute humor for the gains of parity rivalry but instead outsold its competitors by representing its legitimacy. Put another way, for hip hop fans, Pepsi's use of Hammer's music made no real claim to their culture while Sprite gave them the "real thing." Sprite's direct approach to incorporating hip hop would therefore maintain the beverage's credibility with the genre's elite well into the twenty-first century.[44]

When asked about the circulating criticisms of his Pepsi commercials, MC Hammer responded frankly:

> The money they give me, that doesn't tell the whole story. What's going on is pushing the image of MC Hammer to another level. I have found Pepsi to be astute professionals, and they've shown me they are really good at marketing. They have also contributed to my foundation for helping the children, and they also have some things they do with children. There are other corporations in this world who don't do anything for other people.[45]

For Hammer, then, it was Pepsi's promised philanthropy, as well as its vast marketing reach, that made the deal lucrative. Indeed, his album continued to dominate the charts in both the United States and abroad, eventually selling 20 million copies worldwide.[46] "The Switch" thus helped to keep *Please Hammer Don't Hurt 'Em* in the top 10 on the US *Billboard* charts for the next four and a half months. So, despite the skepticism of those in hip hop's inner circles, Hammer's mainstream success confirmed that music and humor were a winning formula.

Old Songs and New Tricks

Once the brand's "The Choice of a New Generation" slogan had run its course, Pepsi would change the venue in which it premiered its biggest pop music commercials. By 1991 the brand elected to reach broader audiences by shifting away from the music industry's televised Grammy Awards shows to what would become America's premiere televised sporting event—the Super Bowl. Rather than catering to lovers of the latest musical hits—typically younger audiences—it moved its advertising to target an all-ages crowd of (mostly male) sports aficionados and those interested in watching the event for its commercials—a trend that gained momentum in the 1990s. At the end of the decade, Pepsi would also premiere a new commercial during the Academy Awards television broadcast. To cater to the diversity of these new audiences, the brand had to change its endorsement content and raise the stakes on the kind of humor it would use. As a result, marketers noticeably employed more direct and sometimes shocking disparagement and arousal safety humor to keep viewers in their seats during the commercial breaks. Although popular music continued to provide the brand with compelling comic material, some of its most successful 1990s spots forewent musical celebrity appearances in favor of showcasing recorded versions or diegetic remakes of older songs and styles.

Many of Pepsi's most memorable 1990s commercials continued to take direct aim at Coke and used musical humor to suggest the disloyalty of the latter's employees. "Diner" (1995) is a fitting example as it was selected as a One Show winner and took second place in *USA Today's* Super Bowl *Ad Meter* ratings.[47] The spot features the late-night encounter of Pepsi and Coke deliverymen who have stopped to rest at a roadside restaurant. Their waitress cues up a record featuring the late 1960s anthem, "Get Together" by The Youngbloods, and the track works to suggest that the two men should put aside their soda differences and be friendly.[48] Predictably, each one admits his affinity for the song, and they move closer together to enjoy a late-night snack, talk, and share a laugh. The camaraderie is broken, however, when they offer one another a sip of their employers' sodas but the Coke representative refuses to give back the Pepsi offered to him. A third repetition of the chorus's plea for "brothers" to "come together" provides humorous incongruity to the final cut to a street view that captures images of breaking windows as the men brawl inside. The campaign's "Nothing Else Is Pepsi" slogan is superimposed over the diner and the commotion that accompanies the peaceful 1960s track.

Here the slogan and the men's physical aggression work to reinforce two of the three mechanisms of humor present in the spot: disparagement (Pepsi tastes better than Coke) and arousal safety (they fight each other for the Pepsi). However, the redaction of the "Get Together" lyrics to fit the onscreen visuals creates the third mechanism—incongruity humor—, which transforms the song into a "comic text" for the spot. Accordingly, the peaceful lyrics sound nonsensical in their narration of the fight, thus breaking the tension onscreen.

Another acclaimed Super Bowl spot called "Dancing Bears" (1997) takes a different approach with its parody of National Geographic's nature documentaries.[49] The spot begins with a monotone narrator who details how California residents witness the annual "coming of age of the adolescent Grizzly Bear." The spot then pans to five bears wandering through a town as the narrator explains that this ritual represents one of the last "vestiges of cubhood" in which they cry out for their "most primal urgent need." The narrated track drops out once the bears line up, single-file in front of a beverage store. Unexpectedly, the syncopated horn lines from The Village People's disco classic "Y.M.C.A." takes over the track.[50] The bears proceed to stand upright and dance to a reworked chorus that spells out "P-E-P-S-I." As the bears groove to the music, an elderly man wheels them a dolly full of soda and hurries back into the shop. Stunned townspeople watch the bears from a distance as one man utters, "Heaven help us if they learn the Macarena."

Humor in the "Dancing Bears" spot occurs on many levels, including the incongruity of the serious opening narration and juxtaposition of the unexpected diegetic performance of the redacted disco hit. As a parody of a well-known piece, it is also hard to miss the campy comedy of the music in the spot—especially as the vehicle for a queer depiction of the bears' ritual of homosocial bonding that leads into their performance as "dancing queens." Although "Y.M.C.A." was certainly a staple at heterosexual wedding receptions at the time, the commercial's innuendo about the bears' desire to exercise their "most primal urgent need"—its arousal safety humor—works with the original artists', song's, and genre's links to the gay community, to make a queer reading of the "Generation Next" subtext inevitable. Despite (or perhaps because of) its queer undertones, "Dancing Bears" ranked as the number-one commercial by the Super Bowl *Ad Meter* that year.

Following Pepsi's brief foray into its "Generation Next" campaign (whose most famous spot featured the globally acclaimed British pop group The Spice Girls), the brand returned to all-ages comedy with its "Joy of Cola" slogan.[51] In these spots, the curly-haired and dimpled child star Hallie Eisenberg captivated audiences by playing a character known for lip-syncing to an overdub of gangster voices from *The Godfather* trilogy each time she was denied a Pepsi. In 1999 Pepsi swapped Eisenberg's gangster shtick for a conjuring of Aretha Franklin's soul style.[52] As the first Pepsi spot ever to premiere during the Academy Awards, it follows Eisenberg as she enters a diner with her grandfather.[53] A server who had received the wrath of the child in previous commercials quickly offers her a Pepsi to avoid hearing one of her "crazy voices." Eisenberg replies with an overdub of Franklin's voice, saying, "Honey, you ain't heard nothing yet." She then jumps on the bar to perform an elaborate and fantastical lip-syncing routine to Franklin's "Joy of Cola" jingle. The performance is completed with miniature African American backup singers, an Afro-haired drummer, and an entourage of dancers. When Franklin-via-Eisenberg hits a high-pitched melisma, the camera unexpectedly pans to the soul queen herself as she appears to be enjoying the performance from a booth.

Franklin exclaims, "You Go Girl!," after which the spot transitions to the "Joy of Cola" logo and a knowing wink from Eisenberg.

Historian Kennell Jackson reads this spot as emblematic of the kinds of black vocal shadowing that had become prominent in 1990s advertising.[54] Indeed, Franklin's soul music style is redacted and made humorous here not just for its reference to past musical eras but for misappropriating her voice to a girl whose age and race create incongruity humor. The caricatured, lip-synced performance of 1960s black soul music by a 1990s white girl is heightened further when the camera rhetorically pans to the very celebrity whose voice is reassigned. Like Pepsi's other humorous spots, this one relies on familiar musical tropes to create comedy by reinforcing existing cultural stereotypes and ideologies. More specifically, in redacting the most prevalent signifiers from soul music in general and Franklin's oeuvre in particular—vocal melismas, syncopation, back-up vocals, and so on—marketers recontextualize musical tropes not humorous on their own, allowing them to take on a comedic reading on the terms of the brand. Put simply, the mid-century soul style that was once loaded with messages of subjectivity for African Americans—and specifically for black women—loses that message and is made comical through the funneling of its signifiers through the soda commodity.

Robin James argues that "'cultural appropriation' is never merely the appropriation of culture, but also of sexuality, class, gender and the like."[55] Pepsi's humorous 1990s commercials exemplify her claims as they rely on the appropriation of music from various stereotyped demographic groups—aging boomers, the working class, the gay community, and black hip hop and soul musicians. In the spots described above, it is obvious that each joke depends on a common cultural understanding of and proficiency with signifiers of difference not only between visual markers that distinguish people from one another but also with the musical codes and communities that both make and consume them. Humor in these commercials thus comes from the role the music takes on to distinguish and defer marginalized cultures from the mainstream. Put another way, it separates Pepsi drinkers from those who consume Coca-Cola. Indeed, advertising scholar Linda C. L. Fu confirms that in many advertisements "the self *needs* the Other in order to have meaning."[56] So no matter how viewers might identify themselves—as the hegemonic self or marginalized Other—by including multiple perspectives, Pepsi promises to (continue to) give its consumers access to musics from African American, women, countercultural, and LGBTQ+ communities.

PART 2: PORTALS INTO MUSIC'S PAST—NOSTALGIC LONGING AND RETRO HUMOR

Turning to the past is a typical reaction to anxieties about the future. It is not surprising, then, that as the twentieth century came to a close, nostalgic texts proliferated in popular culture. Indeed, pop nostalgia permeated much of the entertainment industry as it returned its focus to baby boomers and efforts to recapture their youth with specialized radio formats like "classic rock," fictional historical films such as *Forrest Gump*, and reflective television shows like *The Wonder Years* and VH1's (Video Hits One) *Legends*. The music industry also reinvested in music by former rock stars and hyped releases of unpublished material (such as the Beatles *Anthology*) and new albums (including Eric Clapton's *Unplugged*).

The soda giant, too, became interested again in catering to its original "Pepsi generation" and found nostalgia to be just as effective as humor in appealing to audiences of all ages. As outlined in chapter 1's discussion of the "Now and Then" spot featuring Britney Spears, nostalgic texts are intimately tied to a longing for a different *time*.[57] As Dwyer reminds us, "Nostalgia is the product of an affective engagement with the present that produces a sense of loss. Whether that loss is real or perceived is not the point. The point is that we find something lacking in our current conditions."[58] He further finds it necessary to recognize nostalgia as a "critical affective response" to popular culture's texts—an idea that extends well to some of Pepsi's 1990s spots.

A full decade before Pepsi created "Now and Then," it launched a 1993 campaign with Michael Jackson that exemplified how deploying elements of nostalgia could be used to promote commodified "critical affective responses" to American pop music texts. More specifically, this campaign demonstrated how effective musical redaction could be in creating nostalgia. Just as the process of redaction can alter perceptions of a song's teleology through the fragmentation and rearrangement of its structures (as demonstrated in chapter 4), so, too, can redacted musics successfully mirror the experience of nostalgic longing in their production of fragmented perceptions of time and space.

Accordingly, the soda giant's final campaign with Michael Jackson would bring their co-branding relationship full circle with two commercials that perhaps most fully realized the creative potential for translating the pop video spectacle into corporate advertising contexts. Unlike the other commercials discussed in this chapter, marketers upheld the aesthetic precedents that they had established with Jackson in the mid-1980s—those that they had so rigorously pursued for much of the decade. As with Jackson's two previous Pepsi deals (detailed in chapters 2 and 4), his commercials were intended to promote his newest album *Dangerous* and his accompanying Pepsi-sponsored tour.[59] According to executives, the campaign remained consistent with the image of the long-running "The Choice of a New Generation" campaigns that continued to run overseas.[60]

The first commercial, titled "Dreams," directly transferred Jackson's music video imagery and redacted sections of his new single, "Who is It?," into a spot that circulated on MTV. It was the brand's second commercial, however, that proved most innovative with its nostalgic reflection back to Jackson's fame as a child star. This big-budget spot premiered during the 1993 Super Bowl, although only in overseas markets.[61] Named after the Jackson 5's 1970s hit "I'll Be There," the commercial begins with the King of Pop sitting alone at a piano.[62] The Pepsi commodity allows his memories of touring with his brothers to produce a vision of his childhood self. Intimate pictures of him and his family interweave with performance footage of the five youngsters. Jackson's diegetic performance of fragments to "I'll Be There" support the nostalgic images. Ghostly echoes of a synthesized string track and Jackson's twelve-year-old prepubescent voice eventually merge into a full-fledged duet between him and an apparition of his former self (table 6.2).

Unlike Pepsi's largely fictional tale of nostalgia in its "Make a Wish" commercial with Madonna (discussed in chapter 5), "I'll Be There" uses real historical footage to reflect on Jackson's talent and legacy—a legacy that Pepsi hopes, by now, has been firmly anchored to its brand. The commercial aims for a commodified reading in its disruption of the song's usual temporal unfolding. Fragments of Jackson's performance in the present are thus interspersed with the (added) distant instrumental phrases and clips from his past vocals (table 6.2). These ruptures create nostalgic fractures through which the cola can insert its fiction into the nonfictional relics onscreen. The interweaving of Jackson's multiple voices across time and space here functions analogously with what Jason Stanyek and Benjamin Peikut have termed "the intermundane."[63] Like their reading of the "Unforgettable" duet between Natalie Cole and her late father, Nat King Cole, Pepsi's "I'll Be There" offers a compelling example of late-capitalism's perpetual labor potential—one that is available even after a person is deceased, or in this case when age renders a young body and its prepubescent vocal timbre forever gone. The recording technology and human laborers that make these interactions possible therefore create what the authors refer to as "deadness," "the decisive patterning of inter-

Table 6.2. Pepsi's nostalgic redaction of Michael Jackson's past

"I'll Be There" Commercial Form

Piano intro and grown Jackson vocals:
Melismatic "mmm-hmm," "yeah"

Grown Jackson at piano:
First two phrases of verse 2:
"I'll reach out . . ." / "I'll have faith . . ."

Synthesized string track:
Cuts off refrain/hook and paces slowly between I and iii (2x, 4 mm)

Grown Jackson at piano:
Repetition of the same phrases:
"I'll reach out . . ." / "I'll have faith . . ."

Synthesized string track:
Cuts off refrain/hook and paces slowly between I and iii (2x, 4 mm)

Child Jackson:
Interjects with "Just call my name" and the refrain/hook

Grown Jackson at piano:
Responds with "ooh" and "yeah" and piano comping

Grown Jackson and child Jackson:
Mostly unison duet of verse 3 with refrain/hook:
"Let me fill your heart . . ."

Grown Jackson at piano:
Melismatic "ooh"

Child Jackson:
Distant sounding refrain/hook

Grown Jackson at piano:
"Ooh. I'll, I'll be there" punctuated by the tonic chord in the piano

Note: Transcribed from "I'll Be There," PepsiCo. Inc., 1993.

mundanity based upon ever-replenishable value, ever-resurrectable labor, ever-revertible production processes."[64] In reworking Jackson's preteen vocals to fit the newly arranged duet with his mature voice—notably, a painstaking feat—Pepsi's marketers demonstrated the creative and financial potential of deadness and the intermundane across media formats.

The nostalgic affect produced by this careful redactive process thus proved fundamental to the commercial's aims. Boym notes "the nostalgic desires to obliterate history and return to private or collective mythology, to revisit time like space, refusing to surrender the irreversibility of time that plagues the human condition."[65] Indeed, this spot ignores Pepsi's true historical relationship with Jackson as an endorser of a product he never consumed—a fact of which audiences were now well aware—and instead reimagines the soda as always a part of his iconicity. "I'll Be There" thus returns to the mythology of Jackson as a genius child star and uses real photos and footage to revisit his past while picturing him in the commodity's present space. In this way Pepsi provides its own nostalgic lens through which fans can exalt him as a past and present musical superstar. The purpose here is therefore just as Stanyek and Peikut assert: to "recapitalize the stored star power of [the] residual, spectral celebrity"—a goal that is multiplied by dual re-presentations of Jackson onscreen.[66]

Unfortunately for Pepsi, the public narrative that circulated about Jackson prior to the commercial's release confirms that the brand's intentions once again fell prey to its star's tabloid reputation. As it turned out, blending Jackson's past and present vocals was not the only hurdle facing the spot's creators—of equal concern was how the young apparition of Jackson would *look* after the star had undergone decades of rumored surgeries and skin whitening. This predicament caught the attention of the press, which zeroed in on it. Well ahead of the commercial's release, international media circulated headlines that read, "Michael Jackson Picks White Boy to Play Him" and "Jacko Was a White Baby!"[67] These were followed by reports that the star had replaced the black child originally chosen for the spot with a fair-skinned kid from Australia.[68] Press releases noted that the boy wore an "Afro wig" and his skin was "darkened by video colorization"—practices that were disguised by the low lighting in the spot. Pepsi's executives vaguely sidestepped the story, saying, "We're using techniques to most accurately portray the best of Michael Jackson from yesterday to today."[69]

Going against Pepsi's intentions for the spot, concerns about blackness and whiteness became central to the commercial's reception. Questions about whether a black man was made white or a white child was made black overtook the narrative for a text that used nostalgic longing not only to "obliterate history," as Boym would confirm, but also, as Dwyer suggests (and mentioned in chapter 1), to "remake the present, or at least to imagine corrective alternatives to it." A negotiated reading of the spot might have thus recognized Pepsi's attempt to resolve the tensions of Jackson's current reputation—in this instance, the ambiguities of race (as well as his gender and sexuality, as discussed in chapter 4)—with reverence for his talent as a "once-great" performer. The spot communicated this through the musical and vocal redactions that blended the past and present and also through the visual reworking of the superficial and ideological markers of race that haunted the superstar. But, as an echo of speculation about how Jackson wished to be perceived, the commercial unintentionally plugged his labors and successes as a black child star into a white boy's body, who, in turn, was dressed in blackface. Dwyer asserts, "Once we understand nostalgia as an affective response to representations of the past, we can understand that an array of nostalgic affect can be generated in response to any single pop-nostalgia text."[70] So, in addition to (or perhaps instead of) the preferred celebratory reading of his past, these practices created an oppositional one—a nostalgic reflection of loss for a superstar who had fallen from the height of his fame.

The partnership between the brand and superstar was further overshadowed by various scandals, including Jackson's abrupt cancellation of his tour in order to treat his addiction to painkillers, as well as the child molestation allegations brought against him.[71] As a result, Pepsi would sever its ties with Jackson, ending their mutually fruitful, yet rollercoaster of a 10-year relationship.

Although this particular deal garnered bad press for the brand, it was still riding the success of its relationship with another iconic star—one who had successfully weathered personal and public controversies many decades before and was looking to make a comeback while singing Pepsi's praises. The brand's most successful campaign of the 1990s would not be for its signature cola, nor would it be directed to the teen and 20-something market. It would instead be a multiyear Diet Pepsi campaign that employed the perfect combination of retro gospel and R&B tropes with musical humor to captivate an all-ages audience while venerating Ray Charles (Robinson) as a hip and legendary soda-swigging "genius."[72]

Ray Charles Sings for Diet Pepsi

Retro is closely related to nostalgia, but according to Dwyer their distinction comes in how they are used: retro is a "representational mode," whereas nostalgia is a "critical affective response."[73] Simon Reynolds further defines retro as

> a self-conscious fetish for period stylization (in music, clothes, and design) expressed creatively through pastiche and citation. Retro in its strict sense tends to be the preserve of aesthetes, connoisseurs and collectors, people who possess a near-scholarly depth of knowledge combined with a sharp sense of irony.[74]

A closer look at Ray Charles's early 1990s Diet Pepsi commercials reveals how the brand expertly redacted his iconic style to create retro pastiches and citations that reimagined deep historical connections between the celebrity performer and the product. This connection was further reinforced through the use of musical humor inserted in two of the campaign's early spots.

A feature on WNYW News captured the immense success of Charles's campaign as well as the respect the public afforded the 61-year-old soul music pioneer. Reporter Pablo Guzman begins the feature story by asking, "Yo! What's the hottest piece of music on the air today?" The clip segues to MC Hammer's video for "U Can't Touch This," but after a few seconds the newscaster swipes it aside. saying, "No Way Homeboy! Move over brother, and let a *man* come in." After a brief preview of Charles's newest Diet Pepsi spot, Guzman calls it "the catchiest song being broadcast anywhere" and reports that it had "gone from a TV spot to its own place in pop culture."[75]

The "catchy song" to which Guzman referred was the new jingle that Charles sang in Diet Pepsi spots that ran from 1991 to 1993. The news clip focused on "Orchestra," the retro-styled first commercial in the series.[76] It pictured a tuxedo-clad Charles singing at the piano. He was accompanied by a backup band and the lip-synched stylings of the Uh-huh Girls (a stand-in trio for his famous backup singers, the Raeletts).[77] In hiring Charles, Pepsi likely intended to take a dig at Coca-Cola since the soul singer had been one of its key spokespersons in the 1960s.[78] Moreover, the

USP, "You've Got the Right One, Baby/Uh-huh," bordered close enough to its rival's "Real Thing" motto that it effectively slowed Coke's momentum.[79]

As the news clip alluded, Pepsi's new slogan would become the catch-phrase of the 1990s. When the first promos premiered during Super Bowl XXV in 1991, they took three of the top four positions in viewer polls.[80] The following year *Time* magazine would retrospectively name the campaign number one.[81] Audiences in fact loved the commercials so much that they took on a life of their own. "Uh-huh" references were made in movies and on television, fans wore t-shirts bearing the slogan, Charles and the Uh-huh Girls made mall appearances, President George W. Bush Sr. used the phrase when debating rival Michael Dukakis, and in April 1992 the brand sent 100 million cases of its product to Diet Coke drinkers to prove its superiority during what it called the "Uh-Huh month."[82] Moreover, the success of its third spot, titled "Audition," prompted Pepsi to wander into experiential advertising practices by encouraging audiences to send in their own versions of the jingle for a chance to appear in a commercial and win a $10,000 prize—a challenge that unexpectedly drew 4,000 entries.[83] At the height of the campaign's popularity, Pepsi also sponsored a television special devoted to Charles, which featured a lineup of famous acts that paid tribute to his career.[84]

Prior to the campaign's air date, WLS Chicago offered a sneak peek and noted that the Super Bowl battle that would really count was between the advertisers.[85] The newscast correctly predicted that Charles's commercials would beat their rivals. It also reported that production costs had topped $10 million and Charles had been paid nearly $1 million (a sum considerably less than those earned by 1980s era endorsers). News clips also included a personal interview in which Charles boasted about the recognition he had received from these endorsements, saying that the commercials had allowed him to raise "three or four sets of generations"—not coincidently, the demographic breadth that Pepsi too hoped to attract. The campaign's instant popularity was featured in various media outlets, including a recap of Super Bowl highlights by the nationally syndicated television show *Good Morning America*.[86]

"Orchestra"

Charles's endorsement came at a time when he was working on a musical comeback and had just released *Would You Believe?* on his new label, Warner Brothers. Deviating from the norm Pepsi had established with its "The

Choice of a New Generation" spots, marketers for this campaign chose not to feature any of Charles's pre-existing music. They instead created a retro jingle that cited and pastiched musical tropes from his early 1960s hits. As a result, the musical score quickly became the highlight of the campaign—so much so that during the WNYW story cited above, considerable time was devoted to featuring the marketing firm and the composers it had hired, Sunday Productions' Peter Cofield and Alfred Merrin. During the interview Cofield admitted, "The task was to create a song that Ray could relate to, and all his styles. I mean, he sings so many things so well."[87] The remainder of the interview focused on the music in the "Orchestra" spot—the only commercial in which the full version of the jingle appeared. Cofield demonstrated that its various sections imitated "Georgia on My Mind," "What'd I Say," and "That Lucky Old Sun" (see table 6.3).

As illustrated in table 6.3, "Orchestra" incorporates the unique blend of African American gospel, R&B, and jazz characteristics that had made Charles (in)famous in the late 1950s and early 1960s. Thirty-six years after his controversial 1965 "I Got a Woman" introduced black gospel traditions to white audiences, Pepsi's 1991 spot took viewers back to his roots—this time with a cola twist that hinges on the catchphrase, "Uh-huh." "Orchestra," thus reimagines what his early performances of soul music—his unification of the sacred with the secular—might look and sound like if Diet Pepsi were the inspiration. More specifically, the commercial presents a staged retro mini-revival for the soda commodity. Charles obviously acts as the "church's" leader (a fitting role for his many monikers, "High Priest of Soul," "Brother Ray," and "Righteous Reverend Ray"), and his recognizable yet commanding vocal timbre provides guidance, just as it does on his albums. The grandeur of the retro-revival setting is represented by a large band and orchestra, a female African American vocal trio, and a full chorus line of slim, white female dancers in gold lamé (fig. 6.2). Other than its references to Diet Pepsi, the scenario is not much of a stretch but a pastiche of Charles's performance history.

As demonstrated in table 6.3, the commercial's musical score borrows considerably from gospel idioms in its deployment of abrupt changes in tempo, style, and texture, as well as its frequent use of call-and-response, repeated refrains that praise the superiority of the commodity, and stop-time rhythmic recitations that work to describe its glory. Fluctuations between the flat and natural third (B and B♭) harken to Charles's roots in jazz and blues and allow the track to make sudden transitions to new sec-

Table 6.3. "Orchestra" musical form

Jingle Form	Performing Forces and Lyrics	Characteristics
Intro and verse (Borrowed from "Georgia on My Mind")	<u>Charles solo vocal and piano:</u> You know when it's right . . .	• Rhythm and blues/jazz chords • Languishing vocal delivery • G Major
Transition 1	<u>Backup vocals, band, and piano:</u> Diet Pe-psi.	• Four-note descending line • Accelerando
Hook with refrain (Borrowed from "What'd I Say")	<u>Backup vocals and band:</u> Uh-huh . . . <u>Charles at piano:</u> You got the right one, ba-b-ae . . .	• Rock/pop • Up-tempo • Vocal sliding
Transition 2	<u>Backup vocals, band, and piano:</u> Diet Pe-psi.	• Four-note figure and dominant turn
Bridge recitation 1 with refrain	<u>Backup vocals, band, and horn:</u> Suspended Oooo <u>Charles at piano:</u> If it's irresistibly sippable . . . You got the right one, ba-by.	• Gospel vocal suspension • G minor • Horns punctuate beat three • Rubato • Stop-time scatting down most of a blues scale to G/B♭
Response	<u>Backup vocals:</u> Uh-huh!	• Cadence
Chorus refrain and hook	<u>Full chorus, saxophone, strings, and band:</u> "You've got the right one ba-by."	• Jazz/gospel chorus • Key change to G Major • Horn hits
Verse 1 variation (Borrowed from "That Lucky Old Sun")	<u>Charles at piano:</u> You know when it's ri-ght . . .	• Up-tempo • Tin Pan Alley • Big band
Partial refrain with product name	<u>Full chorus, band, and strings:</u> You've got . . . Diet Pep-si. <u>Charles at piano:</u> Oh Yeah . . . Alright.	• Gospel chorus • Call-and-response
Hook repetition	<u>Charles, backup vocals, band, piano, and strings:</u> Uh-huh.	• Gospel call-and-response

Brief refrain with hook	Charles at piano: You've got . . . Chorus, band, and strings: Uh-huh . . .	• Soulful belting • Gospel call-and-response
Bridge recitation 2 with refrain	Backup vocals and horns: Suspended "Oooo" Charles: If it's ir-refreshably lovable . . . You've got . . .	• Gospel vocal suspension • Rubato • Stop-time scatting down most of a blues scale to G/B♭
Hook	Backup trio, band, strings, and chorus: Uh-Huh!	• Gospel response • Cadence

Note: Transcribed from PepsiCo. Inc., 1991.

tions that could be redacted even further for shorter versions of the spot. A closer analysis of "Orchestra" thus reveals how the fragmentation, citation, and rearrangement of the star's most recognizable styles offers viewers a retro rehearing of his music through this new product-focused setting.

The spot begins with Charles delivering Pepsi's first verse in a backlit, blue hazy room. He sings, "You know when it's right, / you know when you feel it, baby," as his face is superimposed with the hips of one of his backup dancers—a technique alluding to the sexy and slim body that the reduced-calorie soda claims to help its drinkers maintain. Arpeggiated, bluesy chords continue to accompany the next phrase, which is composed in the style of Charles's 1960 cover of "Georgia on My Mind" (table 6.3). The product's name is then highlighted by the entrance of the backup vocals and accompanied with an accelerating chordal descent (See transition 1 in table 6.3). After featuring close-ups of the product, the camera suddenly cuts to new images of a tuxedo-clad Charles surrounded by an entourage of performers. The up-tempo rock/pop energy borrowed from his 1960, "What'd I Say" enters next, and the reference to Charles's iconic song is completed with a flirtatious call-and-response between the star and his lip-syncing backup trio (table 6.3). Not coincidentally, Merrin and Cofield place the most memorable parts of the jingle on this exchange (the "Uh-huh" hook and "You've Got the Right One Baby" refrain), framing it by again calling out the product name—this time with a unexpected deceleration and

Fig. 6.2. Ray Charles jams with the "Uh-huh" girls. (Still from "Orchestra," PepsiCo. Inc., 1991.)

melodic skip down to the dominant (transition 2 in table 6.3). By bookending the "What'd I Say"–style slogan with the varying musical emphases on the product name, the composers not only effectively draw attention to the sales pitch, but sonically solidify the relationship between the commodity and Charles's legacy.

The musical track then shifts to a stop-time recitation that illuminates the wonder of the product in G minor. Reminiscent of rhythmic recitations used by clergymen, Charles's rubato scatting moves down a blues scale and is supported by a halo of backing vocal "Ooos." He teaches us that "If it's irresistibly sippable, uncontestably tasteable, and imminently wonderful" then "You've got the right one, baby" (bridge recitation 1 in table 6.3). The ensuing "Uh-huh" provides a strong cadence on the G tonic, giving a satisfying confirmation to Charles's brief sermon.

A saxophone solo then follows to lead the track into an up-tempo bridge. The melody moves up a step to create climactic energy, thereby removing the flat third (B♭) and moving back into to G major. The full chorus belts out "You've got the right one baby," adding even more power to the key change as it reiterates Charles's message. He follows by repeating some of the spot's opening lines in the crooning style of "That Lucky Old

Sun."[88] The choir then splices part of the refrain ("You've Got") with the product name ("Di-et Pepsi.") This pushes to a second climax with a call-and-response on "Uh-huh" on the seventh degree (F). Melodic relief is provided by another stop-time sermon on a descending blues scale. The spot finally ends on a sung iteration of "Uh-huh" that finishes on the G tonic.

Musically, "Orchestra's" style is clean, comfortable, and catchy. Marketers redact the most familiar parts of not just Charles's signature style but also a lineage that goes back through earlier mainstream American musics: the Tin Pan Alley and big band sounds pastiched in "That Lucky Old Sun," as well as the African American styles outlined above. It is, however, the spot's prevalent use of gospel tropes that most effectively draws in its listeners. The song's passion is communicated by the call-and-response, repeated refrains, rhythmic recitations, and constant tensions and releases aided by changes in tempo, melody, and intensity. These redacted traits are complimented with a grand and retro Hollywood set where the implied "religious" devotion is afforded to the soda brand. Accordingly, "Orchestra"—like many other commercials discussed in this book—exemplifies how pre-existing musical tropes can be reworked to support the replacement of religious icons with the (soda) commodity. This particular setting is unique, however, in that it does not picture Pepsi's devotees: it only shows those at the altar, allowing the potential for anyone in any age group who likes Charles's music and the new jingle to be a part of the brand's congregation.

The pairing of the spot's catchy and retro sonic backdrop also blends well with the brand's cheeky "Uh-huh" slogan, which in turn aligns nicely with the spot's gospel theme.[89] This theme operates according to what Robert Darden calls a "phrase sermonphone"—a practice whereby African American congregations confirm and support their preachers' lessons by speaking short phrases of affirmation.[90] While "Uh-huh" is not typically used in worship, it works well here as a colloquial response to Charles' refrain "You've Got the Right One, Baby." It also adheres to contemporary advertising practices that leaned toward the use of "street" language to attract young audiences.[91] So, despite the glamorous tuxedos and cocktail dresses worn by the performers (a trope that harkens back to a time in Charles's early career when broadcasters worried about making black musicians "presentable" for white middle-class audiences), the relaxed slogan/affirmation works well to create subtle disparity humor and appellate Super Bowl audiences who were (presumably) dressed in jerseys and jeans. The tactic obviously worked, as "Uh-huh" became ingrained in the American vernacular.[92]

Pepsi's marketers boosted "Orchestra's" success by inundating the Super Bowl's commercial breaks with two more Ray Charles commercials. They cleverly designed the content of each ensuing segment to piggyback on "Orchestra's" full version, thus keeping the retro jingle and "street" slogan fresh in viewers' minds.[93] "Worldwide" and "Audition" ran in subsequent quarters and used incongruent musical humor to hype the jingle's (prescribed) success into their story lines. These later commercials planted and reinforced the notion that the "new Pepsi song" was a "hit," even though most audiences were hearing it for the first time.

"Worldwide"

The second spot in the campaign, "Worldwide," employs subtle humor to laud the universal appeal of Diet Pepsi's new endorser. The 60-second commercial ushers viewers into what appears to be the final moments of a rehearsal for Charles and his "Uh-huh" Girls. Following a quick statement of the jingle's refrain and hook, the spot enhances the star's likability by capturing a (staged) personal exchange between Charles and his trio. In this moment of personal revelation, the spokes-singer admits to having doubts about the success of the new jingle. He asks, "Do you think it's caught on yet?"

His question whisks viewers to China, where onscreen "fans" have gathered to sing the jingle's refrain and hook (table 6.4; compare with table 6.3). The exportability of Diet Pepsi's message is inferred by the fact that the crowd sings in English over a subtly pentatonic melody while prominently displaying the product. In the next scene, the commercial pictures a ritual ceremony enacted by an African tribe. Participants wear matching red attire and rhythmically intone a descending set of "Uh-huhs" as they move through their daily routines. Next the camera cuts to a group of Japanese geishas sitting in a circle. The camera focuses on one of the women who teaches the others about Diet Pepsi by reciting the first bridge: "If it's irresistibly sippable . . ." Notably, the lead geisha does not sing but rather speaks over a thin pentatonic melody that again reinforces the location of the scene in Asia—this time in Japan. Before she finishes, the lens whisks viewers to a desolate US mountaintop where a singing cowboy completes the remainder of the phrase on a descending blues scale. This setting is supported with the echo of his bass voice through the canyon and the use of woodblocks to imitate his horse's gallop. Another abrupt cut focuses on a British butler who carries a can of Diet Pepsi atop a silver platter while muttering the product's slogan. Next, a swaying African American gospel choir belts "You've Got the Right One Baby" to an enthusiastic congregation. The religious context then transfers seamlessly to a Buddhist temple where dozens of followers intone a low "Uh-huh" accompanied by a tonic drone that punctuates the second syllable of every other incantation. Finally, the spot returns to America's secular place of worship and the event at hand—a football stadium. Here a faintly syncopated groove accompanies a hypnotized crowd chanting through an unending loop of "Uh-huhs" that are punctuated by the referee's whistle. Unable to concentrate on the game, former Super Bowl MVP Joe Montana calls a time-out and looks around in disbelief. A descending piano motive reminiscent of final bars to "Georgia on My Mind" then segues back to the initial scene, where Ray Charles and the Uh-huh Girls rehearse the jingle. Charles voices his concerns once again, but after a brief pause he laughs and rhetorically answers himself, saying "Nah!" Two tonic horn blasts then signal the end of the spot.

"Worldwide" combines the brand's retro Diet Pepsi jingle with incongruity humor to present viewers with a crude representation of neoliberal glo-

Table 6.4. "Worldwide" at a glance

Jingle Form	Performers and Location
Piano intro with refrain and hook	Charles in a blues club
Spoken dialogue questioning the jingle's success	Charles in a blues club
Hook and refrain	Crowd in China
Hook	Tribe in Africa
Bridge recitation 1	Geishas in Japan, US cowboy, British butler
Refrain	African American gospel choir
Hook	Tibetan monks
Hook and descending piano motive	American football fans in a stadium
Spoken punch line with cadence	Charles in a blues club

Note: Transcribed from PepsiCo. Inc., 1991.

balization in action. The musical styles and performing forces represented here prove essential to conveying Pepsi's message about its diet soda's global success. Charles's jingle is redacted just as much as the cultural stereotypes pictured onscreen, and the track is mixed at a high volume to guide the storyline through the randomly assorted scenes. "Worldwide" therefore suggests the universality of American music and Pepsi's product by using the jingle to create a silly scenario of cultural unification. As discussed in chapter 3, prevalent neoliberal agendas prized the exportation of US goods to a global marketplace. Consequently, Pepsi's suggestion that all nations share an affinity for American products and music once again masked the cultural colonization that occurs when non-American musics are redacted to conform to US styles, commodities, or ideas. This commercial stands out from previous Pepsi spots, however, because marketing creatives not only worked to redact the global musical styles from which they borrowed, but they also stripped their own jingle down in exactly the same way (compare tables 6.3 and 6.4). As a redaction of Pepsi's redaction of Charles's most iconic musical styles—namely, the idioms borrowed from "What'd I Say" that make up the jingle's main hook and refrain—the track to "Worldwide" adds yet another layer of signification to the second order signifiers established in the previous spot.

"Audition"

In her reflection on Pepsi's most iconic Super Bowl commercials, Bonnie Drewnainy locates the company's best tactics in its use of celebrities, music, and humor.[94] Indeed, "Audition," the third and final Diet Pepsi commercial to feature Ray Charles during the 1991 Super Bowl, packed in all three strategies to become an all-time favorite. Notably, Charles's jingle is redacted even further here by cramming the refrain and hook into snippets of an even more diverse array of musical styles performed by various personalities.

The spot begins with a freeze-frame on a title card that reads "Diet Pepsi: Auditions Today." A non-diegetic clip taken from the final bars of "Orchestra" underscores the image to remind viewers of the previous two commercials. This freeze-frame gives way to Charles sitting at a piano in a packed waiting room where he explains that having a "hit song" in today's industry means that everybody else thinks they can "sing it better." His brief monologue then transitions to various clips of other musicians who audition to take his place as the brand's spokesperson.

Many of the commercial's participants are recognizable celebrities, and their appearance adds incongruity humor to the spot. Comedian Jerry Lewis begins by performing a comical version of the slogan. He is followed by Vic Damone, who sings it as slow and sentimental ballad. Tiny Tim then does a falsetto and ukulele rendition, and Charo performs accompanied by Latin percussion. Athlete Bo Jackson appears in a tuxedo and unexpectedly belts in the style of an operatic tenor. Noncelebrity audition clips are also littered throughout, including a cellist, an overly confident blue-grass performer, a group of Indian singers and instrumentalists, an energetic white rapper, a virtuosic female opera singer, a one-man band, a howling dog, and even a cameo polka performance by the jingle's co-composer, Peter Cofield. Not only do the musical styles of each audition clip differ from Charles's version, but the melodies, tempos, performing forces, tessituras, and dynamics also vary considerably—often in unexpected and amusing ways. These musical adjustments aurally reinforce the notion that Charles's rendition is in fact the "best." Accordingly, the disjunctive pace of the fragmented clips along with the extreme fluctuations in style provide the perfect aural evidence for the soul singer's delivery of the commercial's punch line: "There's only one right one, baby." The spot then resolves by seguing back to the final seconds of his performance in "Orchestra," thus bringing "Audition" and the campaign as a whole to a satisfying close.

Charles's biographer calls "Audition" and "Worldwide" "colorful little films" that imply that "Ray's music is universal, and even on a silly tune like the 'Uh-huh' song, no one does it better."[95] While this reading was probably most preferred by the brand, the fundamental reason for the jingle's existence was, of course, to sell more soda. Hence, "The Right One" did not refer merely to Charles but also to Diet Pepsi. "Orchestra" thus venerated the soda giant with a catchy, retro-styled hard-sell message, and its follow-up commercials deployed just enough humor to reinforce the USP and retain viewers' attention. Marketers accomplished this through a continual process of musical redaction that made the jingle central to the campaign. By deploying dozens of styles, the slogan not only became an earworm but also legitimized the claim that consuming Diet Pepsi and its new Ray Charles jingle had become a hot trend. Equally as prominent was the subtext: that liking "classic" African American soul music and Diet Pepsi's new NutraSweet flavor were indicators of "good taste."

These commercials certainly helped Ray Charles to garner the attention he felt his label had failed to generate, but their success also brought a darker reality to celebrity endorsements—that is, they had the potential to eclipse his three-and-a-half-decade career. Charles was put in the position of defending the achievements he had made prior to the campaign and found himself correcting those who referred to it as his "biggest hit."[96] According to the star's biographer, the success of the "Uh-huh" spots surprised everyone in his circle even while it was credited for effectively "sav[ing] his ass." The biographer surmises its success, saying:

> Why did this silliness click, when the albums Ray labored on rolled over and died? There was no way of telling, but the money was certain, as was the surge of fame. . . . Pepsi made him less an old-timer and more a *hip* star of the 90s. In airports the crush of well-wishers grew deeper, and children often recognized Ray before their parents did.[97]

Pepsi's redaction of Charles's music thus surpassed the memory of his oeuvre for many 1990s audiences. His "hipness" was no longer tied to his musical accomplishments but had been successfully transferred to the brand. This campaign therefore confirmed critics' worst fears about "selling out" and added Charles to Pepsi's growing list of marginalized artists from whom it had appropriated hip signifiers.[98]

MILLENNIAL REALITIES

In the 1990s, Pepsi was largely successful in using popular music to distract from its return to a product-focused, hard(er) sell. These campaigns, however, had little effect on the company's profits and ultimately failed to propel its overall soda sales above those of Coca-Cola.[99] Pepsi thus continued for the remainder of the decade to fall behind its rival despite the fact that Coke's image was negatively affected by a string of its own high-profile promotional failures.[100]

As for the music industry, its profits were quickly eroded by factors that incited rapid changes in the way it would (and could) do business by the early years of the twenty-first century. The Telecommunications Act of 1996 in particular dealt labels a serious blow as it decreased restrictions on radio station ownership. This deregulation allowed major monopolies to form, which (among other things) tightened and syndicated playlists all over the country, thus providing fewer opportunities for new and regional artists to break their music.[101] MTV, too, was catering to fewer artists as it opted for reality programming over videos following the success of its first hit reality show, *The Real World*. Writer Steve Knopper further details how the music industry alienated faithful music buyers by pushing album sales over singles—an act that forced consumers to overpay for compact discs that contained a limited number of quality songs.[102] Audiences tired of industry tactics eventually turned to file-sharing services (like the newly formed Napster) as a means to getting free access to the latest singles. Amid these changes, the underground electronic music artist Moby made history by licensing *all* the tracks from his 1999 album *Play* to various commercials, films, and television programs. His act of bypassing the traditional inroads offered by the music industry and instead funneling his music through alternative distribution media set a bold new precedent for future music licensing and synchronization deals as the album attained an unexpected degree of radio play and sales.[103]

It would therefore become the advertising industry's prerogative in the twenty-first century to break new and underground musics. This book's coda investigates the ways in which Pepsi adapted to a commodity-saturated world where the boundaries between the music, entertainment, and corporate advertising industries had eroded. As we will see, the brand's commercials and increased sponsorship of American popular music not only would reveal the extent to which musical marketing had become the norm in the new millennium's early decades, but it would also illuminate the unexpected outcomes of these partnerships.

Pepsi Coda

Twenty-First-Century "Pop" and the Branded Future

In the new millennium Pepsi continued its pursuit of the latest musical trends, and it embraced the digital age by aligning itself with new technologies that had the potential to allow for the consumption of its cola and the music of celebrity endorsers in sophisticated ways. The brand's practices were typical of other companies similarly vying for success in the early twenty-first century "infotainment society"—a time that, according to Douglas Kellner, was ruled by "spectacle culture" and the "synthesis of capital and technology and the information and entertainment industries."[1] Pepsi's early 2000s commercials therefore provided a compelling example of the new look and sound of neoliberal corporate capitalism—what Kellner terms "technocapitalism"—by positioning itself at the high-stakes crossroads of music and technology.[2] In 2004 it paired itself with the unveiling of Apple iTunes's revolutionary online MP3 service and distributed 100 million bottle caps with promotional codes that customers could redeem for iTunes downloads.[3] The following year Pepsi's music marketing agency, Mega Inc., arranged a partnership for the brand with Motorola cellular telephones and musical celebrities, including Mariah Carey, Mary J. Blige, and the All-American Rejects.[4] Pepsi's "Cool Tones" campaign was innovative in offering free ringtones composed, sung, and produced exclusively for the promotion. By allowing branded experiences to occur through multiple touch points, the synthesis of music and technology under the cola giant's umbrella characterized the possibilities of the contemporary infotainment society.[5]

These collaborations, however, did little to resuscitate falling soda sales in an era when continued stagnation across all cola brands was having a significant impact on Pepsi's signature products. In 2008 the soda giant attempted to remedy the situation by making a drastic change to its marketing strategies. In a surprising move, it severed its nearly 50-year partnership with BBD&O and transferred its brands to TBWA\Chiat\Day.[6] Swapping agencies unfortunately did little to help as sales dipped even lower.[7] The severity of the brand's losses became glaringly apparent just a few years later when Diet Coke unseated regular Pepsi from its perennial number-two spot.[8]

Never one to shy away from a challenge, Pepsi embarked on yet another high-profile effort to bounce back in 2011. Dubbed by media outlets as a reinstigation of the cola wars, Pepsi executives decided to follow the example Coca-Cola had set with its lucrative sponsorship of the hit reality singing show *American Idol* and partnered with the inaugural season of its spin-off, the *X Factor–U.S.*[9] It was noted that Pepsi's deal differed from that of its rival by becoming the new show's *sole* national brand sponsor.[10] More significant was the way the arrangement was similar to Coke's relationship with *Idol*. Indeed, Pepsi's deal exemplified the often staggering potential of the type of media convergence that Henry Jenkins identifies as imperative to the "asynchronous participation" that would shape consumer behavior as well as marketing and programming tactics, during this era of reality talent programming.[11] Accordingly, the show's sponsorship and publicity were divided among five corporate entities that had the potential to benefit both collaboratively and individually: PepsiCo. Inc., the Fox Network, and the three companies behind the international *X Factor* franchise: Fremantle Media North America, SycoTV, and Sony Music Entertainment.[12]

As noted in this book's "Introduction," Pepsi used the commercial breaks of the September 21, 2011, *X Factor–U.S.* premiere to unveil its new "Music Icons" spot, a commercial that attempted to elevate perceptions about the brand's influence on, and convergence with, the American popular music industry. An article in *USA Today* confirmed Pepsi's strategy, citing its desire to continue its legacy of supporting new music.

> So, it's back to the future for Pepsi. "We've made a conscious decision to go aggressively back into music," says Frank Cooper, chief global consumer engagement officer at PepsiCo Beverages. "We have a rightful place in music."
>
> Indeed, Pepsi's Jackson and Madonna ads from the 1980s and 1990s were each major events. But several years ago, Pepsi turned more socially conscious and went heavily digital with its Pepsi Refresh campaign.
>
> Now, Pepsi's back re-embracing music. The cola brand makes that abun-

dantly clear at the end of the ad with this new slogan: *"Where there's Pepsi, there's music."*[13]

The unveiling of the "Music Icons" commercial not only confirmed Pepsi's stated intention to take back what executives saw as its "rightful place" in the affairs of the music industry, but, as indicated by its new USP, the commercial also demonstrated the extent to which corporate branding aims would attempt to overtake it.

To accomplish these ends, "Music Icons" takes viewers on a historical tour of Pepsi's most famous musical celebrity spots—most of which are chronicled in previous chapters. It opens with a screaming crowd and the bass line to the synthesized (G major) pentatonic hook of the new single "Tonight Is the Night" by up-and-coming rapper Outasight. Set in a dimly lit backstage corridor (presumably the entrance to the *X Factor* stage), a hooded figure picks up a Pepsi can, drinks from it, and pauses to take in the moment. The can's logo lures the anonymous contestant into the soda giant's world for a recap of successful endorsements done by the biggest names in popular music since the mid-1980s. Accordingly, the first phrases of the chorus give way to a glimpse of Michael Jackson's iconic sparkling socks and black shoes from his 1984 "Concert" spot (fig. 2.1). This is followed by a close-up of his performance in Pepsi's 1988 "The Chase" campaign designed to promote Jackson's newest album, *Bad* (fig. 4.1). The spot then winds back to images of Jackson's young impersonator from 1984's "Street," who famously mimicked the superstar's choreography to a reworked version of "Billie Jean" (fig. 2.2).

Scenes from Ray Charles's early 1990s Diet Pepsi spots accompany Outasight's next verse, in which shots of the soul singer and his 1960s era backup group recall the famous "Uh-huh" jingle that became a cultural phenomenon (fig. 6.2). A stop-time fill gives way to images from Britney Spears's 2001–02 "Joy of Cola" endorsements (chapter 1) and Pepsi's return to hip hop with Kanye West's 2009 "Timeline" commercials.[14] A higher pentatonic melody then segues to shots from Mariah Carey's 2006 joint Motorola and Pepsi "Restaurant" endorsement (mentioned earlier). A coy wink from Britney Spears—taken from the brand's nostalgic 2002 "Now and Then" commercial (fig. intro.1)—finally snaps the shadowy contestant back to reality. Outasight's musical track is then engulfed by the commotion of a screaming audience as the question "Who's Next?" accompanies the *X Factor* logo superimposed over the unidentified figure's entrance onto the stage. This final scene reveals the figure's role in the commercial as a stand-in for the eventual winner of the competition and, presumably, the next in line for the kind of mega–pop stardom that (according to the spot) leads to the pinnacle of fame: Pepsi commercials.

"Music Icons" is straightforward in reinvoking the brand's most successful campaigns over the previous 30 years and in promising the show's winner a shot at the kind of superstardom achieved by previous endorsers. A striking reversal of the once typical trajectory into celebrity status, the commercial suggests that it was the soda giant's campaigns—not the expertise of music industry insiders—that propelled these talented performers to the top. The spot's impressive redactive aims make the brand's intentions clear as distilled images of Jackson, Charles, Spears, and the like are silenced and isolated within the confines of the brand's commodified soda world. And while the clever positioning of Outasight's reworked track communicates the significance of the moment (i.e., "Tonight Is the Night") the onscreen celebrity images actually speak the loudest about the cultural capital and authority Pepsi believes these co-branding deals have afforded it. It is thus through the jingle-ization of rapper Outasight's new single and its placement over redacted campaign images from already redacted superstar performances that "Music Icons" accomplishes Pepsi's greatest feat of redaction yet: spinning the history of the soda brand's pop music commercials into a newly prescribed future for the American music industry—a future beholden to corporate branding and reality show programming. Five months later the debut single released by the *X Factor's* inaugural winner in Pepsi's follow-up commercial would put these claims to the test.

Thus far this book has addressed the questions posed in its introduction by outlining the process by which Pepsi, a forerunner and consistent practitioner of popular music marketing, has, since its acclaimed 1939 "Nickel, Nickel" jingle, employed tactics that have wholly redacted iconic musical and visual signifiers in an attempt to redirect their meanings to fit the commodified worlds of its commercials. The close examination of Pepsi-Cola's advertising history has highlighted pivotal moments in its transition away from the jingle to new popular music, as well as its increased involvement in the dissemination of new music, and its (not always successful) negotiation of aesthetic and capitalist boundaries in commercials. Indeed, in the middle decades of the twentieth century, Pepsi made its slogans into earworms by fastening them to familiar tunes and styles. In the 1960s and 1970s, it emulated youthful styles to gain access to the spending power of the emergent baby boomer generation. From the 1980s onward, the brand set industry trends by making commercials featuring big name musical celebrities that blurred the line between hearing the "art" and the advertisement. A decade later its spots returned to product-focused hard sell approaches, but for these commercials, it paired humorous, retro, and nostalgic tropes with top songs and entertainers.

This final chapter brings this study full circle, using Pepsi's 2011–12 *X Factor* sponsorship and commercials ("Music Icons" and "King's Court") to support the conclusion set up in previous chapters: Despite apparent shifts in the patronage, production, and dissemination practices of American popular music, more than 70 years after its popular "Nickel, Nickel" jingle, the leader of this trend (still) cannot claim responsibility for the successful *creation* of new music icons or pop styles. Instead, Pepsi has continued, by and large, to borrow and *redact* pre-existing pop music texts to benefit increasingly sophisticated branding agendas.

In what follows, part 1 extends scholarship on audience labor and reality talent shows to examine the outcomes and reception of the new star and single promised in Pepsi's *X Factor* "Music Icons" commercial and revealed in its ensuing 2012 Super Bowl spot, "King's Court." Close analysis and public reactions are thus paired with work by Henry Jenkins, Katherine L. Meizel, and Nicholas Carah, among others, to illuminate the falsehood in Pepsi's guarantee that its *X Factor* sponsorship would revolutionize and democratize popular music in the new millennium. The second half of this chapter considers the larger implications of Pepsi's musical marketing practices and reveals that their outcomes say less about what the brand has done for popular music than, perhaps most surprisingly, what popular music has done for (and to) the brand. Part 2 therefore outlines the soda giant's complicated relationships with the musical texts it has borrowed for over seven decades and further illuminates the broader relevance of Pepsi's music-themed commercials within the context of American popular culture. This book concludes by examining the influence that popular music has had on this mainstay American brand and suggests some ways in which Pepsi's marketing practices might offer unique perspectives for future research.

On February 6, 2012, Pepsi aired its much-hyped "King's Court" commercial featuring the first winner of the *X Factor–U.S.*, Melanie Amaro. As Pepsi had done so many times before, it attempted to make its commercial into a not-to-be-missed event, broadcasting the multi-million-dollar spot during what had become the most coveted, expensive, and newsworthy advertising space on American TV: the Super Bowl. The commercial features Sir Elton John dressed as a gaudy medieval king. John sits on a throne made of giant piano keys and ruthlessly presides over his court while searching for an entertainer. The court itself reflects a campy mini-version of the *X Factor* show, and John's character parallels that of Simon Cowell, the executive producer and a member of the judging panel, who was notorious for his swift and harsh criticism.

The first "contestant" to appear before King John is a ginger-haired jester. Recognizable from his role on the hit Fox television show *Glee*, the jester performs an awkward rendition of the hook to rapper Nelly's 2002 hit "Hot in Herre" accompanied by periodesque recorders. King John abruptly cuts off the embarrassing performance of the dance club staple, declaring, "No Pepsi for you." John then expels him through a trapdoor, causing the court to erupt in laughter.

The *X Factor* winner is the next to approach the king. When asked, "And what do *you* do?" Amaro responds with attitude, "I sing." John laughs at her confidence while the track to her inaugural single—a dance remix of Otis Redding's "Respect" made famous by Aretha Franklin's 1967 cover—crescendos into the foreground.[15] Amaro looks and sounds like a version of young Franklin as she belts the soul queen's famous stop-time coda ("R-e-s-p-e-c-t . . .") (fig. coda.1).[16] The entire court, including King John, bobs their heads to the music. When the track stops abruptly, the reality star performs melismatic pyrotechnics on the word "Yeah!," and the sheer force of her voice shatters the elaborate stained glass window above the throne.

Amazed, King John stands up and approaches Amaro in his oversized electric-blue-rimmed glasses and 1970s-inspired gold platform shoes. He begrudgingly says, "Alright, Pepsi for you," and offers her a can. But Amaro refuses his offer and instead grabs the goblet out of his other hand and declares: "Pepsi for all." Acting as the "savior" to free her cola-oppressed

Fig. coda.1. Amaro shatters expectations. (Still from "King's Court," PepsiCo. Inc., 2012.)

people, she tosses the goblet at the trapdoor lever and sends John plummeting into the dungeon below.[17] The court rejoices at the dethroning of the unjust king and runs toward a large bucket of Pepsi. In an ancient-looking font, the campaign slogan "Where There's Pepsi, There's Music" is superimposed over the scene.

Following the resolution of the plot's central conflict and the unveiling of the campaign's USP, the commercial cuts from the court's revolutionary scene to King John's descent into the dungeon below. As he falls on a pile of broken classical instruments, he meets the ousted jester and rapper Flava Flav, who wears a Viking helmet and his signature oversized clock.[18] John rolls around in pain among the instrument scraps while the former member of Public Enemy laughs and revels in the irony that the king has met the same fate as he and the classical instruments that line the dungeon floor. The rapper closes the spot with a recitation of his late 1980s catchphrase "Yeah, boy!"

"King's Court" completes the promise made by "Music Icons" in its literal depiction of the upending of former music industry models in favor of a new (corporate and branded) reality star. Much like its "Music Icons" predecessor, the equivalence of "King's Court" depends on the redacted pop signifiers littered throughout. A preferred reading would therefore recognize that Amaro represents a shift in power from the music industry's old regime of slowly cultivated, artists and repertoire (A&R) discovered talent—represented by Elton John and Flava Flav—to the new reign of (virtually overnight) publicly voted on, reality talent. Hence, the power bestowed on Amaro by the soda giant and the *X Factor* conglomerate allows her to sing forcefully enough to shatter the stained glass in the palace's facade—a likely metaphor for the failing music industry itself. In her rejection of the king's offer of only a portion of the (Pepsi) prize, the spot further seems to call out crooked labels that dupe musicians out of fair pay and royalties. Thus, in the compressed time and space of the commercial's world as a scene set in the medieval past but about the twenty-first century, the *X Factor* prodigy acts as a liberator for the future of popular music in her defeat of a tyrannical and broken system—of course, with the aid of Pepsi-Cola. As the representative of a new guard, Amaro enacts a commodity-filled uprising, using her talent to persuade everyone at the court to dance along with her performance and to rejoice in Pepsi consumption.

The commercial's scapegoat, Elton John, reinforces this reading by acting out the notion that members of the music industry's old guard have been replaced with this new system. His role not only connotes *X Factor* judge Simon Cowell's position as one of the few remaining holdovers from the one-time iron fist of A&R talent scouts, but, as Robert Goldman and Stephen Papson might suggest, John also stands in as a simulation of his own celebrity persona—a "reigning" musical legend who came to prominence during some of the music industry's most prosperous years.[19] So, just as Cowell's often-severe opinions are eventually usurped by the viewer-voting process that determines which singers succeed on the *X Factor* show, so, too, are King John's timeworn values and successes extinguished by Amaro as the representative of that public force. He and his musical aesthetics thus meet the fate of those who had "fallen" out of consumer taste before him: Western classical music, untalented singers who audition for reality shows, and old-school rap. In this way, "King's Court" situates Amaro, Pepsi, and the *X Factor* as the champions and liberators of "pop" consumer taste.

Fraught Reactions, Bland Redactions, and Aesthetic Consequences

Despite Pepsi's much-publicized debut of Amaro and the commercial's array of celebrity cameos, "King's Court" fared poorly in the media. Most reviews of Super Bowl XLVI barely mentioned the spot, and when they did, it was glossed over or dismissed. A review from inside the advertising industry offered one of the few noteworthy public opinions.

Pepsi, the choice of a new generation, may look like it's going old-school in its return to the Super Bowl, what with the castle and court and all. But there's a certain "Hunger Games" vibe to the spot, which may resonate with the kids these days. Then again, Elton John and "X Factor" winner Melanie Amaro aren't exactly the cutting edge of pop culture. And wouldn't a real revolutionary have used social media to depose the king, rather than a cheesy version of "Respect"? The cameo by Flava Flav was worth a laugh.[20]

The spot's unhip and nonrevolutionary content was further criticized in a *New York Times* article that lumped Elton John and Flava Flav together as "overexposed celebrit[ies] whose sell-by date has surely passed."[21] The same article went on to condemn Pepsi for this and another one of its Super Bowl spots, writing, "When the stars were not recycled, concepts were."[22] The spot's lukewarm reception was confirmed by its narrow achievement within the Top 20 ranking of *USA Today*'s annual Super Bowl AdMeter.[23]

As it turned out, the debut single featured in "King's Court" garnered similarly unenthusiastic reviews. Released on iTunes four days prior to the spot's air date, "loyals" (viewers invested in the show) had the opportunity to preview and download Amaro's version of "Respect" before its television premiere.[24] Amaro's fans were thus eager to check it out, but they were equally quick to express their collective disappointment. More specifically, many of the reviews on iTunes blasted her, Simon Cowell, and *X Factor* for the song choice. While many agreed that Amaro has a powerful voice, they bemoaned the fact that her first recording was a cover song, especially one as well known as "Respect." A well-liked comment was incisive in calling out Cowell and his franchise for not understanding what American audiences really wanted: namely, something "original."[25] Another complained about the performance itself and criticized the overproduction of Amaro's voice, the stifling of her creativity, and the track's general lack of "soul."[26] A slightly more forgiving fan seemed exasperated with the cover song choice and demanded to hear "*Melanie's* music!"[27]

Audiences were therefore keen to see (and hear) through the false promises of musical revolution promised by the *X Factor* show and communicated through Pepsi's commercials. These reviews zeroed in on the lack of originality and poor quality that plagued these texts. They further chastised the show's sponsors for trying to garner credibility by clinging to past celebrities and old ideas in new texts that promised innovation. In particular, fans distained the attempt to place Amaro on the coattails of Aretha Franklin's well-established celebrity. Indeed, it was Franklin's version of "Respect" that helped to establish the soul queen's artistic credibility: In 1967 she famously turned Redding's single into an anthem for African American women (and feminists more generally) to fight for fair and equal treatment in the bedroom and beyond.[28] Franklin's revolutionary message was conveyed most recognizably in her spelling out of the hook during the added stop-time coda where her powerful vocals demanded attention and appreciation. The song's success and legacy has lived on ever since through countless pop culture references and covers.

Amaro's handlers thus likely chose "Respect" to encourage familiarity and to map its revolutionary message onto the *X Factor* enterprise. This of course required a careful process of redaction, not only for the purposes of the commercial, but for the single that Sony, Cowell, and his franchise produced beforehand—entities that were concerned most with Amaro's status as an "artist brand" and her potential to promote the show and its sponsors well after the season was over.[29] As noted above, audiences identified the process of redaction in Amaro's iTunes track, noting that her dance-pop version lacked anything "original" and did little to assert her rightful place in the music industry. The single, in fact, simply recycled Franklin's lyrics and emulated her record's call-and-response. These defining characteristics were then remixed with a revised structural form, a narrower melodic line, the insertion of repeated syncopated syllables, and a generous layering of updated production techniques. In the end, Franklin's "Respect" was merely reworked into an overproduced and repetitive dance track that, while sounding contemporary, created an overtly banal result that proved typical of corporate-sponsored musics.[30]

To fit the song within the constraints of the commercial, Pepsi redacted Amaro's redacted version of Franklin's track even further. Marketers therefore chose only to include the stop-time coda and tried to boost Amaro's credibility by surrounding her with other recognizable pop icons. The commercial's lackluster outcome thus epitomized the warning given by Giana M. Eckhardt and Alan Bradshaw that "the unquestioned marriage of the two institutions [popular music and advertising] signals an erasure of political reflexivity within the current consumer culture and a normalization of conservative neoliberalism."[31] Accordingly, the mirrored banality of Amaro's album with her soda commercial performance was supported by the depoliticization of the well-known music icons who accompanied her onscreen—icons whose careers challenged the very ethos of the neoconservative neoliberal ideals to which the reality talent show aimed. More specifically, Pepsi's spot hollowed out and repositioned Elton John, a gay British glam rocker/singer-songwriter who began his career in the late 1960s, beside Flava Flav, an African American activist rapper who rose to prominence in the 1980s. This perplexing juxtaposition of musicians from different eras, backgrounds, lifestyles, aesthetics, and political agendas likely attempted to create the kind of incongruity resolution humor common to the brand's tactics (as described in chapter 6). In reality these signifiers actually created a Brechtian "alienating" moment that in some ways rendered the spot ridiculous but also made the soda giant's claim to usurp the music business alarming.[32] The commercial (perhaps unintentionally) revealed how Pepsi and the *X Factor* franchise had ousted the diverse and unique musical agendas of the past to produce a much blander "brand" of (redacted) popular music that had the potential to appeal to a larger consensus of consumers. While audiences may have been perplexed by the decisions made for Amaro's debut, surrounding her with redacted signifiers of Franklin and other big names from music's past thus best aligned the commercial with the basic principles of television reality talent programming, in which the success of both the contestants and the show at large rested in their resonance with dominant values and beliefs.[33] Indeed, as Alison Slade argues, reality shows intend to attract wide audiences, and in an effort to retain their varied interests, they rarely allow contestants subversive to hegemonic ideologies to win.[34] So, while this type of talent show programming works in some ways, as Katherine L. Meizel asserts, to fetishize the "multivocality" of American identities, its creators simultaneously aimed to stay within the bounds of historically familiar archetypes.[35] Positioning Amaro as the next Aretha Franklin was therefore a safe bet due to the soul queen's well-established and congenial reputation.

Put simply, the promises for musical innovation and democracy made by the *X Factor* show and promoted in "King's Court" hinged on the process of redacting familiar texts as a means for the kind of cultural "gate-keeping" that John Hartley identifies—a process that, in this case, offered audiences a sanitized version of pop's musical past.[36] So, despite the fact that the *X Factor* and its parent show *American Idol* assured democratic ideals through the viewer-voting process, the reality, as posited by Meizel, is that the process "becomes a saleable metonym for democracy itself."[37] The redacted musical texts therefore merely attempted to cash in on the real money-maker, what Jenkins identifies as the "affective economics" of the reality programming model: the means by which media and brands attempt to "quantify desire, to measure connections, and to commodify commitments" as they simultaneously struggle to "understand the emotional underpinnings of consumer decision making as a driving force behind viewing and purchasing decisions."[38] The real bottom line, then, stemmed not from Amaro as the star product or her musical output, but from the process of continually engaging audiences as *laborers* to the show.

Henry Jenkins, Sam Ford, and Joshua Green confirm that "engagement-based models" of television programming view the audience "as a collective of active agents whose labor may generate alternative forms of market value."[39] *X Factor* audiences thus proved essential to the competition as "prosumers"—consumers who helped with the process of the show's production.[40] The role of the reality show audience can be compared to other fans targeted by corporate-sponsored experiential branding techniques, which, according to Nicholas Carah, put audiences to work performing brand-building labor that "'unlocks their latent value."[41] To these ends, Pepsi and the *X Factor* counted on the latent value offered by devoted followers caught up in the spectacle and willing to commit their leisure time to watching, judging, and selecting artists from whom they would (in theory) want to purchase future music. On their own dimes, fans put hours into evaluating performances and dipped into the minutes and texts available on their personal cell phone plans to vote. This system not only granted sponsors the advantage of selling audiences their own work back to them for the wages they earned from their first jobs (i.e., viewers put their paychecks toward the music later produced by the artists they had selected), but it also offered each corporation the added bonus of soliciting demographic information and ratings numbers that could be used to improve individual revenues. Fitting nicely within the confines of experiential branding, these audience laborers also helped to create hype for the show through voting and social media, which in turn allowed *X Factor* and its sponsors to conduct surveillance on their lifestyles.[42] Pepsi, Syco, Sony, *X Factor*, and the Fox television network thus counted on viewers' active involvement in voting and their engagement through multiple technologies and media sources, including television, phones, and computers; and in return for their co-branded partnerships with one another and deployment of various technology platforms, each corporation was promised a better bottom line from the work viewers did for the show. As a result, the *music*, the actual product promised to viewers, acted as a smokescreen for the real conditions of labor and the means for capital generation, thus merely becoming an additional opportunity for income beyond the show's season finale.

In this restructuring of audience labor and leisure through an engagement-based model—a practice Kellner deems typical of the info-tainment society—the corporations involved in the *X Factor* show were given free rein to select, redact, and sell banal musical commodities to consumers.[43] Hence, the "freedoms" promised actually mobilized consumers to perform services for various sponsors, creating what Grant McCracken calls an "*obligation* to decide" and keep deciding.[44] The entrenchment of reality show fans in these conditions is further aligned with what Theodor W. Adorno termed "pseudo-activity"—when consumers attempt to take an active role in the culture industry but end up "entangling" themselves more deeply in the existing system rather than subverting it.[45] It comes as no surprise, then, that Pepsi and its *X Factor* partners did not offer liberation, as consumers were persuaded to use their own time and money to "choose" from a limited number of products—in this case, the musical talents—with which they were presented.[46] In this way, the show exemplified how corporations had come to influence the production and consumption of popular music in the twenty-first century as it sold consumers back their own work at higher prices.

Despite their innovative claims, Pepsi's marketing and sponsorship efforts had merely relapsed into the well-worn redactive tricks the brand had perfected over more than seven decades. "Music Icons" and "King's Court" once again demonstrated the brand's aim to co-opt pre-existing pop signifiers—this time by using them to inscribe Pepsi's soda and the reality show it sponsored into the canon of American music history. But instead of *creating* cultural trends on the cutting edge of pop culture, marketers attached densely coded signifiers from *past* music icons onto the newly created star—ironically the very person who was supposed to incite revolution. Although the commercials suggested a new prospect for popular music—or, as Taylor would say, a "conquest" of its culture—Pepsi's assertion of musical authority and revolution was undermined by the very signifiers it hoped would bring it acclaim.[47] Audiences realized that Amaro did not possess enough cultural capital to push anyone aside or steal the spotlight; she could have been anyone, as indicated by the faceless figure shown in "Music Icon's" promo that hyped the season's first round of competition.

Furthermore, "Kings Court" may have painted Amaro as the symbol of the new guard, but it merely reinscribed her within an old patronage system that proved not to be much different, and certainly no better, than what had traditionally been offered by major music labels. Amaro's five-million-dollar recording contract with the Sony Music Company (one of the show's sponsors and also one of the world's largest labels), as well as her role in the commercial, positioned her in the same situation as most other artists and returned a lackluster result.[48] The only difference between her and the other icons in Pepsi's commercial was that she had become a product sold by corporations that were openly as interested in pushing soda and network ratings as in selling music. Per usual, however, Amaro was the product being sold to the audience, while the audience was being sold to the show, sponsors, and network.[49] Hence, the new system promised by Pepsi and *X Factor* was not new or democratic but in fact autocratic. Amaro's debut track and her corresponding commercial thus exemplified the consequences of the shift from "cultural logics to branding logics" in the creation of new popular music in the twenty-first century, as it had the potential to exploit viewers' labor and redact and neutralize any potentially imaginative or socially meaningful content.[50] Notably, this particular dynasty of media convergence did not last long, as the *X Factor–U.S.* was canceled after only three seasons.[51]

PART 2: OUTCOMES AND EXPECTATIONS

Soda Goes Pop has demonstrated that Pepsi was *not* indeed responsible for steering the history of popular music. But what "Music Icons" and its "Now and Then" predecessor (discussed in chapter 1) do illuminate are the many ways in which Pepsi's advertising history actually *reflects* the triumphs and struggles of the American music industry (and in many ways also those of the nation) over a 73-year period. This is evident, more generally, in the genres, styles, and artists its various pop-themed commercials have re-presented and is realized more profoundly in their mirroring of the industry's (and America's) efforts to negotiate social, cultural, and political ideologies that have challenged hegemonic forces. These moments appear most obviously and consistently in the brand's representations of

African American musical culture, but also in its depictions of gender, the counterculture, religion, and even sexuality.

For Pepsi's 1939 "Nickel, Nickel" jingle (outlined in the "Introduction"), composers drew from a traditional English ballad as well as contemporary Tin Pan Alley and jazz idioms to create a groundbreaking tune that seamlessly combined tensions between old and new, high and low, and black and white musics. Although popular for some time, the Depression era bargain slogan eventually hurt the brand's efforts to beat Coca-Cola by earning a reputation for catering to lower-class and black audiences. This prompted its marketing creatives to (attempt to) counter this image with the "Be Sociable" campaign and a new slogan that carefully emulated the polished sounds of white jazz musicians in order to reflect the aspirational and conservative tastes of 1950s white middle-class consumers (chapter 1).

In the early 1960s, Pepsi's "Think Young" and "Come Alive!" campaigns employed the sound of teen star Joanie Sommers to reflect the optimism of the decade's first years, and in timbre alone these spots subtly alluded to the youthful sounds that had become popular among the up-and-coming baby boomer generation (chapter 1). At the same time, the brand hesitated to include more obvious allusions to racially coded rock and roll and soul musics for fear of alienating older white consumer bases. When the soda giant finally did include African American styles and musicians in its 1966 "Pepsi Pours It On" campaign, its subsequent commercials perfectly echoed the music industry's (and America's) fraught relationship with the black cultural tropes on which executives aimed to capitalize but did not fully understand. Notably, the soda giant began to catch up with the nation's musical trends by the end of the 1960s and early 1970s with "Live/Give" (chapter 1), but again its marketers felt the need to put a positive spin on ideologies that threatened the establishment. Accordingly, in the effort to heal the political and social unrest of the 1960s, Pepsi's commercials featured only a vague depiction of the counterculture and included sonic allusions to anthemic hopefulness and inclusive communities.

In 1984 Pepsi chose just the right moment to bank on the fact that a dazzling onetime child entertainer groomed by a black label (Motown) that taught its artists to cater to white middle-class audiences would be the key to attracting diverse audiences of all ages (see chapter 2). The brand followed industry trends to triumph over Coke with its set of "The Choice of a New Generation" commercials featuring Michael Jackson. It repeated this formula with Lionel Richie—also a former Motown hit maker—whose slick yet older-sounding sentimental tunes similarly appealed across racial lines (chapter 3). Pepsi also achieved moderate success the following year with baby boomer rocker Tina Turner, whose story of liberation from an abusive husband and comeback career had inspired many. The brand also paired her with the theatrics and synth-pop performances of David Bowie in 1987 to create a snapshot of the possibilities for "Modern Love" with a tale of technological innovation and interracial romance.

Not coincidentally, when Pepsi's commercials finally caught up with the music industry's aesthetics in the late 1980s—most notably those of MTV—some of their content incited fierce opposition. Without the usual benefit of a historical buffer, the banal practices typical of corporate advertising could not easily reconcile the volatile political themes that played out in real time through music and video texts created by the world's most famous artists. Michael Jackson's blurring of racial and gender norms (chapters 4 and 6) and Madonna's questioning of racial and religious boundaries (chapter 5) therefore seeped uncomfortably through Pepsi's mini-music-video commercials. The family-friendly cola brand was ill equipped to face the kinds of politically motivated backlash that the music industry had weathered for the much of the century, and it quickly caved to the demands of displeased consumers. Pepsi therefore took a step back from the music industry's aesthetics in the 1990s, but it continued to hire male African American artists, such as MC Hammer and Ray Charles, whose hip yet approachable reputations could bolster the brand's image (chapter 6). Pepsi also garnered a number of industry awards and audience accolades as it worked to stretch its demographic reach by borrowing older pre-existing tracks and styles from groups marginalized by age, sexuality, and gender. These shining moments faded quickly in the early decades of the twenty-first century when the soda giant (much like the music industry) focused too much attention on branding new stars rather than encouraging the expression of unique musical styles and personal identities that audiences craved. As a result, viewers largely found the promotional reality-show musics Pepsi supported uninspiring due to their suppression of essential markers of identity, politics, and creativity.

Thus, in revisiting Pepsi-Cola's advertising history and reading between the (musical) lines, the brand's narrative demonstrates how television commercials, like other cultural texts, divulge their cultural moment, even in conscientious attempts to erase, rewrite, or rectify it. Pepsi's advertising also tells a rich story about the people, ideas, ethos, and ideologies that have affected the production of decades of campaigns. It further illuminates how and why specific musical texts, performances, and performers have not only dominated the music industry but crossed over into many others. A close examination of Pepsi's advertising history has therefore revealed why pop music aesthetics have been absorbed so easily into the interests of corporate advertising and why they continue to pervade it: the sounds of popular music are the sounds of America, and their signifiers encompass all its promises, aspirations, and innovations, as well as its fears, setbacks, and flaws.

Equally important, Pepsi's story illuminates the realities of musical marketing from the perspective of the sponsoring brand. The commercials analyzed throughout this book illustrate how all involved parties, not just the music makers, take calculated risks when making sync and licensing deals. They also verify that the results of musical branding are not in any way predictable and there remains no perfect formula for its success. Sometimes (in fact many times) the application of musical signifiers to commercial contexts subverts expectations to produce negotiated or even oppositional readings that leave marketers surprised with the outcome. And in extreme cases, like Madonna's "Make a Wish," the artist or license holder can benefit from the promised financial rewards and publicity whether or not the brand does. If this and the other lukewarm deals discussed throughout this book prove anything, they show that these co-branding arrangements do not always pay out equally. Musical marketing has the potential to return small dividends and can even have a negative effect on a brand's reputation while simultaneously boosting a star's single up the charts.

Moreover, just as the twenty-first-century infotainment society has opened a space for the prosumer and permitted those in non-music related industries to assert their roles as cultural tastemakers, so, too, have capitalist interests allowed popular music aesthetics to impact the selling propositions and core missions of the brands that use it. Daniel M. Jackson and Douglas Holt allude to this by attributing Pepsi's perpetual underdog status to the fact that its marketing tactics have focused on the music of *others*, thereby positioning it as an "identity brand" rather than an "iconic" one (like Coca-Cola).[52] Indeed, Pepsi has continued to find its sound in what already exists. Taking these hypotheses a step further, *Soda Goes Pop* has shown not only what pre-existing music can do when *mediated* by a corporate brand but also what it can do *to* it: a close study of Pepsi's incorporation of pop music tropes has revealed how its marketing practices made it beholden to the celebrities and hits it promoted, often pushing the marketing of its sodas to a secondary focus.[53] For better or worse, the soda giant's pop-themed deals have not just affected its soda sales but also shifted its motivations. What started as a move toward lifestyle tactics turned into the business of selling specific songs and artists. Pepsi's campaigns have therefore evolved from using past popular music to deliver the message, to current and future songs *becoming* the message. Put another way, Pepsi-Cola advertising has shifted from using *popular music to sell soda* to using *soda to sell popular music*. Perhaps the most startling revelation from Pepsi-Cola's story of musical marketing is that it can have unintended consequences for sponsoring brands. In using music to serve branding aims, brands have the potential to become subservient to the musics they promote.

Musical sponsorship, no doubt, has become a core component and expected outcome of Pepsi's strategies, and despite various efforts to switch tactics at multiple points throughout its history, the sights and sounds of popular music have always crept back into its promotional efforts.[54] The brand's sustained push to keep music central to its message even continues today, as it has put less effort into hyping new Super Bowl commercials in order to sponsor halftime show performances by big name celebrities like Lady Gaga and Justin Timberlake.[55] In the last few years, Pepsi has also made highly publicized deals that feature openly political musicians and musical styles. Most recently, controversy unfolded over its 2017 global YouTube commercial titled "Jump In," featuring model Kendall Jenner and the new single "Lions" by Skip Marley.[56] Pepsi used lyrics from Marley's song (inspired by his reggae icon grandfather, Bob Marley) to put its commodity at the center of a peaceful re-creation of standoffs between disgruntled millennials and police barricades.[57] The spot was picked apart for its trite resolution of pressing social problems, especially racism, Islamophobia, and gender discrimination. Some outlets even compared it to Coca-Cola's co-optation of peaceful counterculture intentions in its 1971 "Hilltop," recognizing that Pepsi's "Jump In," by comparison, comes across as insensitive and insincere with its whitewashed, happy ending of tense scenarios lifted from images of Black Lives Matter protests.[58] Resonating with the outcomes of its 1989 Madonna commercial, outrage over the spot forced Pepsi to release multiple statements explaining its intentions while the threat of boycotts pressured it to pull the commercial after less than 48 hours.[59]

The brand's handling of "Jump In" reiterates how Pepsi's investment in popular music continues to compel it to sell more than soda: pop music's aesthetics and agendas have shaped (and arguably controlled) its branding narratives and identity for more than seven decades, demonstrating the degree to which it has become an inextricable part of the cola's legacy.

Looking Ahead

The prevalence of popular music in advertising has not slackened its pace in recent years, and there seems to be no limit to advertising's reach. Its pervasiveness and effectiveness have in fact accelerated past the point of debate.[60] Recent studies on sonic branding and promotional musics confirm that today's advertising has become just as dependent on the sounds of popular music as musicians have become on branded sponsorship.[61] Music therefore has become an essential component of a sizable portion of the commercials, marketing strategies, and promotions undertaken by businesses, services, and even political campaigns of all sizes.

Ideologies involving the role of music in advertising have also shifted considerably in recent years. Baby boomer anxieties about "selling out" have generally been redirected toward questions about compositional authenticity, authority, and context. Moreover, many consumers (especially millennials) are willing to engage with what Carah calls "brandscapes," which allow them to experience performances of their favorite musicians at corporate-sponsored festivals and concerts where they have opportunities to interact with like-minded peers.[62] Talk of resistance to licensing and sponsorship deals have thus generally become passé due to a shift in cultural priorities, as well as the oft-cited economic realities that new artists face when trying to survive under current conditions of neoliberal capitalism.[63]

In an economy that encourages relentless innovation, future relationships between popular music and corporate advertising will surely continue to evolve in surprising and unpredictable ways. Not only has the music industry been forced to change its business model over the past 30 years; so, too, has the advertising industry now that specialized music licensing and branding services have emerged to weaken the dominance of once mighty firms like BBD&O. Furthermore, as multimedia giants continue to grow, music marketing has increasingly moved back to the purview of music industry insiders. In fact, Meier reports that label executives no longer claim to be in the record business but have instead reconstituted themselves as executives for music companies in the marketing business.[64] The Arcade Creative group, a branch of the Sony Music Company, is a compelling example of how these new in-house marketing firms operate. In an effort to distinguish itself from the middleman firms that pervade the industry, the group promises a direct line to artists in the studio, thereby offering sponsors the opportunity to have a say in how their branding aspirations are integrated into popular tracks, performances, and video media.[65]

As scholarship on the topic of music in advertising proliferates, Pepsi's history will likely resonate with stories of other brands, entities, and services that have similar investments in new music. This study aims to prompt further inquiry into the aesthetic and pragmatic effects that music marketing has had on particular product categories, corporations, or industries. Increased historical distance from twentieth- and early-twenty-first-century advertising practices will also reveal new trends and illuminate novel paths for investigating the aesthetic and formal reworking of various musical styles to fit changing marketing contexts. And, as music marketing relationships become increasingly dependent on partnerships between multiple entities, technologies, and social media platforms, continued attention to nontraditional forms of advertising—sports promos, television show soundtracks, digital banners, social media, political campaigning, and so on—will provide fruitful avenues for study. Additionally, the continued questioning of brands' relationships with evolving constructions of identity that include markers of race, class, gender, sexuality, religion, and region will further untangle the complicated roles that music plays in communicating ideologies through commercial culture at both local and global levels.

As for Pepsi, it remains to be seen if and how it will choose to restrategize future efforts to connect with its aging "generations," the ever-changing youth market, and increasingly omnivorous musical tastes. With its sustained drop in soda sales over the past decade, the soda giant will have to work harder than ever to remain relevant in an increasingly saturated brandscape.[66] Only time will tell if its slogans will continue to proclaim, "Where There's Pepsi, There's Music" or if they will someday read the other way around. But if its summer 2018 "Pepsi Generations" campaign is any indication, it appears that the process of redaction is just about complete as the faces of its biggest celebrity endorsers—Michael Jackson, Ray Charles, and Britney Spears—have been emblazoned on "retro" regular and Diet Pepsi cans.[67] This promotion might indeed be the juncture that best exemplifies how Pepsi can most fully realize the marriage of its iconic soda with celebrity pop.

NOTES

INTRODUCTION

1. Bob Stoddard, *Pepsi: 100 Years* (Los Angeles: General Publishing Group, 1997), 73–83.

2. Nicolai Jørgensgaard Graakjær defines a *jingle* as a "short, rounded, melodic motif" that includes at least two musemes, employs a logo or slogan, and has no other accompanying sounds (nonmusical sounds, talking, etc.). *Analyzing Music in Advertising: Television Commercials and Consumer Choice* (New York: Routledge, 2015), 114–22.

3. Timothy Taylor, *The Sounds of Capitalism: Advertising, Music, and the Conquest of Culture* (Chicago: University of Chicago Press, 2012), 85. The first locally broadcast jingle aired for Wheaties Breakfast Cereal in 1926 in Minneapolis (83).

4. Ibid., 87; J. C. Louise and Harvey Yazijian, *The Cola Wars* (New York: Everest House, 1980), 69.

5. PepsiCo. Inc., "The Pepsi-Cola Story," 2005, www.pepsi.com/PepsiLegacy_Book.pdf. Access dates for online sources not listed in the notes are included in the bibliography.

6. Taylor, *Sounds of Capitalism*, 87–88.

7. Ibid., 88; Stoddard, *Pepsi*, 84.

8. Stoddard, *Pepsi*, 89.

9. Taylor, *Sounds of Capitalism*, 89.

10. Stoddard, *Pepsi*, 83.

11. Walter Mack, interview by Scott Ellsworth, New York City, December 16, 1985, Pepsi Generation Oral History and Documentation Collection, 1938–1986 (hereafter Pepsi Generation), Collection 111, Series 3.1, Box 17, Archives Center, National Museum of American History, Smithsonian Institution, Washington, DC (hereafter NMAH Smithsonian).

12. An example of a *Pepsi and Pete* cartoon featuring an extended version of the jingle can be found at YouTube, "Pepsi Cola Hits the Spot," 1:03, ClassicTVAds.com, 2005, posted by wikievidently, January 19, 2009, https://www.youtube.com/watch?v=RRceI elAB3s

13. "Stop the Music," *Pepsi-Cola World*, June 1958, 21, Pepsi Generation, Collection 111, Series 1.2, Box 3, NMAH Smithsonian. "D'Ye Ken John Peel" was derived from another British Isles folk tune, "Bonnie Annie." The later melody reportedly came to the United States around the time of the War of 1812. Following the death of John Peel in 1854, a re-lyricized version created by John Woodcock Graves became a staple among American glee clubs, college students, and folk aficionados. Theodore Raph, "John Peel: 1945," in *The American Song Treasury: 100 Favorites*, rev. ed. (New York: Dover, 1986), 373.

14. Taylor, *Sounds of Capitalism*, 89.

15. Ibid.

16. Kara Ann Attrep arrives at a similar conclusion in her dissertation, "The Sonic Inscription of Identity: Music, Race, and Nostalgia in Advertising" (PhD diss., University of California, Santa Barbara, 2008), 56–61.

17. Ron Rodman outlines the process of jingle composition and its terminology in *Tuning In: American Narrative Television Music* (Oxford: Oxford University Press, 2010). See especially pages, 84–92.

18. Magazine ads featured the notated versions of the tune's melody and a series of drawings depicting events where customers might enjoy a Pepsi. One version imagined the jingle in the context of a football game by changing the lyrics of the A and B phrases to suit the game's story line and ending with the familiar tag. Stoddard, *Pepsi*, 101. By the 1950s, Pepsi wanted to change its image to "the light refreshment" to keep up with dieting trends. It hired celebrity Polly Bergen for commercials that updated the lyrics to "Nickel, Nickel" to reflect the new slogan. "Pepsi-Cola American Television Commercials," (1946–1975), Pepsi Generation, Collection 111, Series 4, Box 28, NMAH Smithsonian.

19. "New Pepsi Television Ad Features Music Superstars Michael Jackson, Britney Spears, Kanye West, Ray Charles, and Mariah Carey," *PR Newswire: United Business Media*, September 21, 2011, http://www.prnewswire.com/news-releases/new-pepsi-television-ad-features-music-superstars-michael-jackson-britney-spears-kanye-west-ray-charles-and-mariah-carey-130254388.html; Outasight, "Tonight Is the Night," Warner Bros. B005P5OHF4, 2011, MP3; "Music Icons," PepsiCo. Inc., 2011.

20. Leslie Savan, *The Sponsored Life: Ads, TV, and American Culture* (Philadelphia: Temple University Press, 1994), 288.

21. David Huron, "Music in Advertising: An Analytic Paradigm," *Musical Quarterly* 73, no. 4 (1989): 571.

22. Steve Knopper provides a candid account of the ups and downs of the music industry from the late 1970s through the first decade of the new millennium in *Appetite for Self-Destruction: The Spectacular Clash of the Record Industry in the Digital Age* (New York: Free Press, 2009).

23. Simon Frith implies this in "Look! Hear! The Uneasy Relationship of Music and Television," *Popular Music* 21, no. 3 (2002): 277–90.

24. Richard Middleton acknowledges that pop is "marked by the effects of 'consumerism'" in "Pop," in *Grove Music Online*, Oxford Music Online, Oxford University Press, http://www.oxfordmusiconline.com/subscriber/article/grove/music/46845

25. Taylor, *Sounds of Capitalism*, 149. Television commercial director Rick Levine also identified Pepsi's innovative use of music in its campaigns, observing that (unlike other brands) the music came first and acted as the guiding force for creating the brand's campaign storyboards and vignettes. Rick Levine, interview by Scott Ellsworth, New York City, December 18, 1984, Pepsi Generation, Collection 111, Series 3.1, Box 17, NMAH Smithsonian.

26. Television commercials represent only a portion of the company's marketing outreach. Other methods include billboards, promotions, point of purchase displays, newspaper and magazine ads, merchandising, vending machines logos, and product labels.

27. Parity products are those that are fundamentally identical to others on the market. Albert R. Kroeger, "Rising Tide: Soft Drinks and TV," *Television* 20, no. 5 (May 1963): 87.

28. Thomas Frank, *The Conquest of Cool: Business Culture, Counterculture, and the Rise of Hip Consumerism* (Chicago: University of Chicago Press, 1997).

29. Richard S. Tedlow, "The Fourth Phase of Marketing: Marketing History and the Business World Today," in *The Rise and Fall of Mass Marketing*, ed. Richard S. Tedlow and Geoffrey Jones (London: Routledge, 2015), 26.

30. Phil Dusenberry, interview by Scott Ellsworth, New York City, December 11, 1984, Pepsi Generation, Collection 111, Series 3.1, Box 15, NMAH Smithsonian.

31. Don FriField, "The Pepsi Generation: The Phrase Itself Is Now a Generation Old and Has Joined the English Language," n.d., Pepsi Generation, Collection 111, Series 1.1, Box 1, NMAH Smithsonian.

32. Ibid.

33. Tedlow, *Rise and Fall*, 24.

34. Bethany Klein, *As Heard on TV: Popular Music in Advertising* (Burlington, VT: Ashgate, 2009), 79–96.

35. Norman Heller, an authority on Pepsi research and development, believed that Pepsi was more sensitive to Americans' changing lifestyles than Coke was. Interview by Scott Ellsworth, Purchase, New York, January 9, 1985, Pepsi Generation, Collection 111, Series 3.1, Box 16, NMAH Smithsonian.

36. Historically, Pepsi has sold its marketing programs to the bottlers and its sales have depended on the kind and degree of marketing activity done by the independent bottlers who own franchises. "Pepsi Sells Marketing Programs, Not Pop, to Its Dealers," *Marketing*, March 6, 1958, 62, Pepsi Generation, Collection 111, Series 1.1, Box 1, NMAH Smithsonian. African American consumers were reported to prefer Pepsi to other soft drinks by 1950. D. Parke Gibson, *The $30 Billion Negro* (London: Macmillan, 1969).

37. Taylor, *Sounds of Capitalism*, 165.

38. For a reflection on race relations in Coke's and Pepsi's histories, see Adam Clark Estes, "A Brief History of Racist Soft Drinks," *The Atlantic*, January 28, 2013, https://www.theatlantic.com/national/archive/2013/01/brief-history-racist-soft-drinks/318929/

39. As discussed in this book's "Coda," the outrage over Pepsi's 2017 "Jump In" spot eclipsed its debacle with Madonna.

40. Noteworthy videos include *Coca-Cola: The History of an American Icon*, dir. Ray Greene, Orland Park, IL, MPI Home Video, 2002, DVD; *Coca-Cola: The Real Story behind the Real Thing*, dir. Mitch Weitnzer, New York, CNBC Original, 2010; *Coke vs. Pepsi: A Duel between Giants*, dir. Nicolas Glimois, Issy-les-Moulinaux, France 5 and Sunset Presse, 2002.

41. E. J. Schultz and Jeanine Poggi, "Behind Pepsi's 'Meta' Integration into Fox's 'Empire,'" *Advertising Age*, November 19, 2015, http://adage.com/article/media/pep si-s-meta-integration-fox-s-empire/301420/

42. Tiffany Stanley, "What Killed the Jingle?" *The Atlantic*, August 29, 2016, https://www.theatlantic.com/business/archive/2016/08/what-killed-the-jingle/497291/

43. Philip Tagg, *Kojak, 60 Seconds of Television Music: Toward the Analysis of Affect in Popular Music* (Larchmont: NY, Mass Media Music Scholars' Press, 2000); Charles Sanders Peirce, *Values in a Universe of Chance: Selected Writings*, ed. Philip P. Weiner (New York: Dover Press, 1958); Ferdinand de Saussure, *Course in General Linguistics*, trans. Roy Harris (Peru, IL: Open Court, 2000); Roland Barthes, *Elements of Semiology* (London: Jonathan Cape, 1968); Umberto Eco, *A Theory of Semiotics* (Bloomington: Indiana University Press, 1976). See also the foundational structuralist theory that informs semiotic analysis in, for example, Claude Lévi-Strauss, *The Raw and the Cooked (Mythologiques)*, trans. John Weightman and Doreen Weightman (New York: Harper Colophon, 1975).

44. Mark Laver defines flanker products as "ancillary brands with new flavor profiles" that are commonly launched in the summer when soda sales are typically up. Laver, *Jazz Sells: Music, Marketing, and Meaning* (New York: Routledge, 2015), 145.

45. Nicholas Cook, *Analysing Musical Multimedia* (Oxford: Clarendon Press, 1998).

46. Anna Lisa Tota, "'When Orff Meets Guinness': Music in Advertising as a Form of Cultural Hybrid," *Poetics* 29 (2001): 109–23.

47. Rodman, *Tuning In*, 99; Graakjær, *Analyzing Music*, 15. For a list of international scholars working on the topic, see Nicolai Graakjær and Christian Jantzen, eds., *Music in Advertising: Commercial Sounds in Media Communication and Other Settings* (Aalborg: Aalborg University Press, 2009).

48. Laver, *Jazz Sells*, 2015.

49. Klein, *As Heard on TV*, 136–39.

50. Taylor, *Sounds of Capitalism*, 205–29.

51. Taylor's more recent book also critiques musical branding practices in the twenty-first century. Timothy Taylor, *Music and Capitalism: A History of the Present* (Chicago: University of Chicago Press, 2016).

52. David Allan confirms this, noting that global licensing revenue from synchronization (including advertising, television, films, and video games) had reached $3.5 billion by 2011, in his "Turn It Up: That's My Song in That Ad," *International Journal of Music Business Research* 3, no. 1 (April 2014), 27.

53. Anahid Kassabian, *Ubiquitous Listening: Affect, Attention, and Distributed Subjectivity* (Berkeley: University of California Press, 2013), 84–108; Leslie M. Meier, *Popular Music as Promotion: Music and Branding in the Digital Age* (Cambridge:

Polity Press, 2017). See also Meier's "Promotional Ubiquitous Musics: Recording Artists, Brands, and 'Rendering Authenticity,'" *Popular Music and Society* 34, no. 4 (2011): 399–415.

54. David Harvey, *The Condition of Postmodernity: An Enquiry into the Origins of Cultural Change* (Malden, MA: Blackwell, 1990); *A Brief History of Neoliberalism* (Oxford: Oxford University Press, 2005).

55. Douglas Kellner, *Media Culture: Cultural Studies, Identity, and Politics between the Modern and Postmodern* (New York: Routledge, 1995), 263–96; *Media Spectacle* (New York: Routledge, 2003), 1–33.

56. Daniel M. Jackson, *Sonic Branding: An Introduction*, ed. Paul Fulberg (Hampshire: Palgrave Macmillan, 2003).

57. Devon Powers, "Strange Powers: The Branded Sensorium and the Intrigue of Musical Sound," in *Blowing Up the Brand: Critical Perspectives on Promotional Culture*, ed. Melissa Aronczyk and Devon Powers (New York: Peter Lang, 2010), 300.

58. Ibid. (my emphasis).

59. Huron, "Music in Advertising," 560.

60. Ibid., 572.

61. John Hartley, "Communicative Democracy in a Redactional Society: The Future of Journalism Studies," *Journalism: Theory, Practice, and Criticism* 1, no. 1 (2000): 44. Hartley adopted the term *redaction* from Howard Sercombe, "Naming Youth: The Construction of the Youth Category," PhD thesis, Murdoch University, 1996. It can be traced even farther back to a branch of theological studies known as "redaction criticism."

62. John Hartley, *Television Truths: Forms of Knowledge in Popular Culture* (Hoboken, NJ: Wiley-Blackwell, 2007), 26. See also John Hartley, *A Short History of Cultural Studies* (London: Sage, 2003), 58–87. Others have since borrowed the term to explain how redaction contributes to the social and capitalist functions of today's media culture.

63. Hartley, "Communicative Democracy," 45.

64. "Redact, v.," *OED Online*, Oxford University Press, 2017, http://www.oed.com/view/Entry/160138

65. Susan McClary, *Feminine Endings: Music, Gender, and Sexuality* (Minneapolis: University of Minnesota Press, 1991), 148–68.

66. Robert Fink, *Repeating Ourselves* (Berkeley: University of California Press, 2005), 42–47.

67. Stuart Hall, *Encoding and Decoding in the Television Discourse* (Birmingham: Birmingham Centre for Contemporary Cultural Studies, 1973).

68. Chris Wharton redefines and applies Hall's work this way in *Advertising: Critical Approaches* (New York: Routledge, 2015), 103.

69. Vance Packard, *The Hidden Persuaders* (New York: McKay, 1957).

70. Judith Williamson, *Decoding Advertisements: Ideology and Meaning in Advertising* (London: Marion Boyars, 1978) 138–51; Sut Jhally, *The Spectacle of Accumulation: Essays in Culture, Media, and Politics* (New York: Peter Lang, 2006), 85–98; Raymond Williams, "Advertising: The Magic System," in *Media Studies: A*

Reader, ed. Paul Marris and Sue Thornham (New York: New York University Press, 2000), 704–9.

71. Jhally, *Spectacle of Accumulation,* 89.

72. Williamson, *Decoding Advertisements,* 71.

73. Ibid., 43. See also Grant McCracken, *Culture and Consumption: New Approaches to the Symbolic Character of Consumer Goods and Activities* (Bloomington: Indiana University Press, 1988), 71–72, 89; *Culture and Consumption II: Markets, Meaning, and Brand Management* (Bloomington: Indiana University Press, 2005), 104.

74. Williamson, *Decoding Advertisements,* 53.

75. Ibid., 178.

76. Robert Goldman and Steven Papson, *Sign Wars: The Cluttered Landscape of Advertising* (New York: Guilford Press, 1996); *Nike Culture: The Sign of the Swoosh* (London: Sage, 1998), 35.

77. Michael Schudson, *Advertising, the Uneasy Persuasion: Its Dubious Impact on American Society* (New York: Basic Books, 1984), 214.

78. Louise and Yazijian, *Cola Wars,* 1980; Stanley Hollander and Richard Germain, *Was There a Pepsi Generation before Pepsi Discovered It? Youth-Based Segmentation in Marketing* (Chicago: NTC Business Books, 1993); Frank, *Conquest of Cool,* 1997; Taylor, *Sounds of Capitalism,* 2012.

79. Williamson, *Decoding Advertisements;* Schudson, *Advertising,* 1984.

80. Harvey, *Brief History,* 2005; Taylor, *Music and Capitalism,* 2015; Andrea Moore, "Neoliberalism and the Musical Entrepreneur," *Journal of the Society for American Music* 10, no. 1 (2016): 33–53; Marianna Ritchey, "'Amazing Together': Mason Bates, Classical Music, and Neoliberal Values," *Music and Politics* 11, no. 2 (Summer 2017), http://dx.doi.org/10.3998/mp.9460447.0011.202

81. Jean Baudrillard, *Simulacra and Simulation,* trans. Shelia Faria Glaser (Ann Arbor: University of Michigan Press, 1994); Umberto Eco, *Travels in Hyperreality* (Orlando, FL: Harcourt Brace Jovanovich, 1986); Goldman and Papson, *Nike Culture;* Joseph Vogel, *Man in the Music: The Creative Life and Work of Michael Jackson* (Toronto: Sterling, 2011); Ruchi Mital, "Tomorrow Today: Michael Jackson as Science Fiction Character, Author, and Text," in *Michael Jackson: Grasping the Spectacle,* ed. Christopher R. Smit (Burlington, VT: Ashgate, 2012), 131–44.

82. Carla Freccero, "Our Lady of MTV," *Feminism and Postmodernism* 19 (Summer 1992): 163–83; McClary, *Feminine Endings,* 1991.

83. Berthold Brecht, "New Technique of Acting," in *Brecht on Theater,* trans. John Willett (New York: Hill and Wang, 1964).

84. Fred K. Beard, *Humor in the Advertising Business: Theory, Practice, and Wit* (Lanham, MD: Rowman and Littlefield, 2008); Michael D. Dwyer, *Back to the Fifties: Nostalgia, Hollywood, Film, and Popular Music of the Seventies and Eighties* (New York: Oxford University Press, 2015); Simon Reynolds, *Retromania: Pop Culture's Addiction to Its Own Past* (New York: Faber and Faber, 2011).

85. Kellner, *Media Spectacle.*

86. Nicholas Carah, *Pop Brands: Branding, Popular Music, and Young People* (New York: Peter Lang, 2010); Henry Jenkins, "Buying into *American Idol*: How We Are

Being Sold on Reality Television," in *Reality TV: Remaking Television Culture*, ed. Susan Murray and Laurie Ouellette (New York: New York University Press, 2009), 343–62; Katherine L. Meizel, *Idolized: Music, Media, and Identity in American Idol* (Bloomington: Indiana University Press, 2011).

CHAPTER 1

1. "More Bounce to the Ounce" was created by the Biow Company, Inc. *The Advertising Age: Encyclopedia of Advertising*, ed. John McDonough and Karen Egolf, vol. 1 (New York: Fitzroy Dearborn, 2003), 179.

2. Marketers inundated more than 1,000 radio stations with the new campaign. "Pepsi Peels Half-Million Off Bank Roll for Network Radio Saturation Campaign," *Broadcasting*, September 15, 1958, 28–29. Pepsi used the Kenyon & Eckardt agency for this campaign. Actress Joan Crawford was married to the CEO at the time and appeared in promos and at events.

3. John Mcdonough, "Pepsi Turns 100: One of the World's Great Brands Has Been Shaped in Large Measure by its Advertising," *Advertising Age*, July 20, 1998, http://adage.com/article/news/pepsi-turns-100-world-s-great-brands-shaped-large-mea sure-advertising/65046/

4. "Pepsi Peels Half-Million," 28–29.

5. In the end, audiences found "Be Sociable" unrealistic, and the campaign was unable to sustain longevity. Tom Dillon, interview by Scott Ellsworth, New York City, May 23, 1984, Pepsi Generation, Collection 111, Series 3.1, Box 15, NMAH Smithsonian; Taylor, *Sounds of Capitalism*, 148–58.

6. "Pepsi and Coke Accent Youth in Ad Clash," *Printer's Ink*, February 17, 1961, 15, Pepsi Generation, Collection 111, Series 1, Box 1, NMAH Smithsonian.

7. Dwyer, *Back to the Fifties*, 2015; Svetlana Boym, *The Future of Nostalgia* (New York: Basic Books, 2001).

8. Dwyer, *Back to the Fifties*, 10.

9. Ibid.

10. Although the PepsiCo. conglomerate saw an overall sales increase during the first years of the new millennium, its soda sales continued to face the decline experienced by all cola brands since the 1990s. Greg Winter, "Pepsi Has 5th Quarter of Strong Growth," *New York Times*, February 6, 2001, http://www.nytimes.com/2001/02/06/business/pep si-has-5th-quarter-of-strong-growth.html; Scott Leith, "New Soft Drinks Face a Wild Ride: Vanilla Coke, Code Red Slump," *Atlanta Journal-Constitution*, May 13, 2003, 1D.

11. Peter Bart, "Madison Avenue: Think Young," *SR*, December 8, 1962, 66, Pepsi Generation, Collection 111, Series 1, Box 1, NMAH Smithsonian.

12. Rock and roll scandals included the federal prosecution of radio payola deals, the untimely deaths of three major stars (Buddy Holly, Richie Valens, and the Big Bopper), personal scandals involving minors (involving Chuck Berry and Jerry Lee Lewis), and religious and military callings that put the careers of some of its biggest celebrities on hold (Little Richard and Elvis Presley).

13. Frank, *Conquest of Cool*, 170–71.

14. Taylor, *Sounds of Capitalism*, 147–48.

15. Frank, *Conquest of Cool*, 105–30.

16. Taylor, *Sounds of Capitalism*, 153.

17. Bart, "Madison Avenue," 66.

18. Frank, *Conquest of Cool*, 105–30.

19. Taylor, *Sounds of Capitalism*, 165.

20. Ibid., 148.

21. As early as 1947, Pepsi sponsored dances and promotions that linked fashion-wise teenagers to its brand, calling them the "Pepsi Crowd." "Young People Have Fun with Pepsi," *Pepsi-Cola World*, March 1947, 8–11, Pepsi Generation, Collection 111, Series 1.2, Box 3, NMAH Smithsonian.

22. Allen Rosenshine, interview by Scott Ellsworth, New York City, December 10, 1984, Pepsi Generation, Collection 111, Series 3.1, Box 18, NMAH Smithsonian. As discussed throughout this book, the brand would oscillate between targeting youth and the youthful thinking for much of the twentieth century.

23. Frank, *Conquest of Cool*, 175.

24. "Now and Then" was directed by commercial and filmmaker Joe Pytka who had become a veteran collaborator with the brand. The brand hyped the commercial's premiere by allowing audiences in specific markets to choose which of the vignettes would air separately in 30-second versions. Audiences could choose between the 1960s "Doo-Wop" ("Come Alive"), "Surf's Up" ("Pepsi Pours It On"), or the final "New Millennium" ("Joy of Cola") segments. "Pepsi Polls Public for Super Bowl Spot," *Adweek*, January 28, 2002, http://www.adweek.com/news/advertising/pepsi-polls-public-super-bowl-spot-54248

25. For the purposes of this project, Pepsi's early spots are cited from "Pepsi-Cola American Television Commercials."

26. The spot was slated to run about 110 times per week on four major networks for the first two months. "How Pepsi's Web Umbrella Works," *Sponsor*, February 20, 1961, 40–41.

27. Ibid.

28. "Coke-Pepsi Budgets Highest in History," *Sponsor*, June 25, 1962, 29–30. Note that the sales and advertising numbers documented throughout this book mark significant historical moments when increased spending and market share increases coincided with prominent campaigns. It is beyond the purview of this study to provide year-to-year graphs of advertising spending or market share due to the fact that much of the information is proprietary and many of the available numbers are dependent on variable factors, including the fact that PepsiCo. has grown into a multi-brand global corporation. The numbers cited throughout reflect those published in media and trade press sources and are intended to demonstrate the impact of popular music on Pepsi's marketing endeavors.

29. "Pepsi-Cola Uses Old 'Whoopee' Hit as Jingle Theme," *Billboard*, February 13, 1961, 36.

30. "The Pepsi Song," *Pepsi-Cola World*, March 1961, Pepsi Generation, Collection

111, Series 1.2, Box 4, NMAH Smithsonian. Rodman notes that the A-A-B-A form is common in jingle compositions. *Tuning In*, 87.

31. Philip Hinerfeld discusses the ways in which the brand targeted African American audiences in "How Pepsi Cola Talks TO the Market: Negro Radio Reaches Audience with Airborne 'Personality Power,'" *Sponsor*, August 26, 1963, 13–14. Notably, bottlers were offered multiple versions with "open middles"—or, as jingle commercial composers call them, "donuts"—which they would pay local DJs to fill with descriptions of the product. "Pepsi to Pour $59 Mil. into '64 World Market," *Sponsor*, December 9, 1963, 30; Rodman, *Tuning In*, 91.

32. Marketers presented this information at the company's annual convention. "Advertising/The Idea the Power," *Pepsi-Cola World*, March 1961, 14, Pepsi Generation, Collection 111, Series 1.2, Box 4, NMAH Smithsonian.

33. Ibid.

34. Aryes was most famous for being Perry Como's musical director. "Grid Giants Lynch 'Caddying' for Pepsi," *Sponsor*, July 8, 1963, 48.

35. Tom Dillon, an executive at BBD&O, confirmed that marketers believed youth could identify with the vocals while older generations would recognize the melody and remember their own adolescence. Dillon, interview by Ellsworth, 1984.

36. Sommers claimed to have signed a contract that kept her name exonerated from Pepsi marketing. She realized that this was a double-edged sword when she was paid less than other celebrity endorsers (i.e., union scale). She was also denied other gigs once she was identified as Pepsi's spokesperson. Joanie Sommers, interview by Scott Ellsworth, Beverly Hills, CA, January 2, 1985, Pepsi Generation, Collection 111, Series 3.1, Box 15, NMAH Smithsonian.

37. Kroeger, "Rising Tide," 87; "How Pepsi's Web Umbrella Works," 41.

38. Kroeger, "Rising Tide," 87; "How Pepsi's Web Umbrella Works," 41.

39. Alexandra Apolloni identifies media portrayals of the ingénue in 1960s female vocalists in "Authority, Ability, and the Aging Ingénue's Voice," in *Voicing Girlhood in Popular Music: Performance, Authority, Authenticity*, ed. Allison Adrian and Jacqueline Warwick (New York: Routledge, 2016), 143–67.

40. Blondness was an important trope for projecting white femininity throughout the twentieth century. Robynn Stilwell describes how blonde curly hair enhanced the innocence of 1930s child stars like Shirley Temple and figures like Little Orphan Annie. "Vocal Decorum: Voice, Body, and Knowledge in the Prodigious Singer Brenda Lee," in *She's So Fine: Reflections on Whiteness, Femininity, Adolescence, and Class in 1960s Music*, ed. Laurie Stras (Ashgate: Farnham Surrey, 2010), 64. In previous work, bell hooks expands on discussions of blondness in the entertainment industry to discuss how the facade of Madonna's bleached blonde hair reinforced her racial privilege. *Black Looks: Race and Representation* (Boston: South End Press, 1992), 158–59.

41. Stan Hawkins and John Richardson, "Remodeling Britney Spears: Matters of Intoxication and Mediation," *Popular Music and Society* 30, no. 5 (December 2007): 614–15.

42. "Pepsi Alters Theme, Expects to Spend More," *Broadcasting*, September 14, 1964, 40.

43. "Pepsi Launches All-Out Campaign Promoting 'Generation' Theme," *Sponsor*, September 14, 1964, 19.

44. Ramin famously won an Academy Award for arranging *West Side Story*.

45. Sid Ramin, interview by Scott Ellsworth, New York City, December 18, 1984, Pepsi Generation, Collection 111, Series 3, Box 18, NMAH Smithsonian.

46. A famous example occurs in Beethoven's Third Symphony (*Eroica*), which employs the horn's natural fourth interval to signal imminent war.

47. Ramin, interview by Ellsworth, December 18, 1984.

48. Ibid. Instead he cites Billy May and Nelson Riddle as his inspirations for the jingle.

49. Pepsi also partnered with Disney to create the ride "It's a Small World: A Salute to UNICEF" for the 1964–65 World's Fair. Stoddard, *Pepsi*, 138–39, 144–45.

50. Louise and Yazijian, *Cola Wars*, 241–42.

51. Although he is unsure about how to define it, Frank observes that the score opens with a "puzzling musical chord" that conveys "danger." *Conquest of Cool*, 175.

52. Even though the some of the 1963–67 spots marked Pepsi's first use of color in its television advertising, the 2002 version remains in black and white. Hilary Lipsitz, interview by Scott Ellsworth, New York City, April 19, 1985, Pepsi Generation, Collection 111, Series 3.1, Box 17, and Series 1, Box 1, NMAH Smithsonian; "Pepsi Outlay to Reach $15 Million," *Sponsor*, September 21, 1964, 16, Pepsi Generation, Collection 111, Series 1, Box 1, NMAH Smithsonian.

53. Lipsitz, interview by Ellsworth, 1985.

54. Taylor reports that Coke recorded more than 35 arrangements of the tune with top musicians, but The Limelighters folk group was the first to sing it. *Sounds of Capitalism*, 150–51. Louise and Yazijian further list The Shirelles, Roy Orbison, The Four Seasons, The Coasters, and Neil Diamond as Coke endorsers. *Cola Wars*, 234.

55. Ted Ryan, "Pop Songs: How Coca-Cola Invited Music's Biggest Stars to 'Swing the Jingle' in the 1960s," *The Coca-Cola Company*, August 12, 2013, http://www.coca-colacompany.com/stories/pop-songs-how-coca-cola-invited-musics-biggest-stars-to-swing-the-jingle-in-the-1960s. Chapter 6 of this book discusses how both Charles and Franklin eventually became Pepsi endorsers. Franklin would also later endorse Burger King, and its 1985 licensing of the *master* of her *Freeway of Love* is believed to be the first deal of its kind. Mark Lepage, "Who Doesn't Sell Out," *Gazette* (Montreal), November 24, 2007, E1.

56. Frank, *Conquest of Cool*, 176. See also Jackson Lears's hypothesis in his, *Fables of Abundance: A Cultural History of Advertising in America* (New York: Basic Books, 1994).

57. Louis and Yazijian, *Cola Wars*, 235.

58. Ibid.

59. "Come Alive," *Pepsi-Cola World*, October 1964, 2–3, Pepsi Generation, Collection 111, Series 1.2, Box 5, NMAH Smithsonian.

60. "Sweet World of You," *Pepsi-Cola World*, February 1966, 2, Pepsi Generation, Collection 111, Series 1.2, Box 5, NMAH Smithsonian.

61. Ibid.

62. "The 'Now' Club," *Pepsi-Cola World*, June 1966, 12–15, Pepsi Generation, Collection 111, Series 1.2, Box 5, NMAH Smithsonian.

63. The show promised "a curious potpourri of action, songs, and sounds, dances, jokes, visual effects and puns, all populated with entertainment stars of the past, present and future." Its musical acts included popular groups such as Herman's Hermits and Buffalo Springfield. "Here Comes GO!!!," *Pepsi-Cola World*, April 1967, 6, Pepsi Generation, Collection 111, Series 1.2, Box 6, NMAH Smithsonian.

64. Diet Pepsi had recently replaced the brand's former diet drink, Patio Cola, in 1963. It was the first diet soda to be marketed by simply attaching the word *diet* to the brand name. Stoddard, *Pepsi*, 141.

65. Ramin, interview by Ellsworth, 1984.

66. Andy Williams's version, for which the composer asked Tony Velona to write lyrics, also reached number 34. Ibid.

67. The 1970 *Pepsi-Cola Media Ordering Catalog*—packets sent to bottlers so they could choose which marketing items they wanted for their regions—further boasted that in the four years since its debut, there were more than 200 recordings of "Music to Watch Girls By" and that the brand had created three more. It also explained the reasons for the campaign's success, saying that Pepsi had kept the theme music contemporary and even employed "rock," employed beautiful girls to "emphasize sex appeal and humor—tastefully," and featured locations where European men fawned over American "tourist-type" girls. "Live/Give," in *Pepsi-Cola Media Ordering Catalog*, 1970, Pepsi Generation, Collection 111, Series 1.2, Box 9, NMAH Smithsonian.

68. Doo-wop was notably popular but hardly a cutting-edge trend by 1963.

69. Mcdonough, "Pepsi Turns 100."

70. "Pepsi to Pour It on with New 'Cold' Slogan," *Broadcasting*, October 17, 1966, 33; John Corbani, interview by Scott Ellsworth, San Francisco, December 27, 1984, Pepsi Generation, Collection 111, Series 3.1, Box 15, NMAH Smithsonian.

71. Alan Pottasch, interview by Scott Ellsworth, Purchase, NY, May 8, 1984, Pepsi Generation, Collection 111, Series 3.1, Box 19, NMAH Smithsonian.

72. John Bergin, interview by Scott Ellsworth, New York City, February 6, 1985. Pepsi Generation, Collection 111, Series 3.1, Box 15, NMAH Smithsonian.

73. "New Flight," *Pepsi-Cola World*, November 1968, 34–35. Pepsi Generation, 1938–1986, Collection 111, Series 1.2, Box 6, NMAH Smithsonian.

74. Lipsitz, interview by Ellsworth, 1985.

75. "Pepsi to Pour It On," 33.

76. Philip Hughs, interview by Scott Ellsworth, Tulsa, OK, October 19, 1984, Pepsi Generation, Collection 111, Series 3.1, Box 16, NMAH Smithsonian.

77. Frank, *Conquest of Cool*, 177–78.

78. Taylor, *Sounds of Capitalism*, 138–40.

79. Tedlow, "Fourth Phase," 18 (my emphasis).

80. "Live/Give," 1970.

81. Frank, *Conquest of Cool*, 162, 180–81.

82. Ibid., 181–82.

83. Bergin, interview by Scott Ellsworth, 1985.

84. Ibid.; Corbani, interview by Ellsworth, 1984.

85. "You've Got a Lot to Live, and Pepsi's Got a Lot to Give," in *Pepsi-Cola Media Ordering Catalog*, 1969. Pepsi Generation, Collection 111, Series 1.2, Box 9, NMAH Smithsonian.

86. Rosenshine, interview by Ellsworth, 1984.

87. Taylor, *Sounds of Capitalism*, 155.

88. In 1970 Pepsi opened the campaign's radio commercials to popular musical styles that could appeal to diverse demographics. The *Pepsi-Cola Media Ordering Catalog* boasted that it had hired Three Dog Night, Johnny Cash, B. B. King, and Tammy Wynette along with five other hit artists for its radio spots. "Live/Give," 1970.

89. Bill Backer was the creative director for Coca-Cola at the McCann Erikson ad agency. Billy Davis was the spot's musical director, and its songwriters were Roger Cook and Roger Greenaway. Ted Ryan, "The Making of 'I'd Like to Buy the World a Coke,'" Coca-Cola Company, January 1, 2012, http://www.coca-colacompany.com/stories/coke-lore-hilltop-story

90. Ibid.; Travis Andrews and Fred Barbash. "'I'd Like to Buy the World a Coke': The Story Behind the World's Most Famous Ad, in Memoriam Its Creator," *Washington Post*, May 17, 2016, https://www.washingtonpost.com/news/morning-mix/wp/2016/05/17/id-like-to-buy-the-world-a-coke-the-story-behind-the-worlds-most-famous-ad-whose-creator-has-died-at-89/?utm_term=.9d30cd2ce3f5

91. Andrews and Barbash, "I'd Like to Buy the World a Coke."

92. Rodman, *Tuning In*, 205.

93. "The Livin' Is Easy," *Pepsi-Cola World*, November 1968, 20, Pepsi Generation, Collection 111, Series 1.2, Box 7, NMAH Smithsonian.

94. "Live/Give," in *Pepsi-Cola Media Ordering Catalogs*, 1972–73, Pepsi Generation, Collection 111, Series 1.2, Box 9, NMAH Smithsonian.

95. Frank, *Conquest of Cool*, 179.

96. The blurring of binary gender roles here proves reminiscent of synth-pop performers of the era like David Bowie and Annie Lennox. Desexualizing Spears's body and unleashing her vocal timbre also nods to Shania Twain's 1997 video pastiche of "Simply Irresistible" for her female empowerment anthem, "Man! I Feel Like a Woman."

97. "Joy of Pepsi" was renamed from a campaign begun in 1999 featuring child star Hallie Eisenberg called "Joy of Cola." See chapter 6 for more on this campaign. E. J. Schultz and Jeanine Poggi, "Pepsi Brings 'Joy of Pepsi' Back: A Remake of One of the Classic Spots Debuts Tonight During 'Empire,'" *Advertising Age*, October 7, 2015, http://adage.com/article/cmo-strategy/pepsi-brings-joy-pepsi-back-16-year-absence/300810/

98. "Come Alive," 30 (my emphasis).

99. A former member of *The New Mickey Mouse Club*, Britney (Jean) Spears began her solo pop career as the female counterpart to the Backstreet Boys and *NSync. Knopper, *Appetite for Self-Destruction*, 92.

100. Spears was reportedly paid somewhere between 4 and 10 million dollars for

the two-year Pepsi deal, and it eventually cost around $119 million to produce her television spots, in-store promotions, and poster ads. Bruce Horovitz, "Marketers Aim Britney Spears to Appeal to Wider Audience," *USA Today*, February 16, 2001, 12B; Richard Wallace, "Pepsi Dumps Flop Britney," *The Mirror*, December 19, 2002, 11; Bill Hoffmann and Lisa Marsh, "Pepsi Cans Britney: Beyoncé Takes Over as Soda Spokesgirl," *New York Post*, December 19, 2002, 23.

101. Horovitz, "Marketers Aim Britney Spears," 12B.

102. Spears's agency and sexual maturity were questioned after she donned a Catholic schoolgirl's uniform that exposed her midriff in her "Baby One More Time" music video at the age of 16. Christopher R. Smit, *The Exile of Britney Spears: A Tale of 21st Century Consumption* (Chicago: University of Chicago Press, 2011), 51–58. Melanie Lowe discusses how Spears's naive yet hypersexualized, nonbinary, postmodern subjectivity confounded audiences and the media in "Colliding Feminisms: Britney Spears, 'Tweens,' and the Politics of Reception," *Popular Music and Society* 26 no. 2 (2003): 123–40. Hawkins and Richards build off Lowe's work to explore the "mixed signals" in Spears's music video for "Toxic" in "Remodeling Britney Spears," 607.

103. "One Going on Two: "Responsibility Doesn't End with the Making of a Product," *Pepsi-Cola World*, March 1965, 6–9, Pepsi Generation, Collection 111, Series 1.2, Box 5, NMAH Smithsonian. A second LP was created two years later, titled *The Frederick Douglass Years, 1817–1895*. "Adventures II: A Second Album Starts Its Rounds," *Pepsi-Cola World*, April 1966, 22–23, Pepsi Generation, 1938–1986, Collection 111, Series 1.2, Box 6, NMAH Smithsonian.

104. Some of the spots were even made specifically for Mexican American audiences. "Tall in the Saddle," *Pepsi-Cola World*, March 1967, 4, Pepsi Generation, Collection 111, Series 1.2, Box 6, NMAH Smithsonian.

105. "Alive and Living," *Pepsi-Cola World*, August 1968, 38–43, Pepsi Generation, Collection 111, Series 1.2, Box 6, NMAH Smithsonian.

106. "Pepsi's Media Bridge to Black Markets," *Media Decisions*, February 1978, 71, Pepsi Generation, Collection 111, Series 1.2, Box 1, NMAH Smithsonian.

107. Flack sang for the "Join the Pepsi People: Feelin' Free" campaign. "Join the Pepsi People: Feelin' Free," in *Pepsi-Cola Media Ordering Catalog*, 1973, Pepsi Generation, Collection 111, Series 1.2, Box 10, NMAH Smithsonian; "Have a Pepsi Day," in *Pepsi-Cola Media Ordering Catalog*, 1978, Pepsi Generation, Collection 111, Series 1.2, Box 11, NMAH Smithsonian.

108. Frank, *Conquest of Cool*, 173 (my emphasis).

109. "Pepsi Plans New Britney Ad for Bowl," *Billboard*, January 28, 2002, http://www.billboard.com/articles/news/77000/pepsi-plans-new-britney-ad-for-bowl

110. Tony Lofaro, "Britney Is Pepsi's Queen of Pop at Super Bowl: Spears Goes on Nostalgia Kick for Soft Drink Giant." *Ottawa Citizen*, January 31, 2002," F1.

111. Bruce Horovitz, "Bud Light Rules the Advertising Super Bowl," *USA Today*, February 4, 2002, http://usatoday30.usatoday.com/money/advertising/sb02/2002-02-04-ad-meter-bud.htm

112. Wallace, "Pepsi Dumps Flop Britney," 11.

CHAPTER 2

1. Portions of this chapter are revised from Joanna Love, "From Cautionary Chart-Topper to Beverage Anthem: Michael Jackson's 'Billie Jean' and Pepsi's 'Choice of a New Generation' Television Campaign," *Journal for the Society of American Music* 9, no. 2 (2015): 178–203.

2. Michael Jackson, *Thriller*, Epic EK 38112, 1982, long-playing record.

3. Roger Enrico, *The Other Guy Blinked: How Pepsi Won the Cola Wars* (Toronto: Bantam, 1986), 135; Phil Dusenberry, *Then We Set His Hair on Fire: Insights and Accidents for a Hall of Fame Career in Advertising* (New York: Penguin Group, 2005), 232.

4. The special was a response to the publicity storm after the legendary pyrotechnic disaster that severely burned Jackson's scalp. YouTube, "MTV Premiere of Michael Jackson Pepsi," 30:42, from a special televised by MTV in February 1984, posted by Giraldi Media, July 1, 2009, https://www.youtube.com/watch?v=njNwQPrpacs

5. Enrico notes that "Billie Jean," "Beat It," and "Thriller" were being played "to death" on MTV. *The Other Guy Blinked*, 134. Jackson also debuted his version of the famous moonwalk during the *Motown 25* performance.

6. Ibid., 11.

7. Ibid., 134.

8. Dusenberry, *Then We Set His Hair on Fire*, 232–33.

9. *Thriller* has sold about 110 million copies. David Brackett, "Michael Jackson," in *The Grove Dictionary of American Music*, 2nd ed. (Oxford: Oxford University Press, 2013), http://www.oxfordreference.com/view/10.1093/acref/9780195314281.001.0001/acref-9780195314281-e-4149?rskey=0NG1yt&result=1

10. Dusenberry, *Then We Set His Hair on Fire*, 232.

11. Enrico, *The Other Guy Blinked*, 102.

12. Many pop music television endorsements before 1984 featured aging musicians and their songs in order to connect with customers who might have felt nostalgic when hearing a classic they remembered. Taylor reports that the Ford Motor Company's Lincoln Mercury Division licensed 17 classic rock songs that year to reflect baby boomer lifestyles. *Sounds of Capitalism*, 168.

13. Klein, *As Heard on TV*, 79–96; Taylor, *Sounds of Capitalism*, 187–91.

14. See Huron, "Music in Advertising"; Cook, *Analysing Musical Multimedia*; and other works cited in the "Introduction."

15. Lawrence Kramer, *Musical Meaning: Toward a Critical History* (Berkeley: University of California Press, 2002), 8, 149.

16. This aligns with Claudia Gorbman's theory of "mutual implication" for film music. She suggests that this term best describes relationships between the music image and music narrative because it does not privilege the image or treat it as autonomous. See her *Unheard Melodies: Narrative Film Music* (Bloomington: Indiana University Press, 1987), 15.

17. Anders Bonde, "On the Commercialization of Shostakovich's 'Waltz No. 2': A Case Study of Textual, Contextual, and Intertextual Meaning of Music," in *Music*

in *Advertising: Commercial Sounds in Media Communication and Other Settings,* ed. Nicolai Graakjær and Christian Jantzen (Aalborg: Aalborg University Press, 2009), 142.

18. Ibid., 142–43.

19. Rodman, *Tuning In*, 99; Graakjær, *Analyzing Music,* 15.

20. Schudson hypothesizes that "American advertising, like socialist realist art, simplifies and typifies" (*Advertising*, 215).

21. Williamson, *Decoding Advertisements*, 177 (emphasis in the original).

22. Jackson admitted finding himself in a similar position once he became a solo artist. Michael Jackson, *Moonwalk* (New York: Doubleday, 1988), 192.

23. Quincy Jones, Jackson's producer, was essential to composing the score.

24. "Billie Jean" can be read like many other songs with blues influences, making tonal resolution unlikely. This constant slippery motion of the modal areas thus supports the song's unsettling story line.

25. Bruce Swedien, the song's sound engineer, made the drum set sound synthesized by isolating some parts and carefully arranging the pickup possibilities from the microphones. Bruce Swedien, *In the Studio with Michael Jackson* (Milwaukee: Hal Leonard Books, 2009), 36–37. See also Mike Senior, "Bruce Swedien: Recording Michael Jackson," *Sound on Sound*, November 2009, http://www.soundonsound.com/sos/nov09/articles/swedien.htm

26. The passing A minor chord can be read as either the V of the ♭VI or simply as parallel movement. This chapter refers to it as the latter.

27. *Michael Jackson: Video Greatest Hits—HIStory*, "Billie Jean," dir. Martin Scorsese, New York, Epic Music Video, 2001, DVD.

28. At the time the soda giant was growing weary of its international taste test called "The Pepsi Challenge," in which real consumers were asked to "Let Their Taste Decide" as they tried Pepsi and Coke in a blind contest at local supermarkets. The corresponding commercials featured Pepsi as the preferred choice. Enrico, *The Other Guy Blinked*, 6.

29. Ibid., 89.

30. Don King was famously also the manager of the controversial boxer Mike Tyson. Enrico describes King's visit as an "entrance," noting that he wore a long white fur coat, a crown with his name on it, and a "blinding shiny necklace." Ibid., 94.

31. Michael's father, Joe Jackson, mandated that the pop star's brothers be incorporated into the deal. At the time the Jacksons' career as a group was facing a steep decline, and their father attempted to use Michael's solo fame to keep them together. Ironically, it was during the Pepsi-sponsored Victory Tour that the soloist announced he would be leaving the group for good.

32. It is emblematic of Western notions about "selling out" that Jackson expressed reservations about doing a US commercial even though he had already done a campaign for Suzuki motorcycles in Japan that featured snippets of his late 1970s single, "Don't Stop 'Til You Get Enough."

33. Enrico, *The Other Guy Blinked*, 109, 135. Dusenberry alleges that Jackson's time onscreen amounted to even less—about a second and a half. *Then We Set His Hair on Fire*, 225.

34. Enrico, Pepsi's CEO, considered pulling the plug on the deal due to the numerous setbacks caused by Jackson's requests. See chapter seven of his *The Other Guy Blinked*.

35. Dusenberry, *Then We Set His Hair on Fire*, 225.

36. Ibid., 220.

37. Frank, *Conquest of Cool*, 174–78.

38. Ibid., 17–33.

39. Kobena Mercer notes that Jackson's androgynous and racially ambiguous image was responsible for his congenial reputation, although (as discussed in chapter 4) his positive reception would wane in the coming years. See Mercer, "Monster Metaphors: Notes on Michael Jackson's 'Thriller,'" in *Sound and Vision: The Music Video Reader*, ed. Simon Frith, Andrew Goodwin, and Lawrence Grossberg (London: Routledge, 1993), 80–93.

40. As posited by Stanley Hollander and Richard Germain and discussed in chapter 1, the concept of youthfulness was devised by the brand. Hollander and Germain, *Was There a Pepsi Generation?*, 109. This concept paired well with MTV's target audience at the time. Posters and promotional materials for the network proclaimed, "MTV 18–34: They Can't Outgrow It. It's Just Too Enormous," Fred/Alan MTV Network Collection, 1981–1982 (hereafter Fred/Alan MTV), Collection 453, Series 1, Box 4, MTV Folder, Archives Center, National Museum of American History, Smithsonian Institution, Washington DC (hereafter NMAH Smithsonian).

41. The similarities between MTV and commercial advertising practices are well documented in the Fred/Alan MTV archive. The Fred/Alan advertising agency was hired to promote the network, and it worked to co-brand it with other goods and services, including Taco Bell and Samsonite luggage. The philosophies of the agency's marketing campaigns are outlined in press releases, media reports, and promotional items. Fred/Alan MTV, Collection 453, Series 1, Subseries A and H, NMAH Smithsonian.

42. Jaap Kooijman argues that the visual aspects of Jackson's performance demonstrate that previously held ideologies about musical authenticity that had pervaded rock genres faded with the rise of MTV. Jaap Kooijman, "Michael Jackson: *Motown 25*, Pasadena Civic Auditorium, March 25, 1983," in *Performance and Popular Music: History, Place, and Time*, ed. Ian Inglis (Burlington, VT: Ashgate, 2006), 127. Andrew Goodwin outlines a similar argument in *Dancing in the Distraction Factory: Music Television and Popular Culture* (Minneapolis: University of Minnesota Press, 1992), 24–48.

43. The decision to edit the film to look like MTV programming was likely based on the presumption that Pepsi's target audiences would respond well to visual stimulation because of their experience as music video viewers. Frank observes that Pepsi had used "manic visual effects" in its representations of the youth culture for decades, explaining that Pepsi spots in the mid-1960s looked similar to scenes from the Beatles' movie *A Hard Day's Night* and *The Monkees'* television shows. With regard to the "Choice of a New Generation" campaigns he adds that the soda giant hoped that replicating the images and music in MTV pop star videos would lure the commercial's viewers to buy its product. Frank, *Conquest of Cool*, 173–78.

44. Goodwin, *Dancing*, 24–48.

45. Ibid., 33.

46. Kooijman, "Michael Jackson," 127.

47. Douglas Kellner argues that the construction of "spectacle" became a defining trope for MTV artists like Michael Jackson and Madonna. *Media Culture*, 263–96. See also Kellner, *Media Spectacle*, 1–33.

48. Steven Cohan's reading of Astaire's iconicity resonates with how fans experienced Jackson. See his "'Feminizing' the Song-and-Dance Man," in *Screening the Male: Exploring Masculinities in the Hollywood Cinema*, ed. Steven Cohan and Ina Rae Hark (New York: Routledge, 1993), 62. For Mercer's discussion, see his "Monster Metaphors," 93.

49. Kooijman, "Michael Jackson," 127.

50. This interpretation is similar to work done on James Brown, who Jackson openly credited as his idol and inspiration. David Brackett discusses Brown's performance style and how audiences can essentially "see" him when listening to his recordings in *Interpreting Popular Music*, rev. ed. (Berkeley: University of California Press, 2000), 126.

51. A collection of essays published following Jackson's 2009 death theorizes and reflects on the complex web of signifiers that he created throughout his career. See Christopher R. Smit, ed., *Michael Jackson: Grasping the Spectacle* (Surrey: Ashgate, 2012).

52. Enrico, *The Other Guy Blinked*, 110.

53. Pepsi released its version of the track, titled "The Pepsi Generation," as a promotional seven-inch single in *Pepsi World* in 1984.

54. Other subtle differences in Pepsi's mix include the increased prominence of the bass line and altered timbres of some instruments in the rhythm section.

55. Dusenberry, *Then We Set His Hair on Fire*, 231.

56. At this moment the vocal track lies somewhere in what Robynn Stilwell has termed the "fantastical gap." Because Jackson and his brothers are not yet performing either onscreen or onstage, this scene is "in between" diegeses. Jackson's voice thus seems to narrate the scene and also to foreshadow his upcoming entrance. "The Fantastical Gap between Diegetic and Nondiegetic," in *Beyond the Soundtrack: Representing Music in Cinema*, ed. Daniel Goldmark, Lawrence Kramer, and Richard Leppert (Berkeley: University of California Press, 2007), 185–202.

57. Alfonso Ribeiro was known at the time as "the tap dance kid" and later became famous for playing the character Carlton on the TV show *Fresh Prince of Bel-Air*.

58. Carol Vernallis brought the phrase "direct word painting" into video studies to explain moments when the lyrics describe what is happening onscreen. *Experiencing Music Video: Aesthetics and Cultural Context* (New York: Columbia University Press, 2004), 140.

59. Goldman and Papson, *Nike Culture*, 35.

60. Joanna Demers observes that there had been considerable backlash and litigation brought against those who used songs and likenesses of big name stars in commercials in the previous decade. *Steal This Music: How Intellectual Property Law*

Effects Musical Creativity (Athens: University of Georgia Press, 2006), 21–30, 59–70. See also Klein, *As Heard on TV*, 23–40.

61. Schudson, *Advertising*, 209–33.

62. "Music Star Promotions Undergo Cautious Turn," *New York Times*, May 14, 1985, D1.

63. The number and quality of big names attracted to the advertising industry increased dramatically in the years following this campaign. The increasing popularity of using big names was aided by Apple computer's successful "1984" spot, created by director Ridley Scott. Apple's campaign demonstrated (albeit on a smaller scale) that famous names and hefty budgets had the potential to pay off. For a retrospective on the impact of Pepsi's Jackson campaign, see Monica Herrera, "Michael Jackson, Pepsi Made Marketing History," *Billboard*, July 3, 2009, http://www.billboard.com/articles/news/268213/michael-jackson-pepsi-made-marketing-history?page=0%2C1

64. Enrico believed that the pressure Pepsi put on Coke forced it to hire Julio Iglesias for $10 million and to reformulate its recipe into New Coke. Neither move proved successful, and Pepsi finally (though temporarily) beat Coke's sales. *The Other Guy Blinked*, 121.

65. Dusenberry, *Then We Set His Hair on Fire*, 218.

66. "Advertising Age: Best Television Commercials of the Year, 1984 (TV)," AT:29530, Paley Center for Media, Los Angeles (hereafter Paley Center).

67. James R. Walker, "Zapping," Museum of Broadcast Communications, http://www.museum.tv/eotv/zapping.htm

68. "Advertising Age: Best Television Commercials of the Year, 1984 (TV)," AT:29530, Commercials 1984," Paley Center.

69. Ibid.

CHAPTER 3

1. Roger Enrico, interview by Scott Ellsworth, Purchase, NY, January 4, 1985, Pepsi Generation, Collection 111, Series 3.1, Box 15, NMAH Smithsonian.

2. Enrico, *The Other Guy Blinked*, 111.

3. Michael Goldberg, "Live Aid 1985: The Day the World Rocked," *Rolling Stone*, August 15, 1985, https://www.rollingstone.com/music/news/live-aid-1985-the-day-the-world-rocked-19850815

4. Turner had done radio commercials for Pepsi's "Live/Give" campaign in 1972. See "Live/Give," 1972–73.

5. Harvey, *Brief History*, 2005.

6. Ibid.; Wendy Brown, "Neoliberalism and the End of Liberal Democracy," in *Edgework: Critical Essays on Knowledge and Politics* (Princeton: Princeton University Press, 2005), 39–40. See also Manfred B. Steger and Ravi K. Roy, *Neoliberalism: A Very Short Introduction* (New York: Oxford University Press, 2010), 54.

7. It is no coincidence that these words had crept into advertising by the mid-1970s since neoliberal ideology had taken hold following the failures of leftist move-

ments (including the student movement), which struggled to integrate opposing agendas of individualism and social justice. Harvey notes that these ideologies were not just incompatible but that they ultimately took shape from self-interest. See especially pages 40–55 in his *Brief History*.

8. Dusenberry, *Then We Set His Hair on Fire*, 214–15 (my emphasis).

9. Michel Foucault, *The Birth of Biopolitics: Lectures at the College de France, 1978–1979*, ed. Michel Sennelart, trans. Graham Burchell (Basingstoke: Palgrave Macmillan, 2008); Taylor, *Music and Capitalism,* 44–79; Moore, "Neoliberalism," 33–53; Ritchey, "Amazing Together."

10. *RockBill* magazine was a heavy promoter of these relationships in the 1980s. Phil Sutcliffe, "Canned Music: Pop's Cola Wars," *Q*, April 1989, Rock's Backpages, http://www.rocksbackpages.com/Library/Article/canned-music-pops-cola-wars.   Bethany Klein writes specifically about cola endorsements in chapter 5 of *As Heard on TV*, 79–96.

11. Sutcliffe, "Canned Music."

12. "Music Star Promotions," D1.

13. Jonathan Gross, "Pop Culture," *Toronto Star,* April 11, 1987, S18.

14. "Coca-Cola: Max Interview," Video Storyboard Tests, Inc.: Most Outstanding Commercials of 1986, AT88, 1148, Paley Center. Headroom first appeared in a British cyberpunk movie, *Max Headroom: 20 Minutes into the Future*.

15. Gross, "Pop Culture," S18.

16. Lionel Richie, *Can't Slow Down*, Motown 6059MD, 1983, compact disc.

17. The other four were "All Night Long (All Night)," "Hello," "Stuck on You," and "Penny Lover." Stephen Thomas Erlewine, "AllMusic Review: Lionel Richie *Can't Slow Down*," AllMusic, http://www.allmusic.com/album/cant-slow-down-mw0000650685; Sharon Davis, *Lionel Richie: Hello* (London: Equinox, 2009), 84.

18. Richie used some of the money to support charities that served students and families in inner-city schools. Enrico did not confirm the amount of Richie's deal but admitted that it topped Jackson's. *The Other Guy Blinked*, 114. The *Washington Post* and *Ebony* claimed Richie was paid $8 million. Richard Harrington, "Lionel Richie: He Writes the Songs," *Washington Post*, May 24, 1984, K1; Pamela Noel, "TV Ad War's Newest Weapon," *Ebony*, July 1984, 84. According to the *Telegraph*, it was $6 million. "What a Difference a Hit Makes," *Telegraph*, January 26, 1986.

19. News Services and Staff Reports, *Washington Post*, March 10, 1984, G3; Pamela G. Hollie, "A Rush for Singers to Promote Goods," *New York Times*, May 14, 1984, D1.

20. Davis, *Lionel Richie*, 76–82.

21. Tom Shales, "After the Music, the Memories: On TV-Hype, Hoopla and the Whole World," *Washington Post*, July 15, 1985, B1. The campaign would air again during *Live Aid*, the biggest charity music event to date.

22. "Three-Minute Ad Coming to TV," *Globe and Mail* (Canada), February 26, 1985; "Winners: 27th Annual GRAMMY Awards (1984)," The Recording Academy, https://www.grammy.com/grammys/awards/27th-annual-grammy-awards

23. Peter Ainslie, "Commercial Zapping: TV Tapers Strike Back; VCR Owners Are Skipping Station Breaks, and Advertisers Are Getting Worried," *Rolling Stone*, February 28, 1985, 68–69.

24. The *Washington Post* noted that *Entertainment Tonight* hyped the commercial's filming as a "cultural event." Tom Shales, "Television: The Tele-Grammys Pop Stars Send a Self-Serving Message," *Washington Post*, March 3, 1985, G1.

25. Nancy Yoshihara, "3-Minute Pepsi Spot to Launch New Campaign," *Los Angeles Times,* February 25, 1985, http://articles.latimes.com/1985-02-25/business/fi-33515_1_pepsi-spot

26. "Pepsi Cola: New Styles/Homecoming/Block Party," AT:23650.005, Paley Center.

27. "Three-Minute Ad."

28. Yoshihara, "3-Minute Pepsi Spot."

29. Liam Lacey, "Tina Turner Big Grammy Winner," *Globe and Mail* (Canada), February 27, 1985.

30. The progression of musical tracks also outlines the historical progression of Pepsi's twentieth-century musical endorsements. The campaign begins with a staged, specially composed jingle; moves to an older, recognizable pop song; and ends with its slogan laid over the backing track to a newer hit song.

31. "Now Here's the News," *Washington Post*, February 28, 1985, D11.

32. News Services, G3.

33. Consider the jingle's first phrase, "You wear your style, you wear your smile," against the chorus of "You Are." Both are in C Major and have almost identical melodic contours and lyrical rhyme schemes.

34. Adult contemporary music is generally "softer," with a slower tempo and a focus on melody and harmony. A 2011 article in *Billboard* notes that it is intended for all ages to accompany "the workday, and to lull listeners to sleep with gentle ballads." In 1979 adult contemporary took over the easy listening format established in 1961. Gary Trust, "Vanilla Is Licking the Competition," *Billboard*, July 23, 2011, 12–14. Richie's mastery of this style would earn him the moniker "maestro of mellow." Adam Sweeting, "Lionel Richie: Dancing on the Ceiling," *Q*, October 1986, Rock's Backpages, http://www.rocksbackpages.com/Library/Article/lionel-richie-idancing-on-the-ceilingi

35. Phil Hardy and Dave Laing dubbed Lionel Richie "the most popular crossover black ballad singer of the eighties, occupying a similar position to that of Nat 'King' Cole in the sixties and Smokey Robinson in the seventies," in "Lionel Richie," *The Faber Companion to 20th-Century Popular Music*, 2001, Rock's Backpages, http://www.rocksbackpages.com/Library/Article/lionel-richie

36. "Three-Minute Ad."

37. Richie did not appear alongside his fellow Commodores during his *Motown 25* performance but instead sang to Butler in an offstage location. Sickle cell anemia is an inherited red blood cell disorder prevalent among African and Latin Americans.

38. To contribute to the earnestness of the scene, Pepsi hired Richie's biological grandmother for the spot.

39. Taylor describes the industry's move in the mid-1970s toward using music and imagery that evoked a nuanced "mood" in *Sounds of Capitalism,* 101–26.

40. Dwyer, *Back to the Fifties*, 28–35; Harvey, *Brief History*, 81–86.

41. Harvey, *Brief History*, 81–86.

42. It was reported that Pepsi hired 3,000 to 4,000 extras for the set. "Three-Minute Ad," 1985; Frances Phillips, "Advertising: Fit and in Fighting Form for the '80s," *Financial Post*, March 16, 1985, S1.

43. Vernallis, *Experiencing Music Video*, 211–12.

44. These chords are also used in another Pepsi commercial, called "Robots," where they emanate from a car radio. "PepsiCo. Inc., 1985," AT: 52247.020, Paley Center.

45. The camera focuses here on child star Jaleel White, who would play the iconic role of Steve Urkel in the sitcom *Family Matters*.

46. Williams, "Advertising," 704–9.

47. Jhally, *The Spectacle of Accumulation*, 89; Williamson, *Decoding Advertisements*, 138–51.

48. John J. O'Connor, "Grammy Awards Show Finally Comes of Age," *New York Times*, February 28, 1985, C22.

49. Lacey, "Tina Turner Big Grammy Winner," 1985.

50. Shales, "Television," G1.

51. Jonathan Gross, "Trouble Brewing," *Toronto Star*, May 31, 1986, S12.

52. Phillips, "Advertising," S1.

53. Lena Williams, "The Talk of PepsiCo: At PepsiCo, Victory Is Declared," *New York Times,* May 12, 1985, 11WC, 1.

54. "Video Storyboard Tests, Inc.: Most Outstanding Commercials of 1985," AT88:1121, Paley Center.

55. Noel, "TV Ad War's Newest Weapon," 84.

56. Enrico, interview by Scott Ellsworth, 1985.

57. See Mark Anthony Neal's discussion of the role of Motown as a vehicle for black middle-class mobility in *What the Music Said: Black Popular Music and Black Public Culture* (New York: Routledge, 1999), 85–99.

58. Harrington, "Lionel Richie," K1.

59. Richie attempted to balance the affections of both audiences by featuring varied tracks on *Can't Slow Down*. The album showcased not only ballads but also upbeat tunes with Caribbean and even country influences. Davis, *Lionel Richie*, 84; Harrington, "Lionel Richie," K1.

60. Frank, *Conquest of Cool*, 174–78.

61. Hughs, interview by Scott Ellsworth, October 19, 1984.

62. Pottasch, interview by Scott Ellsworth, May 8, 1984.

63. Harrington, "Lionel Richie," K1.

64. Pamela G. Hollie, "Keeping New Coke Alive," *New York Times,* July 20, 1986, 6.

65. Paula Span, "Connecting with the Black Consumer: Lockhart and Pettus, Advertising in the Minority Marketplace," *Washington Post*, December 16, 1986, C1.

66. Hollie, "Rush for Singers," D1.

67. "Hello" was criticized for a story line that revolved around what some saw as a tasteless portrayal of a blind woman falling in love with her teacher. "Running with the Night" also surprised fans with an unconvincing portrayal of Richie as a shadowy figure. Davis, *Lionel Richie*, 86–87.

68. Richie's success would peak the following year when he and Jackson would co-write "We Are the World."

69. Lynn Norment, "Tina Turner Sizzling at 45: 'What's Age Got to Do with It?,'" *Ebony*, May 1985, 78.

70. Turner took Record of the Year and Best Pop Vocal Performance (Female) for "What's Love Got to Do with It?" and Best Rock Vocal Performance (Female) for "Better Be Good to Me." Lacey, "Tina Turner Big Grammy Winner." Recording Academy, "Winners," https://www.grammy.com/grammys/awards/27th-annual-gra mmy-awards

71. Roy Masters, "This Ad Isn't the Real Thing, Tina: What You See Isn't What You Get," *Sydney Morning Herald*, March 15, 1989, 80.

72. Philip H. Dougherty, "Advertising: Tina Turner Helps Global Effort," *New York Times*, March 10, 1986, D 13.

73. Ibid.

74. Jonathan Gross, "Concert Tina," *Toronto Star*, June 13, 1987, S7.

75. Turner claims that she adopted the hairdo one day when she ran out of time to style it. Norment, "Tina Turner," 84.

76. "Show Some Respect" was a single from her the Grammy-award-winning album *Private Dancer*.

77. Another accepted English spelling of her name is Chonkadikij.

78. The push to expand "free markets" worldwide ensured the viability of neoliberal policies and practices. Harvey, *Brief History*, 67–70.

79. YouTube, "Pepsi: Tina vs Anchalee," 1:00, posted by singhagold1, December 9, 2010. https://www.youtube.com/watch?v=LaEL2xzi488

80. This same fan also appears in the Philippine version featuring Gino Padilla. In fact, most of that commercial is identical to the Thai spot, and Padilla is simply inserted in place of Jongkadeekij.

81. Taylor, *Music and Capitalism*, 97. In this passage Taylor references Louise Meintjes, "Paul Simon's *Graceland*, South Africa, and the Mediation of Musical Meaning," *Ethnomusicology* 34 (Winter 1990): 37–73. See also Timothy Taylor, *Global Pop: World Music, World Markets* (New York: Routledge, 1997).

82. Ritchey, "Amazing Together."

83. The two worked for sister labels EMI and Capitol, which was credited to a coincidental moment when Bowie called Turner his "favorite singer" in a room full of EMI executives. David Belcher, "Thigh Time to Call It a Day," *The Herald* (Glasgow), July 1, 2000, 15.

84. Gross, "Pop Culture," S18; "Double Whammy for Pop Drink," *Toronto Star*, July 20, 1987, B6. Bowie's tour, Glass Spider, was his first in four years. Richard Harrington, "David Bowie Unmasked: Rock's Starman Peeling Back the Layers and Finding Himself," *Washington Post*, April 26, 1987, G1.

85. "Big Stars Cashing in on TV Ads," *Telegraph*, September 15, 1987.

86. Gail Belsky, "Pepsi Challenge Back: Jackson Spot on Hold," *Adweek*, March 23, 1987, 2; "Move Over Michael Jackson," *Toronto Star*, August 13, 1987, F1.

87. David Bowie, *Let's Dance*, EMI America 0C 062–400 165, 1983, long-playing

record. "Modern Love" reached number 14 on the US *Billboard* charts. Dave Thompson, "Song Review," AllMusic, http://www.allmusic.com/song/modern-love-mt0019329750

88. Personal computers were growing increasingly popular in the mid-1980s, and commercials regularly featured them. As pointed out during *Advertising Age*'s 1984 awards show, computer graphics also allowed agencies to create more visually provocative ads. "Advertising Age."

89. Philip Auslander discusses Bowie's fraught relationship with rock critics due to his use of theatrics and gender-bending tropes in *Performing Glam Rock: Gender and Theatricality in Popular Music* (Ann Arbor: University of Michigan Press, 2006), 106–49.

90. Audiences familiar with the original may have made the connection between these images and Bowie's opening lyrics to "Modern Love," which metaphorically describe a "paper boy."

91. "Big Stars Cashing in on TV Ads."

92. "Double Whammy for Pop Drink," B6.

93. Lisa Lewis discusses Turner's early career in *Gender Politics and MTV: Voicing the Difference* (Philadelphia: Temple University Press, 1990), 74–81.

94. Turner reported that she had struggled to regain her freedom from an abusive husband who, in a similar way, had "created" her stardom at the cost of her free will.

95. Much has been written about gendered images in advertising. For a fairly recent example, see Kim Bartel Sheehan, *Controversies in Advertising* (Los Angeles: Sage, 2014), 89–111. Linda C. L. Fu also discusses the fetishizing of black bodies in *Advertising and Race: Global Phenomenon, Historical Challenges, and Visual Strategies* (New York: Peter Lang, 2014), 246.

96. Gross, "Pop Culture," S18.

97. N. Roy, "Tina Turner Furthers Pepsi's Musical Hype," *Courier-Mail*, February 3, 1988; M. Jones, "Coke Defector Goes to Pepsi," *Herald*, January 28, 1988.

98. Pepsi would later sponsor a tour featuring the Australian singer Jimmy Barnes. Masters, "This Ad Isn't the Real Thing," 80.

99. John Hay, "Bowie Axed from TV Adverts," *The Advertiser*, November 5, 1987.

100. Niela M. Eliason, "Aging: Later Years Now Mean Prime Time, Not Just Problems," *St. Petersburg Times* (Florida), December 22, 1989.

101. James Erlichman, "The Day the Music Died: Big Business May Be Turning the Pop Industry into Just a Mint with a Hole in the Middle," *The Guardian*, November 24, 1987.

102. Paul Trynka, *David Bowie: Starman* (New York: Little, Brown, 2011), 407.

103. Ibid.

104. Tina Turner and Michael Jackson had also recorded Spanish versions of their commercials, as did the group Menudo, but these commercials did not air on mainstream American television. An entirely Spanish-language Pepsi commercial would not run on a major American network until 1989 with hit artist Chayanne. Stuart Elliott, "Si, Pepsi Habla Español: First Network Spanish Ad," *USA Today*, February 21, 1989, 2B.

105. Fetishizing of the idea of "freedom" is a core tenet of neoliberalism. See Ritchey, "Amazing Together."

106. Zach O'Malley Greenburg, *Michael Jackson, Inc.* (New York: Atria, 2014), 124–26.

CHAPTER 4

1. Enrico, *The Other Guy Blinked*, 269.

2. Pytka also worked on Jackson's music videos for "The Way You Make Me Feel" and "Dirty Diana." Steve Knopper, *The Genius of Michael Jackson* (New York: Scribner, 2015), 169–70.

3. Michael Jackson, *Bad*, Epic EK 40600, 1987, compact disc.

4. Jaimie Hubbard, "The Cola Wars: Coke, Pepsi Keep the Fizz in Their Feud," *Financial Post* (Toronto), December 15, 1986, 12.

5. Ibid., 272. Contemporary reports vary in their accounts of how much money Jackson received. Zach O'Malley Greenburg later claimed that the $10 million figure was correct. *Michael Jackson, Inc.*, 121.

6. Jeffry Scott, "Pepsi Buys Commercial Time on Soviet Television," *Ad Day*, May 5, 1988, 1; "Jackson Commercial Begins in Canada," *Globe and Mail* (Canada), November 16, 1987.

7. Richard Harrington, "Pepsi and the Pop Star: Michael Jackson's $15 Million Cola Deal," *Washington Post*, May 6, 1986, C2; Enrico, *The Other Guy Blinked*, 272; Bob Garfield, "Cola War's TV Extravaganzas: Jackson Gives Pepsi Bad Rap," *Advertising Age*, November 2, 1987; Nancy Giges, "Pepsi-Jackson 'Spectacular' Set for Spring," *Advertising Age*, February 16, 1987, 2; Jon Pareles, "Pop: Michael Jackson's 'Bad,' Follow-Up to a Blockbuster," *New York Times*, August 31, 1987, http://www.nytimes.com/1987/08/31/arts/pop-michael-jackson-s-bad-follow-up-to-a-blockbuster.html; Patricia Winters, "Pepsi 'Bad' Spots Get Good Timing," *Advertising Age,* November 2, 1987, 103; Belsky, "Pepsi Challenge Back"; Sally Rowland, "Pepsi Banks on Jackson as Cola War Fizzes," *Marketing*, September 3, 1987; "MTV to Run Commercial-Free Pepsi Rock Special," *Adweek*, September 15, 1986; Noreen O'Leary, "Pepsi Breaks Its 'Chase' for Michael Tonight," *Ad Day*, March 2, 1988, 1.

8. Michael Lorelli, senior vice-president of marketing at Pepsi-Cola USA, said this in an interview reported by Nancy Giges in "Pepsi Rekindles Cola War: Bottlers Want 'Sure-Fire' Effort to Counter Coke Gains," *Advertising Age*, May 4 1987, 3.

9. Belsky, "Pepsi Challenge Back," 1987.

10. Garfield, "Cola War's TV Extravaganzas," 3.

11. Pareles, "Pop." After the CBS special aired it was sold internationally as a documentary. Goodwin, *Dancing*, 41–42.

12. With the significant rise in sales of VCRs, cable programming, and compact discs, popular music and video were becoming more entwined. See J. Fred Macdonald's account of cable and VCR sales in the 1980s in *One Nation under Television: The Rise and Decline of Network TV* (New York: Pantheon, 1990), 221–63.

13. As discussed in chapter 3, Pepsi's commercials with Richie also followed a similar formula.

14. Nancy Giges, "Pepsi and Jackson in New Link," *Advertising Age*, May 5, 1986, 1, 94.

15. The tour had significant issues with promotion, securing dates, and ticket distribution. Jackson and his brothers were also criticized for high ticket prices that kept economically disadvantaged fans from seeing the show. James McBride, "Fame and Loss in the Kingdom of Rock; Elvis and Michael; The Gloved One: Spinning Glitter into Gold," *Washington Post*, August 16, 1987, F1.

16. The star reportedly wrote the number 100,000,000 on his mirrors as a reminder that his goal was to significantly outsell his former megahit. *Michael Jackson: Bad 25*, dir. Spike Lee, New York, Sony Music, 2013, DVD.

17. Vogel, *Man in the Music*, 95–97.

18. *Michael Jackson: Bad 25*.

19. Vogel reads these signifiers as glam punk. I also read a connection to the contemporary heavy metal scene that similarly stemmed from 1970s punk. *Man in the Music*, 95.

20. Jackson's stylist confirmed that the outfit worn in the *Bad* video was actually made of cotton. Michael Bush, *The King of Style: Dressing Michael Jackson* (San Rafael, CA: Insight Editions, 2012), 101.

21. McBride, "Fame and Loss."

22. Vogel, *Man in the Music*, 95.

23. Barbara Lippert, "Pepsi's 'Chase' Shows Jackson Is a Bad Act to Follow," *Adweek*, March 14, 1988, 22.

24. Pareles, "Pop."

25. Unfortunately for Jackson, *Bad* did not surpass his sales for *Thriller*. Greenburg, *Michael Jackson, Inc.*, 129.

26. Biographers claim that Jackson intentionally planted the hyperbaric chamber and Elephant Man stories as jokes that ultimately backfired. Ibid., 122–24.

27. See Kobena Mercer's "Monster Metaphors," 94; and "Black Hair/Style Politics," in *Welcome to the Jungle: New Positions in Black Cultural Studies* (London: Routledge, 1994), 97–128. Also see Tavia Nyong'o, "Have You Seen His Childhood? Song, Screen, and Queer Culture of the Child in Michael Jackson's Music," *Journal of Popular Music Studies* 23, no. 1 (2011): 40–57; and Harriet J. Manning, "Just Using It: Eminem, the Mask, and a Fight for Authenticity," in *Michael Jackson and the Blackface Mask* (Farnham: Ashgate, 2013), 117–36.

28. James Baldwin, "Freaks and the American Ideal of Manhood," in *Baldwin: Collected Essays*, ed. Toni Morrison (New York: Library of America, 1998), 828.

29. Ibid.

30. Enrico, *The Other Guy Blinked*, 270.

31. Calvin Woodward, "Pop Star and Philanthropist," *Globe and Mail* (Canada), March 2, 1988.

32. "Pepsi Pops TV Spot Touting Jackson Ad," *Adweek*, February 29, 1988, 3.

33. Vogel, *Man in the Music*, 114.

34. Vogel, in fact, suggests that this as the metaphor for the entire album. Ibid., 118–19.

35. Woodward, "Pop Star."

36. Mital, "Tomorrow Today," 135.

37. Schudson notes that surrealism is a typical vehicle for television commercials in *Advertising*, 216.

38. Baudrillard, *Simulacra and Simulation*, 125.

39. Goldman and Papson, *Nike Culture*, 31–32.

40. Schudson, *Advertising*, 213.

41. Eco, *Travels in Hyperreality*, 8.

42. Giges, "Pepsi and Jackson," 1986; Dusenberry, *Then We Set His Hair on Fire*, 222–52.

43. Fink, *Repeating Ourselves*, 42–47.

44. Jackson's "Bad" vocal performance obviously mimics Brown's "Superbad."

45. Vogel notes that Jackson's frequent practice of signifyin(g) (as defined by Henry Louis Gates) was a way for him to play with existing texts. Joseph Vogel, "'I Ain't Scared of No Sheets': Re-Screening Black Masculinity in Michael Jackson's *Black or White*," *Journal of Popular Music Studies* 27, no. 1 (2015): 94–95. Spike Lee's *Bad 25* documentary further contends that Jackson used this as an opportunity to prove his ability to "outfunk" anyone. *Michael Jackson: Bad 25*.

46. Pepsi's treatment of the song as modular units is similar to Bernard Hermann's process for composing music for Hollywood films. Tom Schneller, "Easy to Cut: Modular Form in the Film Scores of Bernard Hermann," *Journal of Film Music* 5, nos. 1–2 (2012): 127–51.

47. This is also known as the "Jimi Hendrix chord" due to its use in "Purple Haze." It is frequently used by jazz guitarists.

48. This note could be analyzed as the 11th of the chord below it, but is better explained as a suspended 7th from the previous A minor chord because of the tension it creates. The A, G, and F♯ are cleverly recycled from the descending synthesizer line that conflicts with the upper voices during the song's verse.

49. The same footage is inserted throughout the campaign. Pytka reportedly added the concert footage to better manage the editing between scenes. Betsy Sharkey, "The Adventure behind Michael Jackson's 'Chase,'" *Adweek*, March 14, 1988, 26.

50. Jackson requested the most absurd sports car available. Ibid., 19.

51. Mital, "Tomorrow Today," 139 (my emphasis).

52. Mercer, "Monster Metaphors," 100.

53. *Adweek* discussed the painstaking process of conceptualizing, filming, and editing the commercial with Jackson's input, noting that, in addition to shooting in various locations in Los Angeles, scenes were filmed in a desert; at Lake Placid, New York; and in San Francisco. Sharkey, "Adventure," 26.

54. B. Baker, "Genius in Wonderland," *Courier-Mail*, April 23, 1988.

55. Susan Jeffords, *Hard Bodies: Hollywood Masculinity in the Reagan Era* (New Brunswick, NJ: Rutgers University Press, 1994), 25.

56. Susan Fast, *Dangerous* (New York: Bloomsbury, 2014), 131.

57. Ibid.

58. Joseba Gabilondo extends André Bazin's ideas about hyperreality in cinema to

an analysis of masculinity in 1990s films in "Morphing Saint Sebastian: Masochism and Masculinity in Forrest Gump," in *Meta-Morphing: Visual Transformation and the Culture of Quick Change*, ed. Vivian Sobchack (Minneapolis: University of Minnesota Press, 2000), 186.

59. The song was intended to be a duet between Prince and Jackson, but Prince turned down the offer. Knopper, *Genius*, 160.

60. Frank, *Conquest of Cool*, 174–78; Phil Ford, *Dig: Sound and Music in Hip Culture* (Oxford: Oxford University Press, 2013), 110.

61. Lippert, "Pepsi's 'Chase,'" 22.

62. Mital, "Tomorrow Today," 144.

63. Fast, *Dangerous*, 102.

64. Judith Hamera, "The Labors of Michael Jackson: Virtuosity, Deindustrialization, and Dancing Work," *Publications of the Modern Language Association of America* 127, no. 4 (2012): 759. Hamera's comment supports the reading of Jackson's dancing as a fusion of masculine (rational) control over the feminine (emotional) body, a dichotomy also unpacked in McClary, *Feminine Endings*.

65. Davitt Sigerson, "Michael Jackson: Bad," *Rolling Stone*, October 22, 1987, Rock's Backpages, http://www.rollingstone.com/music/albumreviews/bad-19871022

66. Ibid.

67. Jeffry Scott, "Roger Enrico, CEO Author: Cola Wars Stir Innovation," *Adweek*, October 13, 1986, 24.

68. Jay Cocks, "The Badder They Come," *Time*, September 14, 1987, http://www.time.com/time/magazine/article/0,9171,965452

69. Winters, "Pepsi 'Bad' Spots."

70. Garfield, "Cola War's TV Extravaganzas."

71. Ibid. This commercial aired before Jackson faced allegations of child molestation.

72. Craig MacInnis, "That's Too Bad: Mikey Jackson Flops and *Graceland* Wins Top Grammy," *Toronto Star*, March 3, 1988, E1; Richard Harrington, "Irish Quartet Takes Album of the Year Award," *Washington Post*, March 3, 1988, D1.

73. Young crooned that those who sang for Pepsi and Coke looked "like a joke." Neil Young, *This Note's for You*, Reprise 9 25719–2, 1988, compact disc.

74. "Michael Jackson Biography," MTV Networks, http://www.mtv.com/music/artist/Jackson_michael/artist.jhtml#bio

75. M. Jones, "Pepsi Brings Cola War to Town" *Herald*, November 16, 1987, 16; Baker, "Genius"; "Michael Jackson Promotions Boost Pepsi Sales in Japan," *Journal of Commerce*, September 22, 1987, 5A.

CHAPTER 5

1. Elliott, "Si, Pepsi habla Español," 2B. Pepsi also aired two non-music-centered spots that looked like television minidramas. "Grammy Awards, 31st: February 22, 1989," VA 7132, University of California, Los Angeles, Film and Television Archive, Los Angeles (hereafter UCLA Film and Television Archive).

2. PepsiCo. Inc., "Madonna Commercial Promo," 1989.

3. This juxtaposition of Western and non-Western musics (gospel and didger-idoo) was a common trope at the time, as evidenced by the fact that Paul Simon's *Graceland* had won the Record of the Year Grammy just a few years earlier.

4. Barbara Lippert, "Pepsi-Cola's 'Make a Wish': Pepsi's Prayer Answered by Madonna's Pop Imagery," *Adweek*, March 6, 1989, 21.

5. Ibid.

6. Betsy Sharkey, "Making a 'Wish': Pytka Directs Madonna for Pepsi," *Adweek*, March 6, 1989.

7. J. Randy Taraborrelli, *Madonna* (New York: Simon and Schuster, 2001), 165–66.

8. Ibid., 165. In the United States it aired during *The Cosby Show*. The fact that it premiered during a program about a wholesome African American middle-class family hints at the brand's target demographic and message.

9. Richard Morgan, "BBDO Slated to Film Madonna for Pepsi Ads," *Ad Day*, January 25, 1989, 1.

10. Joanna Love, "'The Choice of a New Generation': 'Pop' Music, Advertising, and Meaning in the MTV Era and Beyond" (PhD diss., University of California, Los Angeles, 2012). Meier reaches similar conclusions in *Popular Music*, 40.

11. Creative director Phil Dusenberry confirmed, "Viewers were confused. They did not differentiate between Madonna's video and our spot." *Then We Set His Hair on Fire*, 234.

12. Mark Bego, *Madonna: Blonde Ambition* (New York: First Cooper Square Press, 2000), 220; Sharkey, "Making a 'Wish'"; Bruce Haring, "Madonna No Longer Has a Pepsi Prayer," *Billboard*, April 15, 1989, 3, 76; "Pepsi Drops Madonna Ads Because of Boycott Threats," *Pittsburgh Press*, April 5, 1989, D5; "Pepsi Cancels Madonna Ad," *New York Times*, April 5, 1989, 21.

13. Nancy A. Vickers, "Materialism and the Material Girl," in *Embodied Voices: Representing Female Vocality in Western Culture,* ed. Leslie C. Dunn and Nancy A. Jones (Cambridge: Cambridge University Press, 1994), 230–46; Freccero, "Our Lady of MTV," 163–83.

14. Goldman and Papson, *Sign Wars*, 185. Upward mobility was central to neolib-eral politics that encouraged individuality expressed through consumption and socio-economic gains. See Harvey, *Brief History*.

15. Kellner, *Media Culture*, 292.

16. Klein, *As Heard on TV*, 89; Taylor, *Sounds of Capitalism*, 179–204; Meier, *Popular Music*, 2017.

17. McClary, *Feminine Endings*, 163–65.

18. As discussed in chapter 2, Schudson posits that "simplifying" and "typifying" cultural signifiers is essential to creating banal advertising texts. *Advertising*, 209–33.

19. Madonna, *Like a Prayer*, Sire 9 25844-2, 1989, compact disc. See Kellner's dis-cussion of what he calls Madonna's "Who's that girl" stage in *Media Culture*, 275–79. There are a few exceptions to her carefree dance-pop tracks, including "Papa Don't Preach" on *True Blue* (1986).

20. Stephen Holden, "Madonna Re-creates Herself—Again," *New York Times*,

March 19, 1989, http://www.nytimes.com/1989/03/19/arts/madonna-re-creates-her-self-again.html?pagewanted=all&src=pm. Most sources agreed that *Like a Prayer* was an autobiographical album that dealt with the pop star's fraught relationships with her father, siblings, and ex-husband; the death of her mother; and her personal quest for spirituality. McClary demonstrates that Madonna's vulnerability was also apparent in earlier songs. *Feminine Endings*, 158–61.

21. Freccero explains the iconography Madonna adopts in "Our Lady of MTV," 163–83.

22. Madonna dedicated the album to her deceased mother who "taught [her] how to pray." Vickers, "Materialism," 230–46; Freccero, "Our Lady of MTV," 163–83. Her given name also carries an obvious spiritual weight.

23. Leslie Savan, in *The Sponsored Life*, surmises this based on a *Rolling Stone* interview. See also Bill Zehme, "Madonna: The Rolling Stone Interview," *Rolling Stone*, March 23, 1989, http://www.rollingstone.com/music/news/the-rolling-stone-inter view-madonna-19890323

24. hooks, *Black Looks*, 157–64.

25. Holden, "Madonna Re-creates Herself."

26. Taraborrelli, *Madonna*, 162.

27. Kellner *Media Culture*, 277. The "midnight hour" lyric is also an obvious throw-back to Wilson Pickett's soul song of the same name, which uses the phrase to promise his sexual prowess.

28. McClary traces the practice through seventeenth-century opera, Bach's Cantata 140, and into Jerry Lee Lewis's "Whole Lot of Shakin' Goin' on." *Feminine Endings*, 163–64.

29. Holden, "Madonna Re-creates Herself."

30. Ray Charles's "I Got a Woman" is a prevalent example of this. For more on the popularity of secularized gospel tropes, see Brian Ward, "Can I Get a Witness: Civil Rights, Soul, and Secularization," in *Just My Soul Responding: Rhythm and Blues, Black Consciousness, and Race Relations* (London: University College London, 1998), 173–216. See also Robert Fink, "Goal Directed Soul? Analyzing Rhythmic Teleology in African American Popular Music," *Journal of the American Musicological Society* 64 (Spring 2011): 179–238. The song's cowriter, Patrick Leonard, would also have been familiar with these tropes.

31. Brian Hiatt, "Live to Tell," *Rolling Stone,* March 12, 2015, 41.

32. The solo vocal line flirts with these modal areas but resists completing a satis-fying cadence in either one, allowing the song to have two finals. McClary argues that Madonna does make a "decisive" cadence on F at the end of the choruses. Although the cadence does technically happen, it lasts for only a few beats. The melody imme-diately descends back to D minor pentatonic, and the cadences elide over a harmonic move back down to either D minor or B♭. The finality of cadential resolution is there-fore questionable.

33. See Jeremy Day-O'Connell's third chapter, and especially table 3.2, in *Pentatonicism from the Eighteenth Century to Debussy* (Rochester, NY: University of Rochester Press, 2007), 97–142.

34. The prolific use of pentatonic melodies throughout the world makes them non-exclusive to Catholicism. However, when considering Madonna's professed aims for the song and its use of Catholic musical idioms (particularly the organ), this interpretation is valid.

35. Horace Clarence Boyer, *The Golden Age of Gospel* (Urbana: University of Illinois Press, 2000), 24.

36. Gospel songs also use major and minor melodies to oppose allusions to earth and heaven. Soul musicians refer to the relationship between the tonic and submediant as the "major-minor" changes. Fink, "Goal Directed Soul?," 183.

37. The harmonic motion of the major key, joyous sounding choir, and subsequent religious images created for the video and commercial follow a long tradition of thematic "uplift" in African American music and literature from late nineteenth and early twentieth centuries. Henry Louis Gates Jr. and Cornell West provide an overview of the prominent writers of this movement in *The Future of Race* (New York: Random House, 1997).

38. McClary, *Feminine Endings*, 163–65; Freccero, "Our Lady of MTV," 163–83.

39. McClary, *Feminine Endings*, 165.

40. bell hooks makes a similar argument about the images in Madonna's video in *Black Looks*, 161–62. Ronald B. Scott also reads race into the video in "Images of Race and Religion in Madonna's Video 'Like a Prayer,'" in *The Madonna Connection: Representational Politics, Subcultural Identities, and Cultural Theory*, ed. Cathy Schwichtenberg (Boulder, CO: Westview, 1993), 61–63.

41. Kellner, *Media Culture*, 275–76. Notably, like Michael Jackson, Madonna was not a Pepsi drinker. She agreed to hold the can and gesture to drink from it, but she never actually takes a sip.

42. The chord typically moves upward (to VIII) to sound like an "ascension," but here the F chord is inverted and actually moves downward. Nevertheless, the pleasing chord progression (somewhat subtly) signifies hope and transcendence. Day-O'Connell, *Pentatonicism*, 140.

43. As mentioned in previous chapters, Sut Jhally argues that advertising is an institution of advanced capitalism that provides guidance much like religion. *The Spectacle of Accumulation*, 85–98.

44. In light of the pop star's biography, this scene might be read a few ways. It could be revisiting the year Madonna was born (1958); an encounter with youth that could have been her parents or their peers at the time; or, as Vickers suggests, an embodiment of her mother of the same name, who incidentally died at the very age the pop star is in the commercial. "Materialism," 230–46. This moment could also refer intertextually to the star's 1950s tongue-in-cheek sound in *True Blue*.

45. Brecht, "New Technique," 143.

46. This poster was taken from the album art for Madonna's remix compilation *You Can Dance* to signal that the girl onscreen would grow up to be a dance music icon.

47. This scene is reminiscent of the Virginia Slims cigarette slogan, "You've Come a Long Way, Baby." These ads from the mid-1960s (around the time Madonna would

have turned eight) claimed to celebrate women's independence. For more on these ads, see Williamson, *Decoding Advertisements*, 166.

48. Reminiscent of Pink Floyd's, *The Wall*, the commercial follows what Madonna would presumably be thinking during her reflection on the authoritarian rule of her teachers and father.

49. Kellner analyses this moment, writing, "Just as Madonna is the vehicle of morality and liberal integrationism in 'Like a Prayer,' in the Pepsi commercial she 'liberates' a group of Catholic schoolgirls who break into dance when Madonna appears, leading them to self-expression and drinking Pepsi, equated in the commercial with secular salvation and joy." *Media Culture*, 293.

50. As demonstrated in previous chapters, images of people dancing in the street had become a clichéd trademark of Pepsi commercials, and also MTV music videos—including many of Madonna's. Vickers notes that this moment could also be a clichéd reference to Martha and the Vandellas' "Dancing in the Streets." *Materialism*, 237.

51. On the album Madonna's vocal resolution is ineffective because it is momentary and not supported by a root-position tonic harmony. See note 32.

52. In the Pentecostal community Madonna's actions would signify that she is in the ecstatic state of feeling the presence of the Holy Spirit.

53. Other than the glimpse of the "You Can Dance" poster, the crucifix is the one piece of Madonna's fashion iconography preserved in the commercial. She claimed to wear it "ironically" to contrast other aspects of her appearance, namely the tension of the "virgin-whore" dichotomy she sought to complicate. Taraborrelli, *Madonna*, 19.

54. The commercial also removes the distorted opening guitar riff that leads into the slam (Table 5.4).

55. "Pepsi Commercial: March 7, 1989," VA 7495, UCLA Film and Television Archive.

56. MuchMusic (the Canadian version of MTV) discussed the commercial alongside details of its attempt to surpass its US rival with help of Pepsi's sponsorship during its International Video Awards. Mark Evans, "MuchMusic at the Helm for International Video Awards," *Financial Post* (Canada), April 11, 1989.

57. Fox 11 News in Los Angeles reported that the "sexual and religious imagery" was what bothered the Italian Catholic group. "Pepsi Commercial," March 7, 1989.

58. This was first printed in *Advertising Age* in early March 1989 and ran again a month and a half after the commercial aired. Scott Hume, "Pepsi Tops Ad Recall after Madonna Flap," *Advertising Age*, April 24, 1989, 12 (my emphasis).

59. James Cox, "Boycott Aim, Pepsi: Madonna Ridicules Christianity," *USA Today*, March 9, 1989.

60. Ibid. (my emphasis). Canada's *Globe and Mail* also confirmed, "Pepsi had paid the rock idol a reported $5-million (U.S.) to star in a two-minute TV commercial featuring the same music as the video but showing a wholesome Madonna." Aly Sujo, "Sexy Madonna Video Miffs Pepsi," *Globe and Mail*, March 7, 1989.

61. Douglas C. McGill, "The Media Business; Star Wars in Cola Advertising," *New York Times*, March 27, 1989, 1.

62. Richard Morgan, "In Being a Good Corporate Citizen, Pepsi Came to Wrong Conclusion," *Adweek*, April 10, 1989, 2.

63. Ibid.

64. Holden, "Madonna Re-creates Herself."

65. "MuchMusic, MTV Playing Madonna Video," *Globe and Mail* (Canada), March 8, 1989.

66. At first Pepsi executives hesitated to react and only offered to pull the commercial from stations on which the video was also in rotation. Ongoing pressure from the media and religious groups eventually changed their minds.

67. The tenets of neoliberalism are discussed further in chapters 3 and 4. See also Harvey, *Brief History*, 165; and Gérard Duméil and Dominique Lévy, *Capital Resurgent: Roots of the Neoliberal Revolution* (Cambridge, MA: Harvard University Press, 2004).

68. Sources report that Madonna and Mary Lambert, the video's director, considered representing the pop star in an interracial relationship with a black man and getting shot by the Ku Klux Klan. See Liz Smith's column, "Warren Beatty and Madonna Are an Item," *San Francisco Chronicle*, April 19, 1989, E1.

69. The video's religious iconography is discussed further in McClary, *Feminine Endings*, 163–65; and Freccero, "Our Lady of MTV," 180–82. Also see hook's interpretation of the video's images of race and gender in *Black Looks*, 157–64.

70. In a *Rolling Stone* interview, Madonna discussed her reasons for challenging the tendency for people to "blindly" follow rules. Hiatt, "Live to Tell," 40–41.

71. Kellner also suggests that her image and performances, especially those in *Like a Prayer*, lie somewhere between the modern and postmodern. *Media Culture*, 263–95.

72. Williamson posits that audiences construct meaning in the process of "deciphering" an advertisement's signifiers. This deciphering should be relatively effortless for most commercials since they typically use clichéd signifiers. *Decoding Advertisements*, 71.

73. Schudson, *Advertising*, 226–27. In this passage Schudson quotes a market researcher for General Electric, Herbert E. Krugman. See Krugman's "The Impact of Television Advertising: Learning without Involvement," *Public Opinion Quarterly* 29 (1965): 349–56.

74. Schudson, *Advertising*, 214.

75. Vickers, "Materialism," 231.

76. McGill, "Media Business."

77. The look and sound of MTV, commercials, films, and television converged in the 1980s. Following the success of the nostalgic soundtrack for *The Big Chill* in 1983, many movies featured pop and rock songs to attract larger audiences and sell soundtracks. Some even employed new music, such as *Top Gun*'s "Danger Zone," which was the first song to gain popularity from the movie prior to radio play. Additionally, The "Brat Pack" movies (*Sixteen Candles* and *Fast Times at Ridgemont High*) featured the latest hits for teen audiences as a tactic for increasing movie ticket and album sales. Television shows like *Miami Vice* also showcased top-selling popular

music soundtracks. As mentioned in chapter 3, the *Miami Vice* theme song was also featured in a Pepsi commercial.

78. Demers, *Steal This Music*, 21–30, 59–70.

79. "Music Video Awards, 1989," MTV Networks, http://www.mtv.com/ontv/vma/1989/. Winning this particular category confirmed two things: (1) Madonna's message hit home with youth who wanted a say in the culture industry and had the financial means to do it (i.e., those who could afford cable television and the phone charge required to vote); and (2) there is no such thing as bad publicity. She concluded her acceptance speech with a big smile, saying, "And I'd like to thank Pepsi, for causing *so* much controversy." Heightening the irony of the evening, Neil Young's "This Note's for You"—a song about the absurdity and shamefulness of selling out to Pepsi and Coke—won Video of the Year.

80. McGill, "Media Business."

81. Carol Vernallis and Ross Fenimore detail Madonna's commentary on volatile issues explored in her music and videos, including gay rights, marriage, and the AIDS epidemic. Carol Vernallis, *Experiencing Music Video*, 209–35; Ross Fenimore, "Madonna's Confession: Sound, Self, and Survival in a Love Song" (PhD diss., University of California, Los Angeles, 2011).

82. Grant McCracken, *Transformations: Identity Construction in Contemporary Culture* (Bloomington: Indiana University Press, 2008), 305.

83. Harvey notes that the "neoconservatives" born out of the instabilities of the neoliberal state were members of the "disaffected white working class." He summarizes their "moral values" as centered on "nationalism, moral righteousness, Christianity . . . family values, and right-to-life" and their antagonisms to "feminism, gay rights, affirmative action, and environmentalism." *Brief History*, 81–86. "Make a Wish" certainly touches on many of these issues.

CHAPTER 6

1. Pepsi termed this, "Operation Desert Soda." Stoddard, *Pepsi*, 192.

2. Ibid., 189.

3. Pepsi attempted to grow into what it called "a total beverage company" by forming an alliance with Lipton Tea and Ocean Spray to become a distributor of teas, fruit drinks, and sports drinks. Ibid., 189–90.

4. Stuart Elliot, "As Pepsi Regroups, It Strikes a Generational Note Once Again," *New York Times*, January 21, 1997, http://www.nytimes.com/1997/01/21/business/as-pepsi-regroups-it-strikes-a-generational-note-once-again.html?_r=0; Glenda Cooper, "Pepsi Turns Air Blue as Cola Wars Reach for Sky," *Independent*, April 1, 1996, http://www.independent.co.uk/news/pepsi-turns-air-blue-as-cola-wars-reach-for-sky-1302822.html

5. This turned out to be a wise decision at a time when genres such as gangsta rap, grunge, and heavy metal fueled controversies over censorship. By 1990 record

stores were required to label albums that contained lyrics that the Parental Advisory Resource Center and the Recording Industry Association of America (RIAA) deemed "explicit." Many in the music industry opposed this, as well as the requirement that artists must record "clean" versions for sales to minors and for radio play. David Browne, "A Case in Omaha Reopens the Explicit Content Debate: Government Offices and the RIAA Crack Down on Album Sales," *Entertainment Weekly*, May 22, 1992, http://www.ew.com/article/1992/05/22/case-omaha-reopens-explicit-content-debate

6. An exception came at the end of the 1990s with an international bilingual commercial that showcased a love affair between Janet Jackson and Ricky Martin.

7. Stuart Elliott, "Pepsi Widens 'Generation' with New Pitch to All Ages," *New York Times*, January 20, 1992, http://www.nytimes.com/1992/01/20/business/media-business-advertising-pepsi-widens-generation-with-new-pitch-all-ages.html

8. Another 1990 spot not discussed here features Tina Turner singing a cover of Marvin Gaye and Kim Weston's 1965, "It Takes Two" alongside Rod Stewart.

9. Beard, *Humor*, 2.

10. Ibid.

11. Dwyer, *Back to the Fifties*.

12. Reynolds, *Retromania*, 199.

13. Beard, *Humor*, 27. Quotations are from Bob Kuperman, quoted in Anthony Vanoni, "Creative Differences," *Advertising Age* 68, no. 46 (1997): 1, 20, and 28.

14. Beard, *Humor*, 27–28.

15. Ibid., 37–100.

16. Enrique Alberto Arias, *Comedy in Music: A Historical Bibliographical Resource Guide* (Westport, CT: Greenwood Press, 2001), 3–5.

17. Randall Rothenberg, "Advertising: Trained in the School of Hard Yuks," *New York Times*, February 7, 1990, http://www.nytimes.com/1990/02/07/business/the-media-business-advertising-trained-in-the-school-of-hard-yuks.html

18. Barbara Lippert, "Coming of Age: Pepsi Makes Rap Music Its Choice for the Older Generation," *Chicago Tribune*, March 19, 1990, http://articles.chicagotribune.com/1990-03-19/features/9001230004_1_rap-pepsi-pepsi-public-enemy; "Shady Acres," PepsiCo. Inc., 1990.

19. Young MC also created a new rhyme for a Pepsi's short-lived "cool cans" commercial and prize giveaway.

20. Play cues indicate that the situation was meant to be taken as reality. Beard, *Humor*, 52.

21. Rothenberg, "Advertising."

22. Bonnie Drewnainy, "Pepsi's Generation Gap," in *Images That Injure: Pictorial Stereotypes in the Media*, ed. Paul Martin Lester, 3rd ed. (Santa Barbara, CA: Praeger, 2011), 231.

23. Ibid., 237–38.

24. Beard, *Humor*, 48.

25. Ibid., 91.

26. Foster Kamer, "The 40 Biggest Hip-Hop Moments in Pop Culture History,"

Complex, March 26, 2013, http://www.complex.com/music/2013/03/the-40-biggest-hip-hop-moments-in-pop-culture-history/

27. Adam Sweeting, "Hammered Home: Adam Sweeting Sees MC Hammer Let the Rap Rip at the Birmingham NEC on a Night of Music and Moralising," *The Guardian*, May 4, 1991.

28. This outfit is nearly identical to the one he wore in an *Arsenio Hall Show* performance earlier that year.

29. MC Hammer, *Let's Get It Started*, Capitol Records CDP 590924, 1988, compact disc.

30. Tricia Rose, "A Style Nobody Can Deal With: Politics, Style, and the Postindustrial City in Hip Hop," in *Popular Music: Critical Concepts in Media and Cultural Studies*, ed. Simon Frith (London: Routledge, 2004), 341–59. Rose also includes graffiti in this list.

31. Mickey Hess, *Is Hip Hop Dead? The Past, Present, and Future of America's Most Wanted Music* (Westport, CT: Praeger, 2007); Loren Kajikawa, *Sounding Race in Rap Songs* (Oakland: University of California Press, 2015); Charles Hiroshi Garrett, "'Pranksta Rap': Humor as Difference in Hip Hop," in *Rethinking Difference in Music Scholarship*, ed. Olivia Bloechl, Melanie Lowe, and Jeffrey Kallberg (Cambridge: Cambridge University Press, 2015), 315–37.

32. Robin James, *The Conjectural Body: Gender, Race, and the Philosophy of Music* (Lanham, MD: Lexington Books, 2010).

33. Tricia Rose, *Black Noise: Rap Music and Black Culture in Contemporary America* (Middletown, CT: Wesleyan University Press, 1994), 163.

34. Kajikawa, *Sounding Race*, 145.

35. Kamer, "40 Biggest Hip-Hop Moments."

36. Adam Sweeting, "MC Hammer: Me, Jesus, and the President," *The Guardian*, May 7, 1991, Rock's Backpages, http://www.rocksbackpages.com/Library/Article/mc-hammer-me-jesus-and-the-president

37. Rovi Steve Huey, "About Hammer," MTV Artists Beta, http://www.mtv.com/artists/hammer/biography/

38. Dan Charnas, *The Big Payback: The History of the Business of Hip Hop* (New York: New American Library, 2010), 275–77; See also Huey, "About Hammer."

39. Charnas, *Big Payback*, 277. These comments were summarized from the "Summer Music Preview" in *The Source* 3, no. 4 (Summer 1990).

40. Ibid., 280.

41. Ibid., 491–95. Charnas notes that Sprite became an ally to hip hop and even intervened in the East versus West Coast hip hop wars, which left its stars Biggie Smalls and Tupac Shakur dead in the late 1990s, by airing a campaign that encouraged peace between the two factions.

42. Ibid., 493.

43. Ibid., 495; Taylor, *Sounds of Capitalism*, 191.

44. In 1996 Pepsi and BBD&O tried to align its Mountain Dew lemon-lime drink with the hip hop culture it had failed to attract with its Hammer promos. These spots

failed despite the fact that marketers sought help from an African American advertising firm, hired rapper Busta Rhymes as the endorser, and got *The Source* magazine to promote the drink. Douglas Holt, *How Brands Become Icons: The Principles of Cultural Branding* (Boston: Harvard Business School, 2004), 196–98.

45. Sweeting, "MC Hammer."

46. Phil Hardy and Dave Laing, "MC Hammer," *The Faber Companion to 20th-Century Popular Music*, 2001, Rock's Backpages, http://www.rocksbackpages.com/Library/Article/mc-hammer

47. "The One Show: 1996 Winners Reel," AT:45273.021, Paley Center; Dottie Enrico, "Ad Game Was a Blowout, Too: Pepsi Wins/Beverage, Chip Maker Takes 4 of Top 5 Spots," *USA Today*, January 30, 1995, 5B; "Diner," PepsiCo. Inc., 1995.

48. Young Bloods, *Get Together,* RCA Victor LPM-3724, 1967, long-playing record.

49. Alan Siegel, "Watch 5 of the Best Super Bowl Commercials from 1997," *USA Today*, January 16, 2015, http://admeter.usatoday.com/2015/01/16/5-best-super-bowl-commercials-1997-budweiser-bud-light-pepsi-nissan/; "Dancing Bears," PepsiCo. Inc., 1997.

50. The Village People, "Y.M.C.A.," Casablanca NB 945, 1978, 7-inch vinyl single.

51. Skip Wollenberg, "Pepsi to Launch New Adverts at the Oscars: Humour, Humanity, Music; Aretha Franklin, Marlon Brando in Star-Studded Cast," *National Post* (Canada), March 6, 1999, D9.

52. Ibid. This commercial continued what the company's officials called the "key equities of humour, humanity, and music." As mentioned in chapter 1, Franklin had also sung for Coke in the 1960s and 1980s.

53. YouTube, "Pepsi The Joy of Cola Aretha Franklin Commercial," 0:29, posted by Maverick1989, May 14, 2009, https://www.youtube.com/watch?v=3C1I-IrOgyg

54. Kennell Jackson draws from Roland Barthes and Leon Wynte to question advertising's disembodiment of black singers and the cultural trafficking of their music in "The Shadows of Texts: Will Black Singers Sell Everything on Television?," in *Black Cultural Traffic: Crossroads in Global Performance and Popular Culture*, ed. Harry Justin Elam Jr. and Kennell Jackson (Ann Arbor: University of Michigan Press, 2005), 88–107.

55. Robin James, "On Intersectionality and Cultural Appropriation: The Case of Postmillennial Black Hipness," *Journal of Black Masculinity* 1, no. 2 (2011): 2, https://philpapers.org/rec/JAMOIA

56. Fu, *Advertising and Race*, 246.

57. Dwyer, *Back to the Fifties,* 2015; Boym, *Future of Nostalgia*, 2001.

58. Dwyer, *Back to the Fifties*, 10.

59. Michael Jackson, *Dangerous*, Epic EK 45400, 1991, compact disc.

60. Stuart Elliott, "The Media Business-Advertising: Michael Jackson's Revival May Not Win Him Any New Endorsements," *New York Times*, February 18, 1993, D22.

61. David Hay, "Super Bowl Ad Feast to Star Wacko Jacko and Air Jordan," *Sunday Age* (Melbourne), January 31, 1993, 18.

62. The Jackson 5, "I'll Be There," Motown M 1171, 1970, 7-inch vinyl single; "I'll Be There," PepsiCo. Inc., 1993.

63. Jason Stanyek and Benjamin Peikut, "Deadness: Technologies of the Intermundane," *The Drama Review* 54, no. 1 (2010): 14.

64. Ibid., 35.

65. Boym, *Future of Nostalgia*, xv.

66. Stanyek and Peikut, "Deadness," 28.

67. "Michael Jackson Picks White Boy to Play Him," *Evening Standard* (London), December 31, 1992, 5; "Jacko Was a White Baby," *Sunday Mail*, January 3, 1993.

68. Another article identified the boy as Wade Robson, who had won a Michael Jackson dance competition and had the opportunity to perform with the star at age five. "Following in Jacko's Dance Steps," *The Advertiser*, January 13, 1993.

69. "Michael Jackson Picks White Boy," 5.

70. Dwyer, *Back to the Fifties*, 146.

71. "Animal Magic as Jacko Stars in New TV Ad," *Evening Standard* (London), July 23, 1992, 12; Ben Macintyre and Richard Duce, "Pepsi Pulls Plug on Jackson after Pills Confession," *The Times*, November 15, 1993.

72. Frank Sinatra reportedly said that Charles was the only true genius in the business, and this moniker became integral to his legacy.

73. Dwyer, *Back to the Fifties*, 10.

74. Reynolds, *Retromania*, xii.

75. YouTube, "TV News Clips behind the Scenes Ray Charles," Video, 6:33, posted by musickeys 8, March 3, 2013, https://www.youtube.com/watch?v=zvwNBimIGE4. The video is a compilation of news aired on Fox WNYW, ABC's *Good Morning America*, and WLS Chicago in January 1991.

76. YouTube, "Ray Charles Diet Pepsi TV Commercial," 2:45, posted by musickeys8, March 13, 2013, https://www.youtube.com/watch?v=K6AFkk1LVwE. This clip also features "Worldwide" and "Audition," which are discussed below.

77. Martha T. Moore, "Singing for Supper: Uh Huh Girls Think They Can," *USA Today*, January 15, 1993, 2B. Charles's campaign was conceptualized after he had appeared in a successful endorsement the year before with Super Bowl champion Joe Montana. Michael Lydon, *Ray Charles: Man and Music* (New York: Riverhead, 1998), 373.

78. Lydon, *Ray Charles*, 277. Charles's Diet Pepsi commercials came after a decade of pop music endorsements for Diet Coke by Whitney Houston, Elton John, and Paula Abdul. Charles, too, had a long career endorsing products, which included a string of Coke radio commercials that featured duets with Aretha Franklin. He had also appeared in advertisements for multiple food corporations, including McDonalds and the California Raisins. Pepsi first recruited him in 1986 for a series of 60-second radio commercials titled "The Best of the New Generation." Edward Morris, "Hummingbird in Advertising Tie-In: Pepsi Jingles to Become Singles?," *Billboard*, June 28, 1986, 26.

79. Bernice Kanner, *The 100 Best TV Commercials . . . and Why They Worked* (New York: Random House, 1999), 139. Additional spots also aired for the caffeine-free version and international markets. The most famous were: "Orchestra," "Audition," "Worldwide," "Wiseguy," "Blues," and "Courtroom." Bob Stumpel's *Ray Charles Video Museum* blog contains descriptions and links to some of the spots. "Ray Charles

Ft. in Pepsi Commercials (1990–1993)," May 20, 2010, http://raycharlesvideomuseum. blogspot.com/2010/05/ray-charles-ft-in-pepsi-commercials.html

80. "Worldwide," the second spot to air, ranked highest. "Super Bowl Ad Meter: Charting Sales Pitches," *USA Today*, January 28, 1991, 5B.

81. "Best of 1991," *Time*, January 6, 1992, http://content.time.com/time/magazine/ article/0,9171,158750,00.html

82. Lydon, *Ray Charles*, 377; Stoddard, *Pepsi*, 193; Kanner, *100 Best TV Commercials*, 140.

83. "Diet Pepsi Offering a Chance at Spotlight," *Atlanta Journal and Constitution*, February 19, 1991, C2; Tessa Melvin, "Choristers Win Prize of $10,000 from Pepsi," *New York Times*, October 13, 1991, 12WC, 20; Deborah Jones, "Pepsi Got the Right One for Promoting Itself," *Globe and Mail* (Canada), January 30, 1992.

84. The tribute even featured Pepsi's hit slogan in the title: *50 Years in Music, Uh-huh!* Patrick McDonald, "Ode to a Fizzy Drink," *The Advertiser*, August 2, 1991.

85. YouTube, "TV News Clips."

86. Ibid.

87. Ibid.

88. "Lucky Old Sun" was written by Beasley Smith and Haven Gillespie. Many others, including Frank Sinatra and Louis Armstrong, have covered it in a variety of musical styles.

89. Composer Al Merrin calls it "a two syllable grunt that embodies affirmation." Kanner, *100 Best TV Commercials*, 140.

90. Robert Darden, *People Get Ready! A New History of Black Gospel Music* (New York: Continuum, 2004), 62.

91. Stuart Elliott, "More Campaigns Are Taking a Less-Than-Perfect Tone," *New York Times*, March 6, 1992, D5. Elliot reports that Ted Sann of BBD&O confirmed that the phrase "Uh-huh" was intended to "reflect" Diet Pepsi's contemporary target audience.

92. This was precisely the brand's goal according to its vice-president at the time, David Novak. YouTube, "TV News Clips."

93. "Orchestra" premiered during the first commercial break in the game's first quarter. "Super Bowl Ad Meter."

94. Drewnainy, "Pepsi's Generation Gap," 230.

95. Lydon, *Ray Charles*, 377.

96. Ibid., 377–78.

97. Ibid., 377 (my emphasis).

98. Music scholars such as Ingrid Monson have documented how those in privileged positions have appropriated signifiers from male African American artists. "The Problem with White Hipness, Race, Gender, and Cultural Conceptions in Jazz Historical Discourse," *Journal of the American Musicological Society* 48, no. 3 (Autumn 1995): 396–422. Also see Ford, *Dig*; and James, "On Intersectionality."

99. Mark Landler, "'Pepsi's Memorable Ads, Forgettable Sales," *Business Week*, October 21, 1991, 36. Pepsi also met disappointment with its "cool cans" summer promotion, which featured special edition designs with bold images of sunglasses, surf-

ers, and confetti. See Peter Kerr, "Pepsi Gets Facelift to Lure Youth," *New York Times*, September 24, 1991, D1, D4.

100. Customers claimed that Coke cans filled with special prizes for its "Magic Cans" promotion malfunctioned and that the soda inside tasted bad. Coke was also pressured to pull some of its humorous Super Bowl commercials out of respect for the war in the Persian Gulf.

101. Taylor, *Sounds of Capitalism*, 207.

102. Knopper, *Appetite*, 105–12.

103. Klein explains how licensing began to bypass dwindling radio play opportunities in *As Heard on TV*, 59–78.

PEPSI CODA

1. Kellner, *Media Spectacle*, 11.

2. Kellner posits that "technocapitalism" is a result of the move away from industrial models of production and toward the commodification of ideas such as technology, culture, and pharmaceutical research. Ibid., 13.

3. Tristan Donovan claims that Apple founder Steve Jobs modeled the company's image and marketing tactics after the soda brand and its "Pepsi Generation" efforts. *Fizz: How Soda Shook Up the World* (Chicago: Chicago Review Press, 2014), 190. Notably, Pepsi's iTunes co-branding deal was largely a bust since consumers redeemed only five million of the codes due to the fact that bottles with coded caps were not distributed to enough markets before the promotion ended. Ina Fried, "Pepsi's iTunes Promotion Goes Flat," *CNET News*, April 28, 2004, http://news.cnet.com/2100-1025_3-5201676.html

4. "Mariah Carey Hits Perfect Note with Pepsi," *PR Newswire: United Business Media*, April 9, 2006, http://www.prnewswire.com/news-releases/mariah-carey-hits-perfect-note-with-pepsi-56454402html; "New Original Ringtones by Mariah Carey, Mary J. Blige, and The All-American Rejects Now Available Exclusively through the Pepsi Cool Tones and Motorola Phones Promotion," *PR Newswire: United Business Media*, May 15, 2006, http://www.prnewswire.com/news-releases/new-original-ring-tones-by-mariah-carey-mary-j-blige-and-the-all-american-rejects-now-available-ex clusively-through-the-pepsi-cool-tones-motorola-phones-promotion-56349032.html

5. Shazam Entertainment also used mobile technologies to connect consumers with the music heard in its environments and to offer easy links for downloading it through Amazon. Jackson, *Sonic Branding*, 8.

6. Patrick Coffee, "Pepsi and BBDO New York Rekindle Relationship 7 Years after Their Big Breakup," *Adweek,* September 24, 2015, http://www.adweek.com/brand-marketing/pepsi-and-bbdo-new-york-rekindle-relationship-7-years-after-their-big-breakup-167116/

7. Margot Sanger-Katz, "The Decline of Big Soda," *New York Times*, October 2, 2015, http://www.nytimes.com/2015/10/04/upshot/soda-industry-struggles-as-con sumer-tastes-change.html?_r=0

8. Mike Esterl, "Diet Coke Wins the Battle in Cola Wars," *Wall Street Journal*, March 17, 2011, https://www.wsj.com/articles/SB10001424052748703899704576204933906436332

9. "A Not-So-Secret Recipe for Pepsi to Regain Its Footing," *Advertising Age*, March 28, 2011, http://adage.com/article/cmo-strategy/a-secret-recipe-pepsi-regain-footing/149578/

10. Coca-Cola was just one of many national brands that sponsored *American Idol*.

11. Jenkins, "Buying into *American Idol*," 343–47.

12. A report confirmed that Pepsi and *X Factor* would "support each other on the Web and in stores." Brian Stelter, "Deal with Pepsi Lets Fox Have It Both Ways: Agreement on 'X Factor' Adds the 2nd Cola Giant to Network's Sponsor List," *International Herald Tribune*, January 5, 2011, 15; "Sony Music Entertainment and Simon Cowell Launch New Global Venture: 'Syco,'" *PRNewswire: United Business Media*, January 19, 2010, http://www.prnewswire.co.uk/news-releases/sony-music-entertainment-and-simon-cowell-launch-new-global-venture-syco-154865975.html

13. Bruce Horovitz, "'X Factor' Brings Back the Pepsi vs. Coke Cola Wars," *USA Today*, September 9, 2011, https://usatoday30.usatoday.com/money/advertising/story/2011-09-20/cola-wars-pepsi-xfactor/50483082/1 (my emphasis).

14. Drew MacKenzie, "Britney's a $21 Million Pep Star; Teen Queen Signs for Drink Advert," *The Mirror*, February 8, 2001, 24; Nolan Wilder, "Kanye West and Pepsi Take a Trip around the Globe," *Urban Mecca*, August 28, 2009, http://urbanmecca.net/news/2005/08/28/kanye-west-and-pepsi-take-a-trip-around-the-globe/. This spot featured West's new track, "Heard 'Em Say."

15. Melanie Amaro, "Respect," Simco. Ltd./Epic, 2012, downloaded May 2, 2012, iTunes, MP3; Aretha Franklin, "Respect/Dr. Feelgood," Atlantic 45–2403, 1967, long-playing record; Otis Redding, *Otis Blue/Otis Redding Sings Soul*, Volt 412, 1965, long-playing record.

16. A longer version aired during the Grammy Awards the week after the Super Bowl. In that version Amaro also sings the song's opening phrases.

17. Nick Carbone, "Super Bowl Spoiler: Elton John Rules the Middle Ages with Pepsi," *Time*, February 4, 2012, http://newsfeed.time.com/2012/02/04/super-bowl-spoiler-elton-john-rules-the-middle-ages-with-pepsi/

18. Tricia Rose writes that Flava Flav's clock is an emblem of hip hop irony that magnifies the white world's tensions between work, leisure, and time. "A Style Nobody Can Deal With," 351.

19. Goldman and Papson, *Nike Culture*, 31–32.

20. Ken Wheaton, "Forget Ferris: Kia and Chevy Race to the Top; Few Surprises, but Budweiser, Chrysler, and GE Promise Us Things Will Get Better," *Advertising Age*, February 6, 2012, 1.

21. Stuart Elliot, "Judging Super Bowl Commercials, from Charming to Smarmy," *New York Times*, February 6, 2012, 2.

22. Ibid. The brand's other commercial was for Pepsi Max.

23. "How Our Panel Rated the Super Bowl Ads," *USA Today*, February 6, 2012,

https://usatoday30.usatoday.com/money/advertising/story/2012-02-06/how-our-ad-panel-rated-the-Super-Bowl-ads/52981300/1

24. Jenkins, "Buying into *American Idol*," 347.

25. Brian Turner, comment on "Respect-Single," in Customer Reviews, "not sure what is going on here," February 2, 2012, iTunes. This comment received 105 likes.

26. Anita Giulani, comment on "Respect-Single," in Customer Reviews, "No . . . ," February 2, 2012, iTunes. This comment garnered 51 likes.

27. embracethecheese, comment on "Respect-Single," in Customer Reviews, "Melanie's back . . . kind of," February 2, 2012, iTunes (emphasis in the original).

28. Rob Bowman, "Franklin, Aretha," *Grove Music Online*. Oxford Music Online, http://www.oxfordmusiconline.com/subscriber/article/grove/music/45921

29. Meier observes a push both within and outside of the music industry to promote only those deemed potentially successful as "artist brands." *Popular Music*, 74–84.

30. Meier notes that "happy sounds" like this are produced when creativity is suppressed in an effort to capture the positive qualities that sponsoring entities want associated with their brands. Ibid., 120–25.

31. Giana M. Eckhardt and Alan Bradshaw build on Scott Lash and Celia Lury's discussion of the "thingification" of cultural forms in ads in "The Erasure of Antagonisms between Popular Music and Advertising," *Marketing Theory* 14, no. 2 (2014): 181; Scott Lash and Celia Lury, *Global Culture Industry: The Mediation of Things* (Cambridge: Polity Press, 2007).

32. Beard, *Humor*, 39–45; Brecht, "New Technique," 143. For more on the use of Brechtian principles in advertising, see chapter 5.

33. Alison Slade, "Your 'American Idol': The Intersection between Reality Television, Ideology, and the Music Industry in Popular Culture," in *Rock Brands: Selling Sound in a Media Saturated Culture*, ed. Elizabeth Barfoot Christian (Plymouth: Lexington, 2011), 266.

34. Ibid., 257. Slade cites the fate of the openly gay *American Idol* contestant Adam Lambert as an example.

35. Meizel, *Idolized*, 218–19.

36. Hartley, "Communicative Democracy," 45.

37. Meizel, *Idolized*, 17.

38. Jenkins, "Buying into *American Idol*," 345.

39. Henry Jenkins, Sam Ford, and Joshua Green, *Spreadable Media: Creating Value and Meaning in a Networked Culture* (New York: New York University Press, 2013), 116.

40. The term originated with Alvin Toffler, and its applications have proliferated in recent years. *The Third Wave* (New York: Bantam, 1980), 265–88.

41. Carah, *Pop Brands*, xvii.

42. Ibid., 153.

43. Jenkins, Ford, and Green, *Spreadable Media*, 116; Kellner, *Media Spectacle*, 13.

44. McCracken, *Culture and Consumption II*, 112.

45. Theodor W. Adorno, "On the Fetish Character of Music and Regression of Listening," in *Essays on Music*, ed. Richard Leppert, trans. Susan H. Gillespie (Berkeley: University of California Press, 2002), 288–317. Adorno elaborates on this in "Resignation," in *The Culture Industry: Selected Essays on Mass Culture*, ed. Rolf Tiedman, 2nd ed. (London: Routledge, 2001), 198–204.

46. David Harvey confirms that "the assumption that individual freedoms are guaranteed by freedom of the market and of trade is a cardinal feature of neoliberal thinking." *Brief History*, 7.

47. Timothy Taylor, "Advertising and the Conquest of Culture," *Social Semiotics* 19, no. 4 (2009): 405–425.

48. Gerrick D. Kennedy, "Quick Takes: 'X Factor' Champ Signs with Epic," *Los Angeles Times*, January 4, 2012, http://articles.latimes.com/2012/jan/04/entertain ment/la-et-quick-20120104. Amaro's status as a television-made pop star is similar to that of musicians made famous by the late 1960s and 1970s television shows *The Monkees* and *The Partridge Family*.

49. Dallas W. Smythe argued as early as 1983 that the mass media worked to sell audiences as commodities to advertisers and that the act of watching television made viewers "workers" for media outlets. "On Critical and Administrative Research: A New Critical Analysis," *Journal of Communication* 33 (1983): 117–27.

50. Meier, *Popular Music*, 155.

51. Schultz and Poggi, "Behind Pepsi's 'Meta' Integration.'"

52. Jackson, *Sonic Branding*, 90–91; Holt, *How Brands Become Icons*, 10–11.

53. Refer to chapter 2, where Phil Dusenberry, a prominent BBD&O adman, is quoted saying that Pepsi's deal with Jackson placed entertainment above the selling proposition.

54. The switch from "Come Alive! You're in the Pepsi Generation" to "The Taste That Beats the Others Cold, Pepsi Pours It On" is one such example (see chapter 1).

55. "Pepsi Commercial 2017," Super Bowl Commercials 2017, http://www.super bowlcommercials.co/pepsi/. PepsiCo. aired only two commercials during the 2017 event, one for Pepsi Zero Sugar and another for LifeWater, featuring John Legend's "Love Me Now." Notably, the brand signed an agreement with the National Football League for a 10-year deal from 2013 to 2022 to sponsor the event's halftime shows.

56. Skip Marley, "Lions," Island Records/UMG Recordings, Inc., 2017, downloaded April 6, 2017, iTunes, MP4.

57. Erica Gonzales, "The Music Is the Redeeming Quality of Kendall Jenner's Pepsi Commercial: Skip Marley Opens Up about His Track 'Lions,'" *Harper's Bazaar*, April 4, 2017, http://www.harpersbazaar.com/culture/art-books-music/news/a21797/kend all-jenner-pepsi-commercial-skip-marley/

58. Alexander Smith, "Pepsi Ad with Kendall Jenner Echoes Black Lives Matter, Sparks Anger," *NBC News*, April 5, 2017, http://www.nbcnews.com/news/nbcblk/pep si-ad-kendall-jenner-echoes-black-lives-matter-sparks-anger-n742811. Viewers have scrutinized the billion-dollar brand while simultaneously appearing to recognize (and generally accept) Marley's need to license his music in order to succeed in today's music industry. Joanna Love, "Double Bind Taste Test: On the Music in THAT Pepsi

Ad," *Musicology Now*, May 8, 2017, http://musicologynow.ams-net.org/search?q=pepsi

59. Ellie Shechet, "Pepsi Responds to Backlash: Actually, the Kendall Jenner Ad Is Good and Meaningful," *Jezebel*, April 5, 2017, http://jezebel.com/pepsi-responds-to-backlash-actually-the-kendall-jenne-1794030530; Maxwell Strachan, "Pepsi Pulls Kendall Jenner Ad Following Intense Backlash," *Huffington Post*, April 5, 2017, http://www.huffingtonpost.com/entry/pepsi-ad-kendalljenner_us_58 e52783e4b0fe4ce08764d0; Sasha Geffen, "Madonna Has No Sympathy for Kendall Jenner after Pepsi Pulls Controversial Ad," *MTV News*, April 6, 2017, http://www.mtv.com/news/3000427/madonna-kendall-jenner-pepsi-ad/?xrs=_s.fb_main

60. Jonathan Sterne and Anahid Kassabian have documented how popular music helps to promote branded spaces in retail environments in an effort appeal to specific consumer tastes and lifestyles. Jonathan Sterne, "Sounds Like the Mall of America: Programmed Music and the Architectonics of Commercial Space," *Ethnomusicology* 41, no. 1 (1997): 22–50; Kassabian, *Ubiquitous Listening*, 84–108.

61. See Carah, *Pop Brands*, 2010; Jackson, *Sonic Branding*, 2003; Powers, "Strange Powers," 2010; Meier, *Popular Music*, 2017.

62. Carah, *Pop Brands*, 5, 152–75. The proliferation of music festivals over the past decade, as well as soaring attendance numbers for festivals like Coachella, SXSW, and Bonaroo confirm these trends.

63. Taylor, *Music and Capitalism*, 2016.

64. Meier, *Popular Music*, 77.

65. Its slogan reads, "We don't just understand culture, we create it." "About," Arcade Creative Group, a Sony Music Company, http://www.arcadecg.com/about/. Chris Brown's incorporation of the famous Double Mint Gum slogan into his 2007 track "Forever" offers a compelling example of these practices.

66. John Kell, "Soda Consumption Falls to 30-Year Low in the U.S.," *Fortune*, March 29, 2016, http://fortune.com/2015/03/26/soda-sales-drop-2014/; Kate Taylor, "Coke and Pepsi Are Facing a Terrifying Reality," *Business Insider*, March 29, 2016, http://www.businessinsider.com/people-drinking-less-coke-and-pepsi-2016-3

67. E. J. Schultz, "Pepsi Cans Attempt to Reclaim Pop Culture Glory," *Advertising Age*, May 10, 2018, http://adage.com/article/cmo-strategy/michael-jackson-ray-charles-britney-spears-pepsi-cans/313463/

BIBLIOGRAPHY

ABBREVIATIONS

Fred/Alan MTV   Fred/Alan MTV Network Collection, 1981–1982

Pepsi Generation   Pepsi Generation Oral History and
                                       Documentation Collection, 1938–1986

NMAH Smithsonian   Archives Center, National Museum of American
                                       History, Smithsonian Institution, Washington,
                                       DC

Paley Center   Paley Center for Media, Los Angeles

UCLA Film and Television Archive   University of California, Los Angeles, Film and
                                       Television Archive, Los Angeles

MEDIA

"Advertising Age: Best Television Commercials of the Year, 1984 (TV)." AT:29530,
    Paley Center.
Amaro, Melanie. "Respect." Simco Ltd./Epic, 2012, downloaded May 2, 2012, iTunes,
    MP3.
Bowie, David. *Let's Dance*. EMI America 0C 062–400 165, 1983, long-playing record.
"Coca-Cola: Max Interview." Video Storyboard Tests, Inc.: Most Outstanding
    Commercials of 1986, AT88, 1148, Paley Center.
Coca-Cola: The History of An American Icon. Directed by Ray Greene. Orland Park,
    IL, MPI Home Video, 2002. DVD.
Coca-Cola: The Real Story behind the Real Thing. Directed by Mitch Weitnzer. New
    York, CNBC Original, 2010.
Coke vs. Pepsi: A Duel between Giants. Directed by Nicolas Glimois. Issy-les Moulinaux,
    France 5 and Sunset Presse, 2002.

Franklin, Aretha. "Respect/Dr. Feelgood." Atlantic 45-2403, 1967, long-playing record.

"Grammy Awards, 31st: February 22, 1989." VA 7132, UCLA Film and Television Archive.

Hammer, MC. *Let's Get It Started*. Capitol Records CDP 590924, 1988, compact disc.

Jackson, Michael. *Bad*. Epic EK 40600, 1987, compact disc.

Jackson, Michael. *Dangerous*. Epic EK 45400, 1991, compact disc.

Jackson, Michael. *Thriller*. Epic EK 38112, 1982, long-playing record.

The Jackson 5. "I'll Be There." Motown M 1171, 1970, 7-inch vinyl single.

Madonna. *Like a Prayer*. Sire 9 25844-2, 1989, compact disc.

Marley, Skip. "Lions." Island Records/UMG Recordings, Inc., 2017, downloaded April 6, 2017, iTunes, MP4.

Michael Jackson: Bad 25. Directed by Spike Lee. New York, Sony Music, 2013. DVD.

Michael Jackson: Video Greatest Hits—HIStory. "Billie Jean." Directed by Martin Scorsese. New York, Epic Music Video, 2001. DVD.

"The One Show: 1996 Winners Reel." AT:45273.021, Paley Center.

Outasight. "Tonight Is the Night." Warner Bros. B005P5OHF4, 2011, MP3.

"Pepsi Cola: New Styles/Homecoming/Block Party." AT:23650.005, Paley Center.

"Pepsi-Cola American Television Commercials (1946–1975)." Pepsi Generation, Collection 111, Series 4, Box 28, NMAH Smithsonian.

"PepsiCo. Inc., 1985." AT:52247.020, Paley Center.

PepsiCo. Inc. "Backstage." 1987.

PepsiCo. Inc. "Band." 1980.

PepsiCo. Inc. "The Chase" 1988.

PepsiCo. Inc. "Come Alive." 1964.

PepsiCo. Inc. "The Concert." 1984.

PepsiCo. Inc. "The Concert." 1987.

PepsiCo. Inc. "Creation." 1987.

PepsiCo. Inc. "Dancing Bears." 1997.

PepsiCo. Inc. "Diner." 1995.

PepsiCo. Inc. "Have a Pepsi, The Light Refreshment. 1954.

PepsiCo. Inc. "I'll Be There." 1993.

PepsiCo. Inc. "Joy of Cola." 2001.

PepsiCo. Inc. "King's Court." 2011.

PepsiCo. Inc. "Madonna Commercial Promo," 1989.

PepsiCo. Inc. "Make a Wish." 1989.

PepsiCo. Inc. "More Bounce to the Ounce." 1950.

PepsiCo. Inc. "Music Icons." 2011.

PepsiCo. Inc. "New Styles." 1985.

PepsiCo. Inc. "Now and Then." 2002.

PepsiCo. Inc. "Restaurant." 2006.

PepsiCo. Inc. "Robots." 1985.

PepsiCo. Inc. "Shady Acres." 1990.

PepsiCo. Inc. "Street." 1984.

PepsiCo. Inc. "The Switch." 1990.

PepsiCo. Inc. "Timeline." 2009.

PepsiCo. Inc. "We've Got the Taste." 1986.

PepsiCo. Inc. "You've Got a Lot to Live" 1970.

"Pepsi Commercial: March 7, 1989." VA 7495, UCLA Film and Television Archive.

Redding, Otis. *Otis Blue/Otis Redding Sings Soul*. Volt 412, 1965, long-playing record.

Richie, Lionel. *Can't Slow Down*. Motown 6059MD, 1983, compact disc.

"Video Storyboard Tests, Inc.: Most Outstanding Commercials of 1985." AT88:1121, Paley Center.

The Village People. "Y.M.C.A." Casablanca NB 945, 1978, 7-inch vinyl single.

Young, Neil. *This Note's for You*. Reprise 9 25719-2, 1988, compact disc.

Young Bloods. *Get Together*. RCA Victor LPM-3724, 1967, long-playing record.

YouTube. "Commercial-Pepsi-Cola-Be Sociable Have a Pepsi!" 1:14. Posted by Video Archeology6, May 31, 2014, https://www.youtube.com/watch?v=cM5TDiiNpfE

YouTube. "The MTV Premiere of Michael Jackson Pepsi." 30:42. From a special tele-vised by MTV in February 1984. Posted by Giraldi Media, July 1, 2009. https://www.youtube.com/watch?v=njNwQPrpacs

YouTube. "Pepsi Cola Hits the Spot." 1:03. ClassicTVAds.com, 2005. Posted by wikievi-dently, January 19, 2009. https://www.youtube.com/watch?v=RRceIelAB3s

YouTube. "Pepsi: Tina vs Anchalee." 1:00. Posted by singhagold1, December 9, 2010. https://www.youtube.com/watch?v=LaEL2xzi488

YouTube. "Pepsi The Joy of Cola Aretha Franklin Commercial." 0:29. Posted by Maverick1989, May 14, 2009. https://www.youtube.com/watch?v=3C1I-IrOgyg

YouTube. "Ray Charles Diet Pepsi TV Commercial." 2:45. Posted by musickeys8, March 13, 2013. https://www.youtube.com/watch?v=K6AFkk1LVwE

YouTube. "TV News Clips behind the Scenes Ray Charles." 6:33. Posted by musickeys 8, March 3, 2013. https://www.youtube.com/watch?v=zvwNBimIGE4

ARCHIVED INTERVIEWS

Interviews by Scott Ellsworth. Pepsi Generation, Collection 111, NMAH Smithsonian.

Bergin, John. New York City, February 6, 1985, Series 3.1, Box 15.

Corbani, John. San Francisco, December 27, 1984, Series 3.1, Box 15.

Dillon, Tom. New York City, May 23, 1984, Series 3.1, Box 15.

Dusenberry, Phil. New York City, December 11, 1984, Series 3.1, Box 15.

Enrico, Roger. Purchase, NY, January 4, 1985, Series 3.1, Box 15.

Heller, Norman. Purchase, NY, January 9, 1985, Series 3.1, Box 16.

Hughs, Philip. Tulsa, OK, October 19, 1984, Series 3.1, Box 16.

Levine, Rick. New York City, December 18, 1984, Series 3.1, Box 17.

Lipsitz, Hilary. New York City, April 19, 1985, Series 3.1, Box 17, and Series 1, Box 1.

Mack, Walter. New York City, December 16, 1985, Series 3.1, Box 17.

Pottasch, Alan. Purchase, NY, May 8, 1984, Series 3.1, Box 19.

Ramin, Sid. New York City, December 18, 1984, Series 3, Box 18.

Rosenshine, Allan. New York City, December 10, 1984, Series 3.1, Box 18.

Sommers, Joanie. Beverly Hills, CA, January 2, 1985, Series 3.1, Box 15.

TRADE PUBLICATIONS, PRESS, AND WEBSITES

"About." Arcade Creative Group: A Sony Music Company. Accessed June 27, 2017. http://www.arcadecg.com/about/

"Adventures II: A Second Album Starts Its Rounds." *Pepsi-Cola World*, April 1966. Pepsi Generation, Collection 111, Series 1.2, Box 6, NMAH Smithsonian.

"Advertising/The Idea the Power." *Pepsi-Cola World*, March 1961. Pepsi Generation, Collection 111, Series 1.2, Box 4, NMAH Smithsonian.

Ainslie, Peter. "Commercial Zapping: TV Tapers Strike Back; VCR Owners Are Skipping Station Breaks, and Advertisers Are Getting Worried." *Rolling Stone*, February 28, 1985, 68–69.

"Alive and Living." *Pepsi-Cola World*, August 1969. Pepsi Generation, Collection 111, Series 1.2, Box 6, NMAH Smithsonian.

Andrews, Travis, and Fred Barbash. "'I'd Like to Buy the World a Coke': The Story Behind the World's Most Famous Ad, in Memoriam Its Creator." *Washington Post*, May 17, 2016. Accessed June 30, 2017. https://www.washingtonpost.com/news/morning-mix/wp/2016/05/17/id-like-to-buy-the-world-a-coke-the-story-behind-the-worlds-most-famous-ad-whose-creator-has-died-at-89/?utm_term=.9d30cd-2ce3f5

"Animal Magic as Jacko Stars in New TV Ad." *Evening Standard* (London), July 23, 1992. LexisNexis Academic.

Baker, B. "Genius in Wonderland." *Courier-Mail*, April 23, 1988. LexisNexis Academic.

Bart, Peter. "Madison Avenue: Think Young." *SR*, December 8, 1962. Pepsi Generation, Collection 111, Series 1, Box 1, NMAH Smithsonian.

Belcher, David. "Thigh Time to Call It a Day." *The Herald* (Glasgow), July 1, 2000. LexisNexis Academic.

Belsky, Gail. "Pepsi Challenge Back; Jackson Spot on Hold." *Adweek*, March 23, 1987.

"Best of 1991." *Time*, January 6, 1992. Accessed July 6, 2017. http://content.time.com/time/magazine/article/0,9171,158750,00.html

"Big Stars Cashing in on TV Ads." *Telegraph*, September 15, 1987. LexisNexis Academic.

Browne, David. "A Case in Omaha Reopens the Explicit Content Debate: Government Offices and the RIAA Crack Down on Album Sales." *Entertainment Weekly*, May 22, 1992. Accessed October 30, 2016. http://www.ew.com/article/1992/05/22/case-omaha-reopens-explicit-content-debate

Carbone, Nick. "Super Bowl Spoiler: Elton John Rules the Middle Ages with Pepsi." *Time*, February 4, 2012. Accessed June 27, 2017. http://newsfeed.time.com/2012/02/04/super-bowl-spoiler-elton-john-rules-the-middle-ages-with-pepsi/

Cocks, Jay. "The Badder They Come." *Time*, September 14, 1987. Accessed February 20, 2010. http://www.time.com/time/magazine/article/0,9171,965452

Coffee, Patrick. "Pepsi and BBDO New York Rekindle Relationship 7 Years after Their Big Breakup." *Adweek,* September 24, 2015. Accessed June 27, 2017. http://www.adweek.com/brand-marketing/pepsi-and-bbdo-new-york-rekindle-relationship-7-years-after-their-big-breakup-167116/

"Coke-Pepsi Budgets Highest in History." *Sponsor*, June 25, 1962, 27–30, 47.

"Come Alive." *Pepsi-Cola World*, October 1964. Pepsi Generation, Collection 111, Series 1.2, Box 5, NMAH Smithsonian.

Cooper, Glenda. "Pepsi Turns Air Blue as Cola Wars Reach for Sky." *Independent*, April 1, 1996. Accessed November 1, 2016. http://www.independent.co.uk/news/pepsi-turns-air-blue-as-cola-wars-reach-for-sky-1302822.html

Cox, James. "Boycott Aim, Pepsi: Madonna Ridicules Christianity." *USA Today*, March 9, 1989. LexisNexis Academic.

"Diet Pepsi Offering a Chance at Spotlight." *Atlanta Journal and Constitution*, February 19, 1991. LexisNexis Academic.

"Double Whammy for Pop Drink." *Toronto Star*, July 20, 1987, B6. LexisNexis Academic.

Dougherty, Philip H. "Advertising: Tina Turner Helps Global Effort." *New York Times*, March 10, 1986. LexisNexis Academic.

Eliason, Niela M. "Aging: Later Years Now Mean Prime Time, Not Just Problems." *St. Petersburg Times* (Florida), December 22, 1989. LexisNexis Academic.

Elliott, Stuart. "As Pepsi Regroups, It Strikes a Generational Note Once Again." *New York Times*, January 21, 1997. Accessed November 1, 2016. http://www.nytimes.com/1997/01/21/business/as-pepsi-regroups-it-strikes-a-generational-note-once-again.html?_r=0

Elliott, Stuart. "Judging Super Bowl Commercials, from Charming to Smarmy." *New York Times*, February 6, 2012. LexisNexis Academic.

Elliott, Stuart. "The Media Business-Advertising: Michael Jackson's Revival May Not Win Him Any New Endorsements." *New York Times*, February 18, 1993. LexisNexis Academic.

Elliott, Stuart. "More Campaigns Are Taking a Less-Than-Perfect Tone." *New York Times*, March 6, 1992. LexisNexis Academic.

Elliott, Stuart. "Pepsi Widens 'Generation' with New Pitch to All Ages." *New York Times*, January 20, 1992. Accessed November 13, 2016. http://www.nytimes.com/1992/01/20/business/media-business-advertising-pepsi-widens-generation-with-new-pitch-all-ages.html

Elliott, Stuart. "Si, Pepsi Habla Español: First Network Spanish Ad." *USA Today*, February 21, 1989, 2B.

Enrico, Dottie. "Ad Game Was a Blowout, Too: Pepsi Wins/Beverage, Chip Maker Takes 4 of Top 5 Spots." *USA Today*, January 30, 1995. LexisNexis Academic.

Erlewine, Stephen Thomas. "AllMusic Review: Lionel Richie *Can't Slow Down*." AllMusic. Accessed June 29, 2015. http://www.allmusic.com/album/cant-slow-down-mw0000650685

Erlichman, James. "The Day the Music Died: Big Business May Be Turning the Pop Industry into Just a Mint with a Hole in the Middle." *The Guardian*, November 24, 1987. LexisNexis Academic.

Esterl, Mike. "Diet Coke Wins the Battle in Cola Wars." *Wall Street Journal*, March 17, 2011. Accessed June 27, 2017. https://www.wsj.com/articles/SB100014240527487038 99704576204933906436332

Estes, Adam Clark. "A Brief History of Racist Soft Drinks." *The Atlantic*, January 28, 2013. Accessed June 22, 2017. https://www.theatlantic.com/national/ archive/2013/01/brief-history-racist-soft-drinks/318929/

Evans, Mark. "MuchMusic at the Helm for International Video Awards." *Financial Post* (Canada), April 11, 1989. LexisNexis Academic.

"Following in Jacko's Dance Steps." *The Advertiser*, January 13, 1993. LexisNexis Academic.

Fried, Ina. "Pepsi's iTunes Promotion Goes Flat." *CNET News*, April 28, 2004. Accessed June 27, 2007. http://news.cnet.com/2100-1025_3-5201676.html

FriField, Don. "The Pepsi Generation: The Phrase Itself Is Now a Generation Old and Has Joined the English Language." N.d. Pepsi Generation, Collection 111, Series 1.1, Box 1, NMAH Smithsonian.

Garfield, Bob. "Cola War's TV Extravaganzas: Jackson Gives Pepsi Bad Rap." *Advertising Age*, November 2, 1987.

Geffen, Sasha. "Madonna Has No Sympathy for Kendall Jenner after Pepsi Pulls Controversial Ad." *MTV News*, April 6, 2017. Accessed April 6, 2017. http://www. mtv.com/news/3000427/madonna-kendall-jenner-pepsi-ad/?xrs=_s.fb_main

Giges, Nancy. "Pepsi and Jackson in New Link." *Advertising Age*, May 5, 1986.

Giges, Nancy. "Pepsi-Jackson 'Spectacular' Set for Spring." *Advertising Age*, February 16, 1987.

Giges, Nancy. "Pepsi Rekindles Cola War: Bottlers Want 'Sure-Fire' Effort to Counter Coke Gains." *Advertising Age*, May 4 1987.

Goldberg, Michael. "Live Aid 1985: The Day the World Rocked." *Rolling Stone*, August 15, 1985. Accessed December 26, 2017. https://www.rollingstone.com/music/news/ live-aid-1985-the-day-the-world-rocked-19850815

Gonzales, Erica. "The Music Is the Redeeming Quality of Kendall Jenner's Pepsi Commercial: Skip Marley Opens Up about His Track 'Lions.'" *Harper's Bazaar*, April 4, 2017. Accessed April 6, 2017. http://www.harpersbazaar.com/culture/art-books-music/news/a21797/kendall-jenner-pepsi-commercial-skip-marley/

"Grid Giants Lynch 'Caddying' for Pepsi." *Sponsor*, July 8, 1963, 43.

Gross, Jonathan. "Concert Tina." *Toronto Star*, June 13, 1987. LexisNexis Academic.

Gross, Jonathan. "Pop Culture." *Toronto Star,* April 11, 1987, S18.

Gross, Jonathan. "Trouble Brewing." *Toronto Star*, May 31, 1986, S12.

Hardy, Phil, and Dave Laing. "Lionel Richie." *The Faber Companion to 20th-Century Popular Music*, 2001. Rock's Backpages. http://www.rocksbackpages.com/Library/ Article/lionel-richie

Hardy, Phil, and Dave Laing. "MC Hammer." *The Faber Companion to 20th-Century*

Popular Music, 2001. Rock's Backpages. http://www.rocksbackpages.com/Library/Article/mc-hammer

Haring, Bruce. "Madonna No Longer Has a Pepsi Prayer." *Billboard*, April 15, 1989, 3, 76.

Harrington, Richard. "David Bowie Unmasked: Rock's Starman Peeling Back the Layers and Finding Himself." *Washington Post*, April 26, 1987, G1.

Harrington, Richard. "Irish Quartet Takes Album of the Year Award." *Washington Post*, March 3, 1988. LexisNexis Academic.

Harrington, Richard. "Lionel Richie: He Writes the Songs." *Washington Post*, May 24, 1984, K1.

Harrington, Richard. "Pepsi and the Pop Star: Michael Jackson's $15 Million Cola Deal." *Washington Post*, May 6, 1986, C2. LexisNexis Academic.

"Have a Pepsi Day." In *Pepsi-Cola Media Ordering Catalog*, 1978. Pepsi Generation, Collection 111, Series 1.2, Box 10, NMAH Smithsonian.

Hay, David. "Super Bowl Ad Feast to Star Wacko Jacko and Air Jordan." *Sunday Age* (Melbourne), January 31, 1993. LexisNexis Academic.

Hay, John. "Bowie Axed from TV Adverts." *The Advertiser*, November 5, 1987. LexisNexis Academic.

"Here Comes GO!!!" *Pepsi-Cola World*, April 1967. Pepsi Generation, Collection 111, Series 1.2, Box 6, NMAH Smithsonian.

Herrera, Monica. "Michael Jackson, Pepsi Made Marketing History." *Billboard*, July 3, 2009. Accessed April 12, 2012. http://www.billboard.com/articles/news/268213/michael-jackson-pepsi-made-marketing-history?page=0%2C1

Hiatt, Brian. "Live to Tell." *Rolling Stone,* March 12, 2015, 36–41, 64.

Hinerfeld, Philip. "How Pepsi Cola Talks TO the Market: Negro Radio Reaches Audience with Airborne 'Personality Power.'" *Sponsor*, August 26, 1963, 13–14.

Hoffmann, Bill, and Lisa Marsh. "Pepsi Cans Britney: Beyoncé Takes Over as Soda Spokesgirl." *New York Post*, December 19, 2002. LexisNexis Academic.

Holden, Stephen. "Madonna Re-creates Herself—Again." *New York Times*, March 19, 1989. Accessed January 24, 2012. http://www.nytimes.com/1989/03/19/arts/madonna-re-creates-herselfagain.html?pagewanted=all&src=pm

Hollie, Pamela. "Keeping New Coke Alive." *New York Times*, July 20, 1986, 6.

Hollie, Pamela. "A Rush for Singers to Promote Goods." *New York Times,* May 14, 1984. LexisNexis Academic.

Horovitz, Bruce. "Bud Light Rules the Advertising Super Bowl." *USA Today*, February 4, 2002. Accessed June 30, 2017. http://usatoday30.usatoday.com/money/advertising/sb02/2002-02-04-ad-meter-bud.htm

Horovitz, Bruce. "Marketers Aim Britney Spears to Appeal to Wider Audience." *USA Today*, February 16, 2001. LexisNexis Academic.

Horovitz, Bruce. "'X Factor' Brings Back the Pepsi vs. Coke Cola Wars." *USA Today*, September 9, 2011. Accessed June 26, 2017. https://usatoday30.usatoday.com/money/advertising/story/2011-09-20/cola-wars-pepsi-xfactor/50483082/1

"How Our Panel Rated the Super Bowl Ads." *USA Today*, February 6, 2012. Accessed

June 14, 2017. https://usatoday30.usatoday.com/money/advertising/story/2012-02-06/how-our-ad-panel-rated-the-Super-Bowl-ads/52981300/1

"How Pepsi's Web Umbrella Works." *Sponsor*, February 20, 1961, 40–41.

Hubbard, Jaimie. "The Cola Wars: Coke, Pepsi Keep the Fizz in Their Feud." *Financial Post* (Toronto), December 15, 1986. LexisNexis Academic.

Huey, Rovi Steve. "About Hammer." MTV Artists Beta. Accessed October 5, 2016. http://www.mtv.com/artists/hammer/biography/

Hume, Scott. "Pepsi Tops Ad Recall after Madonna Flap." *Advertising Age*, April 24, 1989.

"Jacko Was a White Baby." *Sunday Mail*, January 3, 1993. LexisNexis Academic.

"Jackson Commercial begins in Canada." *Globe and Mail (Canada)*, November 16, 1987. LexisNexis Academic.

"Join the Pepsi People: Feelin' Free." In *Pepsi-Cola Media Ordering Catalog*, 1973. Pepsi Generation, Collection 111, Series 1.2, Box 10, NMAH Smithsonian.

Jones, Deborah. "Pepsi Got the Right One for Promoting Itself." *Globe and Mail* (Canada), January 30, 1992. LexisNexis Academic.

Jones, M. "Coke Defector Goes to Pepsi." *Herald*, January 28, 1988. LexisNexis Academic.

Jones, M. "Pepsi Brings Cola War to Town." *Herald*, November 16, 1987. LexisNexis Academic.

Kamer, Foster. "The 40 Biggest Hip-Hop Moments in Pop Culture History." *Complex*, March 26, 2013. Accessed September 15, 2016. http://www.complex.com/music/2013/03/the-40-biggest-hip-hop-moments-in-pop-culture-history/

Kell, John. "Soda Consumption Falls to 30-Year Low in the U.S." *Fortune*, March 29, 2016. Accessed June 23, 2017. http://fortune.com/2015/03/26/soda-sales-drop-2014/

Kennedy, Gerrick D. "Quick Takes; 'X Factor' Champ Signs with Epic." *Los Angeles Times*, January 4, 2012. Accessed June 27, 2017. http://articles.latimes.com/2012/jan/04/entertainment/la-et-quick-20120104

Kerr, Peter. "Pepsi Gets Facelift to Lure Youth." *New York Times,* September 24, 1991. LexisNexis Academic.

Kroeger, Albert R. "Rising Tide: Soft Drinks and TV." *Television* 20, no. 5 (May 1963): 37–41, 84–93.

Krugman, Herbert E. "The Impact of Television Advertising: Learning without Involvement." *Public Opinion Quarterly* 29 (1965): 349–56.

Lacey, Liam. "Tina Turner Big Grammy Winner." *Globe and Mail* (Canada), February 27, 1985. LexisNexis Academic.

Landler, Mark. "'Pepsi's Memorable Ads, Forgettable Sales." *Business Week*, October 21, 1991. LexisNexis Academic.

Lash, Scott, and Celia Lury. *Global Culture Industry: The Mediation of Things.* Cambridge: Polity Press, 2007.

Leith, Scott. "New Soft Drinks Face a Wild Ride: Vanilla Coke, Code Red Slump." *Atlanta Journal-Constitution*, May 13, 2003, 1D.

Lepage, Mark. "Who Doesn't Sell Out." *Gazette* (Montreal), November 24, 2007. LexisNexis Academic.

Lippert, Barbara. "Coming of Age: Pepsi Makes Rap Music Its Choice for the Older Generation." *Chicago Tribune*, March 19, 1990. Accessed November 1, 2016. http://articles.chicagotribune.com/1990-03-19/features/9001230004_1_rap-pepsi-pepsi-public-enemy

Lippert, Barbara. "Pepsi-Cola's 'Make a Wish': Pepsi's Prayer Answered by Madonna's Pop Imagery." *Adweek*, March, 6, 1989. LexisNexis Academic.

Lippert, Barbara. "Pepsi's 'Chase' Shows Jackson Is a Bad Act to Follow." *Adweek*, March 14, 1988. LexisNexis Academic.

"Live/Give." In *Pepsi-Cola Media Ordering Catalog*, 1970. Pepsi Generation, Collection 111, Series 1.2, Box 9, NMAH Smithsonian.

"Live/Give." In *Pepsi-Cola Media Ordering Catalogs*, 1972–73. Pepsi Generation, Series 1.2, Box 9, NMAH Smithsonian.

"The Livin' Is Easy." *Pepsi-Cola World*, November 1968. Pepsi Generation, Collection 111, Series 1.2, Box 7, NMAH Smithsonian.

Lofaro, Tony. "Britney Is Pepsi's Queen of Pop at Super Bowl: Spears Goes on Nostalgia Kick for Soft Drink Giant." *Ottawa Citizen*, January 31, 2002, F1.

MacInnis, Craig. "That's Too Bad: Mikey Jackson Flops and *Graceland* Wins Top Grammy." *Toronto Star*, March 3, 1988, E1.

Macintyre, Ben, and Richard Duce. "Pepsi Pulls Plug on Jackson after Pills Confession." *The Times*, November 15, 1993. LexisNexis Academic.

MacKenzie, Drew. "Britney's a $21 Million Pep Star: Teen Queen Signs for Drink Advert." *The Mirror*, February 8, 2001. LexisNexis Academic.

"Mariah Carey Hits Perfect Note with Pepsi." *PR Newswire: United Business Media*, April 9, 2006. Accessed April 20, 2012. http://www.prnewswire.com/news-releases/mariah-carey-hits-perfect-note-with-pepsi-56454402html

Masters, Roy. "This Ad Isn't the Real Thing, Tina: What You See Isn't What You Get." *Sydney Morning Herald*, March 15, 1989. LexisNexis Academic.

McBride, James. "Fame and Loss in the Kingdom of Rock: Elvis and Michael, the Gloved One, Spinning Glitter into Gold." *Washington Post*, August 16, 1987. LexisNexis Academic.

McDonald, Patrick. "Ode to a Fizzy Drink." *The Advertiser*, August 2, 1991. LexisNexis Academic.

Mcdonough, John. "Pepsi Turns 100: One of the World's Great Brands Has Been Shaped in Large Measure by Its Advertising." *Advertising Age*, July 20, 1998. Accessed June 22, 2017. http://adage.com/article/news/pepsi-turns-100-world-s-great-brands-shaped-large-measure-advertising/65046/

McGill, Douglas C. "The Media Business: Star Wars in Cola Advertising." *New York Times*, March 27, 1989. LexisNexis Academic.

Melvin, Tessa. "Choristers Win Prize of $10,000 from Pepsi." *New York Times*, October 13, 1991. LexisNexis Academic.

"Michael Jackson Biography." MTV Networks. Accessed November 3, 2010. http://www.mtv.com/music/artist/Jackson_michael/artist.jhtml#bio

"Michael Jackson Picks White Boy to Play Him." *Evening Standard* (London), December 31, 1992. LexisNexis Academic.

"Michael Jackson Promotions Boost Pepsi Sales in Japan." *Journal of Commerce*, September 22, 1987, 5A. LexisNexis Academic.

Moore, Martha T. "Singing for Supper: Uh Huh Girls Think They Can." *USA Today*, January 15, 1993. LexisNexis Academic.

Morgan, Richard. "BBDO Slated to Film Madonna for Pepsi Ads." *Ad Day*, January 25, 1989.

Morgan, Richard. "In Being a Good Corporate Citizen, Pepsi Came to Wrong Conclusion." *Adweek*, April 10, 1989, 2.

Morris, Edward. "Hummingbird in Advertising Tie-In: Pepsi Jingles to Become Singles?" *Billboard*, June 28, 1986, 26.

"Move over Michael Jackson." *Toronto Star*, August 13, 1987. LexisNexis Academic.

"MTV 18–34: They Can't Outgrow It, It's Just Too Enormous." Fred/Alan MTV, NMAH Smithsonian.

"MTV to Run Commercial-Free Pepsi Rock Special." *Adweek*, September 15, 1986. LexisNexis Academic.

"MuchMusic, MTV Playing Madonna Video." *Globe and Mail* (Canada), March 8, 1989. LexisNexis Academic.

"Music Star Promotions Undergo Cautious Turn." *New York Times*, May 14, 1985, D1. LexisNexis Academic.

"Music Video Awards, 1989." MTV Networks. Accessed December 1, 2011. http://www.mtv.com/ontv/vma/1989

"New Flight." *Pepsi-Cola World*, November 1968. Pepsi Generation, NMAH Smithsonian.

"New Original Ringtones by Mariah Carey, Mary J. Blige, and the All-American Rejects Now Available Exclusively through the Pepsi Cool Tones and Motorola Phones Promotion." *PR Newswire: United Business Media*, May 15, 2006. Accessed June 27, 2017. http://www.prnewswire.com/news-releases/new-original-ringtones-by-mariah-carey-mary-j-blige-and-the-all-american-rejects-now-available-exclusively-through-the-pepsi-cool-tones-motorola-phones-promotion-56349032.html

"New Pepsi Television Ad Features Music Superstars Michael Jackson, Britney Spears, Kanye West, Ray Charles, and Mariah Carey." *PR Newswire: United Business Media*, September 21, 2011. Accessed June 22, 2017. http://www.prnewswire.com/news-releases/new-pepsi-television-ad-features-music-superstars-michael-jackson-britney-spears-kanye-west-ray-charles-and-mariah-carey-130254388.html

News Services and Staff Reports. *Washington Post*, March 10, 1984. LexisNexis Academic.

Noel, Pamela. "TV Ad War's Newest Weapon." *Ebony*, July 1984, 81–86.

Norment, Lynn. "Tina Turner Sizzling at 45: 'What's Age Got to Do with It?'" *Ebony*, May 1985, 76–80, 84.

"A Not-So-Secret Recipe for Pepsi to Regain Its Footing." *Advertising Age*, March 28, 2011. Accessed June 27, 2017. http://adage.com/article/cmo-strategy/a-secret-recipe-pepsi-regain-footing/149578/

"Now Here's the News." *Washington Post*, February 28, 1985, D11.

O'Connor, John J. "Grammy Awards Show Finally Comes of Age." *New York Times*, February 28, 1985, C22.

O'Leary, Noreen. "Pepsi Breaks Its 'Chase' for Michael Tonight." *Ad Day*, March 2, 1988, 1.

"One Going on Two: "Responsibility Doesn't End with the Making of a Product." *Pepsi-Cola World*, March 1965. Pepsi Generation, Collection 111, Series 1.2, Box 5, NMAH Smithsonian.

Pareles, Jon. "Pop: Michael Jackson's 'Bad,' Follow-Up to a Blockbuster." *New York Times*, August 31, 1987. Accessed July 17, 2017. http://www.nytimes.com/1987/08/31/arts/pop-michael-jackson-s-bad-follow-up-to-a-blockbuster.html

"Pepsi Alters Theme, Expects to Spend More." *Broadcasting*, September 14, 1964, 40.

"Pepsi and Coke Accent Youth in Ad Clash." *Printer's Ink*, February 17, 1961. Pepsi Generation, Collection 111, Series 1, Box 1, NMAH Smithsonian.

"Pepsi Cancels Madonna Ad." *New York Times*, April 5, 1989. LexisNexis Academic.

"Pepsi Commercial 2017." Super Bowl Commercials 2017. Accessed June 27, 2017. http://www.superbowlcommercials.co/pepsi/

"Pepsi Drops Madonna Ads Because of Boycott Threats." *Pittsburg Press*, April 5, 1989. LexisNexis Academic.

"The Pepsi Generation." *Pepsi World*, Winter 1984. Pepsi Generation, NMAH Smithsonian.

"Pepsi Launches All-Out Campaign Promoting 'Generation' Theme." *Sponsor*, September 14, 1964, 19.

"Pepsi Outlay to Reach $15 Million." *Sponsor*, September 21, 1964. Pepsi Generation, Collection 111, Series 1, Box 1, NMAH Smithsonian.

"Pepsi Peels Half-Million Off Bank Roll for Network Radio Saturation Campaign." *Broadcasting*, September 15, 1958, 28–29.

"Pepsi Plans New Britney Ad for Bowl." *Billboard*, January 28, 2002. Accessed June 30, 2017. http://www.billboard.com/articles/news/77000/pepsi-plans-new-britney-ad-for-bowl

"Pepsi Polls Public for Super Bowl Spot." *Adweek*, January 28, 2002. Accessed June 30, 2017. http://www.adweek.com/news/advertising/pepsi-polls-public-super-bowl-spot-54248

"Pepsi Pops TV Spot Touting Jackson Ad." *Adweek*, February 29, 1988. LexisNexis Academic.

"Pepsi Sells Marketing Programs, Not Pop, to Its Dealers." *Marketing*, March 6, 1958, 62. Pepsi Generation, Collection 111, Series 1.1, Box 1, NMAH Smithsonian.

"The Pepsi Song." *Pepsi-Cola World*, March 1961. Pepsi Generation, Collection 111, Series 1.2, Box 4, NMAH Smithsonian.

"Pepsi to Pour $59 Mil. into '64 World Market." *Sponsor*, December 9, 1963, 30.

"Pepsi to Pour It on with New 'Cold' Slogan." *Broadcasting*, October 17, 1966, 33.

PepsiCo. Inc. "The Pepsi-Cola Story." 2005. Accessed June 22, 2017. www.pepsi.com/PepsiLegacy_Book.pdf

"Pepsi-Cola Uses Old 'Whoopee' Hit as Jingle Theme." *Billboard*, February 13, 1961, 36.

"Pepsi's Media Bridge to Black Markets." *Media Decisions*, February 1978. Pepsi Generation, Series 1.2, Box 1, NMAH Smithsonian.

Phillips, Frances. "Advertising: Fit and in Fighting Form for the '80s." *Financial Post*, March 16, 1985, S1.

Recording Academy. "Winners: 27th Annual GRAMMY Awards (1984)." The Recording Academy. Accessed July 3, 2017. https://www.grammy.com/grammys/awards/27th-annual-grammy-awards

Rothenberg, Randall. "Advertising: Trained in the School of Hard Yuks." *New York Times*, February 7, 1990. Accessed October 13, 2016. http://www.nytimes.com/1990/02/07/business/the-media-business-advertising-trained-in-the-school-of-hard-yuks.html

Rowland, Sally. "Pepsi Banks on Jackson as Cola War Fizzes." *Marketing*, September 3, 1987. LexisNexis Academic.

Roy, N. "Tina Turner Furthers Pepsi's Musical Hype." *Courier-Mail,* February 3, 1988. LexisNexis Academic.

Ryan, Ted. "The Making of 'I'd Like to Buy the World a Coke.'" *The Coca-Cola Company.* January 1, 2012. Accessed June 30, 2017. http://www.coca-colacompany.com/stories/coke-lore-hilltop-story

Ryan, Ted. "Pop Songs: How Coca-Cola Invited Music's Biggest Stars to 'Swing the Jingle' in the 1960s." Coca-Cola Company, August 12, 2013. Accessed June 30, 2017. http://www.coca-colacompany.com/stories/pop-songs-how-coca-cola-invited-musics-biggest-stars-to-swing-the-jingle-in-the-1960s

Sanger-Katz, Margot. "The Decline of Big Soda." *New York Times*, October 2, 2015. Accessed June 27, 2017. http://www.nytimes.com/2015/10/04/upshot/soda-industry-struggles-as-consumer-tastes-change.html?_r=0

Schultz, E. J. "Pepsi Cans Attempt to Reclaim Pop Culture Glory." *Advertising Age*, May 10, 2018. Accessed May 17, 2018. http://adage.com/article/cmo-strategy/michael-jackson-ray-charles-britney-spears-pepsi-cans/313463/

Schultz, E. J., and Jeanine Poggi. "Behind Pepsi's 'Meta' Integration into Fox's 'Empire.'" *Advertising Age*, November 19, 2015. Accessed June 22, 2017. http://adage.com/article/media/pepsi-s-meta-integration-fox-s-empire/301420/

Schultz, E. J., and Jeanine Poggi. "Pepsi Brings 'Joy of Pepsi' Back: A Remake of One of the Classic Spots Debuts Tonight During 'Empire.'" *Advertising Age*, October 7, 2015. Accessed June 30, 2017. http://adage.com/article/cmo-strategy/pepsi-brings-joy-pepsi-back-16-year-absence/300810/

Scott, Jeffry. "Pepsi Buys Commercial Time on Soviet Television." *Ad Day*, May 5, 1988. LexisNexis Academic.

Scott, Jeffry. "Roger Enrico, CEO Author: Cola Wars Stir Innovation." *Adweek,* October 13, 1986, 24.

Senior, Mike. "Bruce Swedien: Recording Michael Jackson." *Sound on Sound*, November 2009. Accessed July 3, 2017. http://www.soundonsound.com/sos/nov09/articles/swedien.htm

Shales, Tom. "After the Music, the Memories: On TV-Hype, Hoopla and the Whole World." *Washington Post*, July 15, 1985, B1.

Shales, Tom. "Television: The Tele-Grammys Pop Stars Send a Self-Serving Message." *Washington Post*, March 3, 1985, G1.

Sharkey, Betsy. "The Adventure behind Michael Jackson's 'Chase.'" *Adweek*, March 14, 1988, 19, 26.

Sharkey, Betsy. "Making a 'Wish': Pytka Directs Madonna for Pepsi." *Adweek*, March 6, 1989. LexisNexis Academic.

Shechet, Ellie. "Pepsi Responds to Backlash: Actually, the Kendall Jenner Ad Is Good and Meaningful." *Jezebel*, April 5, 2017. Accessed April 6, 2017. http://jezebel.com/pepsi-responds-to-backlash-actually-the-kendall-jenne-1794030530

Siegel, Alan. "Watch 5 of the Best Super Bowl Commercials from 1997." *USA Today*, January 16, 2015. Accessed July 6, 2017. http://admeter.usatoday.com/2015/01/16/5-best-super-bowl-commercials-1997-budweiser-bud-light-pepsi-nissan/

Sigerson, Davitt. "Michael Jackson: Bad." *Rolling Stone*, October 22,1987. Rock's Backpages. http://www.rollingstone.com/music/albumreviews/bad-19871022

Smith, Alexander. "Pepsi Ad with Kendall Jenner Echoes Black Lives Matter, Sparks Anger." *NBC News*, April 5, 2017. Accessed April 6, 2017. http://www.nbcnews.com/news/nbc-blk/pepsi-ad-kendall-jenner-echoes-black-lives-matter-sparks-anger-n742811

Smith, Liz. "Warren Beatty and Madonna Are an Item." *San Francisco Chronicle*. April 19, 1989, E1.

"Sony Music Entertainment and Simon Cowell Launch New Global Venture: 'Syco.'" *PRNewswire*, January 19, 2010. Accessed March 1, 2017, http://www.prnewswire.co.uk/news-releases/sony-music-entertainment-and-simon-cowell-launch-new-global-venture-syco-154865975.html

Span, Paula. "Connecting with the Black Consumer: Lockhart and Pettus, Advertising in the Minority Marketplace." *Washington Post*, December 16, 1986. LexisNexis Academic.

Stanley, Tiffany. "What Killed the Jingle?" *The Atlantic*, August 29, 2016. Accessed June 22, 2017. https://www.theatlantic.com/business/archive/2016/08/what-killed-the-jingle/497291/

Stelter, Brian. "Deal with Pepsi Lets Fox Have It Both Ways; Agreement on 'X Factor' Adds the 2nd Cola Giant to Network's Sponsor List." *International Herald Tribune*, January 5, 2011. LexisNexis Academic.

"Stop the Music." *Pepsi-Cola World*, June 1958. Pepsi Generation, Collection 111, Series 1.2, Box 3, NMAH Smithsonian.

Strachan, Maxwell. "Pepsi Pulls Kendall Jenner Ad Following Intense Backlash." *Huffington Post*, April 5, 2017. Accessed April 6, 2017. http://www.huffingtonpost.com/entry/pepsi-ad-kendalljenner_us_58e52783e4b0fe4ce08764d0

Stumpel, Bob. "Ray Charles Ft. in Pepsi Commercials (1990–1993)." *Ray Charles Video Museum* (blog), May 20, 2010. Accessed October 30, 2016. http://raycharlesvideomuseum.blogspot.com/2010/05/ray-charles-ft-in-pepsi-commercials.html

Sujo, Aly. "Sexy Madonna Video Miffs Pepsi." *Globe and Mail* (Canada), March 7, 1989. LexisNexis Academic.

"Super Bowl Ad Meter: Charting Sales Pitches." *USA Today*, January 28, 1991. LexisNexis Academic.

Sutcliffe, Phil. "Canned Music: Pop's Cola Wars." *Q*, April 1989. Rock's Backpages. http://www.rocksbackpages.com/Library/Article/canned-music-pops-cola-wars

"Sweet World of You." *Pepsi-Cola World*, February 1966, Pepsi Generation, Collection 111, Series 1.2, Box 5, NMAH Smithsonian.

Sweeting, Adam. "Hammered Home: Adam Sweeting Sees MC Hammer Let the Rap Rip at the Birmingham NEC on a Night of Music and Moralising." *The Guardian*, May 4, 1991. LexisNexis Academic.

Sweeting, Adam. "Lionel Richie: Dancing on the Ceiling." *Q*, October 1986. Rock's Backpages. http://www.rocksbackpages.com/Library/Article/lionel-richie-idancing-on-the-ceilingi

Sweeting, Adam. "MC Hammer: Me, Jesus, and the President." *The Guardian*, May 7, 1991. Rock's Backpages. http://www.rocksbackpages.com/Library/Article/mc-hammer-me-jesus-and-the-president

"Tall in the Saddle." *Pepsi-Cola World*, March 1967. Pepsi Generation, Collection 111, Series 1.2, Box 6, NMAH Smithsonian.

Taylor, Kate. "Coke and Pepsi Are Facing a Terrifying Reality." *Business Insider*, March 29, 2016. Accessed June 23, 2017. http://www.businessinsider.com/people-drinking-less-coke-and-pepsi-2016-3

Thompson, Dave. "Song Review." AllMusic. Accessed July 5, 2017. http://www.allmusic.com/song/modern-love-mt0019329750

"Three-Minute Ad Coming to TV." *Globe and Mail* (Canada), February 26, 1985. LexisNexis Academic.

Toffler, Alvin. *The Third Wave*. New York: Bantam, 1980.

Trust, Gary. "Vanilla Is Licking the Competition." *Billboard*, July 23, 2011, 12–14.

Walker, James R. "Zapping." Museum of Broadcast Communications. Accessed July 2, 2015. http://www.museum.tv/eotv/zapping.htm

Wallace, Richard. "Pepsi Dumps Flop Britney." *The Mirror*, December 19, 2002, 11.

"What a Difference a Hit Makes." *Telegraph*, January 26, 1986. LexisNexis Academic.

Wheaton, Ken. "Forget Ferris: Kia and Chevy Race to the Top; Few Surprises, but Budweiser, Chrysler, and GE Promise Us Things Will Get Better." *Advertising Age*, February 6, 2012. LexisNexis Academic.

Wilder, Nolan. "Kanye West and Pepsi Take a Trip around the Globe." *Urban Mecca*, August 28, 2009. Accessed June 27, 2017. http://urbanmecca.net/news/2005/08/28/kanye-west-and-pepsi-take-a-trip-around-the-globe/

Williams, Lena. "The Talk of PepsiCo: At PepsiCo, Victory Is Declared." *New York Times*, May 12, 1985. LexisNexis Academic.

Winter, Greg. "Pepsi Has 5th Quarter of Strong Growth." *New York Times*, February 6, 2001. Accessed June 30, 2017. http://www.nytimes.com/2001/02/06/business/pepsi-has-5th-quarter-of-strong-growth.html

Winters, Patricia. "Pepsi 'Bad' Spots Get Good Timing." *Advertising Age*, November 2, 1987, 103.

Wollenberg, Skip. "Pepsi to Launch New Adverts at the Oscars: Humour, Humanity, Music; Aretha Franklin, Marlon Brando in Star-Studded Cast." *National Post* (Canada), March 6, 1999. LexisNexis Academic.

Woodward, Calvin. "Pop Star and Philanthropist." *Globe and Mail* (Canada), March 2, 1988. LexisNexis Academic.

Yoshihara, Nancy. "3-Minute Pepsi Spot to Launch New Campaign." *Los Angeles Times,* February 25, 1985. Accessed July 10, 2015. http://articles.latimes.com/1985-02-25/business/fi-33515_1_pepsi-spot

"Young People Have Fun with Pepsi." *Pepsi-Cola World*, March 1947. Pepsi Generation, Collection 111, Series 1.2, Box 3, NMAH Smithsonian.

"You've Got a Lot to Live, and Pepsi's Got a Lot to Give." In *Pepsi-Cola Media Ordering Catalog*, 1969. Pepsi Generation, Series 1.2, Box 9, NMAH Smithsonian.

Zehme, Bill. "Madonna: The Rolling Stone Interview." *Rolling Stone,* March 23, 1989. Accessed July 18, 2017. http://www.rollingstone.com/music/news/the-rolling-stone-interview-madonna-19890323

BOOKS, DISSERTATIONS, AND ARTICLES

Adorno, Theodor W. "On the Fetish Character of Music and the Regression of Listening." In *Essays on Music*. Edited by Richard Leppert, translated by Susan H. Gillespie, 288–317. Berkeley: University of California Press, 2002.

Adorno, Theodor W. "Resignation." In *The Culture Industry: Selected Essays on Mass Culture*. Edited by Rolf Tiedman, 2nd ed., 198–204. London: Routledge, 2001.

The Advertising Age: Encyclopedia of Advertising. Edited by John McDonough and Karen Egolf. 3 vols. New York: Fitzroy Dearborn, 2003.

Allan, David. "Turn It Up: That's My Song in That Ad." *International Journal of Music Business Research* 3, no. 1 (April 2014): 26–51.

Apolloni, Alexandra. "Authority, Ability, and the Aging Ingénue's Voice." In *Voicing Girlhood in Popular Music: Performance, Authority, Authenticity*, edited by Allison Adrian and Jacqueline Warwick, 143–68. New York: Routledge, 2016.

Arias, Enrique Alberto. *Comedy in Music: A Historical Bibliographical Resource Guide*. Westport, CT: Greenwood, 2001.

Attrep, Kara Ann. "The Sonic Inscription of Identity: Music, Race, and Nostalgia in Advertising." PhD diss., University of California, Santa Barbara, 2008.

Auslander, Philip. *Performing Glam Rock: Gender and Theatricality in Popular Music*. Ann Arbor: University of Michigan Press, 2006.

Baldwin, James. "Freaks and the American Ideal of Manhood." In *Baldwin: Collected Essays*, edited by Toni Morrison, 814–39. New York: Library of America, 1998.

Barthes, Roland. *Elements of Semiology*. London: Jonathan Cape, 1968.

Baudrillard, Jean. *Simulacra and Simulation*. Translated by Shelia Faria Glaser. Ann Arbor: University of Michigan Press, 1994.

Beard, Fred K. *Humor in the Advertising Business: Theory, Practice, and Wit*. Lanham, MD: Rowman and Littlefield, 2008.

Bego, Mark. *Madonna: Blonde Ambition*. New York: First Cooper Square Press, 2000.

Bonde, Anders. "On the Commercialization of Shostakovich's 'Waltz No. 2': A Case Study of Textual, Contextual, and Intertextual Meaning of Music." In *Music in*

Advertising: Commercial Sounds in Media Communication and Other Settings, edited by Nicolai Graakjær and Christian Jantzen, 141–67. Aalborg: Aalborg University Press, 2009.

Bowman, Rob. "Franklin, Aretha." *Grove Music Online.* Oxford Music Online. Accessed June 27, 2017. http://www.oxfordmusiconline.com/subscriber/article/grove/music/45921

Boyer, Horace Clarence. *The Golden Age of Gospel.* Urbana: University of Illinois Press, 2000.

Boym, Svetlana. *The Future of Nostalgia.* New York: Basic Books, 2001.

Brackett, David. *Interpreting Popular Music.* Rev. ed. Berkeley: University of California Press, 2000.

Brackett, David. "Michael Jackson." In *The Grove Dictionary of American Music,* 2nd ed. Oxford: Oxford University Press, 2013. Accessed August 4, 2017. http://www.oxfordreference.com/view/10.1093/acref/9780195314281.001.0001/acref-9780195314281-e-4149?rskey=0NG1yt&result=1

Brecht, Berthold. "New Technique of Acting." In *Brecht on Theater.* Translated by John Willett, 136–47. New York: Hill and Wang, 1964.

Brown, Wendy. "Neoliberalism and the End of Liberal Democracy." In *Edgework: Critical Essays on Knowledge and Politics.* Princeton: Princeton University Press, 2005.

Bush, Michael. *The King of Style: Dressing Michael Jackson.* San Rafael, CA: Insight Editions, 2012.

Carah, Nicholas. *Pop Brands: Branding, Popular Music, and Young People.* New York: Peter Lang, 2010.

Charnas, Dan. *The Big Payback: The History of the Business of Hip Hop.* New York: New American Library, 2010.

Cohan, Steven. "'Feminizing' the Song-and-Dance Man." In *Screening the Male: Exploring Masculinities in the Hollywood Cinema,* edited by Steven Cohan and Ina Rae Hark, 46–69. New York: Routledge, 1993.

Cook, Nicholas. *Analysing Musical Multimedia.* Oxford: Clarendon Press, 1998.

Darden, Robert. *People Get Ready! A New History of Black Gospel Music.* New York: Continuum, 2004.

Davis, Sharon. *Lionel Richie: Hello.* London: Equinox, 2009.

Day-O'Connell, Jeremy. *Pentatonicism from the Eighteenth Century to Debussy.* Rochester, NY: University of Rochester Press, 2007.

De Saussure, Ferdinand. *Course in General Linguistics.* Translated by Roy Harris. Peru, IL: Open Court, 2000.

Demers, Joanna. *Steal This Music: How Intellectual Property Law Effects Musical Creativity.* Athens: University of Georgia Press, 2006.

Donovan, Tristan. *Fizz: How Soda Shook Up the World.* Chicago: Chicago Review Press, 2014.

Drewnainy, Bonnie. "Pepsi's Generation Gap." In *Images That Injure: Pictorial Stereotypes in the Media,* edited by Paul Martin Lester, 3rd ed., 228–41. Santa Barbara, CA: Praeger, 2011.

Duméil, Gérard, and Dominique Lévy. *Capital Resurgent: Roots of the Neoliberal Revolution*. Cambridge, MA: Harvard University Press, 2004.

Dusenberry, Phil. *Then We Set His Hair on Fire: Insights and Accidents for a Hall of Fame Career in Advertising*. New York: Penguin Group, 2005.

Dwyer, Michael D. *Back to the Fifties: Nostalgia, Hollywood, Film, and Popular Music of the Seventies and Eighties*. New York: Oxford University Press, 2015.

Eckhardt, Giana M., and Alan Bradshaw. "The Erasure of Antagonisms between Popular Music and Advertising." *Marketing Theory* 14, no. 2 (2014): 167–83.

Eco, Umberto. *A Theory of Semiotics*. Bloomington: Indiana University Press, 1976.

Eco, Umberto. *Travels in Hyperreality*. Orlando, FL: Harcourt Brace Jovanovich, 1986.

Enrico, Roger. *The Other Guy Blinked: How Pepsi Won the Cola Wars*. Toronto: Bantam, 1986.

Ewen, Stuart. *Captains of Consciousness: Advertising and the Social Roots of the Consumer Culture*. New York: McGraw-Hill, 1976.

Fast, Susan. *Dangerous*. New York: Bloomsbury, 2014.

Fenimore, Ross. "Madonna's Confession: Sound, Self, and Survival in a Love Song." PhD diss., University of California, Los Angeles, 2011.

Fink, Robert. "Goal Directed Soul? Analyzing Rhythmic Teleology in African American Popular Music." *Journal of the American Musicological Society* 64 (Spring 2011): 179–238.

Fink, Robert. *Repeating Ourselves*. Berkeley: University of California Press, 2005.

Ford, Phil. *Dig: Sound and Music in Hip Culture*. Oxford: Oxford University Press, 2013.

Foucault, Michel. *The Birth of Biopolitics: Lectures at the College de France, 1978–1979*. Edited by Michel Sennelart, translated by Graham Burchell. Basingstoke: Palgrave Macmillan, 2008.

Frank, Thomas. *The Conquest of Cool: Business Culture, Counterculture, and the Rise of Hip Consumerism*. Chicago: University of Chicago Press, 1997.

Freccero, Carla. "Our Lady of MTV." *Feminism and Postmodernism* 19 (Summer 1992): 163–83.

Frith, Simon. "Look! Hear! The Uneasy Relationship of Music and Television." *Popular Music* 21, no. 3 (2002): 277–90.

Fu, Linda C. L. *Advertising and Race: Global Phenomenon, Historical Challenges, and Visual Strategies*. New York: Peter Lang, 2014.

Gabilonda, Joseba. "Morphing Saint Sebastian: Masochism and Masculinity in Forrest Gump." In *Meta-Morphing: Visual Transformation and the Culture of Quick Change*, edited by Vivian Sobchack, 183–208. Minneapolis: University of Minnesota Press, 2000.

Hiroshi Garrett, Charles. "'Pranksta Rap': Humor as Difference in Hip Hop." In *Rethinking Difference in Music Scholarship*, edited by Olivia Bloechl, Melanie Lowe, and Jeffrey Kallberg, 315–37. Cambridge: Cambridge University Press, 2015.

Gates, Henry Louis, Jr., and Cornell West. *The Future of Race*. New York: Random House, 1997.

Gibson, D. Parke. *The $30 Billion Negro*. London: Macmillan, 1969.

Goldman, Robert, and Stephen Papson. *Nike Culture: The Sign of the Swoosh*. London: Sage, 1998.

Goldman, Robert, and Stephen Papson. *Sign Wars: The Cluttered Landscape of Advertising*. New York: Guilford Press, 1996.

Goodwin, Andrew. *Dancing in the Distraction Factory: Music Television and Popular Culture*. Minneapolis: University of Minnesota Press, 1992.

Gorbman, Claudia. *Unheard Melodies: Narrative Film Music*. Bloomington: Indiana University Press, 1987.

Graakjær, Nicolai Jørgensgaard. *Analyzing Music in Advertising: Television Commercials and Consumer Choice*. New York: Routledge, 2015.

Greenburg, Zach O'Malley. *Michael Jackson, Inc*. New York: Atria, 2014.

Hall, Stuart. *Encoding and Decoding in the Television Discourse*. Birmingham: Birmingham Centre for Contemporary Cultural Studies, 1973.

Hamera, Judith. "The Labors of Michael Jackson: Virtuosity, Deindustrialization, and Dancing Work." *Publications of the Modern Language Association of America* 127, no. 4 (2012): 751–65.

Hartley, John. "Communicative Democracy in a Redactional Society: The Future of Journalism Studies." *Journalism: Theory, Practice, and Criticism* 1, no. 1 (2000): 39–48.

Hartley, John. *A Short History of Cultural Studies*. London: Sage, 2003.

Hartley, John. *Television Truths: Forms of Knowledge in Popular Culture*. Hoboken, NJ: Wiley-Blackwell, 2007.

Harvey, David. *A Brief History of Neoliberalism*. Oxford: Oxford University Press, 2005.

Harvey, David. *The Condition of Postmodernity: An Enquiry into the Origins of Cultural Change*. Malden, MA: Blackwell, 1990.

Hawkins, Stan, and John Richardson. "Remodeling Britney Spears: Matters of Intoxication and Mediation." *Popular Music and Society* 30, no. 5 (December 2007): 605–29.

Hess, Mickey. *Is Hip Hop Dead? The Past, Present, and Future of America's Most Wanted Music*. Westport, CT: Praeger, 2007.

Hollander, Stanley, and Richard Germain. *Was There a Pepsi Generation before Pepsi Discovered It? Youth-Based Segmentation in Marketing*. Chicago: NTC Business Books, 1993.

Holt, Douglas. *How Brands Become Icons: The Principles of Cultural Branding*. Boston: Harvard Business School, 2004.

hooks, bell. *Black Looks: Race and Representation*. Boston: South End Press, 1992.

Huron, David. "Music in Advertising: An Analytic Paradigm." *Musical Quarterly* 73, no. 4 (1989): 557–74.

Jackson, Daniel M. *Sonic Branding: An Introduction*. Edited by Paul Fulberg. Hampshire: Palgrave Macmillan, 2003.

Jackson, Kennell. "The Shadows of Texts: Will Black Singers Sell Everything on Television?" In *Black Cultural Traffic: Crossroads in Global Performance and Popular Culture*, edited by Harry Justin Elam Jr. and Kennell Jackson, 88–107. Ann Arbor: University of Michigan Press, 2005.

Jackson, Michael. *Moonwalk*. New York: Doubleday, 1988.

James, Robin. *The Conjectural Body: Gender, Race, and the Philosophy of Music*. Lanham, MD: Lexington Books, 2010.

James, Robin. "In but not of, of but not in: On Taste, Hipness, and White Embodiment." *Contemporary Aesthetics* 6, no. 4 (2008). Accessed September 30, 2015. http://www.contempaesthetics.org/newvolume/pages/article.php?articleID=549

James, Robin. "On Intersectionality and Cultural Appropriation: The Case of Postmillennial Black Hipness." *Journal of Black Masculinity* 1, no. 2 (2011). Accessed September 5, 2015. https://philpapers.org/rec/JAMOIA

Jeffords, Susan. *Hard Bodies: Hollywood Masculinity in the Reagan Era*. New Brunswick, NJ: Rutgers University Press, 1994.

Jenkins, Henry. "Buying into *American Idol*: How We Are Being Sold on Reality Television." In *Reality TV: Remaking Television Culture*, edited by Susan Murray and Laurie Ouellette, 343–62. New York: New York University Press, 2009.

Jenkins, Henry, Sam Ford, and Joshua Green. *Spreadable Media: Creating Value and Meaning in a Networked Culture*. New York: New York University Press, 2013.

Jhally, Sut. *The Spectacle of Accumulation: Essays in Culture, Media, and Politics*. New York: Peter Lang, 2006.

Kajikawa, Loren. *Sounding Race in Rap Songs*. Oakland: University of California Press, 2015.

Kanner, Bernice. *The 100 Best TV Commercials . . . And Why They Worked*. New York: Random House, 1999.

Kassabian, Anahid. *Ubiquitous Listening: Affect, Attention, and Distributed Subjectivity*. Berkeley: University of California Press, 2013.

Kellner, Douglas. *Media Culture: Cultural Studies, Identity, and Politics between the Modern and Postmodern*. New York: Routledge, 1995.

Kellner, Douglas. *Media Spectacle*. New York: Routledge, 2003.

Klein, Bethany. *As Heard on TV: Popular Music in Advertising*. Burlington, VT: Ashgate, 2009.

Knopper, Steve. *Appetite for Self-Destruction: The Spectacular Crash of the Record Industry in the Digital Age*. New York: Free Press, 2009.

Knopper, Steve. *The Genius of Michael Jackson*. New York: Scribner, 2015.

Kooijman, Jaap. "Michael Jackson: *Motown 25*, Pasadena Civic Auditorium, March 25, 1983." In *Performance and Popular Music: History, Place, and Time*, edited by Ian Inglis, 119–27. Burlington, VT: Ashgate, 2006.

Kramer, Lawrence. *Musical Meaning: Toward a Critical History*. Berkeley: University of California Press, 2002.

Laver, Mark. *Jazz Sells: Music, Marketing, and Meaning*. New York: Routledge, 2015.

Lears, Jackson. *Fables of Abundance: A Cultural History of Advertising in America*. New York: Basic Books, 1994.

Lévi-Strauss, Claude. *The Raw and the Cooked (Mythologiques)*. Translated by John Weightman and Doreen Weightman. New York: Harper Colophon, 1975.

Lewis, Lisa. *Gender Politics and MTV: Voicing the Difference*. Philadelphia: Temple University Press, 1990.

Louise, J. C., and Harvey Yazijian. *The Cola Wars*. New York: Everest House, 1980.

Love, Joanna. "'The Choice of a New Generation': 'Pop' Music, Advertising, and Meaning in the MTV Era and Beyond." PhD diss., University of California, Los Angeles, 2012.

Love, Joanna. "Double Bind Taste Test: On the Music in THAT Pepsi Ad." *Musicology Now*, May 8, 2017. Accessed June 28, 2017. http://musicologynow.ams-net.org/search?q=pepsi

Love, Joanna. "From Cautionary Chart-Topper to Beverage Anthem: Michael Jackson's 'Billie Jean' and Pepsi's 'Choice of a New Generation' Television Campaign." *Journal for the Society of American Music* 9, no. 2 (2015): 178–203.

Lowe, Melanie. "Colliding Feminisms: Britney Spears, 'Tweens,' and the Politics of Reception." *Popular Music and Society* 26, no. 2 (2003): 123–40.

Lydon, Michael. *Ray Charles: Man and Music*. New York: Riverhead, 1998.

Macdonald, J. Fred. *One Nation under Television: The Rise and Decline of Network TV*. New York: Pantheon, 1990.

Manning, Harriet J. "Just Using It: Eminem, the Mask, and a Fight for Authenticity." In *Michael Jackson and the Blackface Mask*, 117–36. Farnham: Ashgate, 2013.

McClary, Susan. *Feminine Endings: Music, Gender, and Sexuality*. Minneapolis: University of Minnesota Press, 1991.

McCracken, Grant. *Culture and Consumption: New Approaches to the Symbolic Character of Consumer Goods and Activities*. Bloomington: Indiana University Press, 1988.

McCracken, Grant. *Culture and Consumption II: Markets, Meaning, and Brand Management*. Bloomington: Indiana University Press, 2005.

McCracken, Grant. *Transformations: Identity Construction in Contemporary Culture*. Bloomington: Indiana University Press, 2008.

Meier, Leslie M. *Popular Music as Promotion: Music and Branding in the Digital Age*. Cambridge: Polity Press, 2017.

Meier, Leslie M. "Promotional Ubiquitous Musics: Recording Artists, Brands, and 'Rendering Authenticity.'" *Popular Music and Society* 34, no. 4 (2011): 399–415.

Meintjes, Louise. "Paul Simon's *Graceland*, South Africa, and the Mediation of Musical Meaning." *Ethnomusicology* 34 (Winter 1990): 37–73.

Meizel, Katherine L. *Idolized: Music, Media, and Identity in American Idol*. Bloomington: Indiana University Press, 2011.

Mercer, Kobena. "Black Hair/Style Politics." In *Welcome to the Jungle: New Positions in Black Cultural Studies*, 97–128. London: Routledge, 1994.

Mercer, Kobena. "Monster Metaphors: Notes on Michael Jackson's 'Thriller.'" In *Sound and Vision: The Music Video Reader*, edited by Simon Frith, Andrew Goodwin, and Lawrence Grossberg, 80–93. London: Routledge, 1993.

Middleton, Richard. "Pop." In *Grove Music Online*. Oxford Music Online, Oxford University Press. Accessed June 30, 2017. http://www.oxfordmusiconline.com/subscriber/article/grove/music/46845

Mital, Ruchi. "Tomorrow Today: Michael Jackson as Science Fiction Character, Author, and Text." In *Michael Jackson: Grasping the Spectacle*, edited by Christopher R. Smit, 131–44. Burlington, VT: Ashgate, 2012.

Monson, Ingrid. "The Problem with White Hipness, Race, Gender, and Cultural Conceptions in Jazz Historical Discourse." *Journal of the American Musicological Society* 48, no. 3 (Autumn 1995): 396–422.

Moore, Andrea. "Neoliberalism and the Musical Entrepreneur." *Journal of the Society for American Music* 10, no. 1 (2016): 33–53.

Neal, Mark Anthony. *What the Music Said: Black Popular Music and Black Public Culture*. New York: Routledge, 1999.

Nyong'o, Tavia. "Have You Seen His Childhood? Song, Screen, and Queer Culture of the Child in Michael Jackson's Music." *Journal of Popular Music Studies* 23, no. 1 (2011): 40–57.

Packard, Vance. *The Hidden Persuaders*. New York: David McKay Co. Inc., 1957.

Peirce, Charles Sanders. *Values in a Universe of Chance: Selected Writings*. Edited by Philip P. Weiner. New York: Dover Press, 1958.

Powers, Devon. "Strange Powers: The Branded Sensorium and the Intrigue of Musical Sound." In *Blowing up the Brand: Critical Perspectives on Promotional Culture*, edited by Melissa Aronczyk and Devon Powers, 285–306. New York: Peter Lang, 2010.

Raph, Theodore. "John Peel: 1945." In *The American Song Treasury: 100 Favorites*. Rev. ed., 373. New York: Dover, 1986.

Reynolds, Simon. *Retromania: Pop Culture's Addiction to Its Own Past*. New York: Faber and Faber, 2011.

Ritchey, Marianna. "'Amazing Together': Mason Bates, Classical Music, and Neoliberal Values." *Music and Politics* 11, no. 2 (Summer 2017). http://dx.doi.org/10.3998/mp.9460447.0011.202

Rodman, Ron. *Tuning In: American Narrative Television Music*. Oxford: Oxford University Press, 2010.

Rose, Tricia. *Black Noise: Rap Music and Black Culture in Contemporary America*. Middletown, CT: Wesleyan University Press, 1994.

Rose, Tricia. "A Style Nobody Can Deal With: Politics, Style, and the Postindustrial City in Hip Hop." In *Popular Music: Critical Concepts in Media and Cultural Studies*, edited by Simon Frith, 341–59. London: Routledge, 2004.

Savan, Leslie. *The Sponsored Life: Ads, TV, and American Culture*. Philadelphia, Temple University Press, 1994.

Schneller, Tom. "Easy to Cut: Modular Form in the Film Scores of Bernard Hermann." *Journal of Film Music* 5, nos. 1–2 (2012): 127–51.

Schudson, Michael. *Advertising, the Uneasy Persuasion: Its Dubious Impact on American Society*. New York: Basic Books, 1984.

Scott, Ronald B. "Images of Race and Religion in Madonna's Video 'Like a Prayer.'" In *The Madonna Connection: Representational Politics, Subcultural Identities, and Cultural Theory*, edited by Cathy Schwichtenberg, 57–79. Boulder, CO: Westview Press, 1993.

Sheehan, Kim Bartel. *Controversies in Advertising.* Los Angeles: Sage, 2014.

Slade, Alison. "Your 'American Idol': The Intersection between Reality Television, Ideology, and the Music Industry in Popular Culture." In *Rock Brands: Selling Sound in a Media Saturated Culture,* edited by Elizabeth Barfoot Christian, 255–71. Plymouth: Lexington, 2011.

Smit, Christopher R. *The Exile of Britney Spears: A Tale of 21st Century Consumption.* Chicago: University of Chicago Press, 2011.

Smit, Christopher R., ed. *Michael Jackson: Grasping the Spectacle.* Surrey: Ashgate, 2012.

Smythe, Dallas W. "On Critical and Administrative Research: A New Critical Analysis." *Journal of Communication* 33 (1983): 117–27.

Stanyek, Jason, and Benjamin Peikut. "Deadness: Technologies of the Intermundane." *The Drama Review* 54, no. 1 (2010): 14–38.

Steger, Manfred B., and Ravi K. Roy. *Neoliberalism: A Very Short Introduction.* New York: Oxford University Press, 2010.

Sterne, Jonathan. "Sounds Like the Mall of America: Programmed Music and the Architectonics of Commercial Space." *Ethnomusicology* 41, no. 1 (1997): 22–50.

Stilwell, Robynn. "The Fantastical Gap between Diegetic and Nondiegetic." In *Beyond the Soundtrack: Representing Music in Cinema,* edited by Daniel Goldmark, Lawrence Kramer, and Richard Leppert, 184–204. Berkeley: University of California Press, 2007.

Stilwell, Robynn. "Vocal Decorum: Voice, Body, and Knowledge in the Prodigious Singer Brenda Lee." In *She's So Fine: Reflections on Whiteness, Femininity, Adolescence, and Class in 1960s Music,* edited by Laurie Stras, 57–87. Ashgate: Farnham Surrey, 2010.

Stoddard, Bob. *Pepsi: 100 Years.* Los Angeles: General Publishing Group, 1997.

Swedien, Bruce. *In the Studio with Michael Jackson.* Milwaukee: Hal Leonard Books, 2009.

Tagg, Philip. *Kojak, 60 Seconds of Television Music: Toward the Analysis of Affect in Popular Music.* Larchmont, NY: Mass Media Music Scholars' Press, 2000.

Taraborrelli, J. Randy. *Madonna.* New York: Simon and Schuster, 2001.

Taylor, Timothy. "Advertising and the Conquest of Culture." *Social Semiotics* 19, no. 4 (2009): 405–25.

Taylor, Timothy. "The Changing Shape of the Culture Industry; or, How Did Electronica Music Get into Television Commercials?" *Television and New Media* 8, no. 3 (2007): 235–58.

Taylor, Timothy. *Global Pop: World Music, World Markets.* New York: Routledge, 1997.

Taylor, Timothy. *Music and Capitalism: A History of the Present.* Chicago: University of Chicago Press, 2016.

Taylor, Timothy. *The Sounds of Capitalism: Advertising, Music, and the Conquest of Culture.* Chicago: University of Chicago Press, 2012.

Tedlow, Richard S. "The Fourth Phase of Marketing: Marketing History and the Business World Today." In *The Rise and Fall of Mass Marketing,* edited by Richard S. Tedlow and Geoffrey Jones, 8–35. London: Routledge, 2015.

Tota, Anna Lisa. "'When Orff Meets Guinness': Music in Advertising as a Form of Cultural Hybrid." *Poetics* 29 (2001): 109–23.

Trynka, Paul. *David Bowie: Starman.* New York: Little Brown, 2011.

Vernallis, Carol. *Experiencing Music Video: Aesthetics and Cultural Context.* New York: Columbia University Press, 2004.

Vickers, Nancy A. "Materialism and the Material Girl." In *Embodied Voices: Representing Female Vocality in Western Culture,* edited by Leslie C. Dunn and Nancy A. Jones, 230–46. Cambridge: Cambridge University Press, 1994.

Vogel, Joseph. "'I Ain't Scared of No Sheets': Re-screening Black Masculinity in Michael Jackson's *Black or White.*" *Journal of Popular Music Studies* 27, no. 1 (2015): 90–123.

Vogel, Joseph. *Man in the Music: The Creative Life and Work of Michael Jackson.* Toronto: Sterling, 2011.

Ward, Brian. "Can I Get a Witness: Civil Rights, Soul, and Secularization." In *Just My Soul Responding: Rhythm and Blues, Black Consciousness, and Race Relations,* 173–216. London: University College London, 1998.

Wharton, Chris. *Advertising: Critical Approaches.* New York: Routledge, 2015.

Williams, Raymond. "Advertising: The Magic System." In *Media Studies: A Reader,* edited by Paul Marris and Sue Thornham, 704–9. New York: New York University Press, 2000.

Williamson, Judith. *Decoding Advertisements: Ideology and Meaning in Advertisements.* London: Marion Boyars, 1978.

INDEX

Academy Awards shows, 192, 194

adult contemporary genre, 93, 95, 96, 99, 103, 254n34

Adventures in Negro History (Pepsi LP), 55

Advertising Age, 84, 146–47, 168, 257n88, 265n58

Adweek magazine, 126, 169

African American demographic, 228, 243n31; artists highlighted, 11, 55, 229; Mountain Dew and, 269n44; Richie campaign and, 101–2; Sprite and, 191, 269n41; upward mobility, 102

African American musical tropes: gospel music, 154, 156, 158, 203, 207, 264n36; in "Like a Prayer," 154, 156, 158

African American Pentecostal churches, 207

age demographic targets, multiple brackets, 181; Richie, 93, 99–100, 102, 103; Sommers, 243n35

age demographic targets, older adults, 69, 149; fears of alienating, 37, 228; Jackson's mature look and sound, 124; Richie, 93, 103

age demographic targets, youth, 118, 207, 242n22; age stereotyping, 183–84; Jackson, 68, 69, 103; MTV aesthetic, 60; redaction in "Now and Then," 30, 44, 45–46, 50–54. *See also* youthfulness target

age demographic targets, youth marketing development, 9–10, 23–24, 35, 242n21; baby boomers and, 19, 29,

30–32, 218; BBD&O and, 29, 45–46, 48; "Be Sociable" campaign failure, 28; race and, 11; scholarship on, 24, 29; "Soda Fountain," 34, 36, 37, 164; Sommers, 37, 243n35

age stereotyping, 183–84

the All-American Rejects, 214

Amaro, Melanie, 27, 219–24, 226–27, 276n48

AMC network, 12

American Bandstand (television show), 9, 42

American cultural changes, 11, 31, 179, 237n35

American Family Association, 168

American Idol (reality talent show), 215, 218, 275n33

American values, neoliberalism and. *See* neoliberalism

"Amphibicar" (commercial), 41

"Amusement Park" (commercial), 41

Anderson, Lynn, 34, 50

Andrew, Richard (Outasight), 6–7, 216, 217

appellate (how ads invite audiences in), 22–23, 97, 117

Apple, 214, 252n63

Arcade Creative group, 233, 277n65

arousal safety humor, 182, 192, 193

artist brands, 223, 275n29

Aryes, Michell, 243n34

Atlantic, The (magazine), 13

audience interpretation, 61

audience labor, 218, 225–27, 276n49

"Audition" (1991 commercial), 202, 210–12

Australian Cola Wars, 117

baby boomer demographic, 29, 118, 181; influence of, 30–33; nostalgia and, 196, 248n12; youth marketing development for, 19, 29, 30–32, 218. *See also* age demographic targets

"Baby One More Time" (Spears), 247n102

Backer, Bill, 49, 246n89

"Backstage" (1987 commercial), 122, 127, 147

Bad (album, Jackson), 125, 128–29, 146–48, 259n25; concert tour, 25, 121–22, 123, 148; delayed release, 113, 122–23; other promotional texts, 142–43. *See also* "The Choice of a New Generation" (campaigns)

Bad (video, Jackson), 123, 128

"Bad" (Jackson), redaction of: "Backstage," 122, 127, 147; "Concert," 122, 127–28, 146–47, 216; lyrical analysis, 25, 132–35, 136, 138, 147–48; musical analysis, 131–33, 135, 137, 138–40, 144–45, 260n47, 260n58. *See also* "The Chase" (1988 episodic commercial)

"Bad" chord, 134, 135, 138

Baldwin, James, 127

banality, 23, 168, 171, 223, 226, 229

Barthes, Roland, 14

Batten, Barton, Durstine, & Osborn (BBD&O) agency, 10, 28, 42, 150, 243n35; creative awards for, 60; humor and, 183; Pepsi ends partnership with, 215; youth marketing development, 29, 45–46, 48

Batten, Barton, Durstine, & Osborn (BBD&O) agency, campaigns by: "Girl Watchers," 43–44; "Live/Give," 34–35, 47–49, 50–51, 54, 252n4; "Pepsi Pours It On," 34–35, 45, 46–47, 228; "Soda Fountain," 34, 36, 37, 164; "Surf Football," 34, 44–47; "Think Young," 12, 34, 35–37, 42, 45, 52, 228, 242n26. *See also* "The Choice of a New Generation" (campaign); "Come Alive! You're in the Pepsi Generation" (campaign); "Joy of Cola" (1999 campaign); "You've Got the Right One, Baby, Uh-huh" (campaign)

beach movie imagery, 44–47

Beard, Fred K., 26, 181, 182, 184

"Beat It" (Jackson), 59, 77, 78–79

the Beatles, 48, 119

Beethoven, Ludwig Van, 244n46

Bergin, John, 45, 46

"Be Sociable" campaign, 28, 228, 241n5

"Best Soft Drink Commercial" award, 44

"Better Be Good to Me" (Turner), 256n70

Beverage Products Corporation, 102–3

"Be Young, Have Fun, Drink Pepsi" (slogan), 180

Billboard charts. *See* chart topping

Billie Jean (video, Jackson), 66–67

"Billie Jean" (Jackson), 24–25, 59, 62–67; lyrical analysis, 62, 64, 65; musical analysis, 62–66, 72, 249n26; offered to Pepsi, 68; sound engineering on, 249n25; success of, 69

"Billie Jean" (Jackson), redaction of: "The Concert," 59, 60, 71–77, 79; lyrics, 73, 74–76, 79; musical elements, 24–25, 72–73, 80, 81–82; "Street," 59, 77–80, 127, 216

Black Journal (Pepsi-sponsored PBS show), 55

Black Lives Matter protests, 231–32

black masculinity, 188–89

black vocal shadowing, 195

Blige, Mary J., 214

"Block Party" (1985 commercial), 92, 96–99, 101, 255n42

blondness, 243n40

Bonde, Anders, 61, 73

bottling companies, 11, 36–37, 237n36, 245n67

Bowie, David, 25, 86, 112–19, 121, 122, 228, 256n83

Boym, Svetlana, 29–30, 199, 200

Bradham, Caleb D., 3

Bradshaw, Alan, 223

brand awareness, 17–18; retail environments and popular music, 277n60

brand logo, 3
brandscapes, 232
brand switching, 181
Britney Spears (Spears), 53. *See also* Spears, Britney
Brooks, Joe, 34, 48, 50
Brown, James, 34, 50
Brown, Wendy, 87
Burger King, 244n55
Burrell, Stanley Kirk (MC Hammer). *See* MC Hammer
Bush, George W., Sr., 202
"Bust a Move" (Young MC), 183
Butler, Lynette, 93, 254n37

cable television, 84
Canada Dry beverage company, 89
Canadian market, 117
Can't Slow Down (Richie), 89, 255n59
capitalist realism, 23; in "Billie Jean" redaction, 81–82; in "The Chase," 129, 142; in "Make a Wish," 26, 153, 163, 172, 176
Capitol Records label, 256n83
Carah, Nicholas, 27, 218, 225, 232
Carey, Mariah, 214, 216
cartoon comic strips as marketing, 3
CBS television network, 90, 128
celebrity commercial compensations: for Charles, 202; for Hammer, 192; for Jackson, 67, 83, 89, 253n18; for Madonna, 150, 265n60; for Richie, 89, 253n18; for Spears, 246n100; for Turner and Bowie, 113
celebrity endorsement template, 82, 124, 180–81
censorship and record label rating requirements, 267n5
Charles, Ray, 12, 181, 182, 200–213, 244n55, 271n78; in Coca-Cola marketing, 42; monikers, 203, 271n72; in "Music Icons," 216; Pepsi campaign eclipses oeuvre, 212. *See also* "You've Got the Right One, Baby, Uh-huh" (campaign)
Charnas, Dan, 190, 191
Charo, 211
chart topping: "I'd Like to Teach the

World to Sing," 13, 49; jingles' popularity, 13, 44, 49; jingles' sound as antithetical, 46; *Like a Prayer*, 151; *Please Hammer Don't Hurt 'Em*, 184, 192; *Thriller*, 60, 127; trend changes, 32; Turner, Tina, 104
"The Chase" (1988 episodic commercial), 128–48, 216; "Bad" licensed for before airing, 123–24; "The Chase" (episode 1), 128, 131–37; "The Chopper" (episode 2), 128, 132, 137–39; "The Museum" (episode 3), 128, 132, 140–41; "The Finale" (episode 4), 128, 132, 141–42; production cost and difficulties, 128, 260n53; Pytka directs, 121, 122, 130, 260n49; reception of, 147–48; surrealism in, 129–30. *See also* Jackson, Michael
Chayanne, 149
Cheetahs (dance club), 43
choice ideology, 87, 91–92, 119, 252n7
"The Choice of a New Generation" (campaigns), 12, 24, 59–85, 86–120, 121–48, 197; "Backstage," 122, 127, 147; "Block Party," 92, 96–99, 101, 255n42; "Concert," 122, 127–28, 146–47, 216; "The Concert," 59, 60, 71–77, 79; "Creation," 112–19, 122; entertainment's centrality to, 68–69, 81, 173; "Homecoming," 90, 92–96, 254n38; "I'll Be There," 197–200; Jackson's creative control over, 68, 83, 250n34; marketing budget, 90, 121–22, 128; MTV aesthetics of, 70, 91, 250n43; neoliberalism and, 25, 87–88; "New Styles," 90–92, 93, 99; in "Now and Then" segment, 34, 51, 54; Pepsi sales following, 59–60, 69, 81, 82, 86, 120, 150; Pytka directs commercials in, 121, 122, 260n49; reception of, 146–48, 228–29; slogan, 87, 180; "Street," 59, 77–80, 127, 216; "We've Got the Taste," 104, 105–11, 112, 256n80. *See also* "The Chase" (1988 episodic commercial); "The Switch" (1990 commercial)
"The Chopper." *See* "The Chase" (1988 episodic commercial)

Coca-Cola marketing, 10, 31, 149; budget, 242n28; Charles in, 42; failed campaigns, 273n100; Franklin in, 42, 271n78; Headroom in, 89; "Hilltop," 12–13, 49–50, 231, 246n89; Houston markets Diet Coke, 147; Iglesias in, 89, 252n64; "Obey Your Thirst" (1994 Sprite campaign), 191; "Things Go Better with Coca-Cola," 42, 244n54

Cofield, Peter, 202, 205, 211

cola wars (Pepsi-Coke rivalry), 12–13, 28, 42–43, 89, 215; Australian, 117; disparaging humor, 183–84, 193; Frank on, 31, 42, 53; taste tests, 249n28

Coleman, Jay, 67, 103, 121

Collins, Phil, 149

"Come Alive! You're in the Pepsi Generation" (campaign), 12, 42–43, 45, 228; jingle, 34–35, 37, 40–41, 43; in "Now and Then," 40–41, 41–42, 44, 244n52

the Commodores, 89, 102

computer technology, 113, 116, 257n88

"Concert" (1987 commercial), 122, 127–28, 146–47, 216

"The Concert" (1984 commercial), 59, 60, 71–77, 79, 105; musical analysis, 72, 75–76

concert tours: Glass Spider (Bowie), 113, 118, 256n84; Jackson's problems on, 88, 124–25, 200, 259n15; MC Hammer, 190; Turner opens for Richie, 104; Victory Tour (Jackson), 88–89, 117, 125, 126, 249n31

concert tour sponsorship, 88–89, 112–13, 257n98; for Bowie, 113, 118; celebrity endorsement template and, 124; for Jackson/*Bad*, 25, 121–22, 123, 148; for Jackson/*Dangerous*, 197; for Jackson/*Thriller*, 60, 67, 125, 126, 249n31; for Madonna, 150, 174; for Richie, 89; for Turner, 104, 113, 117

consumerism, 87; anti-consumerism values, 119

Cook, Nicholas, 16

Cook, Roger, 246n89

"Cool Tones" campaign, 214

Cooper, Frank, 215

copyright law, 119

Corbin, Darryl, 191

cotextual elements, 61

counterculture movement, industry monetization of, 119–20; "Hilltop," 49–50; "Jump In," 231–32, 237n39, 276n58; "Live/Give," 47–51

Cowell, Simon, 219, 221, 222

Crawford, Joan, 241n2

"Creation" (1987 commercial), 112–19, 122, 129

Crewe, Bob, 44

critical affective response, 30, 196

Croom-Johnson, Austin H., 3, 4–5

Crouch, Andraé, 158

Crystal, Billy, 119, 121

cultural appropriation, 195–96, 212, 272n98

cultural assimilation, 105

Damone, Vic, 211

"Dancing Bears" (1997 commercial), 193–94

dancing in streets, as trope, 265n50

Dangerous (album, Jackson), 197

Danzig, Fred, 84–85

Darden, Robert, 207

Davis, Billy, 246n89

Day-O'Connell, Jeremy, 158, 163

Demers, Joanna, 251n60

demographic targets. *See* age demographic targets; youthfulness target

demographic targets, racial, 11, 28, 55, 228, 243n31. *See also* African American demographic

Diet Coke, 215, 271n78. *See also* Coca-Cola marketing

Diet Pepsi, 43–44, 119, 200. *See also* Charles, Ray; "You've Got the Right One, Baby, Uh-huh" (campaign)

Dillon, Tom, 243n35

"Diner" (1995 commercial), 193

direct word painting, 78, 94, 98, 141, 251n58

Disney, 41, 244n49

disparagement humor, 182, 183–84, 192, 193

diversification of revenue streams (PepsiCo.), 179
Donaldson, Walter, 34, 35–36
"Don't Stop 'Til You Get Enough" (Jackson), 249n32
doo-wop music, 245n68
"Dreams" (1993 commercial), 197–200
Drewnainy, Bonnie, 183, 184, 210
Dukakis, Michael, 202
Dusenberry, Phil, 10, 83, 262n11; on Jackson campaigns, 60, 68–69, 249n33; on slogan choice rationale, 87, 180
Dwyer, Michael D., 95; on nostalgia, 26, 29–30, 181, 196, 200, 201; on retro, 201

earworms, 108, 211, 218
easy listening genre, 254n34
Ebony magazine, 101
Eckhardt, Giana M., 223
Eco, Umberto, 130
Ed Sullivan Show (television show), 9
Eisenberg, Hallie, 194–95, 246n97
EMI, 256n83
Empire (television show), 12
encoding and decoding, 21–22
Enrico, Roger, 86, 249n30, 250n34, 252n64, 253n18; on Jackson campaigns, 59, 67, 69, 71, 121, 248n5
entertainment, 68–69, 81, 142, 173–74, 276n53
Entertainment Tonight, 168
equivalence (link between product and results), 23, 220–21

Family Ties (television show), 122
family values, 95–96. *See also* neoliberalism
Farr, Teri, 119
Fast, Susan, 143, 145
"Feelings" (Morris), 187, 188
female ingénue, 35, 38, 40, 54, 243n39
Ferraro, Geraldine, 119
film music, 248n16, 266n77
"The Finale." *See* "The Chase" (1988 episodic commercial)
Fink, Robert, 21, 130
Flack, Roberta, 55

flanker products, 15, 238n44
Flava Flav, 220, 222, 224, 274n18
Ford, Sam, 225
Foucault, Michel, 87
The Four Tops, 34, 45
Fox, Michael J., 119, 121, 122
Fox Network, 12, 215, 225
Frank, Thomas, 24, 29, 55; on cola wars, 31, 42, 53; on early Pepsi campaigns, 44, 45, 47–48, 49, 50, 244n51; on hip consumerism, 10, 31, 69; on imagery, 44, 250n43
Franklin, Aretha, 34, 219, 223, 244n55; Amaro and, 224; in Coca-Cola marketing, 42, 271n78; "You Go Girl," 194–95, 270n52
Freccero, Carla, 152, 154, 158
Fred/Alan advertising agency, 250n41
Fremantle Media North America, 215
Frey, Glenn, 118–19
Fu, Linda C. L., 195

Gabilonda, Joseba, 143
Garfield, Bob, 146–47
Garfinkel, Lee, 183
Gates, Henry Louis, 260n45
gender, 11, 51, 125–26, 163, 195, 228; androgyny, 79, 127, 143, 200, 229, 246n96, 250n39, 261n64; female ingénue, 35, 38, 40, 54, 243n39; masculinity, 143, 188–89
"A Generation Ahead" (1989 campaign), 150
"Generation Next" (campaign), 180, 194
"Georgia on My Mind" (Charles), 203, 204, 205
Germain, Richard, 24, 29, 250n40
"Get Together" (The Youngbloods), 193
Giraldi, Bob, 70, 78–79, 91, 99, 100
"Girl Watchers" (1966 campaign), 43–44
Glass Spider (Bowie tour), 113, 118, 256n84
globalization, 108, 111, 170, 176, 208–10, 256n78. *See also* neoliberalism
Go!!! (variety television show), 43, 245n63
Goldman, Robert, 22–23, 129, 152–53, 221
Goodwin, Andrew, 70, 250n42

Gorbman, Claudia, 248n16

gospel music, 125, 200, 264n36; in "Like a Prayer," 154, 156, 158, 171; in "Make a Wish," 150, 164, 165, 166–68, 171; in "Orchestra," 203, 204, 207; in "Worldwide," 209

"Gotta Have It" (slogan), 180

Graakjær, Nicolai Jørgensgaard, 16, 61, 235n2

Graceland (Simon), 111–12

Grammy Awards shows, 89–90, 100, 149, 192, 256n70; "The Chase" premieres during, 122, 128, 147; Richie campaign premieres during, 104

Green, Joshua, 225

Greenaway, Roger, 246n89

Guzman, Pablo, 201

Hall, Stuart, 21

Hamera, Judith, 146, 261n64

hard-sell approach (product-focused marketing), 28, 42, 49, 180, 205, 211; return to, in 1990s, 212, 218; soft-sell approach, 10, 31–32, 68–69, 182; in "Surf Football," 44–47. *See also* humor; nostalgia; retro; "You've Got the Right One, Baby, Uh-huh" (campaign)

Hardy, Phil, 254n35

Hartley, John, 19, 224, 239n61

Harvey, David, 17; on neoliberalism, 25, 87, 95, 253n7, 267n83, 276n46

"Have a Pepsi, the Light Refreshment" (1954 commercial), 28

"Have a Pepsi Day," 55

Hayes, Issac, 34

Headroom, Max, 89, 253n14

Heller, Norman, 237n35

"Hello" (Richie), 255n67

Herb Alpert and the Tijuana Brass, 43

Hess, Mickey, 188

Hidden Persuaders, The (Packard), 22

Hill, Faith, 34

the Hillside Singers, 49

"Hilltop" (1971 Coca-Cola commercial), 12–13, 49–50, 231, 246n89

Hinerfeld, Philip, 29

hip consumerism, 10, 31, 69

hip hop music, 184–92; black masculinity and, 188–89; celebrity endorsements by hip hop artists, 190; reception of, MC Hammer and, 189–90; Sprite and, 191, 269n41; video aesthetic, 184–85

Hiroshi Garrett, Charles, 188

hits. *See* chart topping

Hollander, Stanley, 24, 29, 250n40

Holt, Douglas, 230

"Homecoming" (1985 commercial), 90, 92–96, 254n38

The Hondells, 34, 43

hooks, bell, 159, 243n40

Houston, Whitney, 89, 147, 149

Hudson, Dawn, 53

Hughs, Philip, 102–3

humor, 26, 181–96; arousal safety, 182, 192, 193; "Audition," 202, 210–12; BBD&O praised for, 183; "Dancing Bears," 193–94; "Diner," 193; disparagement, 182, 183–84, 192, 193; incongruity resolution, 182, 184, 193, 224; redacted musical styles and imagery, 182–84, 185–89, 193–95; "Shady Acres," 183–84, 188; "You Go Girl," 194–95. *See also* "The Switch" (1990 commercial)

Huron, David, 18

hyperreality, 129–30, 141, 143, 145

"I'd Like to Teach the World to Sing" (New Seekers), 13, 49

Iglesias, Julio, 89, 252n64

"I Got a Woman" (Charles), 203

"I'll Be There" (1993 commercial), 197–200

"I'll Be There" (Jackson 5), 197

imagery. *See* visual imagery

imagery, scholarship on, 22, 44, 61, 152–53, 254n39

imagetext, 61

"I'm Not a Girl, Not Yet a Woman" (Spears), 53

incongruity resolution humor, 182, 184, 193, 224

individualism, 153, 169–70, 276n46. *See also* neoliberalism

infotainment, 214, 226
intermundane, 198–99
international marketing, 104, 105–8, 117, 121–22
iTunes, 214, 273n3

Jackson, Bo, 211
Jackson, Daniel M., 18, 230
Jackson, Joe, 68, 249n31
Jackson, Kennell, 195
Jackson, Michael, 59–85, 228; child molestation allegations, 200, 261n71; costuming of, 70–71, 73, 79, 83, 137, 141, 259n20; co-writes "We Are the World," 256n68; dance moves, 146, 248n5; doesn't drink Pepsi, 88–89, 104, 199; global marketing appeal, 117; iconography of, 125–26, 127, 130, 137, 142–43; image ambiguity, 143, 199–200, 229; leaves Jackson 5, 249n31; in "Music Icons," 216; Pepsi releases from contract, 147, 200; rebrands self-image, 125–26, 145–46, 259n19; reputation, 124, 126–27, 199, 250n39, 259n26; solicited by other companies, 67–68; Suzuki motorcycle commercials, 249n32; wins Grammy awards, 59. *See also* *Bad* (album, Jackson); "Billie Jean" (Jackson)
Jackson, Michael, "The Choice of a New Generation" campaign, 9, 11, 12, 120, 181; acclaim for, 150; "Backstage," 122, 127, 147; "Concert," 122, 127–28, 146–47, 216; "The Concert," 59, 60, 71–77, 79; creative control in, 68, 70–71, 83, 130, 250n34; face time limits, 68, 70–71, 130; "I'll Be There," 197–200; pyrotechnic burns, 248n4; racial demographic targets and, 101; sales following, 13; "Street," 59, 77–80, 127, 216; youth demographic target, 68, 69, 103; youthfulness target, 69, 77, 79, 82, 135. *See also* "The Chase" (1988 episodic commercial)
Jackson, Michael, concert tours: for *Bad*, 25, 121–22, 123, 148; for *Dangerous*, 197; problems on, 88, 124–25, 200, 259n15; for *Thriller*, 60, 67, 125, 126, 249n31;

Victory Tour, 88–89, 117, 124–25, 126, 249n31
Jackson, Michael, costuming, 79, 83; "Bad"-related, 125–26, 137, 141, 259n20; used in lieu of face time, 68, 70–71, 73, 74, 130
Jackson, Michael, signifiers, 61–66; "Bad"-related, 125–26, 127, 137, 141; iconic costuming, 68, 70–71, 73, 74; musical analysis in "Billie Jean," 62–66; offered in lieu of face time, 68, 70–71, 74, 130
Jackson 5, 62, 197, 249n31
Jackson siblings, 71, 77, 78–79
James, Robin, 188, 195
Jeffords, Susan, 143
Jenkins, Henry, 27, 215, 218, 225
Jenner, Kendall, 231
Jhally, Sut, 22, 264n43
jingles, 19; "Be Sociable," 28; "Come Alive!," 34–35, 37, 40–41, 43; definition of, 235n2; "Hilltop" (Coca-Cola), 13, 49, 50, 246n89; "Joy of Cola," 34, 194; "Joy of Pepsi," 34, 51–52; "Live/Give," 34–35, 47–49, 50–51; locally broadcast, 235n3; "Madison Avenue choir" sound, 45–46; "Makin' Whoopee/ Pepsi Song," 35–36; "Music Icons," 7; "Nickel, Nickel," 3–6, 228, 235n13; notated, in magazine ads, 236n18; "Pepsi Feels So Right," 90, 92, 98–99; by Phillips, 34, 46; popularity of, 4, 13, 44, 49; by Ramin, 34, 40–41, 43–44, 244n44; by Richie, 89, 90, 91, 92–93, 98–99, 101; *vs.* sonic branding, 18, 232; transition away from, 13, 25, 60, 85, 124, 152, 217; "We've Got the Taste," 104, 106–8, 110, 112; "You're Looking Pepsi Style," 90, 91, 99, 254n33; "You've Got the Right One, Baby," 202, 203–4, 205–6, 208–11. *See also* Sommers, Joanie
John, Elton, 219, 221, 222, 224
"John Peel" (nineteenth-century English hunting ballad), 4, 236n13
Johnson, Don, 118, 121
Jones, Grace, 89
Jones, Quincy, 69, 123

Jongkadeekij, Pu Anchalee, 108–11, 112, 256n80

Jovan perfume, 9

"Joy of Cola" (1999 campaign), 53, 216, 246n97, 246–47n100; jingle, 34, 194; slogan, 180, 194; "You Go Girl," 194–95, 270n52

"Joy of Pepsi" (2002 jingle), 34, 51–52. *See also* "Now and Then" (2002 commercial)

"Jump In" (2017 commercial), 231–32, 237n39, 276n58

Kahn, Gus, 34, 35–36

Kajikawa, Loren, 188, 189

Kassabian, Anahid, 17

Kellner, Douglas, 153, 155, 226, 265n49, 266n71; on spectacle, 18, 214, 251n47; on technocapitalism, 27, 214, 273n2

Kennedy, John F., 31

Kent, Alan B., 3, 4–5

Kenyon & Eckardt agency, 241n2

King, Don, 67, 249n30

"King's Court" (2012 commercial), 27, 218, 219–27, 274n16; reception of, 221–24

Kingston Trio, 33

Klein, Bethany, 10, 16–17, 153

Knopper, Steve, 213

Knowles, Beyoncé, 56

Kooijman, Jaap, 70, 250n42

Kramer, Lawrence, 61

Laing, Dave, 254n35

Lambert, Mary, 168, 170, 171, 266n68

Lane, Clifford, 34

Latin American audiences, 118

Latino consumers, 11, 55, 191

Laver, Mark, 16

Let's Dance (Bowie), 113

Let's Get It Started (album, MC Hammer), 185

Levine, Rick, 237n25

Lewis, Jerry, 211

licensing new music before or concurrent with release, 19, 123–24, 150–51, 152

lifestyle-focused marketing (soft-sell

approach), 10, 31–32, 42–43, 68–69, 182

Like a Prayer (album, Madonna), 151, 153–54, 263n20

Like a Prayer (video, Madonna): Lambert directs, 168, 170, 171, 266n68; "Make a Wish" conflation, 168–69, 171, 172; wins MTV Viewer's Choice Award, 151, 174, 267n79. *See also* "Make a Wish" (1989 commercial)

"Like a Prayer" (Madonna), 149–50, 151, 153–59; "miracle" cadence, 162, 163, 264n42; musical analysis, 156–58, 162–63, 171, 264n42, 265n51; redacted musical elements, 165–66, 171, 172, 174; song structure, 157–58, 160–61, 263n32

The Limelighters, 42, 244n54

"Lions" (Marley), 231

Lippert, Barbara, 144

Lipsitz, Hilary, 42

lip-syncing, 70

Live Aid charity concert, 86, 253n21

"Live/Give" (campaign). *See* "You've Got a Lot to Live, and Pepsi's Got a Lot to Give" (1972 campaign)

Loft Inc., 3

Los Angeles Times, 90

Louise, J. C., 4, 24, 29, 41

lyrical analysis: "Billie Jean," 62, 64, 65; "Like a Prayer," 154–56, 158, 171; "Modern Love," 114, 115–16, 257n90; "You've Got the Right One, Baby," 204–5. *See also* redacted lyrics

Mack, Walter, 3, 4

MacKenzie, Tod, 169

"Madison Avenue choir" sound, 45–46

Mad Max: Beyond Thunderdome (film), 86

Mad Men (television show), 12–13

Madonna, 12, 26, 149–76, 229, 264n44; blondness of, 243n40; concert tours, 150, 174; doesn't drink Pepsi, 264n41; iconic costuming, 163, 265n53; Pepsi releases from contract, 151; racial identity, 154; record sales, 125; religious struggles, 154, 155; reputation prior to *Like a Prayer*, 153, 262n19; vocal timbre, 153. *See also Like a*

Prayer (video, Madonna); "Like a Prayer" (Madonna); "Make a Wish" (1989 commercial)

magazine ads, music notation in, 236n18

"Make a Wish" (1989 commercial), 12, 26, 149, 151–53, 159–72, 174–76; controversy benefits Madonna, 174, 230; gospel choir, 150, 164, 165, 166–68, 171; imagery in, 152–53, 162, 163–64, 170, 172, 264n46, 265n48; "Like a Prayer" redaction in, 160–61, 162–63, 165–66; pulled from broadcast, 151, 152, 169, 266n66; Pytka directs, 151; scholarship on, 152–53, 158, 265n49

"Makin' Whoopie" (Kahn and Donaldson), 34, 35–37, 243n35

Manhattan Transfer, 89

"Man in the Mirror" (Jackson), 147

Manning, Harriet J., 127

marginalized groups, 11, 117, 175, 229; cultural appropriation and, 195–96, 212, 272n98

Marino, Dan, 119

marketing budget, 35, 242n28; "The Choice of a New Generation" spots, 90, 121–22, 128; "Come Alive!" campaign, 40; concert tour sponsorship, 117; "Joy of Cola" campaign, 246n100; "Now and Then," 56; other companies increase, after "The Choice of a New Generation" campaign, 83, 252nn63–64

marketing research and focus groups, 18, 45

marketing strategies, 237n26, 241n2; baby boomers' influence on, 30–33; bottling companies buy programs, 11, 237n36; celebrity endorsement template, 82, 124, 180–81; for "Come Alive!" campaign, 40; entertainment, 173–74; iTunes bottlecaps, 214, 273n3; licensing music, 19, 123–24, 150–51, 152; "Madison Avenue choir" sound, 45–46; mobile technologies, 214, 216, 271n5; Pepsi distributed to troops, 179, 267n1; soft-sell (lifestyle-focused), 10, 31–32, 42–43, 68–69, 182; synchronization, 17, 213, 238n52. *See also* hard-sell

approach (product-focused marketing); humor; nostalgia

market saturation, 179

Marley, Skip, 231, 276n58

Martha and the Vandellas, 34, 43

masculinity, 143, 188–89. *See also* gender

Master of Love (Franklin), 244n55

McCann Erikson ad agency, 246n89

McClary, Susan, 21, 153, 155, 158–59, 263n32

McCracken, Grant, 22, 226

McGill, Douglas, 173–74, 176

MC Hammer, 181, 184–92; iconic costuming, 184–85, 269n28; reception of Pepsi ads, 189–92; reputation of, 189–90, 229. *See also* "The Switch" (1990 commercial)

meaning making in multimedia formats, scholarship on, 60–61, 248n16

meaning potentials, 61, 73, 76, 80, 139

meanings as currency, 82

meaning value chain, 21

Mega, Inc., 214

Meier, Leslie, 17, 153, 233, 275nn29–30

Meizel, Katherine L., 27, 218, 224

Mercer, Kobena, 127, 142, 250n39

Merrin, Alfred, 202, 205

Miami Sound Machine, 118–19

Miami Vice television show, 118, 266n77

Michael, George, 149

Michael Jackson: The Magic Returns (CBS special), 122, 123

Michelob, 149

Miss America Pageant, 35, 40

Mital, Ruchi, 25, 129, 141

mixed media, 10

mobile technologies, 214, 271n5

Moby, 213

"Modern Love" (Bowie), 113, 114, 115–16, 228, 257n87

Montana, Joe, 119, 209

Moonwalk (Jackson), 62

Moonwalker (Jackson's promotional film), 129, 141, 143

Moore, Andrea, 87

"More Bounce to the Ounce" (1950 commercial), 28

Morgan, Richard, 169

Morris, Albert, 185, 189

Motorola cell phones, 214, 216

Motown 25: Yesterday, Today, and Forever (television special), 59, 70, 73, 93, 254n37

Motown label, 42, 69, 93–94, 228, 250n40

Mountain Dew, 269n44

MP3s, 214

MTV, 9, 24, 59, 103, 169, 250n41; global reach, 105; moves away from music videos, 213; target audience, 60, 102, 250n40; Video Music Awards, 151, 174, 267n79

MTV video aesthetics, 83, 86, 102, 151, 229, 250n43; in 1980s media, 266n77; Giraldi directs both videos and commercials, 70, 78–79, 91, 99, 100; hip hop videos, 184–85

multimedia convergence, 17, 123, 213, 238n52

multimodal interactions, 61

"The Museum." *See* "The Chase" (1988 episodic commercial)

musical market saturation, 87

musical modes, in "Billie Jean," 62–63, 64, 65–66

music charts. *See* chart topping

music festivals, 232, 277n62

"Music Icons" (2011 commercial), 6–8, 27, 215–18, 226, 227

music industry: file-sharing services, 213; future of corporatization, 232–33; in-house marketing, 233, 277n65; "King's Court" as critique, 220–21; neoliberalism's influence on, 87; Telecommunications Act changes, 212–13

music marketing, historical scholarship, 16–17

"Music to Watch Girls By" (1966 jingle), 43–44, 245nn66–67

music video editing, 71. *See also* MTV video aesthetics

mutual implication, 248n16

Neilsen ratings, 50

neoconservative values, 95–96, 99

neoliberalism, 24, 86–88, 92, 214; Brown on, 87; freedom ideology, 17, 87, 252n7, 257n105; globalization and, 108, 111, 170, 176, 208–10, 256n78; Harvey on, 25, 87, 95, 253n7, 267n83, 276n46; individualism and, 153, 169–70, 276n46; Moore on, 87; Ritchey on, 87, 112; Taylor on, 87, 111

neoliberalism, influence on advertising: "Block Party," 92, 96–99, 101, 255n42; "Creation," 112–19, 122; "Homecoming," 90, 92–96, 254n38; "Make a Wish," 153, 169–70; "New Styles," 90–92, 93, 99; "We've Got the Taste," 104, 105–11, 112, 256n80

Neverland Ranch, 126

New Coke, 89, 101

Newell-Emmet advertising agency, 3

the New Seekers, 49

"New Styles" (1985 commercial), 90–92, 93, 99

New York Times, 100, 101, 126, 154, 173, 183, 222

"Nickel, Nickel" (Kent and Croom-Johnson), 3–6, 228, 235n13

Nike, 119

9/11, 55–56

nonwhite consumers, 11. *See also* African American demographic

nostalgia, 44, 53, 95, 196–201, 248n12; extension of Dwyer's definition (critical affective response), 30, 196; scholarship on, 26, 29–30, 181, 196, 200, 201. *See also* redacted musical elements, in "Now and Then"

"Nothing Else Is Pepsi" (slogan), 180, 193

"Now and Then" (2002 commercial), 7, 24, 29, 33–35, 38–40, 216; "The Choice of a New Generation" segment, 34, 51, 54; "Come Alive!" segment, 34, 40–41, 41–42, 44, 244n52; "Joy of Pepsi" segment, 34, 51–52; "Live/Give" segment, 47, 50–51; nostalgia and, 44, 196; omissions from, 54–55; "Pepsi Pours It On" segment, 46–47; Pytka directs, 242n24; reception of, 56; "Simply Irresistible" segment, 34, 51; "Soda Fountain" segment, 34, 38–39,

51, 54; "Surf Football" segment, 34, 44, 46–47; "Thing Young" segment, 35–37. *See also* redacted musical elements, in "Now and Then"

"Now It's Pepsi, for Those Who Think Young" (campaign), 34, 42, 45, 52, 228, 242n26; acclaim, 12; in "Now and Then" segment, 35–37

Nyong'o, Tavia, 127

"Obey Your Thirst" (1994 Sprite campaign), 191

Ogilvy and Mather agency, 104

Olympics (1984), 89

"Orchestra" (1991 commercial), 201–8, 211; musical analysis, 203–5, 206

originality, consumer desire for, 222, 223

The Other Guy Blinked: How Pepsi Won the Cola Wars (Enrico), 67

Outasight (Richard Andrew), 6–7, 216, 217

Oxford English Dictionary (OED), 20, 21

Packard, Vance, 22

Padilla, Gino, 256n80

Palmer, Robert, 34, 51, 149

paparazzi and fans, 125, 128–29, 143

Papson, Stephen, 22–23, 129, 152–53, 221

Pareles, Jon, 126

parity products, 9, 28, 237n27. *See also* cola wars (Pepsi-Coke rivalry)

patriotism and nationalism, 56

Peikut, Benjamin, 198, 199

Peirce, Charles Sanders, 14

Penn, Irving, 37

Penn, Sean, 154

pentatonic melodies, 156, 157–58, 264n34, 264n42; in "Music Icons," 7, 216; in "We've Got the Taste," 106, 108–10; in "Worldwide," 208

Pentecostal churches, 207

Pepsi and Pete (comic strip), 3

"The Pepsi Challenge" (campaign), 249n28

Pepsi-Cola, Bradham invents, 3

"Pepsi-Cola Hits the Spot" (full version of "Nickel, Nickel"), 4

Pepsi-Cola International, 104

Pepsi-Cola Media Ordering Catalog, 47–48, 245n67, 246n88

Pepsi-Cola World Magazine, 35, 50

"Pepsi Feels So Right" (Richie), 90, 92, 98–99

"Pepsi Generation" (campaign), 29, 37, 52

"Pepsi Generation" (slogan), 10, 75–76

"Pepsi Generation" (Smithsonian oral history project), 12

"The Pepsi Generation" (Pepsi's version of "Billie Jean"), 72–73, 251nn53–54

"Pepsi Generations" (2018 campaign), 233–34

"Pepsi Pours It On" ("The Taste That Beats the Others Cold, Pepsi Pours It On," 1966 campaign), 34–35, 45, 46–47, 228

"The Pepsi Song" ("Now It's Pepsi, for Those Who Think Young"), 34, 35–37, 42, 45, 52, 242n26

Peters, Michael, 79

philanthropy of Pepsi, 192

Phillips, Anne, 34, 46

Phoenix Securities firm, 3

Play (album, Moby), 213

play cues, 183, 268n20

Please Hammer Don't Hurt 'Em (album, MC Hammer), 184, 192

the Pointer Sisters, 89

Pottasch, Alan, 45, 52, 103, 175

Powell, Jane, 35

Powers, Devon, 18

price of Pepsi, 3, 11

Prince, 125

Private Dancer (Turner), 86, 256n76

product-centered slogans, 180

product distribution, 43

product-focused marketing. *See* hard-sell approach (product-focused marketing)

product redesign, 179, 272n99

profits. *See* sales

prosumers, 225, 275n40

psychographic targets, 10, 33. *See also* age demographic targets; youthfulness target

Pytka, Joe, 121, 122, 151, 242n24, 258n2, 260n49

race: "I'll Be There" casting, 199–200; Jackson's ambiguous image, 125–26, 199–200; *Like a Prayer* video and, 170, 172, 266n68; Madonna's racial identity, 154; MC Hammer and, 190; other identity markers and, 188–89; racial uplift, 264n37; rock and roll and, 31; Spears's whiteness, 39, 55; of Sprite consumers, 191; whitewashing, 55–56

racial demographic targets, 11, 28, 55, 101, 228, 243n31. *See also* African American demographic

radio commercials, 45, 52, 243n31, 252n4; "Come Alive!," 34, 44; "Have a Pepsi Day," 55; "Live/Give," 34, 49, 50; "Music to Watch Girls By," 43–44, 245nn66–67; "Nickel, Nickel," 4; "Now It's Pepsi, For Those Who Think Young," 34, 35–37, 242n26; "Pepsi Pours It On," 34, 45; "Things Go Better with Coca-Cola," 42, 244n54; "We've Got the Taste," 117

Ramin, Sid, 34, 40–41, 43–44, 244n44

rap music. *See* hip hop music

Reagan, Ronald, 86–87, 95

reality television, 224–26, 275n33, 275n40

"Real Thing" (Coca-Cola slogan), 202

The Real World (MTV reality show), 213

recombinant teleologies, 21, 130, 132, 135, 138–39, 144–45

redacted lyrics: "Bad," 25, 132–35, 136, 138, 147–48; "Billie Jean," 73, 74–76, 79; "Modern Love," 115–16; "Running with the Night," 96, 98–99, 101. *See also* lyrical analysis

redacted musical elements: "Bad," 131–33, 135, 137, 138–40, 144–45, 260n47, 260n58; "Billie Jean," 24–25, 72–73, 80, 81–82; "I'll Be There," 198–99; "Like a Prayer," 165–66, 171, 172, 174; "Modern Love," 115–16; "Music Icons," 216–17, 226; recombinant teleologies evoke emotion, 21, 130, 135, 138–39; "Respect," 223–26; "Running with the Night," 96–97

redacted musical elements, in "Now and Then," 29, 30, 35, 45–47, 50–56;

"Come Alive!" segment, 41–42, 44; "Live/Give" segment, 50–51; "Simply Irresistible" segment, 51; "Soda Fountain" segment, 36–40; "Surf Football" segment, 46–47; whitewashing, 55–56. *See also* "Now and Then" (2002 commercial)

redacted musical styles and imagery: humor and, 182–84, 185–89, 193–95; nostalgia and, 197–200; retro and, 201, 203–5, 210, 212. *See also* imagery

redaction, 19–23; defined, 19, 20–21; as gatekeeping, 20, 224; scholarly use, 19, 239nn61–62

Redding, Otis, 219

religious iconography, 170, 172, 175, 267n83

religious pentatonic composition, 158

remote control devices (RCDs), 84

replication and dissemination (of musical media), 87

"Respect" (Redding), 219, 222, 223–26

"Restaurant" (2006 commercial), 216

retro, 181, 201–13; celebrity endorsers on cans, 234; defined, 201; redacted musical styles and imagery, 201, 203–5, 210, 212. *See also* "You've Got the Right One, Baby, Uh-huh" (campaign)

"Revolution" (the Beatles), 119

"Revolution in Motion" (Nike campaign), 119

Reynolds, Simon, 26, 169, 201

Ribeiro, Alfonso, 78, 251n57

Richie, Lionel, 25, 86, 121, 228–29; adult contemporary and, 93, 95, 96, 99, 103, 254nn34–35; concert tours, 89, 104; co-writes "We Are the World," 256n68; hit singles, 89, 253n17; jingles by, 89, 90, 91, 92–93, 98–99, 101; *Motown 25* performance, 93, 254n37; reputation, 102, 103, 255n59; selling out accusations, 100–101. *See also* "Running with the Night" (Richie)

Richie, Lionel, "The Choice of a New Generation" campaign, 90–104, 228–29; appeals to multiple age brackets, 93, 99–100, 102, 103; "Block Party," 92, 96–

99, 101, 255n42; disagreements about purpose for hiring, 103; "Homecoming," 90, 92–96, 254n38; length of spots, 90, 101; musical structure of, 90, 91, 254n30; "New Styles," 90–92, 93, 99; production costs, 90; reception of, 99–103
risk taking, 10, 11, 230
Ritchey, Marianna, 87, 112
"Robots" (1985 commercial), 255n44
rock and roll, 30–31, 48; as blanket term for popular music, 32, 43; scandals involving, 31, 241n12
RockBill magazine, 67, 103, 121, 253n10
Rockin' the Pepsi Generations (MTV special), 122
Rodman, Ron, 16, 49, 61
Rolling Stone magazine, 146
the Rolling Stones, 9
Rose, Tricia, 185, 188–89, 274n18
Rosenshine, Allen, 48
Run D.M.C., 189
"Running with the Night" (Richie), 89, 90, 92, 255n67; Giraldi films video, 91; redacted lyrics, 96, 98–99, 101; redacted musical elements, 96–97

sales, music industry, 87, 88, 125, 150–51, 259n25; after "The Choice of a New Generation" campaign, 82–83; film and television soundtracks, 266n77; Telecommunications Act, 212–13; *Thriller*, 248n9, 259n25
sales, Pepsi products, 52, 237n36, 242n28; after "The Choice of a New Generation" campaign, 59–60, 69, 81, 82, 86, 120, 150; after "Girl Watchers" campaign, 44; after "Live/ Give" campaign, 50; after "Nickel, Nickel," 3, 4; after "Think Young" campaign, 35; Australian market, 117; declining, 30, 233; exceed Coca-Cola's, 13, 252n64; increase, despite industry decline, 241n10; market saturation and product diversification, 179; racial demographics and, 55; stagnation, 212; trail behind Coca-Cola's, 212

sales, soda industry, 238n44; of Coca-Cola after "Hilltop," 49; declining, 233, 241n10; of Sprite after "Obey Your Thirst," 191; stagnation, 214–15
sampling (musical), 185, 190
Saussure, Ferdinand de, 14
Schudson, Michael, 61, 73, 142, 170, 249n20; on capitalist realism, 23, 26, 81–82; on surrealism, 129–30, 260n37
Scorsese, Martin, 123
Scott, Ridley, 252n63
Scott, Ronald B., 159
selling out, 82–83, 212, 249n32; baby boomer anxieties about, 119–20; Charles and, 212; Jackson and, 249n32; MC Hammer and, 190; Richie accused of, 100–101; scholarship on, 17; in today's industry, 39, 232; Young articulates through parody, 147, 261n73, 267n79
Sennett, Mack, 3
September 11, 2001, 55–56
7 Up, 33
sex (in music and advertising industries), 175
sexual connotations in "Like a Prayer," 155
sexual orientation, 125–26, 194
"Shady Acres" (1990 commercial), 183–84, 188
Shannon, Del, 34, 43
Shazam Entertainment, 271n5
"Show Some Respect" (Turner), 105, 107, 256n76
Sigerson, Davit, 146
signifyin(g), 260n45
Simon, Paul, 111–12
"Simply Irresistible" (1989 commercial), 149; in "Now and Then" segment, 34, 51
"Simply Irresistible" (Palmer), 34, 51
simulacra, 129–30, 141, 145
simulation: in "The Chase," 25, 131, 135, 140, 142, 145; in "King's Court," 221; scholarship on, 25, 129–30
skywriting promotions, 3
Slade, Alison, 224, 275n33

slogans, 5, 34, 36, 45, 132, 136; "The Choice of a New Generation," 87, 100; "Joy of Cola," 180, 194; "Nothing Else is Pepsi," 180, 193; "Pepsi Generation," 10, 75–76; "Pepsi Pours It On," 45; rationale in selecting, 87, 100; "Real Thing" (Coca-Cola), 202; "Where There's Pepsi, There's Music," 216, 220; "You've Got the Right One, Baby," 202

Smithsonian Institution, 12

Smithsonian National Museum of American History, 29

Smooth Criminal (video, Jackson), 143

Snipes, Wesley, 123

socialist realism, 81–82

"Soda Fountain" (1958 "Now and Then" segment), 34, 36–40, 51, 54

"Soda Fountain" (1961 commercial), 34, 36, 37, 164

soft-sell approach (lifestyle-focused marketing), 10, 31–32, 42–43, 68–69, 182. *See also* hard-sell approach (product-focused marketing)

Sommers, Joanie, 12, 34, 43, 243n35; "Come Alive!" campaign, 40, 228; contract, 243n36; offscreen performance, 37–38, 39, 44; vocal timbre, 37–38, 228

sonic branding, 18, 232

Sony Music Entertainment, 215, 225, 227, 233

soul music, 203

sound engineering, on "Billie Jean," 249n25

The Source (magazine), 190, 270n44

Spanish-language Pepsi commercials, 149, 262n1

Spears, Britney, 53–54, 246n99, 247n102; dropped as Pepsi spokesperson, 56; "Joy of Cola" compensation, 246n100; in "Music Icons," 6, 7, 216

Spears, Britney, "Now and Then" commercial, 29, 34, 38–40, 56; "The Choice of a New Generation" segment, 54; "Come Alive!" segment, 41–42; "Joy of Pepsi" segment, 51–52; "Live/Give" segment, 47, 54; onscreen performance, 37–38, 39, 44; "Simply Irresistible"

segment, 51; "Soda Fountain" segment, 38–39, 54; "Surf Football" segment, 44, 46–47; vocal timbre, 42, 54; whiteness, 39, 55. *See also* "Now and Then" (2002 commercial)

special markets, 11, 55

spectacle, trope of, 70, 71, 107; Kellner on, 18, 214, 251n47

"Speed Demon" (Jackson), 128–29, 137

Sponsor magazine, 35

sponsorship. *See* concert tour sponsorship

Sprite marketing, 191, 269n41

Stanyek, Jason, 197–98, 199

Steele, Alfred, 28

Stilwell, Robynn, 243n40, 251n56

streaming music, 214

"Street" (1984 commercial), 59, 77–80, 127, 216

stroboscopic effect, 45

Super Bowl, commercials aired during, 192; "Dancing Bears," 193–94; "Diner," 193; "I'll Be There," 197; "King's Court," 218, 219, 222; "Music Icons," 6; "Now and Then," 56, 242n24; "You've Got the Right One, Baby," 202, 208

Super Bowl, half-time sponsorship, 231, 276n55

The Supremes, 42

"Surf Football" (1968 commercial), 34, 44–47

surrealism, 129–30, 168, 260n37

Swedien, Bruce, 249n25

"The Switch" (1990 commercial), 184–96; form outlined, 186; hip hop reception after, 189–90; musical analysis of, 185, 186, 187, 188; reception of, 189–92. *See also* MC Hammer

SycoTV, 215, 225

Sylvern, Hank, 28

synchronization, 17, 123, 213, 238n52

Tagg, Phillip, 14

target demographics. *See* age demographic targets; youthfulness target

target demographics, racial, 11, 28, 55, 101, 228, 243n31. *See also* African American demographic

"The Taste That Beats the Others Cold, Pepsi Pours It On" (1966 campaign), 34–35, 45, 46–47, 228

Taylor, Timothy, 4, 16–17, 29, 226; on "The Choice of a New Generation," 9, 60; on "Live/Give" campaign, 48; on "Make a Wish," 153; on neoliberalism, 87, 111; on Sprite marketing, 191; on youth marketing, 9, 24, 32, 33, 60

TBWAChiatDay agency, 215

technocapitalism, 27, 214, 273n2

technology, 214

Tedlow, Richard S., 10, 46

Telecommunications Act (1996), 212–13

television commercials: "Amphibicar," 41; "Amusement Park," 41; "Audition," 202, 210–12; "Backstage," 122, 127, 147; "Block Party," 92, 96–99, 101, 255n42; "Concert," 122, 127–28, 146–47, 216; "The Concert," 59, 60, 71–77, 79; "Creation," 112–19, 122, 129; "Dancing Bears," 193–94; "Diner," 193; "Dreams," 197–200; "Girl Watchers," 43–44; "Have a Pepsi, the Light Refreshment," 28; "Have a Pepsi Day," 55; "Hilltop," 12–13, 49–50, 231, 246n89; "Homecoming," 90, 92–96254n38; humor and, 56; "I'll Be There," 197–200; "Jump In," 231–32, 237n39, 276n58; "King's Court," 27, 218, 219–27, 274n16; "Live/Give," 34–35, 47–49, 50–51, 54, 252n4; "More Bounce to the Ounce," 28; "Music Icons," 6–8, 27, 215–16, 226, 227; "New Styles," 90–92, 93, 99; "Orchestra," 201–8, 211; other marketing methods, 237n36; Pepsi as first soda brand to use, 9–10; "Pepsi Pours It On," 34–35, 45, 46–47, 228; "Restaurant," 216; "Robots," 255n44; "Shady Acres," 183–84, 188; "Simply Irresistible," 34, 51, 149; "Soda Fountain," 34, 36, 37, 164; "Street," 59, 77–80, 127, 216; "Surf Football," 34, 44–47; "Timeline," 216; "We've Got the Taste," 104, 105–11, 112, 256n80; "Worldwide," 208–10, 211, 272n80; "You Go Girl," 194–95; zipping and zapping, 84. See also "The Chase" (1988 episodic commercial); "Come Alive! You're in the Pepsi Generation" (campaign); "Joy of Cola" (1999 campaign); "Make a Wish" (1989 commercial); "Now and Then" (2002 commercial); "The Switch" (1990 commercial)

television show music, 266n77, 276n48

"That Lucky Old Sun" (Charles), 206–7

"Things Go Better with Coca-Cola," 42, 244n54

"Think Young" (campaign). See "Now It's Pepsi, for Those Who Think Young" (campaign)

"This Note's For You" (Young), 147, 261n73, 267n79

Thriller (Jackson): acclaim, 59, 124, 127; concert tour, 60, 67, 125, 126, 249n31; sales, 248n9, 259n25; tops charts, 60, 127

"Thriller" (short film, Jackson), 142

"Timeline" (2009 commercial), 216

Time magazine, 146, 202

Tiny Tim, 211

Toffler, Alvin, 275n40

"Tonight Is the Night" (Outasight), 6–7, 216

Tota, Anna Lisa, 16

the Trade Masters, 34

traditional advertising approach, 10

The Trials of O'Brien (television show), 43

Trynka, Paul, 118

Turner, Tina, 256n83, 257n94, 268n8; concert tours, 104, 113, 117; Grammys won by, 104, 256n70; iconic symbols of, 104–5, 108, 117; "Live/Give" campaign and, 34, 50, 252n4; as Pepsi consumer, 104; vocal timbre, 106

Turner, Tina, "The Choice of a New Generation" campaign, 25, 86, 104–19, 121; "Creation," 112–19, 122, 229. See also "We've Got the Taste" (1986 commercial)

The Turtles, 34, 45

Tyson, Mike, 249n30

Uh-huh Girls, 201
unique selling proposition (USP). *See* slogans
upward mobility, 102, 153, 169, 262n14
USA Today, 193, 194, 215–16

Velona, Tony, 245n66
Vernallis, Carol, 97, 251n58
Vickers, Nancy A., 152, 172
Victory Tour (Jackson), 88–89, 117, 124–25, 126, 249n31
videocassette recorders (VCRs), 84
Video Storyboard Tests, Inc., 101
The Village People, 193
Virginia Slims marketing, 264n47
visual imagery, 125; in *Billie Jean*, 67; evoking youth, 44, 45, 46, 70; Frank on, 44, 250n43; Jackson's costuming iconography, 68, 70–71, 73, 83, 137, 141, 259n20; lyrical suggestions of religious, in "Like a Prayer," 156, 163; in "Make a Wish," 152–53, 162, 163–64, 170, 172, 264n46, 265n48; in "Music Icons," 6; music video aesthetic, 70, 102, 184–85; in "New Styles," 91; scholarship on advertising and, 22, 44, 61, 152–53, 254n39; in "Shady Acres," 183; in "We've Got the Taste," 107–8. *See also* redacted musical styles and imagery
vocal timbre: of Madonna, 153; of Sommers, 37–38, 228; of Spears, 42, 54; of Turner, 106
Vogel, Joseph, 25, 126, 128, 259n19, 260n45
volume of ads, 185

Warner Brothers, 202
Washington Post, 49, 100–101, 125–26, 147
"The Way You Make Me Feel" (Jackson), 147, 258n2
"We Are the World" (Jackson and Richie), 256n68
West, Kanye, 216
Western musicians, "world music" collaborations and, 111–12, 150, 262n3
"We've Got the Taste" (1986 commercial), 104, 105–11; musical analysis,

106–7, 108, 109–11; Thai/Jongkadeekij version, 105, 108–11, 112, 256n80; US/solo version, 105–8
"What'd I Say" (Charles), 203, 204, 205, 206, 210
"What's Love Got to Do with It?" (Turner), 256n70
Wheaties Breakfast Cereal, 235n3
"Where There's Pepsi, There's Music" (slogan), 216, 220
White, Jaleel, 255n45
white consumers, 101, 228
white femininity, 37–38, 39, 55
"Who Is It?" (Jackson), 197
Wildmon, Donald, 168, 169
Williams, Andy, 245n66
Williams, Raymond, 22
Williamson, Judith, 22, 61, 73, 82
women rappers, 188–89
Wood, Mary Frisbie, 34
"world music," 111–12
"Worldwide" (1991 commercial), 208–10, 211, 272n80
Would You Believe? (Charles), 202

X Factor–U. S. (reality talent show), 26–27; "King's Court" and, 219–27; "Music Icons" and, 6–8, 27, 215–18, 220, 226

Yazijian, Harvey, 4, 24, 29, 41
"Y.M.C.A." (The Village People), 193–94
"You Are" (Richie), 91, 95, 254n33
"You Belong to the City" (*Miami Vice* theme song), 118
"You Go Girl" (1999 commercial), 194–95
"You Got the Right One Baby" (slogan), 202
"You Mean More to Me" (Richie), 90, 92, 93, 99
Young, Neil, 147, 261n73, 267n79
"Young America" (1970), 34, 47
The Youngbloods, 193
Young MC, 183, 268n19
"You're Looking Pepsi Style" (Richie), 90, 91, 92, 99, 254n33
youth culture, 30–31, 41; imagery evoking, 44, 45, 46, 70

youthfulness target, 11, 33, 102–3, 242n22; BBD&O and, 29; "The Choice of a New Generation" slogan, 87, 180; freedom ideology and, 87–88; Jackson and, 69, 77, 79, 82, 135; MTV and, 250n40; neoliberalism and, 87–88, 92; "Now It's Pepsi, for Those Who Think Young," 12, 34, 35–37, 42, 45, 52, 228, 242n26

youth marketing, return to, 102–3. *See also* age demographic targets, youth marketing development

YouTube, 231

"You've Got a Lot to Live, and Pepsi's Got a Lot to Give" (1972 campaign): jingle, 34–35, 47–49, 50–51, 54; Turner on radio spots, 34, 50, 252n4

"You've Got the Right One, Baby, Uh-huh" (campaign), 182, 200–213; "Audition," 210–12; inspiration for, 271n77; "Orchestra," 201–8; "Worldwide," 208–10. *See also* Charles, Ray

zapping (remotely changing channels), 84, 86, 90, 101

zipping (VCR fast-forwarding), 84, 86, 90, 101